CONTRACT LAW

This book gives an introduction to the English law of contract. The third edition has been fully updated to cover recent developments in case law and recent statutes such as the Consumer Rights Act 2015. However, this new edition retains the primary focus of the earlier editions: it is designed to introduce the lawyer trained in a civil law jurisdiction to the method of reasoning in the common law, and in particular to the English law of contract. It is written for the lawyer—whether student or practitioner—from another jurisdiction who already has an understanding of a (different) law of contract, but who wishes to discover the way in which an English lawyer views a contract. However, it is also useful for the English law student: setting English contract law generally in the context of other European and international approaches, the book forms an introductory text, not only demonstrating how English contract law works but also giving a glimpse of different ways of thinking about some of the fundamental rules of contract law from a civil law perspective. After a general introduction to the common law system—how a common lawyer reasons and finds the law—the book explains the principles of the law of contract in English law covering all the aspects of a contract from its formation to the remedies available for breach, whilst directing attention in particular to those areas where the approach of English law is in marked contrast to that taken in many civil law systems.

Contract Law

An Introduction to the English Law of Contract for the Civil Lawyer

Third Edition

John Cartwright

·HART·
OXFORD · LONDON · NEW YORK · NEW DELHI · SYDNEY

HART PUBLISHING

Bloomsbury Publishing Plc

Kemp House, Chawley Park, Cumnor Hill, Oxford, OX2 9PH, UK

1385 Broadway, New York, NY 10018, USA

HART PUBLISHING, the Hart/Stag logo, BLOOMSBURY and the Diana logo are trademarks of Bloomsbury Publishing Plc

This edition, first published in Great Britain 2016

Reprinted 2018, 2019, 2020

First edition, 2007

Second edition, 2013

Copyright © John Cartwright

John Cartwright has asserted his right under the Copyright, Designs and Patents Act 1988 to be identified as Author of this work.

All rights reserved. No part of this publication may be reproduced or transmitted in any form or by any means, electronic or mechanical, including photocopying, recording, or any information storage or retrieval system, without prior permission in writing from the publishers.

While every care has been taken to ensure the accuracy of this work, no responsibility for loss or damage occasioned to any person acting or refraining from action as a result of any statement in it can be accepted by the authors, editors or publishers.

All UK Government legislation and other public sector information used in the work is Crown Copyright ©. All House of Lords and House of Commons information used in the work is Parliamentary Copyright ©. This information is reused under the terms of the Open Government Licence v3.0 (http://www.nationalarchives.gov.uk/doc/open-government-licence/version/3) except where otherwise stated.

All Eur-lex material used in the work is © European Union, http://eur-lex.europa.eu/, 1998–2018.

A catalogue record for this book is available from the British Library.

Library of Congress Cataloging-in-Publication data

Names: Cartwright, John, 1957– author.

Title: Contract law : an introduction to the English law of contract for the civil lawyer / John Cartwright.

Description: Third edition. | Oxford ; Portland, Or. : Hart Publishing, 2016. | Includes bibliographical references and index.

Identifiers: LCCN 2016007374 (print) | LCCN 2016008234 (ebook) | ISBN 9781509902910 (pbk. : alk. paper) | ISBN 9781509902927 (Epub)

Subjects: LCSH: Contracts—England. | Contracts—Wales.

Classification: LCC KD1554 .C368 2016 (print) | LCC KD1554 (ebook) | DDC 346.4202/2—dc23

LC record available at http://lccn.loc.gov/2016007374

ISBN: PB: 978-1-50990-291-0
ePDF: 978-1-50990-293-4
ePub: 978-1-50990-292-7

Typeset by Compuscript Ltd, Shannon
Printed and bound in Great Britain by TJ International Ltd, Padstow, Cornwall

To find out more about our authors and books visit www.hartpublishing.co.uk.
Here you will find extracts, author information, details of forthcoming events
and the option to sign up for our newsletters.

Preface

The primary purpose of the new edition of this book remains as it was in the first two editions: to provide an introduction to the English law of contract for the lawyer trained in a civil law jurisdiction—whether as a student who is discovering English law in order to compare it with his or her own law, or as a practitioner who needs to understand how English lawyers view a contract and why they draft their contracts as they do. In giving first (in Part I) a general introduction to the common law system—how a common lawyer reasons and finds the law; and then (in Part II) an explanation of the principles of the law of contract in English law, directing attention in particular to those areas where the approach of English law is in marked contrast to that taken in many civil law systems, the book is intended to provide an overview of the English law which will enable any civil lawyer to see the similarities and differences with his or her own system. The book is not exclusively for the civil lawyer, however: it can also form a useful introductory text for the English student, who will see not only how English contract law works but also get a glimpse of different ways of thinking about some of the fundamental rules of contract law from a civil law perspective—a glimpse which might even encourage the English student to go further and discover more about contract law in other legal systems.

This new edition does not change the scope of the book, but has been prepared in order to take into account some very significant developments in the English law of contract over the last three years, particularly by legislation such as the Consumer Rights Act 2015 (which alters significantly the law governing consumer contracts, replacing and extending the special regime of remedies for breach of consumer contracts for goods, digital content and services, amends the Unfair Contract Terms Act 1977 and replaces the Unfair Terms in Consumer Contracts Regulations 1999), together with the Consumer Contracts (Information, Cancellation and Additional Charges) Regulations 2013 (which impose duties of disclosure on traders) and the Consumer Protection (Amendment) Regulations 2014 (which provide private rights to redress for consumers under the Consumer Protection from Unfair Trading Regulations 2008). By the time of the last edition we already had the Consumer Insurance (Disclosure and Representations) Act 2012, but now we also have the Insurance Act 2015 (which comes into force in August 2016) to complete the reform of the old common law duties of disclosure in the formation of insurance contracts. This has been an unusually active period of legislative intervention in contract law, and the effect of these changes tends to pull the English law—or, at least, the law of consumer contracts—towards a model which will seem familiar to the civil lawyer. But these are particular statutory exceptions to the general rules of the common law that still define the essential nature of a contract in English law.

In revising the text I have continued to be greatly helped not only by comments I have received from those who have used the book in their own teaching both in England and in civil law jurisdictions in continental Europe and in other parts of the world, but also by the reactions I received to the last edition from my own students in Leiden, Oxford and Paris, and from civil law practitioners. Contract law can provide a natural focus for the dialogue between common lawyers and civil lawyers, to enable them to learn about their own legal systems as well as about each other's, and I hope that this book can contribute to that dialogue.

John Cartwright
January 2016

Contents

Preface v
List of Abbreviations xvii
Table of Cases xxi
Table of Legislation xxxv

Part I: An Introduction to the Common Law

1. The 'Common Law' 3
   I. The 'Common Law' of England 3
      1. Meanings of 'Common Law' 3
      2. Common Law and Equity 5
      3. Common Law and Civil Law 8
   II. Common Law Systems Around the World 9
      1. The Range of the Common Law 9
      2. Differences Between Common Law Systems 10
      3. Some General Features of the Common Law Systems 12

2. Finding the Law 15
   I. The Sources of Law 15
      1. Legal Reasoning in the Common Law:
         Where Shall We Begin? 15
      2. Legislation and Case-Law as Sources of Law 17
   II. The Judge as Interpreter and as Law-Maker 19
      1. Different Judicial Approaches to the Different
         Sources 19
      2. The 'Binding' Force of Case-Law:
         The Doctrine of Precedent 20
         (a) Case-Law as an Authority 20
         (b) Case-Law as Binding 21
         (c) The Rules of Precedent in English Law 22
         (d) Understanding the Case-Law in the Light
             of the Doctrine of Precedent 27
      3. The Interpretation of Legislative Texts 28
         (a) The Basic Test: Applying the Normal,
             Objective Meaning of the Words of the Statute 28
         (b) Some General Principles and Presumptions
             of Interpretation 29

    (c) Interpretation of European Law and Compliance with the European Convention on Human Rights 30
    (d) The Relevance of the Context of the Statute at the Time of its Enactment 31
    (e) The Court Does Not Generally Reason Beyond the Statute 33
  4. Reasoning from the Cases in the Common Law 34
    (a) The Judge Develops the Common Law and Does Not Simply Declare it 34
    (b) Reasoning in the Common Law 36
    (c) An Illustration of Common Law Reasoning: *Donoghue v Stevenson* and its Aftermath 38
 III. English Statutory Drafting 44
  1. The General Style of Statutory Drafting in England 44
  2. An Illustration: The Contracts (Rights of Third Parties) Act 1999 45

Part II: The Law of Contract

3. Introduction to the English Law of Contract 51
 I. The Place of Contract in Private Law 51
  1. Contract within the Law of Obligations 51
  2. Contract and Tort 53
  3. Contract and Property 55
 II. A General Law of Contract: The Place of 'Special' Contracts 57
  1. 'General' and 'Special': A Different Starting-Point 57
  2. The (Limited) Role of 'Special Contracts' in English Law 58
    (a) Formation of the Contract 58
    (b) The Terms of the Contract 59
    (c) Remedies 61
    (d) Significance of the Adoption of a General Rule Rather than 'Special' Contracts in English Law 62
 III. Some General Features and Some Fundamental Starting-Points 63
  1. The Role of 'Good Faith' 64
  2. Objectivity, Reasonableness and Reliance 67
  3. The Significance of the 'Intentions of the Parties' 68
  4. Contract as an Economic Instrument: Contractual Freedom, Certainty and the Commercial Model of Contracting 69

		5.	Contract Drafting in the Common Law 71
	IV.		English Contract Law in a European Context 71
4.	The Negotiations for a Contract 74
	I.		The Starting Point: No General Duty between Negotiating Parties 75
		1.	The General Approach 75
		2.	No General Duty Because of a Reluctance to Use General Principles? 75
		3.	Difficulties in Defining the Duty? 76
		4.	The Relationship between Negotiating Parties is Adversarial; The Allocation of Risk in Negotiations 78
		5.	Negotiations 'Subject to Contract' 79
		6.	No General Duty of Disclosure 80
		7.	Breaking off Negotiations is Not a Tort 81
		8.	No General Liability Based on Estoppel 82
	II.		Particular Liabilities Arising During the Negotiations 83
		1.	Particular Liabilities Rather than General Duties 83
		2.	Misrepresentation: Remedies in Tort 84
		3.	Contractual Liability in the Precontractual Phase 86
			(a) Express Contracts: Options, Rights of Pre-emption, Lock-out Agreements and 'Letters of Intent' 86
			(b) Implied Contracts: Duties to Consider Tenders 90
			(c) Implied Duty to Maintain Offer of Unilateral Contract 91
		4.	Unjust Enrichment 92
		5.	Breach of Confidence 94
5.	Formation of the Contract: Contract as 'Agreement' 95
	I.		The Meaning of 'Agreement': The 'Objective Test' 95
		1.	An 'Agreement' Requires Communication between the Parties 95
		2.	'Objectivity' and 'Subjectivity' 96
		3.	Arguments in Relation to the Different Approaches 97
		4.	The 'Objective' Test in English Law 100
		5.	The Objective Test in Context in the English Law of Contract 103
	II.		The Mechanisms of Contract Formation: The Rules of Offer and Acceptance 103
		1.	'Offer and Acceptance' as a *Rule* 103
			(a) Problems and Benefits of the 'Offer and Acceptance' Analysis 104

    (b) Rejection of the 'Offer and Acceptance'
Analysis by Lord Denning..107
    (c) Insistence on the 'Offer and Acceptance'
Analysis by the House of Lords 107
    (d) 'Offer and Acceptance' is Normally a Rule................109
   2. The Particular Rules of 'Offer and Acceptance'.................109
    (a) Offer..110
    (b) Termination of Offer by the Offeror
or the Offeree..113
    (c) Acceptance 114
    (d) Time and Place of Acceptance 117
   3. Unresolved Negotiations: 'Battles of Forms' 120
  III. Minimum Content and Certainty..122
   1. An Agreement (and the Offer) Must Be Complete..............122
   2. An Agreement (and the Offer) Must Be Certain 122

6. Form, Consideration and Intention...125
  I. Formality in the Formation of Contracts.................................126
   1. Specific Formalities for Specific Contracts.........................126
   2. A General Formality: The Deed 127
   3. The Avoidance of Formalities..129
  II. The Doctrine of Consideration 131
   1. Consideration: The Basic Principle 131
   2. Consideration: Particular Rules 132
    (a) Consideration is provided by B when he does,
or promises to do, something at A's request 132
    (b) Consideration involves B doing or promising
something which is to his detriment and/or
to A's benefit 133
    (c) For B's promise or act to be consideration it
must have some (economic) value 134
    (d) B's promise or act must be done at the same
time as A's promise: 'past consideration'
is insufficient..138
    (e) An act done, or promise made, by B which
he is already under a contractual obligation
to perform in favour of a third party can be
good consideration 138
    (f) An act done, or promise made, by B which he is
already under a contractual obligation to perform
in favour of A, or which he has a legal obligation
to perform, cannot be good consideration, unless
A obtains some additional benefit 139
    (g) Part-payment of a debt is not consideration
for the release of the balance 142

III. Promissory Estoppel 143
  1. The Core Principle of Estoppel: Reliance on a
     Representation 143
  2. The Modern Development of Promissory
     Estoppel in English Law 144
  3. The Elements of Promissory Estoppel in English Law........147
     (a) The Doctrine is Limited to the Variation of an
         Existing Contract, in the Absence of Fresh
         Consideration 148
     (b) The Representation..149
     (c) The Representee Must Have Relied on the
         Representation—Altered His Position 149
     (d) The Representor Can Revoke His Promise:
         Estoppel is Normally Only Temporary 150
     (e) The Representation May Be Irrevocable 150
     (f) Promissory Estoppel Does Not Create New
         Rights—It is a 'Shield' Not a 'Sword' 152
  4. The Relationship between Consideration and Estoppel:
     Differences within the Common Law, and Possible
     Developments in England 153
IV. Contractual Intention..155
  1. The Role of the Parties' 'Intentions' in the Formation
     of a Contract 155
  2. 'Intention to Create Legal Relations' 156

7. Vitiating Factors: Void, Voidable and Unenforceable Contracts..........158
  I. The Vitiating Factors in English Law; Void
     and Voidable Contracts 159
     1. An Overview of the Vitiating Factors 159
     2. 'Void' and 'Voidable' Contracts...160
     3. The Range of Remedies for the Vitiating Factors 162
  II. Mistake 163
     1. Different Ways of Categorising Mistakes..........................163
     2. Mistakes About the Terms of the Contract 164
        (a) Mistake in the Formation of a Contract 164
        (b) Written Contracts: Rectification for Mistake 165
        (c) Written Contracts: *Non Est Factum*..........................167
     3. Mistakes About the Identity of the Other Party 167
        (a) Identity is Not Normally of Determining
            Significance...167
        (b) A Mistake of Identity Prevents the Formation
            of the Contract 168
     4. Mistakes About the Subject-Matter....................................171
        (a) The 'Subject-Matter'..171

			(b) Unilateral Mistake...171

        (b) Unilateral Mistake...171
        (c) Common (Shared) Mistake 172
  III. Misrepresentation and Non-disclosure.....................................176
     1. Misrepresentation Contrasted with Mistake 176
     2. The Range of Remedies for Misrepresentation 177
     3. Rescission of the Contract..179
     4. Damages in Tort 180
     5. Damages under Section 2(1) of the
        Misrepresentation Act 1967 182
     6. Right to Redress under the Consumer Protection
        from Unfair Trading Regulations 2008 183
     7. Remedies for Breach of Contract..183
     8. Choosing between the Remedies..184
     9. Exclusion of Remedies for Misrepresentation....................185
     10. Non-disclosure 186
  IV. Duress, Undue Influence and Unconscionable Bargains............189
     1. Pressure and Abuse of Position 189
     2. Duress 191
     3. Undue Influence 194
     4. Unconscionable Bargains 197
  V. Capacity...198
  VI. Illegality and Public Policy..199

8. Finding the Terms of the Contract...201
  I. The 'Terms' of a Contract...201
  II. Finding and Interpreting the Express Terms 202
     1. Contracts Not Reduced to Writing......................................203
        (a) Finding the Terms 203
        (b) Interpreting the Terms 205
     2. Written Contracts..205
        (a) Finding the Terms 205
        (b) Interpreting the Terms 207
  III. Implied Terms...210
     1. Obvious Terms; Regular and Customary Terms 211
     2. Terms Necessary to Give the Contract
        'Business Efficacy' 212
     3. Particular Terms in Particular Types of Contract 213
        (a) Terms Implied at Common Law 213
        (b) Terms Implied by Statute..214
     4. The Exclusion of Implied Terms: Drafting Styles in
        the Common Law 215

9. Controlling the Content of the Contract: 'Unfair' Contracts 218
  I. Indirect Controls over the 'Fairness' of the Contract 219
     1. Procedural and Substantive Unfairness 219

		2.	Judicial Controls over Unfair Terms: Incorporation and Construction..220
			(a) Incorporation of the Term...221
			(b) Interpretation of the Term: Construction *Contra Proferentem*..221
	II.	Direct Controls over the 'Fairness' of the Contract..224
		1. Control by the Common Law 224
		2. Control by Statute 226
			(a) Exclusion and Limitation Clauses in Non-consumer Contracts: The Unfair Contract Terms Act 1977..227
			(b) Exclusion and Restriction of Liability for Misrepresentation by Clauses in Non-consumer Contracts: Section 3 of the Misrepresentation Act 1967 229
			(c) Exclusion and Limitation Clauses in Consumer Contracts: The Consumer Rights Act 2015 230
			(d) Unfair Terms in Consumer Contracts: Part 2 of the Consumer Rights Act 2015 230
			(e) Other Statutory Controls over Particular Types of Term 233
10.	Who has the Benefit of the Contract? Who is Bound by the Contract? 235
	I.	Who is a 'Party' to the Contract? The Doctrine of Privity of Contract 236
		1. A Party to the Agreement or to the Bargain?......................236
		2. The Link between Privity and Consideration: *Tweddle v Atkinson*..237
		3. Development of Judicial Attitudes to the Doctrine of Privity During the Twentieth Century 239
	II.	Avoiding the Doctrine of Privity 241
		1. Creating Rights for the Third Party 242
			(a) Make the Third Party a Party 242
			(b) Trusts..242
			(c) Assignment..243
			(d) Agency 243
			(e) Tort...244
			(f) Property Law...245
			(g) Third-Party Rights by Statute...................................247
		2. Enforcement of the Contract by the Promisee for the Benefit of a Third Party 247
			(a) The Problem: The Loss is Suffered by the Third Party 247
			(b) Specific Performance 247

(c) Damages Calculated to Cover the Third
Party's Losses 249
III. Reform by the Contracts (Rights of Third Parties)
Act 1999 250
1. The Law Commission's Proposals for Reform 250
2. The Contracts (Rights of Third Parties) Act 1999 250
   (a) Which Contracts are Covered? 251
   (b) In what Circumstances does a Third Party
       Acquire the Right to Enforce a Term? 251
   (c) Parties can Always Contract out of the
       Act Expressly 252
   (d) What Rights does the Third Party Acquire? 252
   (e) The Act also Applies to Exemption Clauses 253
   (f) Can the Third Party's Right to Enforce be
       Taken Away by the Contracting Parties? 253
   (g) The Position of the Promisor 253
   (h) The Position of the Promisee 254
   (i) Interaction of the Act with Other Remedies for
       Third-Party Losses 254
3. Interaction of the Doctrines of Privity of Contract
   and Consideration after the 1999 Act 255
IV. Assignment and Novation of Contractual
    Rights and Duties 256
    1. Assignment 256
       (a) Assignment is of Only the Benefit,
           Not the Burden 256
       (b) Legal and Equitable Assignments 257
       (c) Rights Which are Capable of Assignment 257
       (d) The Effect of a Valid Assignment 258
    2. Novation 259

11. Change of Circumstances 260
    I. The Doctrine of Frustration 261
       1. Development of the Doctrine of Frustration 261
       2. Application of the Test for Frustration 264
       3. Consequences of Frustration 266
    II. Using Contract Terms to Anticipate Changes
        of Circumstances 269

12. Remedies for Breach of Contract 272
    I. 'Breach of Contract' 272
       1. What is a Breach of Contract?
          The Significance of the Obligation to Perform 272
       2. The Range of Remedies 274
    II. Specific Performance and Injunction 275

		1.	Specific Performance and Injunction as Equitable Remedies..275
		2.	The Content of the Order and the Remedy for Non-compliance...276
		3.	Specific Performance in the Modern Law........................277
		4.	Injunction 280
		5.	Damages in Place of Specific Performance or Injunction 281
	III.	Termination for Breach..281	
		1.	The Nature of Termination...281
		2.	Availability of Termination...281
			(a) Breach of Condition 282
			(b) Fundamental Breach 282
		3.	Exercising the Right to Terminate..................................283
		4.	Consequences of Termination...285
		5.	Contractual Termination Clauses 285
		6.	Deposits; Relief against Forfeiture..................................286
		7.	No General Right of Suspension 287
	IV.	Damages..288	
		1.	Damages are to Compensate the Claimant's Failed Expectation..288
		2.	Valuing the Expectation..289
		3.	Damages for Distress and Other Intangible Losses..........291
		4.	Whose Expectation? Losses Suffered by Third Parties 292
		5.	Punitive Damages 292
		6.	Damages to Deprive the Defendant of a Profit................293
		7.	Limits on Recovery and Defences: Remoteness, Mitigation, Contributory Negligence and Limitation Periods 294
			(a) Remoteness of Damage 294
			(b) Mitigation of Loss; Contributory Negligence..........295
			(c) Limitation Periods 296
		8.	Damages for Delay 296
	V.	Debt 297	
	VI.	Consumer Contracts for the Supply of Goods, Digital Content or Services: Rejection, Repair, Replacement, Reduction in Price and Repeat Performance..........................297	
	VII.	Agreed Remedies..299	
	VIII.	Learning About a Contract from the Remedies for Breach..300	

Appendix..303
Index...311

List of Abbreviations

Case Reports

AC or App Cas	Appeal Cases
Aleyn	Aleyn's Reports
All ER	All England Law Reports
All ER (Comm)	All England Law Reports (Commercial Cases)
All ER (D)	All England Law Reports (Digests)
ALR	Australian Law Reports
B & Ald	Barnewall & Alderson's Reports
B & S	Best and Smith's Reports
Beav	Beavan's Reports
Bing	Bingham's Reports
BLR	Building Law Reports
Burr	Burrow's Reports
C & P	Carrington & Payne's Reports
CA	Court of Appeal
Camp	Campbell's Reports
CB (NS)	Common Bench Reports (New Series)
Ch or ChD	Chancery Division
Cl & Fin	Clark and Finnelley's Reports
CLC	Commercial Law Cases
CLR	Commonwealth Law Reports [Australia]
CMLR	Common Market Law Reports
Co Rep	Coke's Reports
Com LR	Commercial Law Reports
Comm	Commercial Court
CP or CPD	Common Pleas Division
DC	Divisional Court
De GJ & S	De Gex, Jones & Smith's Reports
DLR	Dominion Law Reports [Canada]
Drew	Drewry's Reports
EGLR	Estates Gazette Law Reports
El & Bl	Ellis and Blackburn's Reports
EMLR	Entertainment and Media Law Reports
ER	English Reports
EWCA Civ	England and Wales Court of Appeal, Civil Division
EWHC	England and Wales High Court
Ex or Exch	Exchequer

F & F   Foster and Finlason's Reports
FLR   Family Law Reports
H & N   Hurlstone & Norman's Reports
HCA   High Court of Australia
HL   House of Lords
HL Cas   Clark's House of Lords Reports
HL Sc   House of Lords (appeal from Scotland)
KB   King's Bench Division
Lloyd's Rep   Lloyd's Law Reports
Lord Raym   Lord Raymond Reports
L & TR   Landlord and Tenant Reports
LR   Law Reports
LT   Law Times Reports
M & W   Meeson and Welsby's Reports
NSWCA   New South Wales Court of Appeal [Australia]
NWSLR   New South Wales Law Reports [Australia]
NW   North Western Reporter [US]
P & CR   Property, Planning and Compensation Reports
PC   Privy Council
PD   Probate, Divorce and Admiralty Division
Ph   Phillips' Reports
QB or QBD   Queen's Bench Division
RPC   Reports of Patent, Design and Trade Mark Cases
SCC   Supreme Court of Canada
SLT   Scots Law Times
Swans   Swanston's Reports
TCLR   Trade and Competition Law Reports [New Zealand]
TLR   Times Law Reports
TR   Term Reports
UKHL   United Kingdom House of Lords
UKPC   United Kingdom Privy Council
UKSC   United Kingdom Supreme Court
WLR   Weekly Law Reports

Legislative References

art(s)   article(s)
BGB   *Bürgerliches Gesetzbuch* (German Civil Code)
C Civ   *Code civil* (French civil code)
para(s)   paragraph(s)
pt   part
reg(s)   regulation(s)
s(s)   section(s)
sch   schedule
SI   Statutory Instrument

Journals

CLJ	Cambridge Law Journal
CLP	Current Legal Problems
Colum L Rev	Columbia Law Review
Harv L Rev	Harvard Law Review
LQR	Law Quarterly Review
LS	Legal Studies
MLR	Modern Law Review
OJLS	Oxford Journal of Legal Studies

Other

B	Baron
C	Chancellor
CJ	Chief Justice
CJEU	Court of Justice of the European Union
Cm or Cmd or Cmnd	Command Paper [UK Government publication]
CPR	Civil Procedure Rules
DPSC	Deputy President of the Supreme Court
J	Justice [judge at first instance]
JSC	Justice of the Supreme Court
LC	Lord Chancellor
LJ	Lord (or Lady) Justice [judge of the Court of Appeal]
MR	Master of the Rolls
PSC	President of the Supreme Court

Table of Cases

Actionstrength Ltd v International Glass Engineering
 IN.GL.EN SpA [2003] UKHL 17, [2003] 2 AC 541 .... 59, 131
Adam Opel GmbH v Mitras Automotive UK Ltd [2007]
 EWHC 3252 (QB) 142
Adams v Lindsell (1818) 1 B & Ald 681, 106 ER 250 .... 117, 119
Addis v Gramophone Co Ltd [1909] AC 488 (HL) 292
Ailsa Craig Fishing Co Ltd v Malvern Fishing Co Ltd
 (The Strathallan) [1983] 1 WLR 964 (HL Sc) 223
Ajayi v RT Briscoe (Nigeria) Ltd [1964] 1 WLR 1326 (PC) 147
Alcock v Chief Constable of South Yorkshire Police [1992]
 1 AC 310 (HL) 44
Alfred McAlpine Construction Ltd v Panatown Ltd [2001]
 1 AC 518 (HL) 249
Allcard v Skinner (1887) 36 Ch D 145 (CA) 194, 195
Allen v Hounga [2014] UKSC 47; [2014] 1 WLR 2889 (SC) 200
Allied Marine Transport v Vale do Rio Doce Navegacao SA
 (The Leonidas D) [1985] 1 WLR 925 (CA) 115, 116, 149
André et Compagnie SA v Marine Transocean Ltd
 (The Splendid Sun) [1981] QB 694 (CA) 116
Andrews v Hopkinson [1957] 1 QB 229 (QB) 42, 203
Anglia Television Ltd v Reed [1972] 1 QB 60 (CA) 79, 288
Antaios Compania Naviera SA v Salen Rederierna AB
 (The Antaios) [1985] AC 191 (HL) 209
Arnold v Britton [2015] UKSC 36; [2015] AC 1619 209
Associated Japanese Bank (International) Ltd v Crédit du
 Nord SA [1989] 1 WLR 255 (QB) 173
Atlas Express Ltd v Kafco (Importers and Distributors) Ltd
 [1989] QB 833 (QB) 192
Attorney-General v Blake [2001] 1 AC 268 (HL) 38, 293
Attorney-General v R [2003] UKPC 22, [2003] EMLR 24 196
Attorney-General of Belize v Belize Telecom Ltd [2009]
 UKPC 10, [2009] 1 WLR 1988 210
Axa Sun Life Services plc v Campbell Martin Ltd [2011]
 EWCA Civ 133, [2011] 1 CLC 312 186
Aziz v Caixa d'Estalvis de Catalunya, Tarragona i Manresa
 (Catalunyacaixa) (C-415/11) [2013] 3 CMLR 5;
 [2013] All ER (EC) 770 (ECJ) 233
Baird Textile Holdings Ltd v Marks & Spencer plc [2001]
 EWCA Civ 274, [2002] 1 All ER (Comm) 737 .... 83, 153, 155
Balfour v Balfour [1919] 2 KB 571 (CA) 157

Bank of Credit and Commerce International SA v Aboody
[1990] QB 923 (CA)..195
Bank of Credit and Commerce International SA v Ali
[2001] UKHL 8, [2002] 1 AC 251..208
Banque Financière de la Cité SA v Westgate Insurance Co
[1991] 2 AC 249 (HL)..187
Barclays Bank plc v O'Brien [1994] 1 AC 180 (HL)...194
Barton v Armstrong [1976] AC 104 (PC)...191
Bell v Lever Bros Ltd [1932] AC 161 (HL).................................. 164, 173, 175, 176
Benedetti v Sawiris [2013] UKSC 50, [2014] AC 938 94
Beswick v Beswick [1968] AC 58 (HL) 27, 241, 248, 254, 278
BICC plc v Burndy Corp [1985] Ch 232 (CA)..287
Bilta (UK) Ltd (In Liquidation) v Nazir [2015] UKSC 23;
[2015] 2 WLR 1168 (SC) 200
Black-Clawson International Ltd v Papierwerke Waldhof-Aschaffenburg
AG [1975] AC 591 (HL)...31
Blackpool and Fylde Aero Club v Blackpool BC [1990] 1 WLR 1195 90
Bourhill v Young [1943] AC 92 (HL Sc)...44
BP Exploration Co (Libya) Ltd v Hunt (No 2) [1979] 1 WLR 783 (QB)...............268
Bremer Handelsgesellschaft mbH v Vanden Avenne-Izegem
PVBA [1978] 2 Lloyd's Rep 109 (HL)...149
Brennan v Bolt Burdon [2004] EWCA Civ 1017,
[2005] QB 303 (CA).. 175, 177
Brewer Street Investments Ltd v Barclays Woollen
Co Ltd [1954] 1 QB 428 (CA)..92, 93
Brikom Investments Ltd v Carr [1979] QB 467 (CA)...149
Brimnes, The [1975] QB 929 (CA)..119
Brinkibon Ltd v Stahag Stahl und Stahlwarenhandelsgesellschaft
[1983] 2 AC 34 (HL)... 106, 118, 119
British Car Auctions Ltd v Wright [1972] 1 WLR 1519 (QB)................................110
British Crane Hire Corp Ltd v Ipswich Plant
Hire Ltd [1975] QB 303 (CA) 211, 212
British Groundschool Ltd v Intelligent Data
Capture Ltd [2014] EWHC 2145 (Ch) 67
British Steel Corp v Cleveland Bridge & Engineering Co Ltd
[1984] 1 All ER 504 (QB)...93
British Westinghouse Electric and Manufacturing Co Ltd v Underground
Electric Railways Co of London Ltd [1912] AC 673 (HL) 295
Brogden v Metropolitan Railway Co (1876) LR 2 App Cas 666 (HL)...................115
Brown v Gould [1972] Ch 53 (Ch)... 123, 124
Bunge Corp, New York v Tradax Export SA Panama
[1981] 1 WLR 711 (HL) 282
Bunge SA v Nidera BV (formerly Nidera Handelscompagnie BV)
[2015] UKSC 43; [2015] 3 All ER 1082..289
Butler Machine Tool Co v Ex-Cell-O Corp (England)
Ltd [1979] 1 WLR 401 (CA)...99, 107, 120, 121
Byrne & Co v Van Tienhoven & Co (1880) 5 CPD 344 .... 113, 114

Cable & Wireless plc v IBM United Kingdom Ltd [2002]
    EWHC 2059 (Comm), [2002] 2 All ER (Comm) 1041 .... 78, 271
Callisher v Bischoffsheim (1870) LR 5 QB 449 137
Campbell Discount Co Ltd v Bridge [1962] AC 600 (HL) 286
Caparo Industries plc v Dickman [1990] 2 AC 605 (HL) 44, 181
Car and Universal Finance Co Ltd v Caldwell [1965] 1 QB 525 (CA) 179
Carewatch Care Services Ltd v Focus Caring Services Ltd
    [2014] EWHC 2313 (Ch) 67
Carlill v Carbolic Smoke Ball Co [1893] 1 QB 256 (CA) 91, 110, 112, 115,
    116, 134, 238
Carter v Boehm (1766) 3 Burr 1905, 97 ER 1162 187
Cassell & Co Ltd v Broome [1972] AC 1027 (HL) 27
Cavendish Square Holding BV v Makdessi; ParkingEye Ltd v
    Beavis [2015] UKSC 67; [2015] 3 WLR 1373 .... 225, 300
CCC Films (London) v Impact Quadrant Films [1985] QB 16 (QB) 289
Central London Property Trust v High Trees House [1947]
    KB 130 (KB) 38, 145, 146, 147,
    150, 151, 152
Centrovincial Estates v Merchant Investors Assurance
    Co [1983] Com LR 158 (CA) 100, 134
Chapelton v Barry UDC [1940] 1 KB 532 (CA) 205
Chartbrook Ltd v Persimmon Homes Ltd [2009] UKHL 38,
    [2009] 1 AC 1101 .... 27, 165, 208
CIBC Mortgages plc v Pitt [1994] 1 AC 200 (HL) 196
Clarke v Earl of Dunraven (The Satanita) [1897] AC 59 (HL) 105, 108
Coatsworth v Johnson (1886) 54 LT 520 (CA) 278
Cobbe v Yeoman's Row Management Ltd [2008]
    UKHL 55, [2008] 1 WLR 1752 130
Coggs v Bernard (1703) 2 Lord Raym 900, 92 ER 107 54
Collier v P & MJ Wright (Holdings) Ltd [2007] EWCA
    Civ 1329, [2008] 1 WLR 643 .... 143, 147, 151
Collins v Hopkins [1923] 2 KB 617 (KB) 214
Combe v Combe [1951] 2 KB 215 (CA) 83, 132, 152,
    153, 155, 199
Commission for the New Towns v Cooper (Great Britain)
    Ltd [1995] Ch 259 (CA) 127, 166
Commonwealth v Verwayen (1990) 95 ALR 321 (HCA) 153, 154
Conlon v Simms [2006] EWCA Civ 1749, [2008] 1 WLR 484;
    [2006] EWHC 401 (Ch), [2006] 2 All ER 1024 .... 81, 86, 187, 188
Continental Illinois National Bank & Trust Co of Chicago v
    Papanicolaou (The Fedora) [1986] 2 Lloyd's Rep 441 (CA) 223
Cook v Wright (1861) 1 B & S 559, 121 ER 822 137
Co-operative Insurance Society Ltd v Argyll Stores
    (Holdings) Ltd [1998] AC 1 (HL) 277, 278, 279, 290
Co-operative Insurance Society Ltd v Argyll Stores
    (Holdings) Ltd (No 2) 1999 SLT 685 (Outer House, Ct of Session) 278
Couchman v Hill [1947] KB 554 (CA) 203

Courtney & Fairbairn Ltd v Tolaini Brothers (Hotels) Ltd
 [1975] 1 WLR 297 (CA) 65, 76, 123
Coward v Motor Insurers' Bureau [1963] 1 QB 259 (CA) 157
Cresswell v Potter [1978] 1 WLR 255 (Ch) 197
Crossco No 4 Unlimited v Jolan Ltd [2011] EWHC 803 (Ch),
 [2011] All ER (D) 13 (Apr) 165
CTN Cash and Carry Ltd v Gallaher Ltd [1994]
 4 All ER 714 (CA) 192, 193
Cundy v Lindsay (1878) 3 App Cas 459 (HL) 169
Currie v Misa (1875) 10 Exch 153 .... 70, 133
Curtis v Chemical Cleaning and Dyeing Co [1951] 1 KB 805 (CA) 207
Customs and Excise Commissioners v Barclays Bank plc
 [2006] UKHL 28, [2007] 1 AC 181 44
D & F Estates Ltd v Church Commissioners for England
 [1989] AC 177 (HL) 39, 44
Dahl v Nelson (1881) 6 App Cas 38 263
Dandara Holdings Ltd v Co-operative Retail Services Ltd [2004]
 EWHC 1476 (QB), [2004] 2 EGLR 163 89
Darlington BC v Wiltshier Northern Ltd [1995]
 1 WLR 68 (CA) 156, 239, 240,
 249, 255
Daulia Ltd v Four Millbank Nominees Ltd [1978] Ch 231 92
Davis Contractors v Fareham UDC [1956] AC 696 (HL) 263, 266
Dawson v Great Northern and City Railway Co
 [1905] 1 KB 260 (CA) 258
De Francesco v Barnum (1890) 45 Ch D 438 (CA) 277
De la Bere v Pearson [1908] 1 KB 280 (CA) 137
Denny Mott & Dickson Ltd v James B Fraser & Co Ltd
 [1944] AC 265 (HL Sc) 265
Derry v Peek (1889) 14 App Cas 337 (HL) 84, 180
Dick Bentley Productions Ltd v Harold Smith (Motors)
 Ltd [1965] 1 WLR 623 (CA) 204
Dickinson v Dodds [1876] 2 Ch D 463 (CA) 114
Dies v British and International Mining and Finance Corp
 Ltd [1939] 1 KB 724 (KB) 287
Dimmock v Hallett (1866) 2 Ch App 21 177
Dimskal Shipping Co SA v International Transport Workers
 Federation (The Evia Luck) [1992] 2 AC 152 (HL) 192
Director General of Fair Trading v First National Bank plc
 [2001] UKHL 52, [2002] 1 AC 481 233
Don King Productions Inc v Warren [2000] Ch 291 (CA) 258
Donoghue v Stevenson [1932] AC 562 (HL Sc) 35, 38, 39, 40, 41,
 42, 43, 44, 54, 76
Dunhill v Burgin [2014] UKSC 18; [2014] 1 WLR 933 (SC) 198
Dunlop Pneumatic Tyre Co Ltd v New Garage and Motor
 Co Ltd [1915] AC 79 (HL) 224, 300
Dunlop Pneumatic Tyre Co Ltd v Selfridge & Co Ltd
 [1915] AC 847 (HL) 10, 27, 238, 240

Durham Fancy Goods Ltd v Michael Jackson (Fancy Goods)
   Ltd [1968] 2 QB 839 (QB) 148
Earl of Aylesford v Morris (1873) 8 Ch App 484 197
Edgington v Fitzmaurice (1885) 29 ChD 459 (CA) 86, 97, 178
Edwards v Skyways [1964] 1 QB 349 (QB) 157
EE Caledonia Ltd v Orbit Valve Co Europe [1994]
   1 WLR 1515 (CA) 223
Entores Ltd v Miles Far East Corp [1955] 2 QB 327 (CA) 118, 119
Errington v Errington [1952] 1 KB 290 (CA) 91
Esso Petroleum Co Ltd v Mardon [1976] QB 801 (CA) 85, 181
Esso Petroleum Co Ltd v Niad Ltd [2001] EWHC 6 (Ch),
   [2001] All ER (D) 324 293
Experience Hendrix LLC v PPX Enterprises Inc [2003]
   EWCA Civ 323, [2003] 1 All ER(Comm) 830 .... 293, 294
Exxonmobil Sales & Supply Corp v Texaco Ltd [2003]
   EWHC 1964 (QB), [2003] 2 Lloyd's Rep 686 206
Factortame Ltd v Secretary of State for Transport [1990] 2 AC 85 (HL) 18
Fairline Shipping Corp v Adamson [1975] QB 180 (QB) 116
Falcke v Gray (1859) 4 Drew 651, 62 ER 250 280
Farley v Skinner [2001] UKHL 49, [2002] 2 AC 732 291
Felthouse v Bindley (1862) 11 CB NS 869, 142 ER 1037 .... 115, 116
Fibrosa Spolka Akcyjna v Fairbairn Lawson Combe
   Barbour Ltd [1943] AC 32 (HL) 267
First National Securities Ltd v Jones [1978] Ch 109 (CA) 128
Fisher v Bell [1961] 1 WLR 394 (DC) 110
Fitzpatrick v Sterling Housing Association Ltd [2001] 1 AC 27 (HL) 33
Foakes v Beer (1884) 9 App Cas 605 .... 21, 25, 142,
                                                                                                       143, 147, 151
Foley v Classique Coaches Ltd [1934] 2 KB 1 (CA) 78, 123
Forsikringsaktieselskapet Vesta v Butcher [1989] AC 852 (HL) 296
Frederick E Rose (London) Ltd v William H Pim Junior &
   Co Ltd [1953] 2 QB 450 (CA) 99, 166
Freeman v Cooke (1848) 2 Exch 654, 154 ER 652 .... 100, 101
Fry v Lane (1889) LR 40 Ch D 312 (Ch) 197
G Percy Trentham Ltd v Archital Luxfer Ltd [1993]
   1 Lloyd's Rep 25 (CA) 103
G Scammell and Nephew Ltd v HC and JG Ouston
   [1941] AC 251 (HL) 123
Gamerco SA v ICM/Fair Warning (Agency) Ltd [1995]
   1 WLR 1226 (QB) 268
Gee v Pritchard (1818) 2 Swans 402, 36 ER 670 6
Geys v Société Générale, London Branch [2012] UKSC 63,
   [2013] 1 AC 523 283
Ghaidan v Godin-Mendoza [2004] UKHL 30, [2004] 2 AC 557 33
Gibson v Manchester City Council [1979] 1 WLR 294 (HL);
   [1978] 1 WLR 520 (CA) 99, 107, 108,
                                                                                                       109, 120, 121

Gillespie Bros & Co Ltd v Roy Bowles Transport Ltd
  [1973] QB 400 (CA) 222
Glasbrook Bros Ltd v Glamorgan County Council
  [1925] AC 70 (HL) 139
Goddard's Case (1584) 2 Co Rep 4b, 76 ER 396 128
Golden Strait Corp v Nippon Yusen Kubishika Kaisha
  (The Golden Victory) [2007] UKHL 12, [2002] 2 AC 353 289
Golden Ocean Group Ltd v Salgaocar Mining Industries PVT
  Ltd [2012] EWCA Civ 265, [2012] 1 WLR 3674 (CA) 127
Gordon v Selico Co Ltd [1985] 2 EGLR 79 (Ch) 177
Gore v Gibson (1845) 13 M & W 623, 153 ER 260 198
Grainger & Son v Gough [1896] AC 325 (HL) 111
Granatino v Radmacher [2010] UKSC 42, [2011] 1 AC 534 157
Great Peace Shipping Ltd v Tsavliris Salvage (International) Ltd
  (The Great Peace) [2002] EWCA Civ 1407, [2003] QB 679 .... 26, 38, 99, 172,
                                                                                   173, 174,
                                                                                   175, 176
Greenclose Ltd v National Westminster Bank plc [2014] EWHC
  1156 (Ch), [2014] 1 CLC 562 119
Greenwood v Greenwood (1863) 2 De GJ & S 28, 46 ER 285 187
Grundt v Great Boulder Pty Gold Mines Ltd (1937) 59 CLR 641 154
Hadley v Baxendale (1854) 9 Ex 341, 156 ER 145 .... 70, 294, 295
Hallett's Estate, In re: Knatchbull v Hallett (1880) 13 ChD 696 35
Halpern v Halpern [2007] EWCA Civ 291, [2008] 1 QB 195 193
Hamilton v Watson (1845) 12 Cl & Fin 109, 8 ER 1339 (HL Sc) 187
Hardwick Game Farm v Suffolk Agricultural and Poultry
  Producers Association Ltd [1966] 1 WLR 287 (CA) 213
Harris v Great Western Railway (1876) 1 QBD 515 .... 205, 207
Hart v O'Connor [1985] AC 1000 (PC) 198, 219
Hartley v Ponsonby (1857) 7 El & Bl 872, 119 ER 1471 140
Harvela Investments Ltd v Royal Trust Co of Canada
  (CI Ltd) [1986] AC 207 (HL) 90, 113
Haseldine v CA Daw & Son Ltd [1941] 2 KB 343 (CA) 42
Hedley Byrne & Co Ltd v Heller & Partners Ltd
  [1964] AC 465 (HL) 39, 42, 44, 52,
                                                                                  54, 85, 137, 181
Heilbut, Symons & Co v Buckleton [1913] AC 30 (HL) 203
Helby v Matthews [1895] AC 471 (HL) 87
Henderson v Merrett Syndicates Ltd [1995] 2 AC 145 (HL) 53
Henthorn v Fraser [1892] 2 Ch 27 (CA) 117
Herbert v Doyle [2010] EWCA Civ 1095, [2011] 1 EGLR 119 130
Herschtal v Stewart and Ardern Ltd [1940] 1 KB 155 (KB) 42
Heywood v Wellers [1976] QB 446 (CA) 292
HIH Casualty and General Insurance Ltd v Chase Manhattan
  Bank [2003] UKHL 6, [2003] 2 Lloyd's Rep 61; [2001] EWCA
  Civ 1250, [2001] 2 Lloyd's Rep 483 .... 188, 224
Hirji Mulji v Cheong Yue Steamship Co Ltd [1926] AC 497 (PC) 263

Hochster v De La Tour (1852) 2 El & Bl 678, 118 ER 922 283
Hoenig v Isaacs [1953] 2 All ER 176 (CA) 288
Hoffman v Red Owl Stores Inc 133 NW 2d 267 .... 83, 153
Hollier v Rambler Motors (AMC) Ltd [1972] 2 QB 71 (CA) 211
Holwell Securities v Hughes [1974] 1 WLR 155 (CA) 117, 118
Home Office v Dorset Yacht Co Ltd [1970] AC 1004 (HL) 44
Hongkong Fir Shipping Co Ltd v Kawasaki Kisen Kaisha
 Ltd (The Hongkong Fir) [1962] 2 QB 26 (CA) 283
Howe v Smith (1884) 27 Ch D 89 (CA) 286
Hughes v Metropolitan Railway Co (1877) 2 App Cas 439 (HL) 146, 149
Huyton SA v Peter Cremer GmbH & Co [1999]
 1 Lloyd's Rep 620 (QB) 193
Hyde v Wrench (1840) 3 Beav 334, 49 ER 132 114
Inche Noriah v Shaik Allie Bin Omar [1929] AC 127 (PC) 195
Ingram v Little [1961] 1 QB 31 (CA) 168, 170
Inntrepreneur Pub Co (GL) v East Crown Ltd [2000]
 2 Lloyd's Rep 611 (Ch) 186, 206
Interfoto Picture Library Ltd v Stiletto Visual Programmes
 Ltd [1989] QB 433 (CA) 65, 76, 220, 221
Investors Compensation Scheme Ltd v West Bromwich
 Building Society [1998] 1 WLR 896 (HL) 208, 209, 211
J Lauritzen AS v Wijsmuller BV (The Super Servant Two)
 [1990] 1 Lloyd's Rep 1 (CA) 265
J Pereira Fernandes SA v Mehta [2006] EWHC 813 (Ch),
 [2006] 1 WLR 1543 127
Jackson v Horizon Holidays Ltd [1975] 1 WLR 1468 (CA) 249
Jackson v Union Marine Insurance Co Ltd (1874) LR 10 CP 125 .... 263, 266
Jaggard v Sawyer [1995] 1 WLR 269 (CA) 280
Jarvis v Swan Tours Ltd [1973] QB 233 (CA) 292
Jennings v Rice [2002] EWCA Civ 159, [2003] 1 P & CR 8 .... 145, 154
John Grimes Partnership Ltd v Gubbins [2013] EWCA Civ 37;
 [2013] BLR 126 295
Johnson v Agnew [1980] AC 367 (HL) 281, 285
Johnson v Unisys Ltd [2001] UKHL 13, [2003] 1 AC 518 292
Jones v Kaney [2011] UKSC 13, [2011] 2 AC 398 12
Jones v Padavatton [1969] 1 WLR 328 (CA) 157
Jones v Secretary of State for Social Services [1972] AC 944 (HL) 27
Jorden v Money (1854) 5 HL Cas 185, 10 ER 868 .... 144, 145, 146
Kay v Lambeth LVC [2006] UKHL 10, [2006] 2 AC 465 .... 25, 27
Kennedy v Panama New Zealand and Australian
 Royal Mail Co (1867) LR 2 QB 580 262
King's Motors (Oxford) v Lax [1970] 1 WLR 426 (Ch) 123
King's Norton Metal Co Ltd v Edridge, Merrett and
 Co Ltd (1897) 14 TLR 98 (CA) 169
Kleinwort Benson Ltd v Lincoln City Council
 [1999] 2 AC 349 (HL) 35, 36, 37
Kleinwort Benson Ltd v Malaysia Mining Corp Bhd
 [1989] 1 WLR 379 (CA) 156

Koufos v C Czarnikow Ltd (The Heron II) [1969] 1 AC 350 (HL) 295
Krell v Henry [1903] 2 KB 740 (CA) 265
Kuddus v Chief Constable of Leicestershire Constabulary [2001]
 UKHL 29, [2002] 2 AC 122..292
Les Laboratoires Servier v Apotex Inc [2014] UKSC 55;
 [2015] AC 430 (SC)..200
L'Estrange v Graucob [1934] 2 KB 394 (CA)..207
Lewis v Averay [1972] 1 QB 198 (CA) 168, 170
Linden Gardens Trust Ltd v Lenesta Sludge Disposals Ltd
 [1994] 1 AC 85 (HL)..14, 249, 257, 258
Lindsay Petroleum Co v Hurd (1873) 5 PC 221..166
Little v Courage (1994) 70 P & CR 469 (CA)...77
Liverpool CC v Irwin [1977] AC 239 (HL)..60, 212, 214, 216
Lloyds Bank Ltd v Bundy [1975] QB 326 (CA) 190
Lloyds Bank Ltd v Marcan [1973] 1 WLR 1387 (CA)...123
Lloyds Bank plc v Waterhouse [1993] 2 FLR 97 (CA)..207
Lloyds TSB Foundation for Scotland v Lloyds Banking
 Group plc [2013] UKSC 3, [2013] 1 WLR 366...269
Lord Strathcona Steamship Co Ltd v Dominion Coal Co Ltd
 [1926] AC 108 (PC)...246
Lordsvale Finance plc v Bank of Zambia [1966] QB 752 (QB) 224
Lumley v Gye (1852) 2 El & Bl 216, 118 ER 749..245
Malik v Bank of Credit and Commerce International SA
 [1998] AC 20 (HL)..214
Malik Co v Central European Trading Agency [1974]
 2 Lloyd's Rep 279 (QB) 77
Manchester Diocesan Council of Education v Commercial &
 General Investments Ltd [1970] 1 WLR 241 (Ch)..116
Mannai Investment Co Ltd v Eagle Star Life Assurance
 Co Ltd [1997] AC 749 (HL).. 208, 209
Maredelanto Compania Naviera SA v Bergbau–Handel
 GmbH (The Mihalis Angelos) [1971] 1 QB 164 (CA)..284
Markham v Paget [1908] 1 Ch 697 (Ch) 214
Marks & Spencer Plc v BNP Paribas Securities Services
 Trust Co (Jersey) Ltd [2014] EWCA Civ 603, [2014] L &
 TR 26, [2015] UKSC 72; [2015] 3 WLR 1843 .... 211, 213
Martel Building Ltd v Canada (2000) 193 DLR (4th) 1 ....82, 91
May and Butcher v The King [1934] 2 KB 17 (HL)..123
McCutcheon v David MacBrayne Ltd [1964] 1 WLR 125 (HL Sc) 211
McIlkenny v Chief Constable of the West Midlands
 [1980] QB 283 (CA)..144
McRae v Commonwealth Disposals Commission
 (1951) 84 CLR 377 (HCA)..173
Mid Essex Hospital Serives NHS Trust v Compass
 Group UK & Ireland Ltd [2013] EWCA Civ 200 67
Miliangos v George Frank (Textiles) Ltd [1976] AC 443 (HL)................................24
Miller Paving Ltd v B Gottardo Construction Ltd (2007)
 285 DLR (4th) 568 176

Milner v Carnival plc [2010] EWCA Civ 389, [2010] 3 All ER 701 292
Ministry of Health v Simpson [1951] 1 AC 251 (HL) 238
Moorcock, The (1889) 14 PD 64 (CA) 212
Multiservice Bookbinding Ltd v Marden [1979] Ch 84 (Ch) 198, 226
National Westminster Bank Ltd v Morgan [1985] AC 686 (HL) 34, 190
New Zealand Shipping Co Ltd v AM Satterthwaite & Co
 Ltd (The Eurymedon) [1975] AC 154 (PC) 104, 107, 139, 244
Nicolene v Simmonds [1953] 1 QB 543 (CA) 124
Nordenfelt v Maxim Nordenfelt Guns and Ammunition Co
 Ltd [1894] AC 535 (HL) 199
North Ocean Shipping Co v Hyundai Construction Co
 (The Atlantic Baron) [1979] QB 705 (QB) 193
OBG Ltd v Allan [2007] UKHL 21, [2007] 2 WLR 920 245
Occidental Worldwide Investment Corp v Skibs A/S Avanti
 (The Siboen and The Sibotre) [1976] 1 Lloyd's Rep 293 (QB) 192
Ocean Tramp Tankers Corp v V/O Sovfracht (The Eugenia)
 [1964] 2 QB 226 (CA) 265
Office of Fair Trading v Abbey National plc [2009]
 UKSC 6, [2010] 1 AC 696 232
Olley v Marlborough Court Ltd [1949] 1 KB 532 (CA) 205
Omak Maritime Ltd v Mamola Challenger Shipping Co Ltd
 [2010] EWHC 2026 (Comm), [2010] 2 CLC 194 289
Onyx Group Ltd v Auckland City Council (2003) 11 TCLR 40 82
Oscar Chess Ltd v Williams [1957] 1 WLR 370 (CA) 99, 204
Paal Wilson & Co A/S v Partenreederei Hannah Blumenthal
 (The Hannah Blumenthal) [1983] 1 AC 854 (HL) 101, 102, 116
Page v Smith [1996] AC 155 (HL) 44
Pankhania v Hackney LBC [2002] EWHC 2441 (Ch),
 [2002] All ER (D) 22 (Aug) 177
Pannon GSM Zrt v Sustikne Gyorfi (C-243/08) [2010]
 1 All ER (Comm) 640; [2009] E.C.R. I-4713 (ECJ) 232
Pao On v Lau Yiu Long [1980] AC 614 (PC) 138, 192
Paradine v Jane (1647) Aleyn 26, 82 ER 897 261
Parker v South Eastern Railway (1877) 2 CPD 416 204
ParkingEye Ltd v Beavis. See Cavendish Square Holding
 BV v Makdessi; ParkingEye Ltd v Beavis
ParkingEye Ltd v Somerfield Stores Ltd [2012] EWCA Civ 1338;
 [2013] QB 840 (CA) 200
Partridge v Crittenden [1968] 1 WLR 1204 (QB) 110, 111
Pearce v Brooks (1866) LR 1 Exch 213 199
Peek v Gurney (1873) LR 6 HL 377 .... 81, 86, 188
Peekay Intermark Ltd v Australia and New Zealand Banking
 Group Ltd [2006] EWCA Civ 386, [2006] 2 Lloyd's Rep 511 .... 185, 207
Pell Frischmann Engineering Ltd v Bow Valley Iran Ltd [2009]
 UKPC 45, [2011] 1 WLR 2370 294
Pepper v Hart [1993] AC 593 (HL) 31
Peter Pan Manufacturing Corp v Corsets Silhouette Ltd [1976]
 1 WLR 923 (CA) 94

Petromec Inc v Petroleo Brasileiro SA [2005] EWCA Civ 891,
  [2006] 1 Lloyd's Rep 121 .... 79, 271
Peyman v Lanjani [1985] Ch 457 (CA) 283
Pharmaceutical Society of Great Britain v Boots Cash
  Chemists (Southern) Ltd [1953] 1 QB 401 (CA),
  [1952] 2 QB 795 (QBD) 110, 111, 112
Philips Hong Kong Ltd v Attorney-General of
  Hong Kong (1993) 61 BLR 41 (PC) 228, 300, 301
Phillips Products v Hyland [1987] 1 WLR 659 (CA) 228
Photo Production Ltd v Securicor Transport Ltd
  [1980] AC 827 (HL) 33, 202, 220, 222, 223,
  225, 274, 281, 282,
  284, 285
Pinnel's Case (1602) 5 Co Rep 117a, 77 ER 237 .... 21, 142, 143, 151
Pinner v Everett [1969] 1 WLR 1266 (HL) 29
Pioneer Container, The [1994] 2 AC 324 (PC) 247
Pioneer Shipping Ltd v BTP Tioxide Ltd (The Nema)
  [1982] AC 724 (HL) 263
Pitt v PHH Asset Management Ltd [1994]
  1 WLR 327 (CA) 87, 88, 137
Port Jackson Stevedoring Pty Ltd v Salmond & Spraggon
  (Australia) Pty Ltd (The New York Star) [1981] 1 WLR 138 (PC) 244
Port Line Ltd v Ben Line Steamers Ltd [1958] 2 QB 14 (QB) 246
Practice Statement (Judicial Precedent) [1966] 1 WLR 1234 26
Pratt Contractors Ltd v Transit New Zealand
  [2003] UKPC 83, [2004] BLR 143 90
Prenn v Simmonds [1971] 1 WLR 1381 (HL) 208
Quinn v Leathem [1901] 1 AC 495 (HL) 38
R (Jackson) v Attorney General [2005] UKHL 56, [2006] 1 AC 262 32
Rainy Sky SA v Kookmin Bank [2011] UKSC 50,
  [2011] 1 WLR 2900 209
Ramsden v Dyson and Thornton (1866) LR 1 HL 129 144
Ramsgate Victoria Hotel Co Ltd v Montefiore (1866)
  1 LR 1 Exch 109 113
Rann v Hughes (1778) 7 TR 350n, 101 ER 1014 128
Recher's Will Trusts, Re [1972] Ch 526 (Ch) 105
Record v Bell [1991] 1 WLR 853 (Ch) 206
Redgrave v Hurd (1881) 20 Ch D 1 (CA) 179
Regalian Properties Plc v London Docklands Development
  Corp [1995] 1 WLR 212 (Ch) 80, 94
Reichman v Beveridge [2006] EWCA Civ 1659, [2007] 1 P & CR 20 284
Republic of India v Indian Steamship Co Ltd (No 2)
  [1998] AC 878 (HL) 144
Rice v Great Yarmouth BC [2000] All ER (D) 902 (CA) 286
Robb v Green [1895] 2 QB 315 (CA) 214
Robinson v Harman (1848) 1 Ex 850, 154 ER 363 .... 70, 288
Robophone Facilities Ltd v Blank [1966] 1 WLR 1428 (CA) 300
Rookes v Barnard [1964] AC 1129 (HL) 193

TABLE OF CASES xxxi

Roscorla v Thomas (1842) 3 QB 234, 114 ER 496..138
Rose & Frank Co v JR Crompton & Bros Ltd
  [1925] AC 445 (HL)..156
Routledge v Grant (1828) 4 Bing 653, 130 ER 920...113
Royal Bank of Scotland plc v Etridge (No 2) [2001]
  UKHL 44, [2002] 2 AC 773... 180, 187, 194,
                                                                 195, 196, 220
Royscot Trust Ltd v Rogerson [1991] 2 QB 297 (CA)...182
RTS Flexible Systems Ltd v Molkerei Alois Müller GmbH &
  Co KG [2010] UKSC 14, [2010] 1 WLR 753 ....79, 100, 156
Rugby Group Ltd v ProForce Recruit Ltd [2005] EWHC 70 (QB).........................79
Ruxley Electronics & Construction Ltd v Forsyth [1996]
  AC 344 (HL) 290, 291, 292,
                                                                      301, 302
S Pearson & Son Ltd v Dublin Corporation [1907] AC 351 (HL) 224
Saleh v Romanous [2010] NSWCA 274, (2010) 79 NSWLR 453......................154
Saltman Engineering Co v Campbell Engineering Co
  (1948) 65 RPC 203 (CA) 94
Samuel v Jarrah Timer and Wood Paving Corp Ltd
  [1904] AC 323 (HL).. 61, 226
Saunders v Anglia Building Society [1971] AC 1004 (HL) 167
Scandinavian Trading Tanker Co AB v Flota Petrolera
  Ecuatoriana (The Scaptrade) [1983] 2 AC 694 (HL)..287
Scarf v Jardine (1882) 7 App Cas 345 (HL)...259
Schebsman, Re [1944] Ch 83 (CA)...243
Scotson v Pegg (1861) 6 H & N 295, 158 ER 121 139
Scruttons Ltd v Midland Silicones Ltd [1962] AC 446 (HL) 27, 240
Seager v Copydex Ltd (No 2) [1969] 1 WLR 809 (CA)..94
Selectmove, Re [1995] 1 WLR 474 (CA)...25, 142, 143
Sempra Metals Ltd (formerly Metallgesellschaft Ltd) v IRC
  [2007] UKHL 34; [2008] 1 AC 561..296
Shah v Shah [2001] EWCA Civ 527, [2002] QB 35 130
Shirlaw v Southern Foundries Ltd [1939] 2 KB 206 (CA) 211
Shogun Finance Ltd v Hudson [2003] UKHL 62,
  [2004] 1 AC 919 .... 11, 56, 162, 168,
                                                                      169, 170
Sky Petroleum Ltd v VIP Petroleum Ltd [1974] 1 WLR 576 (Ch).........................280
Smith New Court Securities Ltd v Scrimgeour Vickers
  (Asset Management) [1997] AC 254 (HL) 181
Smith v Hughes (1871) LR 6 QB 597..70, 80, 81, 100, 101,
                                                                 171, 172, 186, 205
Smith v Morgan [1971] 1 WLR 803 (Ch) 88
Société Italo–Belge Pour le Commerce et L'Industrie SA (Antwerp) v
  Palm and Vegetable Oils (Malaysia) Sdn
  Bhd (The Post Chaser) [1982] 1 All ER 19 (QB) 150
Solle v Butcher [1950] 1 KB 671 (CA)...38, 99, 164,
                                                                      175, 176

South Caribbean Trading Ltd v Trafigura Beheer BV [2004]
  EWHC 2676 (Comm), [2005] 1 Lloyd's Rep 128...24, 142
Southcott Estates Inc v Toronto Catholic District School
  Board, 2012 SCC 51, (2012) 351 DLR (4th) 476 (SC) 280
Southern Pacific Co v Jensen (1917) 244 US 205...36
Spencer v Harding (1870) LR 5 CP 561 ....90, 110, 113
Spiro v Glencrown Properties Ltd [1991] Ch 537 87
Springwell Navigation Corp v JP Morgan Chase Bank
  [2010] EWCA Civ 1221, [2010] 2 CLC 705 ....185, 186
Spurling v Bradshaw [1956] 1 WLR 461 (CA)...205
Staffordshire Area Health Authority v South Staffordshire
  Waterworks Co [1978] 1 WLR 1387 (CA) 264, 259
Statoil ASA v Louis Dreyfus Energy Services LP (The Harriette N)
  [2008] EWHC 2257 (Comm), [2008] 2 Lloyd's Rep 685 171
Stennett v Hancock [1939] 2 All ER 578 (KB)..42
Stevenson, Jacques & Co v McLean (1880) 5 QBD 346 (QB)................................114
Stewart Gill Ltd v Horatio Myer & Co Ltd [1992] QB 600 (CA)..........................229
Stilk v Myrick (1809) 2 Camp 317, 170 ER 1168...140, 141
Stockloser v Johnson [1954] 1 QB 476 (CA)...287
Sudbrook Trading Estate Ltd v Eggleton [1983] 1 AC 444 (HL) 78, 123
Sumpter v Hedges [1898] 1 QB 673 (CA) 288
Supershield Ltd v Siemens Building Technologies FE Ltd
  [2010] EWCA Civ 7, [2010] 1 Lloyd's Rep 349 295
Swain v Law Society [1983] 1 AC 598 (HL)..241
Swainland Builders Ltd v Freehold Properties Ltd [2002]
  EWCA Civ 560, [2002] 2 EGLR 71 165
Swiss Bank Corp v Lloyds Bank Ltd [1979] Ch 548 (Ch)......................................246
Sylvia Shipping Co Ltd v Progress Bulk Carriers Ltd [2010]
  EWHC 542 (Comm), [2010] 2 Lloyd's Rep 81 295
TSG Building Services plc v South Anglia Housing Ltd [2013]
  EWHC 1151 (TCC)...67
Tamplin v James (1880) 15 Ch D 215 97
Tang v Grant Thornton International Ltd [2012] EWHC 3198 (Ch),
  [2014] 2 CLC 663 ....78, 123
Taylor v Caldwell (1863) 3 B & S 826, 122 ER 309...70, 262
Taylor v Johnson (1982–1983) 151 CLR 422..99
Tekdata Interconnection Ltd v Amphenol Ltd [2009] EWCA
  Civ 1209, [2010] 1 Lloyd's Rep 357 ....106, 121
Thomas v Thomas (1842) 2 QB 851, 114 ER 330..135
Thomas Bates & Son Ltd v Wyndham's (Lingerie) Ltd [1981]
  1 WLR 505 (CA)..165
Thomas Borthwick (Glasgow) Ltd v Faure Fairclough Ltd
  [1968] 1 Lloyd's Rep 16 (QB)..270
Thomas Witter Ltd v TBP Industries Ltd [1996] 2 All ER 573 (Ch) 222
Thompson v Palmer (1933) 49 CLR 507...154
Thornton v Shoe Lane Parking Ltd [1971] 2 QB 163 (CA) 205
Tilden Rent-a-Car Co v Clendinning (1978) 83 DLR
  (3d) 400 (CA Ontario)..207

Timothy v Simpson (1834) 6 C & P 499, 172 ER 1337 110
Tinn v Hoffmann & Co (1873) 29 LT 271 .... 96, 116
Tinsley v Milligan [1994] 1 AC 340 (HL) 200
Transfield Shipping Inc v Mercator Shipping Inc
 (The Achilleas) [2008] UKHL 48, [2009] 1 AC 61 295
Tulk v Moxhay (1848) 2 Ph 774, 41 ER 1143 246
Turnbull & Co v Duval [1902] AC 429 (PC) 194
Tweddle v Atkinson (1861) 1 B & S 393, 121 ER 762 .... 70, 237, 238,
 241, 251
Tye v House (1998) 79 P & CR 188 (Ch) 89
Union Bank v Munster (1887) 37 Ch D 51 (Ch) 14
Union Eagle Ltd v Golden Achievement Ltd [1997] AC 514 (PC) 286
United Scientific Holdings Ltd v Burnley BC [1978] 1 AC 904 8
Universe Tankships Inc of Monrovia v International Transport
 Workers Federation (The Universe Sentinel)
 [1983] 1 AC 366 (HL) 38, 192
Van der Garde v Force India Formula One Team Ltd [2010]
 EWHC 2373 (QB) 294
Vandepitte v Preferred Accident Insurance Corp of New York
 [1933] AC 70 (PC) 243
Wade v Simeon (1846) 2 CB 548, 135 ER 1061 137
Wagon Mound, The [1961] AC 388 (PC) 181
Walford v Miles [1992] 2 AC 128 (HL) 65, 66, 77, 78,
 88, 123, 271
Walsh v Lonsdale (1882) 21 Ch D 9 (CA) 56, 280
Waltons Stores (Interstate) Ltd v Maher (1988) 164
 CLR 387 (HCA) 82, 153, 154
Ward v Byham [1956] 1 WLR 496 (CA) 139, 140
Warner Bros Pictures Inc v Nelson [1937] 1 KB 209 (KB) 280
Way v Latilla [1937] 3 All ER 759 (HL) 94
Western Fish Products Ltd v Penwith DC [1981] 2 All ER 204 (CA) 144
White v Jones [1995] 2 AC 207 (HL) 245
White & Carter (Councils) Ltd v McGregor [1962] AC 413 (HL Sc) 284
Whittaker v Kinnear [2011] EWHC 1479 (QB) 130
Wickman Machine Tool Sales Ltd v L Schuler
 AG [1974] AC 235 (HL) 282
William Lacey (Hounslow) Ltd v Davis [1957] 1 WLR 932 (QB) 93
Williams v Bayley (1866) LR 1 HL 200 194
Williams v Roffey Bros & Nicholls (Contractors)
 Ltd [1991] 1 QB 1 (CA) 24, 25, 134, 138, 140, 141, 142,
 143, 148, 156, 192, 240
Wilmott v Barber (1880) 15 Ch D 96 144
Wilson v First County Trust Ltd (No 2) [2003] UKHL 40,
 [2004] 1 AC 816 32
Wood v Scarth (1858) 1 F & F 293, 175 ER 733 96
Woodar Investment Development Ltd v Wimpey Construction
 UK Ltd [1980] 1 WLR 277 (HL) 241, 249, 284

Woodhouse AC Israel Cocoa SA v Nigerian Produce
  Marketing Co Ltd [1972] AC 741 (HL) 149
Workers Trust & Merchant Bank Ltd v Dojap Investments
  Ltd [1993] AC 573 (PC) 287
Wrotham Park Estate Co Ltd v Parkside Homes Ltd
  [1974] 1 WLR 798 (CA) 280, 293
WWF World Wide Fund for Nature (formerly World Wildlife Fund) v
  World Wrestling Federation Entertainment Inc [2007] EWCA Civ 286,
  [2008] 1 WLR 445 294
Yam Seng Pte Ltd v International Trade Corp Ltd [2013]
  EWHC 111 (QB), [2013] 1 Lloyd's Rep 526 .... 64, 66, 67,
                                                                                                                77, 271, 286
Yaxley v Gotts [2000] Ch 162 (CA) 129, 130, 131
Young v Bristol Aeroplane Ltd [1944] KB 718 (CA) 25, 27

Table of Legislation

UK Statutes

Bill of Rights 1689
    art 9 31
Chancery Amendment Act 1858
    s 2 281
Common Law Procedure Act 1852 39
Common Law Procedure Act 1854
    s 68 162
Companies Act 1989 199
    s 108 199
    s 130 129
Companies Act 2006 128
    s 33 105
    s 39 199
    s 44 129
Constitutional Reform Act 2005
    s 40 7
    s 59 7
    Sch 11 para 1 7
Consumer Credit Act 1974 ....34, 70, 234
    Pt 5 ....58, 126
    ss 137–140 234
    ss 140A–140C 234
Consumer Credit Act 2006
    ss 19–21 234
Consumer Insurance (Disclosure and Representations) Act 2012 ....5, 187
Consumer Protection Act 1987
    Pt I 18, 40
    s 2(6) 40
    s 6(7) 18
Consumer Rights Act 2015 ....61, 184, 187, 204, 216, 226,
                                                  227, 230, 231, 282, 298
    Pt 1 ....5, 62, 71, 230
    Pt 2 ....5, 66, 71, 72, 186, 230, 287, 299
    s 1 230
    s 2 ....226, 230
    s 3 ....214, 227
    s 9 ....60, 138, 172, 214, 230
    s 10 ....138, 172, 189, 214, 230
    s 11 ....184, 214, 230
    s 12 ....184, 230

xxxvi TABLE OF LEGISLATION

s 13	214, 230
s 17	214, 230
s 19(12)	298
ss 20–24	298
s 31	62, 215, 230
s 34	230
s 35	230
s 36	184, 230
s 37	184
s 41	230
s 42(8)	298
ss 43–45	298
s 47	62, 230
s 49	60, 215, 230
s 50	184, 230
s 51	122, 230
s 54(7)	299
s 55	299
s 56	299
s 57	62, 215, 230
s 58	299
s 61	230
s 62	231
s 64	232
s 65	230
(4)	230
s 68	231
s 69(1)	231
s 70	231
s 71	232
Sch 2 Pt 1	232
Consumer Safety Act 1978	34
Contracts (Rights of Third Parties) Act 1999	5, 17, 18, 28, 29, 45, 69, 70, 236, 241, 247, 250, 251, 252, 255, 256, 292, 303
s 1	303, 304
(1)	251
(2)	251, 253
(3)	251, 268
(5)	252
(6)	253
s 2	46, 253, 304, 305
(1)(a)	253
(b), (c)	253
s 3	252, 305, 306
(2)	254
(3)	254

(4)	254
(5)	254
s 4	306
s 5	252, 254, 306
s 6	251, 307
s 7	254, 309
s 8	309, 310
s 9	310
s 10	310
Crime and Courts Act 2013	
Sch 9	
Pt 3 para 71	305
Defamation Act 1952	19
Defamation Act 1996	19
Defamation Act 2013	19
Employment Rights Act 1996	233
Pt X	62
s 203	61, 233
Equality Act 2010	110
European Communities Act 1972	18
Financial Services and Markets Act 2000	
s 80	188
s 81	188
s 90	188
Government of Wales Act 1998	3
Hire Purchase Act 1964	
s 27(1), (2)	169
Human Rights Act 1998	18, 32, 33
s 3	18, 31
s 4	18
s 6(7)	18
Identity Cards Act 2006	168
Identity Documents Act 2010	168
Inheritance (Provision for Family and Dependants) Act 1975	
s 10	136
Inheritance Tax Act 1984	
s 3	136
Insolvency Act 1986	
s 238	136
s 423	136
Insurance Act 2015	187
Insurance Companies Act 1982	34
Interpretation Act 1978	29
s 6	29
Sch 1	127
Judicature Act 1873	7, 8, 39, 197, 275
s 25(11)	7, 276

Judicature Act 1875 .... 7, 39, 197, 275, 276
Land Charges Act 1972 19
   s 2(5)(ii) 246
   s 4(6) 246
Land Registration Act 1925 129
Land Registration Act 2002 .... 19, 129
   s 29 246
Landlord and Tenant Act 1985
   s 8 .... 60, 62
   s 11 .... 60, 62, 215
   s 12 .... 62, 215, 233
Late Payment of Commercial Debts (Interest) Act 1998 296
Law of Property Act 1925 19
   s 40 .... 59, 126
   s 49(2) 287
   s 136 257
   s 146 283
Law of Property (Miscellaneous Provisions) Act 1989
   s 1 .... 128, 130
   s 2 .... 59, 126, 127, 130
      (1) 87, 206
Law Reform (Enforcement of Contracts) Act 1954 59
Law Reform (Frustrated Contracts) Act 1943 .... 5, 18, 267, 302
   s 1(2) 268
   s 2(5) 5
Law Reform (Miscellaneous Provisions) Act 1934
   s 1 19
Limitation Act 1980
   s 3 56
      (2) 162
   s 4 .... 56, 162
   s 5 296
   s 8 .... 127, 296
   s 11 296
Marriage (Same Sex Couples) Act 2013 33
Marine Insurance Act 1906
   s 22 126
Married Women's Property Act 1882
   s 11 .... 236, 247
Misrepresentation Act 1967 18
   s 2 .... 180, 182, 183
      (1) 178, 182, 184, 229
      (2) 180
      (4) 180, 183
   s 3 .... 186, 226, 229
Money-lenders Act 1900 234
   s 1 234

National Assistance Act 1948
  s 42 139
Northern Ireland Act 1998 3
Occupiers' Liability Act 1957 .... 19, 227, 230
Occupiers' Liability Act 1984 19
Official Secrets Act 1989 293
Road Traffic Act 1988
  s 148(7) 247
Sale of Goods Act 1893 215
  s 14(2) 60
  s 55 215
Sale of Goods Act 1979 .... 71, 216, 228, 282, 298
  s 6 .... 29, 228
  s 8 122
  s 9 123
  s 12 214
    (5A) 282
  s 13 214
    (1A) 282
  s 14 .... 138, 172, 214
    (2) 60
    (3) 189
    (6) 282
  s 15 214
  s 15A 184
  s 17(2) 55
  s 18 55
  s 51 289
  s 61 29
  Sch 1 6
Sale and Supply of Goods Act 1994 284
Scotland Act 1998 3
Senior Courts Act 1981 .... 7, 171
  s 49 7
    (1) 7, 276
  s 50 281
  s 69 171
Statute of Frauds 1677 .... 59, 126, 127, 131
  s 4 .... 59, 126
  s 17 59
Supply of Goods (Implied Terms) Act 1973 .... 34, 228
Supply of Goods and Services Act 1982 .... 34, 298
  ss 2–4 214
  s 4 60
  ss 7–9 214
  s 11 215
  s 13 .... 60, 215

s 15 .... 92, 122
s 16 215
Supreme Court Act 1981 *see* Senior Courts Act 1981
Theft Act 1968
   s 21(1) 192
Torts (Interference with Goods) Act 1977
   s 3 162
   s 5 162
Trade Union and Labour Relations (Consolidation) Act 1992
   s 236 277
Tribunals, Courts and Enforcement Act 2007
Pt 2 14
Unfair Contract Terms Act 1977 .... 5, 33, 70, 204, 226, 227,
229, 230, 232, 299
   s 1(1) 227
      (3) 227
   s 2 227
   s 3 227
      (2)(b) 228
   s 6 .... 62, 215, 227, 228, 229
   s 7 .... 62, 228, 229
   s 8 229
   s 11 .... 62, 66, 228
      (5) 229
   s 13(1) 228
   Sch 2 .... 228, 232

UK Statutory Instruments

Civil Procedure Rules 1998 (SI 1998/3132) 38, 39
   Pt 52 24
      PD 52A 24
   Pt 70
      r 70.2A 276
Companies Act 2006 (Consequential Amendments, Transitional
   Provisions and Savings) Order 2009 (SI 2009/1941)
   reg 2 307
   Sch 1, para 179 307
Consumer Contracts (Information, Cancellation and
   Additional Charges) Regulations 2013 (SI 2013/3134) 72, 184, 187
   reg 6 187
Consumer Protection (Amendment) Regulations
   2014 (SI 2014/870) 163, 183, 193, 196
Consumer Protection from Unfair Trading Regulations
   2008 (SI 2008/1277) 110, 163, 183, 193, 196
   Pt 4A 180, 182
   reg 29 183
Financial Services (Distance Marketing) Regulations
   2004 (SI 2004/2095) 188

Limited Liability Partnerships Regulations 2001 (SI 2001/1090)
  reg 9(1) 307
  Sch 5 para 20 307
Railways (Convention on International Carriage by Rail)
Regulations 2005 (SI 2005/2092)
  reg 9(2) 308
  Sch 3 para 3 308
Sale and Supply of Goods to Consumers Regulations 2002
  (SI 2002/3045) 62, 71, 298
Unfair Terms in Consumer Contracts Regulations
  1994 (SI 1994/3159) 230, 233
Unfair Terms in Consumer Contracts Regulations
  1999 (SI 1999/2083) 5, 70, 226, 230,
                                                                        231, 232
  Sch 2 233

Non-UK Legislation

European Union

Convention on Human Rights and
  Fundamental Freedoms 18, 25, 30, 31, 33
Treaty on the Functioning of the European Union
  art 267 (ex art 234 EC) 30
Directive 85/374/EEC on Liability for Defective Products 18, 40
Directive 93/13/EC on Unfair Terms
  in Consumer Contracts 5, 66, 72, 230
  Preamble 233
Directive 1999/44/EC on Certain Aspects of the Sale
  of Consumer Goods and Associated Guarantees 5, 72, 298
Directive 2002/65/EC concerning the distance marketing
  of consumer financial services 188
Directive 2005/29/EC on Unfair Commercial Practices................................. 110, 183
Directive 2011/83/EU on Consumer Rights 72, 187

Belgium

Burgerlijk Wetbook 8
Code civil 8

France

Code civil 8, 9, 270
  art 1121 46
  art 1131 135
  art 1138 55
  art 1150–1 294

Germany

Bürgerliches Gesetzbuch 4, 46
  art 328(2) 46

Italy

Codice civile 8
    art 1411 46

Netherlands

Burgerlijk Wetboek 8

United Nations

Convention on Contracts for the International Sale of Goods (1980)
    art 19 120

United States

Uniform Commercial Code 11, 79
    para 1–304 269
    para 2–302 197

Part I

An Introduction to the Common Law

The primary focus of this book is the English law of contract. However, it is designed to be accessible to the civil lawyer: that is, to a reader who is already trained as a lawyer, but in a jurisdiction which belongs to the civil law tradition rather than the common law tradition. In any legal system the detail of a particular area of law can be fully understood only in the context which the legal system itself sets. When reading about any area of substantive law in a common law legal system, therefore, the civil lawyer should bear in mind some general features of the common law, and how a common lawyer thinks, reasons and finds the sources of law.

The aim of this Part is to give the reader an introduction to the common law, and to set English law within the common law more generally. However, it is only introductory. It is not intended to provide a full account of the common law system, or of the English legal system in particular, but is more narrowly intended to form an introduction to English private law, to give a proper context for the substantive discussion of the English law of contract in Part II.

1

The 'Common Law'

Although the 'common law' extends beyond English law[1] and covers many other legal systems in the English-speaking world, the origin of the 'common law' is found in England, and the other modern 'common law' legal systems trace their genealogy historically to their roots in English law.

I. The 'Common Law' of England

1. Meanings of 'Common Law'

The term 'common law' is used in different senses. In its narrowest sense it can mean the law found in or traced back to the decisions of a particular group of courts which existed in England from the early middle ages until the late nineteenth century—the King's courts, also referred to as the common law courts. In the modern law this generally means the law found in the line of modern developments from old decisions of those courts. The law as applied by those courts in their earliest days was 'common', in that in

---

[1] 'English law' is the law of the jurisdiction of England and Wales. Within the United Kingdom there are three separate *legal* systems: England and Wales; Scotland; and Northern Ireland. The *political* structures, however, are separated for (i) the United Kingdom as a whole (based on the UK Parliament at Westminster); and (ii) Scotland (the Scottish Parliament, created by the Scotland Act 1998), Wales (the Welsh Assembly, created by the Government of Wales Act 1998) and Northern Ireland (the Northern Ireland Assembly, created by the Northern Ireland Act 1998). The scope of the devolved powers varies—the most significant devolution is in relation to Scotland. One speaks of the 'British Constitution'; but at least in relation to private law one should not speak of 'British' law, or the law of the United Kingdom: for example, there is no such thing as the 'British' law of contract. Indeed, there are significant differences between the English and Scots law of contract, Scots law having adopted many of the characteristics of the Roman law within its law of contract: see below, n 20.

4 THE 'COMMON LAW'

principle it consisted of a general set of legal rules which were applied equally across the country, superseding the purely local jurisdictions which had been exercised until then. But in this narrow sense the 'common law' is contrasted with 'equity', the law which can be found in or traced back to the decisions of a separate group of courts which grew up initially under the control of the King's Chancellor (and so known as the Chancery courts, or the courts of equity) and developed from the late fourteenth or early fifteenth century, after the King's courts of common law were already established, until the late nineteenth century. This distinction between 'common law' and 'equity' is discussed further below.

On the other hand, the term 'common law' is often used more widely to refer to the law found in the decisions of the courts in general, contrasted with the law found in legislative enactments.[2] The dual use of 'common law' is illustrated in the tabular illustration of the sources of law in England, in Figure 1.

```
                    SOURCES OF LAW
                   /              \
    LEGISLATIVE SOURCES         THE 'COMMON LAW'
                                 /            \
    European Union legislation;  'COMMON LAW':  'EQUITY':
    Acts of the UK Parliament;   rules from the rules from the
    delegated legislation.       old Common Law old Courts of
                                 Courts.        Equity.
```

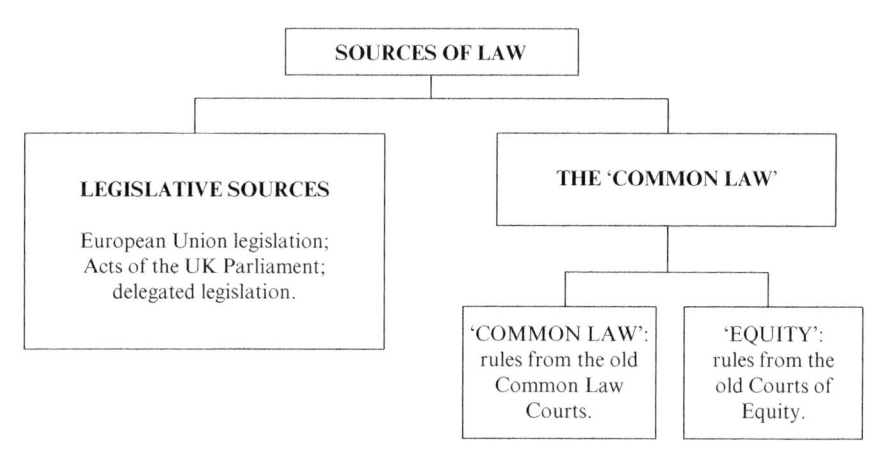

Figure 1

It is this latter, wider sense which is reflected in the use of the term 'common law' to describe the essential characteristics of a legal system. On this basis, what makes English law a common law system is that it contains a body of legal rules, many of which are found simply in the decisions of particular cases, and have no origin in any legislative enactment. The 'common law' is judge-made law. Of course there are very many areas of English law whose rules are contained wholly or mainly in legislation. For example, much of company law has now been taken over by statute; most (but not all)

---

[2] For the hierarchy of legislative sources (EU legislation, UK Acts of Parliament, delegated legislation), see below, pp 17–18.

criminal offences are statutory; and it is legislation, not the common law, which provides the legal authority for taxation and the regulation of financial services. But some very significant areas continue to be based in the common law—their authority is found in the case-law, not in legislation. This book is concerned with the law of contract, most of which is to be found in the cases. Legislation has changed or added to the common law rules of contract; for example, since the later twentieth century, legislative intervention has enhanced consumer protection in the field of contract law, sometimes on the initiative of the UK Parliament, but sometimes in order to implement European Directives,[3] and occasionally to take inspiration from a Directive, but to give greater protection to consumers.[4] Another very significant legislative change to the common law occurred in 1999, when Parliament reformed the common law rule of 'privity of contract', to allow a third party in certain circumstances to sue to enforce a term in a contract which was made for his benefit.[5] And there are many other particular statutory changes to the common law of contract which apply either generally[6] or for particular types of contract.[7] But the essential rules of the law of contract remain those which the modern courts continue to apply and to develop based on the earlier decisions of their predecessors.

2. Common Law and Equity

The relationship between the common law and equity must be understood from the outset.[8]

We have already mentioned that the courts of equity were developed as a jurisdiction separate from the common law courts. During the fifteenth and sixteenth centuries the practice grew of litigants applying to the King directly for justice, to circumvent the application of the law as dispensed by the common law courts. The hearing of such direct petitions by the Chancellor on behalf of the King was the origin of the Chancery jurisdiction; and the Chancellor decided cases according to what 'equity' required; a decision of 'conscience', based on the Chancellor's discretion to find an appropriate result, and an appropriate remedy, to resolve the case in hand even if this

---

[3] Eg Unfair Contract Terms Act 1977 (domestic legislation) and Consumer Rights Act 2015 pt 2 (re-implementing Directive 93/13/EC); below, ch 9.
[4] Eg Consumer Rights Act 2015 pt 1 (re-implementing Directive 1999/44/EC on consumer sales, but also covering consumer contracts for digital content and for services); below, pp 297–99.
[5] Contracts (Rights of Third Parties) Act 1999; below, ch 10.
[6] Eg Law Reform (Frustrated Contracts) Act 1943; below, ch 11 (some types of contract are, however, excluded: s 2(5)).
[7] Eg Consumer Insurance (Disclosure and Representations) Act 2012; below, p 187.
[8] JH Baker, *An Introduction to English Legal History*, 4th edn (London, Butterworths LexisNexis, 2002) chs 2, 6.

meant going beyond or even directly against the law as it would be applied in such a case by the common law courts.

This historical background must not, however, be read into the modern law. Over the years and the centuries the courts of equity developed principles and rules by reference to which they would grant remedies—just as much as the common law courts applied the legal rules which had been developed over the years by the common law judges. In 1818, the Lord Chancellor, Lord Eldon, said:

> The doctrines of this Court ought to be as well settled and made as uniform almost as those of the common law, laying down fixed principles, but taking care that they are to be applied according to the circumstances of each case. I cannot agree that the doctrines of this Court are to be changed with every succeeding judge. Nothing would inflict on me greater pain, in quitting this place, than the recollection that I had done any thing to justify the reproach that the equity of this Court varies like the Chancellor's foot.[9]

The result of the operation of the equitable jurisdiction was the creation of rights which were not known in the common law courts, as well as the creation of remedies which were different from those available in the common law courts and which were awarded in order to protect not only the new equitable rights but also the established common law rights. For our purpose, it is important to notice that the core notions of the law of contract were developed by the common law courts. But the courts of equity devised remedies to supplement the common law remedies. Apart from recognising that apparent contracts in certain defined situations would be void or otherwise unenforceable, the common law courts generally limited the remedies in this context to the award of sums of money, either by way of damages to compensate losses flowing from breach of contractual duties, or by way of the enforcement of an undertaking to pay a particular sum, such as a debt. But the courts of equity devised the remedies of *specific performance* and *injunction* to enable them to issue a direct order to a party to perform an obligation, or to refrain from committing a particular act or to do an act defined in the order; and the remedy of *rectification*, by which the court could order that a document which failed to reflect the intentions of the parties be given effect in a re-written form. However, although in the modern law these remedies still contain an element of discretion for the court in deciding when and how to invoke them, they are not based only on what is 'fair' for the parties in the view of the particular judge hearing the case: the test is not simply what is 'equitable' in a non-legal, non-technical sense. As we shall see in chapters 7 and 12, the courts' discretion in relation to such remedies is now a principled discretion, and the outcome of a claim for an equitable remedy is in general as predictable now as a claim for a common law remedy.

---

[9] *Gee v Pritchard* (1818) 2 Swans 402, 414; 36 ER 670, 674.

In the twenty-first century these 'equitable' rules and remedies still coexist with the common law rules and remedies, and they continue to be developed by the courts today. Until 1875, the development of the common law and equity proceeded in parallel. Separate court structures were developed for the two separate jurisdictions, even with separate appeal courts, although the House of Lords was the final court of appeal in both common law and equity cases. However, this jurisdictional separation was ended by the Judicature Acts 1873 and 1875[10] which joined the separate courts into what was then called[11] the 'Supreme Court of Judicature'—a single Court of Appeal, and a single High Court of Justice which contained divisions in which judges would sit who specialised in particular types of case, but in which *all* courts could and should apply all the relevant rules of law, whether the common law rules devised by the old common law courts, or the rules of equity devised by the old courts of equity. The superiority of the old equitable jurisdiction under which the courts of equity could recognise rights and award remedies even where they were contrary to the position at common law, was retained by the general provision that 'where there is a conflict between the rules of equity and the rules of the common law with reference to the same matter, the rules of equity shall prevail'.[12]

In summary, therefore: the court structure was developed from the middle ages onwards, and was reformed in the late nineteenth century. The 'common law'—the body of rules of law which are recognised and given effect by the judges even though they do not originate in any statute—was developed through those courts and (within the rules of the 'common law' in this wider sense) the separate rules of 'common law' and 'equity' were developed by the separate courts of common law and equity. The courts were fused into a single new court structure in the late nineteenth century. But the reform of the courts did not itself reform the rules of common law and equity, which remain applicable by all courts in the reformed court structure. These separate 'streams' of rules—common law and equity—continue to be developed by the courts in the modern law, and inevitably with the passage of time the old rules become more mixed in their modern development. Lord Diplock put this argument in its most extreme form:

> Your Lordships have been referred to the vivid phrase traceable to the first edition of *Ashburner, Principles of Equity* where, in speaking in 1902 of the effect of the Supreme Court of Judicature Act he says (p. 23) 'the two streams of jurisdiction'

---

[10] Now Senior Courts Act 1981 (formerly known as Supreme Court Act 1981: below, n 11) s 49.

[11] Under the Constitutional Reform Act 2005 s 40 the appeal jurisdiction of the House of Lords (which was exercised through the Judicial Committee of the House), was transferred on 1 October 2009 to a new 'Supreme Court': below, p 24. The High Court and the Court of Appeal are in consequence now known as the 'Senior Courts', and the Supreme Court Act was renamed the Senior Courts Act: Constitutional Reform Act 2005 s 59 and sch 11 para 1.

[12] Senior Courts Act 1981 s 49(1), replacing Supreme Court of Judicature Act 1873 s 25(11).

(sc. law and equity)—'though they run in the same channel, run side by side and do not mingle their waters.' My Lords, by 1977 this metaphor has in my view become both mischievous and deceptive. The innate conservatism of English lawyers may have made them slow to recognise that by the Supreme Court of Judicature Act 1873 the two systems of substantive and adjectival law formerly administered by courts of law and Courts of Chancery (as well as those administered by courts of admiralty, probate and matrimonial causes), were fused. As at the confluence of the Rhône and Saône, it may be possible for a short distance to discern the source from which each part of the combined stream came, but there comes a point at which this ceases to be possible. If Professor Ashburner's fluvial metaphor is to be retained at all, the waters of the confluent streams of law and equity have surely mingled now.[13]

In spite of the mingling of the jurisdictions, the substantive rules have not in fact been fully merged, and the rules of the modern law can often be understood only by reference to their origins in the common law or in equity.[14] And the language of the old law is often retained. Specific performance is still spoken of as an 'equitable remedy'; damages are available 'at common law' for breach of contract.

3. Common Law and Civil Law

'Common law' systems are often contrasted with 'civil law' systems. This contrast is drawn in the title of this book. A common feature of many modern civil law systems is that their private law is based on a systematic set of general rules of law contained in legislative enactments—typically, a 'code', such as the *Code civil* in France or Belgium,[15] the *Bürgerliches Gesetzbuch* in Germany, the *Codice civile* in Italy and the *Burgerlijk Wetboek* in the Netherlands. The difference does not reside only the existence of a civil code, however, since Scandinavian countries are generally recognised to fall within the civil law tradition although they do not have complete, systematic codifications. They do, however, share with the codified European systems (and other systems outside Europe which are now based on the European civil law model) features which mark them apart from the common law, and which the civil lawyer will immediately recognise by way of contrast with the general features of the common law which are discussed below.[16] But one feature which certainly marks out the common law by contrast with its civilian neighbours is the limited

---

[13] *United Scientific Holdings Ltd v Burnley BC* [1978] 1 AC 904, 924–25.
[14] The consequences of the fusion of the courts of common law and of equity are not identical in all common law jurisdictions: eg equity is seen by some as still having a more significant, independent role in developing the modern law in Australia: cf K Mason, 'Fusion: Fallacy, Future or Finished?' in S Degeling and J Edelman (eds), *Equity in Commercial Law* (Sydney, Lawbook Co, 2005) 41, 42.
[15] The Dutch (Flemish) version of the Belgian civil code is the *Burgerlijk Wetboek*.
[16] Below, pp 12–14.

reception in English law of Roman law principles. The term civil law is used to describe these European jurisdictions because of their reception of the language, ideas and structures of Roman law in the revival and rediscovery of Justinian's *Corpus Iuris Civilis* which began in Italy at the end of the eleventh century and spread with varying degrees of influence into the several countries of the Continent.[17] There was a real sense in which the received Roman law rules, as refined and explained by scholars, became the common law of continental Europe—the *ius commune*. But the revival of Roman law did not have the same impact on the law in England, where the King's courts and the legal profession were already (and in parallel with the European developments) developing their own law—the common law of England—without the same academic influence which was so strong on the Continent.[18] In England the common law was developed in the courts, not in the universities: there was no common law degree in the English universities before the late nineteenth century, and the tradition was that the lawyer learned his law 'at the Bar': in the Inns of Court in London.[19]

II. Common Law Systems Around the World

1. The Range of the Common Law

Common law legal systems around the world have drawn their legal system from England, typically in the context of having been British colonies—in the same way that many other parts of the world owe the basis of their current legal system to former colonisation, such as the influence of the legal systems of Belgium, France and Portugal in their former colonies in Africa. Amongst the common law systems would be counted such countries as Australia, Canada (except Quebec, which has a civil law code: it was a French colony before it passed to the British crown in 1763), India, the Republic of Ireland, Hong Kong, New Zealand, Singapore and the states within the United States of America except for Louisiana (which has a civil law code: it was held by Spain and France before it passed to the United States in 1803). Other countries have received the common law only in part, and are generally

---

[17] B Nicholas, *An Introduction to Roman Law* (Oxford, Clarendon Press, 1962) 45–54.
[18] Baker, *An Introduction to English Legal History* (above, n 8) 27–29.
[19] FH Lawson, *The Oxford Law School, 1850–1965* (Oxford, Clarendon Press, 1968) ch 1; C Stolker, *Rethinking the Law School* (Cambridge, Cambridge University Press, 2014) 17.

referred to as 'mixed' jurisdictions—such as Scotland, which already had a civilian basis to its legal system before the union with England in 1707, and despite the influence of English law in many areas has largely retained it (indeed, the language and underlying principles of the Scots law of contract more closely resemble that of Continental civil law systems than the English common law);[20] and South Africa, in which a civil law system based on Roman-Dutch law was already well established by the time of the British occupation at the end of the eighteenth century, and became overlaid with, rather than replaced by, common law rules and principles. The legal and political links between the United Kingdom and the countries which received the common law system during their period of British rule, have changed over time. Ireland, for example, was part of the United Kingdom until independence in 1922 and so Irish law has had considerably less time to develop independently of its common origins with English law than the law of the United States which declared independence in 1776. And although Australia, Canada and New Zealand became politically independent nations at various times during the nineteenth and early twentieth centuries, they each initially retained legal links with England by virtue of the fact that they retained the King or Queen as Head of State, and that the monarch's Privy Council—sitting in London and comprised largely of the same judges who sat to hear appeals in the House of Lords in English cases—was a final court of appeal. The right of final appeal to the Privy Council in Canadian cases continued until 1949, rights of appeal from Australian courts were gradually limited and finally abolished in 1986, and for New Zealand the appeal jurisdiction was abolished for cases heard by the Court of Appeal of New Zealand after the end of 2003.

2. Differences Between Common Law Systems

Understanding the range of the common law is important for the civil lawyer who wishes to discover the common law. It will be obvious that there is no such thing as, for example, the 'common law of contract'. Just as the civil law is not a unity and there are significant differences between, say, French, Dutch and German law as regards their law of contract, so too there are significant differences between American, Australian and English law. These differences are sometimes on points of detail, but also sometimes go beyond mere detail to more fundamental questions about the nature of contracts and

---

[20] Eg Scots law does not have the doctrine of consideration (below, ch 6) and in consequence could accept the enforceability of third-party rights more easily than English law: *Dunlop Pneumatic Tyre Co Ltd v Selfridge & Co Ltd* [1915] AC 847 (HL) 853 (Viscount Haldane, quoted below, p 239); and specific performance is one of the ordinary remedies and therefore more readily available than in English law: below, p 278, n 16.

the role of the law in regulating particular relationships. For example, the place of *reliance* in the creation of obligations in the contractual context, through the doctrine of *estoppel*, is much more fully developed in American law; Australian law has taken some steps in this direction but English law is the least receptive to such ideas.[21] And principles of *good faith* have been developed within the American and Australian law of contract more than in English law.[22] Some such differences reflect different responses to questions as they have arisen in the various common law jurisdictions, but sometimes they also reflect underlying structural and jurisdictional differences. For example, in the United States the common law of contract is not federal law, but is the common law of each separate state, and there are differences between states in their acceptance of new developments, although there is also a concern to harmonise the law amongst the states.[23] English law and Irish law contain various rules by virtue of the transposition of European Directives[24] whereas the other common law systems, which are all outside Europe, do not have this influence. Domestic legislative policy will also vary within all the jurisdictions; and the development of the common law around legislative enactments will also be correspondingly different. The focus of this book is English law; and its principal purpose is to introduce the civil lawyer to the English law of contract. Part II will therefore generally explain the approach taken by the case-law and legislation in England, although where appropriate it will also mention briefly key differences of detail in other major common law jurisdictions.

The influence of the several common law jurisdictions on each other must also be understood. English judges will sometimes consider the case-law of other jurisdictions in order to assist them to decide a particular point of law, either where there is a lack of English case-law on the point, or where another jurisdiction has made relevant (and often recent) developments which it might be thought that English law should follow. There has been a growing tendency in recent years for the English judges to consider the law in European civil law jurisdictions, because of the developing pressure for convergence, or harmonisation, of European private law, and in particular the law of contract.[25] But more commonly, and historically, the English courts look

---

[21] Below, pp 153 ff.
[22] Below, p 64.
[23] Notably through: (a) the American Law Institute's 'Restatements of the Law', such as the *Restatement of Contracts*, first published in 1932, and now the *Restatement 2d Contracts* since 1981: below, p 153, n 113; (b) the National Conference of Commissioners on Uniform State Laws which have produced such acts as the Uniform Commercial Code, although these uniform laws must still be enacted by each of the State legislators: RE Barnett, *Contracts* (New York, Oxford University Press, 2010) xxii–xxv.
[24] For the European context of English contract law, see below, p 71.
[25] Eg *Shogun Finance Ltd v Hudson* [2003] UKHL 62, [2004] 1 AC 919 [84]–[85], below, pp 169–70. See also below, p 71.

across to the major common law jurisdictions with which they have strong links—and in particular Australia, Canada and New Zealand.[26] Similarly, the courts of these jurisdictions still look to the English case-law in coming to their own decisions. The fact that the Privy Council retained its status as final court of appeal in private law in these jurisdictions until relatively recently means that there is a greater affinity with them than with, say, American law. The Privy Council sat as the final court of appeal within the jurisdiction in question—and therefore heard argument, and made its recommendations to the Monarch—on the basis of the relevant local law. However, the Privy Council in practice provided something of a unifying force to the common law. After the legal separation of these major jurisdictions became complete, and the final appeal was fully devolved to each jurisdiction, the direct influence between the several jurisdictions certainly reduced; but it is still not uncommon for an English court to be invited by the parties to a dispute to consider relevant developments in other common law jurisdictions. This is not because the English court is bound by such developments elsewhere (and, indeed, even when the Privy Council had made a decision on a particular point it was only formal authority within the jurisdiction in question) but simply as evidence of a development in a system which has a common legal heritage with England, and which might properly be made also here. But this reinforces the point that to understand not only the current law of contract in England but also its possible development, it is important to have a broader view of how some key areas of the law are seen differently in other jurisdictions from which there may possibly be some influence in due course.

3. Some General Features of the Common Law Systems

Chapter two will discuss in more detail some of the features of common law systems which have a practical relevance to an understanding of how the common lawyer approaches an area of law such as the law of contract. Here it should simply be noted—partly by way of summary of what has already been discussed in this chapter, and partly by way of introduction to what follows—that lawyers in one of the common law jurisdictions would generally recognise the following features of their legal system:

(A) *It is based on the common law of England,* even if it has developed separately (and differently) from English law from the time at which the particular legal system ceased to be influenced directly by English law. We have already noted that the separation of the common law systems

---

[26] Cf *Jones v Kaney* [2011] UKSC 13, [2011] 2 AC 398 [76]: 'It is highly desirable that at this appellate level, in cases where issues of legal policy are concerned, the court should be informed about the position in other common law countries. This court is often helped by being referred to authorities from other common law systems, including the United States' (Lord Collins of Mapesbury JSC).

from English law has taken place in different ways and over an extended period of time; and that the independent development of the substantive rules of law in the various common law jurisdictions is correspondingly varied.

(B) *There is no single coherent set of principles of law from which the answer to a legal question can be deduced.* The legal reasoning of a common lawyer does not start from a general principle—such as a general legislative principle which might typically be found in a 'code' in a civil law system. The answers to legal questions—and the solutions to legal disputes—are generally based on the facts of the case in question and the particular solutions of earlier individual cases, rather than generalised statements of principle. The common law does, of course, recognise general rules of law, and common law jurisdictions see a very significant role for legislative texts. But the process of reasoning is different from that typically engaged in by the civil lawyer—reflecting different approaches to 'finding the law'. The nuances of this are explored in more detail in chapter two.

(C) *Case-law is a principal source of law.* This follows from (a) and (b) above. Historically the development of the general body of legal rules in the English common law was through the case-law of the common law courts and the courts of equity—and although there have been significant legislative interventions to introduce new legal rules or to modify the rules developed by the courts, much of English law is still contained in the modern case-law developments of the old lines of cases. The law is often therefore found in a case or in a group of cases. The other common law jurisdictions, whose law originates in this common law of England, are still also based on the same principle: that the legislator may have intervened on particular issues, and may in consequence have given an impetus to the development of substantive rules of law differently from the development within England. But the core rules remain those of the original case-law which has been inherited from the historic English roots, and which continues to be developed in broadly the same way—by the local case-law.

(D) *Judges have a significant and individual status.* The significance of case-law as a source of law places the court at the centre of the law-making process. In consequence, the role of the judge is significant—to the point where the judges of the higher courts in common law jurisdictions have a high status within the legal system, and tend to be known for their individual judgments and for particular developments to which they have contributed.[27] The status of judges is also linked to the

---

[27] Eg E Heward, *Lord Denning: A Biography* (2nd edn, Chichester, Barry Rose) 1997; JL Jowell and JPWB McAuslan (eds), *Lord Denning: The Judge and the Law* (London, Sweet & Maxwell, 1984); and Lord Denning's autobiography, *The Family Story* (London, Butterworths, 1981) and his own account of his contributions to the law in *The Discipline of Law* (London, Butterworths, 1979); *The Due Process of Law* (London, Butterworths, 1980); *What Next in the Law* (London, Butterworths, 1982); and *The Closing Chapter* (London, Butterworths, 1983).

procedure for their selection: students leaving the law schools in common law jurisdictions do not generally have the choice of a judicial career: they become practising lawyers, and the judges are recruited from practitioners—particularly, in the higher courts, very senior practitioners who have expertise in their field. In England the eligibility for judicial appointment includes experience as a practitioner.[28]

(E) *Academic writing is not so significant.* The interplay between the legislator, the courts and academic writing in the common law is different from that generally encountered in civil law systems. Civil lawyers see a role for the academic writer in explaining the significance of the general principles to be found in the legislative texts; and the academic is involved in the process of law-making that flows from the development of general principles by their interpretation and concretisation to particular cases. In the common law, by contrast, the recognition of the status of the judge as contributing to the law not only by interpretation of legislative texts but in the development of the rules of the common law—and the fact that in performing this role a common law judge will generally give a detailed exposition of his reasoning within his judgment—means that less reliance has traditionally been placed on academic writing where a court needs to discover the law from the earlier cases. However, we have moved forward a long way from the old view that it was not acceptable to cite the writings of living authors as part of an argument in court:

> It is to my mind much to be regretted, and it is a regret which I believe every Judge on the bench shares, that text-books are more and more quoted in Court—I mean of course text-books by living authors—and some Judges have gone so far as to say that they shall not be quoted.[29]

Judges in modern cases frequently refer explicitly to academic writing; and sometimes even encourage legal scholars to explore areas of law ready for future cases in which there might be a need for the courts to take a particular step in developing the common law:

> I am reluctant to express a concluded view on this point since it may have profound effects on commercial contracts which effects were not fully explored in argument. In my view the point merits exposure to academic consideration before it is decided by this House.[30]

But this still does not give the body of academic writers in a common law legal system the same role as 'legal science' or 'doctrine' in civil law systems.

---

[28] Tribunals, Courts and Enforcement Act 2007 pt 2. See also the general information published by the Judicial Appointments Commission: *www.jac.judiciary.gov.uk.*
[29] *Union Bank v Munster* (1887) 37 ChD 51 (Ch) 54 (Kekewich J).
[30] *Linden Gardens Trust Ltd v Lenesta Sludge Disposals Ltd* [1994] 1 AC 85 (HL) 112 (Lord Browne-Wilkinson).

2

Finding the Law

The purpose of this book is to enable the lawyer who is not already trained in the common law to understand some of the significant features of the English law of contract. In this chapter, we consider some of the practical consequences of the general features of a common law legal system which were outlined in chapter one. In essence, the common lawyer's general approach to finding the law is different from the civil lawyer's approach; and this means that a common lawyer who looks at a contract makes certain assumptions about the legal context within which the contract is to be analysed. This is not simply a matter of the different substantive rules on particular points—the comparison of any area of law in any two legal systems, civil law or common law, will reveal differences in the detailed rules and therefore differences of result in similar cases. It is more fundamental: the common lawyer's approach to legal reasoning, to the significance of the different sources of law, and to the questions of where to look for the law and how to interpret the different sources of law, are part of the common lawyer's background which set the context for the approach to be taken to any area of law. In this chapter we shall look at these questions using examples from various areas of private law, including where appropriate the law of contract. Contract is discussed in more detail in Part II.

I. The Sources of Law

1. Legal Reasoning in the Common Law: Where Shall We Begin?

The lawyer needs to know where to look for the law—where to find the legal rules which are relevant to the case in hand, and how to discover the meaning of the rules and their application to the particular case. In practice, the lawyer in any jurisdiction—common law or civil law—may start his search by looking at the relevant textbooks. For example, there are standard works on the law of contract, both general texts which the lawyer may have used during the course of his own professional training, and specialised works aimed at practitioners of the law in particular areas. But for our purposes this is not the answer. We need to know where the textbook writers themselves find the law: and so where the lawyer should look in the authoritative sources in order to check the detail which he reads in the textbooks, or to find the answer which is not contained in the textbooks because the case involves a variation on the standard situation on which the books have based their discussion and analysis.

We have already seen that the principal feature of a civil law system is that its legal rules are to be found in a systematic set of general principles of law, typically found in legislative enactments (a 'code').[1] The civil lawyer therefore reaches for his copy of the code and turns up the relevant provision. The bare text of the provision of the code is insufficient, because it is stated in broad and general terms—that is the point of a general principle. Its interpretation is therefore critical. And so the civil lawyer proceeds to consider the discussions of the provision of the code which are contained in the commentaries on it (typically written by legal scholars); and the cases which have been decided under that provision. His purpose is to interpret it—to predict how a court in his legal system might apply it to the case in hand. The detail of this search for the law will vary from one system to another. Some codes are more detailed in their drafting than others; the decisions of courts in some systems are more detailed and explicit in their reasoning than others, and therefore the relative usefulness of court decisions and academic commentaries in understanding the legislative provisions and how they are to be interpreted will vary from system to system.[2] But the starting point of the civil lawyer is the general principle of law in his legal system's legislative provisions: his code.

The common lawyer, however, has no 'code' to reach for. He does not expect to be able to find a relevant legislative text containing a statement of general principle, or a more specific provision, in order to provide a framework for the question which he has to answer. This is not to say that there is no legal principle or legal rule which can answer his question; simply that there is no

---

[1] Above, p 8.
[2] The most laconic decisions are perhaps those of the French *Cour de cassation*, which typically run to rather less than a page and contain no discussion of the legal reasoning—simply a statement of the relevant legislative text, the key question of law as it was decided by the lower court, and the solution as decided by the *Cour*. Decisions of the German *Bundesgerichtshof*, by contrast, are more discursive and contain a discussion of the reasons for the decision. But in each of these—and other—civil law systems there is also a developed role for academic writing in explaining the application of the codes in the courts, and in theory the courts act only to interpret and apply the legislative texts (not as formal sources of law themselves)—although the interpretative role is of course in itself formative of the legal rules as they are developed through their application in successive cases.

collection of general principles in a legislative form. There may be a legislative text; but there may not be. The common lawyer starts from the case in hand, the facts of the particular question to which he needs an answer; and he looks to one or other of the sources of law—legislation or case-law—to predict the answer which the court would give to his question. And his own reading of the sources will depend on whether the relevant source is in legislation or in the case-law, just as a court's own reading of these different sources varies.

2. Legislation and Case-Law as Sources of Law

We have already noted that within a common law legal system, such as English law, there are both legislative and non-legislative sources of law.[3] The relative importance of these sources must be understood.

In the sense of priority within the hierarchy of legal rules, legislative sources are more important. Legislative enactments take precedence over non-legislative sources where they relate to the same subject-matter. For example, under the doctrine of 'privity of contract', the English courts developed the rule that only a party to a contract could sue to enforce it; a third party could not sue, even to enforce a benefit which was expressed to be for his benefit and to be enforceable by him. This common law rule was overridden by an Act of Parliament enacted in 1999,[4] which now allows a third party in certain defined circumstances to enforce a term in a contract for his own benefit. The Act did not abolish the doctrine of privity of contract; but in cases in which it applies it provides a direct recourse for a third party which the common law rule denies. Therefore, in cases covered by the Act, it is the provisions of the Act which apply—the common law rule is overridden, or excluded. But in other cases the common law rule remains in force. To this extent, the legislator has power to remove, override or amend the rules of the common law as devised and developed by the courts. But the courts—subject, of course, to their role in interpreting legislation—have no power to remove, override or amend a legislative enactment.

Within the British constitution there is also in a sense a hierarchy within the legislative sources—a hierarchy which itself rests on the authority of the courts because, in the absence of a written constitution or any other constitutional documents which lay down the rules,[5] it is the courts who have settled the rules on such matters. The courts have accepted that European Union law takes priority over domestic legislation since by passing the European

---

[3] Above, p 4, Fig 1.
[4] Contracts (Rights of Third Parties) Act 1999; see below, p 45 and ch 10.
[5] AW Bradley, KD Ewing and CJS Knight, *Constitutional and Administrative Law*, 16th edn (Harlow, Pearson, 2015) ch 1.

Communities Act 1972, the UK Parliament accepted limitations on its sovereignty which continue as long as the 1972 Act is in force.[6] EU regulations and directly effective provisions of EU directives can therefore be relied upon by individuals in domestic courts in accordance with European Union law even where this involves overriding an Act of the UK Parliament. Below Acts of Parliament in the hierarchy is secondary, or 'delegated', legislation which takes effect under the authority of specific provisions in Acts of Parliament, but which must be created strictly within the procedures laid down by the Act in question and—unlike an Act of Parliament—may be reviewed by the courts and struck down if its terms contravene the provisions of the enabling Act, or another Act of Parliament, or constitutional principle.[7]

If, however, we are looking for the more 'important' source of law in the sense of the greater body of legal rules which apply in private law, then the non-legislative sources predominate. The fundamental rules of the building-blocks of private law—contract, tort and property—are contained in no statute. The core rules governing the formation of a contract, its terms and remedies for breach were devised by the courts through successive cases, and remain within the common law. Statutes sometimes refer to contracts, and statutes have changed some of the rules of the law of contract. For example, we have noted that the common law rule of 'privity of contract' was changed by the Contracts (Rights of Third Parties) Act 1999. Similarly, the remedies following frustration of a contract were changed by the Law Reform (Frustrated Contracts) Act 1943;[8] and the law on precontractual misrepresentation was reformed by the Misrepresentation Act 1967.[9] But reference has to be made to the common law for the meaning of the word 'contract' in such statutes since the statutes contain no definition of 'contract' but are drafted on the basis that the common law applies. In similar fashion there is no general statutory definition of tort, nor any provision covering tort liability in general. There are some specific statutory causes of action which are in the nature of tort, such as the claim under Part I of the Consumer Protection Act 1987[10] for damages for death, personal injury or loss of or damage to

---

[6] *Factortame Ltd v Secretary of State for Transport* [1990] 2 AC 85 (HL). The European Convention on Human Rights is not, however, directly enforceable in the same way within the UK courts in order to override a UK Act. Under the Human Rights Act 1998 s 3 primary and subordinate legislation must be read and given effect in a way which is compatible with the Convention rights, so far as it is possible to do so, but the court cannot give effect to a Convention right over a clear provision of domestic legislation, and is limited under s 4 to making a declaration of incompatibility whilst still enforcing the domestic provision. International treaties, even when ratified, are not directly enforceable in the UK courts without an Act of the UK Parliament which enables or requires that they be given effect in domestic law.

[7] P Craig, *Administrative Law*, 7th edn (London, Sweet & Maxwell, 2012) ch 10.

[8] Below, pp 267–68.

[9] Below, ch 7.

[10] See s 6(7). The Act implemented Council Directive No 85/374/EEC (25 Jul 1985) on Liability for Defective Products.

property caused by a defect in a product. And statutes have overridden and therefore changed the existing case-law rules in some particular areas of tort, such as the reform of the law on the liability of occupiers to their visitors and non-visitors, under the Occupiers' Liability Acts 1957 and 1984, the reform of many particular rules of the tort of defamation (libel and slander) by a series of statutes,[11] and the reversal in 1934 of the general common law rule that on the death of a tortfeasor, or of the victim of a tort, the cause of action dies with him.[12] But the principal torts—such as negligence, nuisance, trespass and defamation—are creations of the common law courts and in their continuing development their core elements remain part of the common law, even where these torts have also been changed or developed by statute. The example of the development of the tort of negligence will be explored in further detail in section II below. In the law of property, too, the fundamental rules remain those of the common law. There has been significant statutory intervention in the law relating to land and interests in land: in particular, Parliament enacted a group of statutes in 1925 which might look like a codification of the land law. Some of these have been revised and replaced by later Acts: the principal statutes currently in force are the Law of Property Act 1925 (as amended), the Land Charges Act 1972 and the Land Registration Act 2002. However, these statutes are not a complete codification; they very significantly changed the old common law, but recourse still has to be made to the pre-1926 land law, which is largely contained in the case-law, in order to understand the underlying concepts to which the statutes make reference.[13]

II. The Judge as Interpreter and as Law-Maker

1. Different Judicial Approaches to the Different Sources

The law which is relevant to answer a particular question may therefore be found *either* in a legislative text, *or* in the common law authorities—the cases. The lawyer who looks for the law to advise a client must therefore be able to predict how a court would interpret the statutory text, or the cases, in order to extract the legal rule to apply to the case in hand. And it is important to

---

[11] Defamation Acts 1952, 1996 and 2013.
[12] Law Reform (Miscellaneous Provisions) Act 1934 s 1 (claims for defamation are excluded).
[13] EH Burn and J Cartwright, *Cheshire & Burn's Modern Law of Real Property*, 18th edn (Oxford, Oxford University Press, 2011) 1.

understand that the judicial approach to these two different types of legal source is different. Put rather simplistically, one could say that where the case raises an issue which is governed by a legislative text, the role of the judge is to interpret the text, looking back to earlier cases which have themselves interpreted the same text, for both guidance and (where the rules of precedent apply) as binding authority; and then faithfully to apply the text as so interpreted but not to go beyond it. But where the case raises an issue which is governed by the common law (that is, case-law) the judge looks back to the earlier cases which have devised and interpreted the common law rule, for both guidance and (where the rules of precedent apply) as binding authority; and then he applies the rule to the case in hand but with the possibility, in the absence of contrary binding precedent, of extending or changing the rule beyond that which has been accepted in the earlier cases. That is, the courts have a greater freedom to develop the common law rules than legislative rules. This requires some elaboration of the role of the courts and the English law rules of precedent, as well as of their general approach to the interpretation of legislative texts and to finding and developing the common law.

2. The 'Binding' Force of Case-Law: The Doctrine of Precedent

(a) Case-Law as an Authority

In any legal system, civil law or common law, the decisions of the courts have a certain authority. Of course—subject to any possible appeal or other similar challenge in the particular case[14]—a decision is binding on the parties to the dispute, in relation to the subject-matter of the dispute. But legal systems vary as to the significance which they give to case-law beyond this. Even in a civil law system which takes the strongest position of principle under which the decisions of the courts are perceived to be only applying the legislative provision (the Code) and not in any sense having any binding force on later cases, the decisions of the courts still have significance for the later cases. A judge in interpreting a provision will naturally consider earlier decisions of his fellow judges on the same provision, and there will be a natural tendency for similar cases to be decided in the same way—not simply because of the

---

[14] Some legal systems distinguish between an appeal (designed to re-hear the case and decide whether the first decision should be confirmed or reversed) and *cassation*, where the court hearing the challenge may decide that the lower court applied the wrong principles of law and so the decision should be quashed and the case referred back to a new court for a fresh hearing. English law knows a form of cassation in the case of a quashing order following judicial review of administrative decision-making (Craig, *Administrative Law*, above, n 7, para 26–010), but in private law the challenges against a decision are in the nature of an appeal: the Supreme Court of the United Kingdom, even where it hears a second appeal (against the first appeal which was heard first by, typically, the Court of Appeal) is therefore not, in this sense, a cassation court.

view that fairness (sometimes in this context referred to as 'the rule of law') requires it to be so, to enable parties to conduct themselves with some degree of predictability as to the outcome of any future dispute about their rights and obligations; nor because it may sometimes be seen as a pragmatic and efficient solution to follow the earlier decisions (why not take advantage of an earlier court's time and effort in exploring the legal issue?); but also because the earlier decisions of the courts have an influence on the later court's own interpretation of the provision. If earlier judges—particularly those who individually or collectively command respect within the legal system—have interpreted the provision in a particular sense, then it should not be surprising to find that later judges do likewise. The legal rule is contained in the text. So an application of the same text to similar cases should, in principle, produce the same answer.

(b) Case-Law as Binding

However, English law goes further than this and in certain circumstances gives a formal binding force to particular decisions. It should be noted from the outset that the rule of precedent is not an inherent rule of the common law: each common law jurisdiction has developed its own version of the doctrine of precedent and therefore its own view of the status of particular judgments as regards their binding force in later cases. The doctrine of precedent in the United States, for example, is significantly less strict than in England.[15] But the general approach to legal reasoning on the basis of previous cases with a view to discovering the law to apply to the case in hand, and in consequence the general view of the judge as a law-maker—one of the hallmarks of the 'common law'—is shared by the American judge. And, as we shall see, many decisions in England are not in fact binding on later courts under the rules of precedent. But they are still part of the development of the law through the cases, and there is a tendency for judges to respect earlier cases even if they are not technically binding, in order to maintain stability in the legal order. Even the Supreme Court may be reluctant to overturn a well-established line of cases from the lower courts on which parties will have acted and which have become accepted as stating a principle of the common law, even if there appears to be good reason to doubt it. The older the case-law, the more cautious the courts are in changing it.[16]

---

[15] R Cross and JW Harris, *Precedent in English Law*, 4th edn (Oxford, Clarendon Press, 1991) 26–27.
[16] Eg, see the reluctance of the House of Lords in *Foakes v Beer* (1884) 9 App Cas 605 to overturn the principle in *Pinnel's Case* (1602) 5 Co Rep 117a, 77 ER 237; below, p 143.

It is therefore important to keep separate the role of case-law as creating and developing the law in a common law system, and the rules of precedent as regards the binding force of decisions within the particular common law legal system. That said, however, within English law the doctrine of precedent has a firm basis which is part of the particular approach of English law to the development of the law through the cases, and it is very important to understand the rules of the doctrine within English law in order to appreciate how the law—for example, individual rules or doctrines within the law of contract—has developed and is likely to develop in the future.

(c) The Rules of Precedent in English Law

There are two key aspects to the general doctrine of precedent. First, it is necessary to identify *what* is capable of binding later courts. Secondly, *which courts* are bound. *What* can bind a later court is the *ratio decidendi* of a case— the 'reason for the decision'—commonly referred to simply as the 'ratio'. In essence, this means the point(s) of law which were applied by the court as a necessary part of its reasoning in reaching its decision on the facts.[17] Other statements of law by judges (*obiter dicta*—'things said in passing') may be useful for a later court and may have a persuasive force but cannot be formally binding. For the later court, therefore, or for the lawyer who wishes to predict how a later court will view the significance of a particular earlier case, it is crucial to assess the judgments in the earlier case and especially the judges' reasoning. Where the court was composed of a single judge, only one judgment requires analysis in order to discover the ratio. But in the case of a decision taken by a larger court—such as the Court of Appeal, which is commonly composed of three judges, or the Supreme Court (and formerly the House of Lords), which commonly has five members but may occasionally sit as a court of seven or even nine—the ratio of the case is to be found in the reasoning of a majority of the judges who agreed in the final result, even if other judges agreed in the result but gave different reasons. This approach to discovering the ratio of an earlier case is inextricably bound up with the common lawyer's general method of reasoning from the cases. This will be discussed further and illustrated below.

Which courts are bound by previous decisions in civil cases depends on the relative place of the courts in the hierarchy of the civil courts in England, which is illustrated by Figure 2.

Civil cases dealing with matters of general private law, such as contract, are heard at first instance in either the County Court (which has centres across the country) or the High Court (based in London but there are court centres across the country at which High Court business can be heard).

---

[17] Cross and Harris, *Precedent in English Law* above, n 15, ch II.

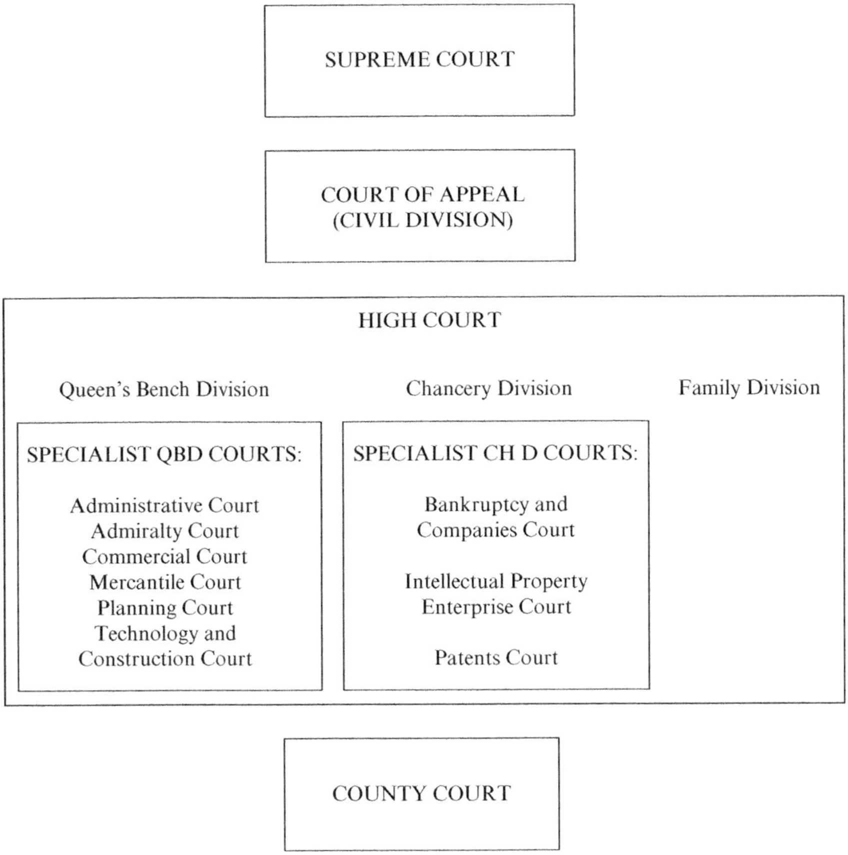

THE JUDGE AS INTERPRETER AND AS LAW-MAKER 23

```
                    ┌─────────────────────┐
                    │   SUPREME COURT     │
                    └─────────────────────┘

                    ┌─────────────────────┐
                    │  COURT OF APPEAL    │
                    │  (CIVIL DIVISION)   │
                    └─────────────────────┘
```

HIGH COURT		
Queen's Bench Division	Chancery Division	Family Division
SPECIALIST QBD COURTS: Administrative Court Admiralty Court Commercial Court Mercantile Court Planning Court Technology and Construction Court	**SPECIALIST CH D COURTS:** Bankruptcy and Companies Court Intellectual Property Enterprise Court Patents Court	

```
                    ┌─────────────────────┐
                    │    COUNTY COURT     │
                    └─────────────────────┘
```

Figure 2

The distribution of business between the County Court and the High Court is based on the type and value of the claim, but very many more cases are heard in the County Court than in the High Court. The High Court is divided into Divisions according to specialisation (Queen's Bench Division,[18] Chancery Division and Family Division), and the Queen's Bench and Chancery Divisions have further sub-divisions within which specialist courts hear cases of particular kinds.[19] Appeal from the County Court is either to a senior judge in the County Court or to the High Court or the Court of Appeal,

---

[18] When the monarch is a King, this division is known as the King's Bench Division (KBD).
[19] The QBD has the Administrative, Admiralty, Commercial, Mercantile, Planning, and Technology and Construction Courts; the ChD has the Bankruptcy and Companies Court, the Intellectual Property Enterprise Court and the Patents Court. For further details of the courts and their jurisdiction, see *www.judiciary.gov.uk*.

24 FINDING THE LAW

depending on the nature of the claim; and an appeal from a first instance decision of a High Court Judge is generally to the Court of Appeal. Appeals normally require the permission of either the trial court or the court to which appeal is to be made: there is no automatic right of appeal.[20] There is a limited possibility of further appeal to the Supreme Court.[21] Until 1 October 2009 the final court of appeal was the House of Lords, which exercised its appeal functions through its Judicial Committee.[22] The appeal jurisdiction was then transferred to the newly-created Supreme Court, but the general scope of jurisdiction is unchanged.

The general rule is that a court is bound to follow the ratio of an earlier relevant decision of a court which is higher in the court hierarchy; and the Court of Appeal is bound by its own previous decisions. To be more precise:[23]

(i) The County Court is bound to follow a decision of the Court of Appeal or the Supreme Court (and older decisions of the House of Lords); and it is generally assumed that it is also bound to follow a decision of the High Court. It is not bound by its own decisions. In any event, County Court judgments are not generally published and so there is no readily identifiable body of case-law from the County Court.

(ii) A judge in the High Court is bound to follow a decision of the Court of Appeal[24] or the Supreme Court (and older decisions of the House of Lords), but is not bound by earlier decisions of the High Court, although the reasoning in an earlier relevant decision will be considered carefully and may well be followed in practice. However, there is some uncertainty about how a High Court judge should deal with the situation where he considers that a decision of the Court of Appeal is inconsistent with an earlier decision of the Supreme Court or the House of Lords. It has been said that the duty of the judge is to follow the (more recent) decision of the Court of Appeal,[25] although there are examples of judges refusing to do this on the ground that the Court

---

[20] CPR pt 52 and Practice Direction 52A.

[21] Statistics are published on *www.gov.uk/government/statistics*. See eg Ministry of Justice, 'Civil Justice Statistics Quarterly, England and Wales, January to March 2015 and Appellate Court Statistics 2014' (published 4 June 2015, with associated tables): in 2014, 247 petitions for permission to appeal were presented to the Supreme Court, of which 156 (67%) were refused without a hearing and 77 were allowed to proceed for hearing in due course (p 23, Table 3.4). In that year, 1,037 final appeals were disposed of by the Civil Division of the Court of Appeal (Table 3.9), but only 68 cases were decided by the Supreme Court: they are listed on the Supreme Court website, *www.supremecourt.uk*. The Supreme Court hears appeals only on arguable points of law of general public importance.

[22] Above, p 7.

[23] See generally Cross and Harris, *Precedent in English Law* above, n 15, chs III, IV.

[24] Eg *South Caribbean Trading Ltd v Trafigura Beheer BV* [2004] EWHC 2676 (Comm), [2005] 1 Lloyd's Rep 128 [108]: 'But for the fact that *Williams v Roffey Bros* [below, n 26] was a decision of the Court of Appeal, I would not have followed it' (Colman J).

[25] *Miliangos v George Frank (Textiles) Ltd* [1976] AC 443 (HL) 478.

of Appeal had failed properly to take into account a binding decision of the House of Lords—in other words, the Judge discounts the decision of the Court of Appeal on the grounds that it was reached '*per incuriam*' (in error).

(iii) The Court of Appeal is bound to follow a decision of the Supreme Court (and older decisions of the House of Lords). This therefore places a greater constraint on the Court of Appeal in an area of the common law in which the Supreme Court or the House of Lords has taken a decision than in an area in which there is a well-established common law rule which has not been subject to such a decision.[26] The House of Lords has emphasised the importance of adherence to the rules of precedent, and has made clear that the Court of Appeal should normally follow the domestic rules even in a case which raises an issue under the European Convention on Human Rights and where there is an argument that the House of Lords (or, now, the Supreme Court) might itself decide otherwise on the basis of the case-law of the European Court of Human Rights.[27] The Court of Appeal is also bound by its own previous decisions *except* where:[28]

(a) there are conflicting decisions of the Court of Appeal, in which case it is free to decide which to follow;

(b) a decision of the Court of Appeal is inconsistent with a *later* decision of the House of Lords, which therefore impliedly overrules it; or

(c) it decides that the previous decision of the Court of Appeal was given *per incuriam*: it was in error because it failed to consider a binding legal rule (such as an earlier decision of the House of Lords) which would have affected the decision. This has sometimes been extended to cover the case where the Court decides that the previous decision was plainly wrong because it failed properly to give effect to a binding earlier decision which was considered—a controversial extension of the freedom of the Court of Appeal to depart from its own previous decision, but one which has significance in the context of this book because it includes a case

---

[26] Cf the approach in *Re Selectmove* [1995] 1 WLR 474 (where CA was bound by the decision in *Foakes v Beer*, above, n 16) and in *Williams v Roffey Bros & Nicholls (Contractors) Ltd* [1991] 1 QB 1 (CA) (where there was no HL decision to inhibit the court's development of the law); below, pp 139–43.

[27] *Kay v Lambeth LBC* [2006] UKHL 10, [2006] 2 AC 465 [40]–[45]. On matters of EU law, the courts follow decisions of the Court of Justice of the European Union (CJEU); for arguments about how to deal with a conflict between English precedents and decisions of the CJEU see Cross and Harris, *Precedent in English Law* above, n 15, 182–85.

[28] *Young v Bristol Aeroplane Co Ltd* [1944] KB 718 (CA) 729–30.

where the Court of Appeal applied it in 2002 to reject a line of case-law which had extended the scope of the doctrine of mistake in contract.[29]

(iv) The Supreme Court is not bound by its own previous decisions or those of the House of Lords. By the end of the nineteenth century the House of Lords had established the rule that it would be bound by its own decisions—which had the consequence that, in principle, only an Act of Parliament could change the ratio of a decision of the House of Lords. In 1966, however, the Lord Chancellor, Lord Gardiner, on behalf of himself and the other Lords of Appeal in Ordinary (the judges of the House of Lords) made the following Practice Statement:

> Their Lordships regard the use of precedent as an indispensable foundation upon which to decide what is the law and its application to individual cases. It provides at least some degree of certainty upon which individuals can rely in the conduct of their affairs, as well as a basis for orderly development of legal rules.
>
> Their Lordships nevertheless recognise that too rigid adherence to precedent may lead to injustice in a particular case and also unduly restrict the proper development of the law. They propose, therefore, to modify their present practice and, while treating former decisions of this House as normally binding, to depart from a previous decision when it appears right to do so.
>
> In this connection they will bear in mind the danger of disturbing retrospectively the basis on which contracts, settlements of property and fiscal arrangements have been entered into and also the especial need for certainty as to the criminal law.
>
> This announcement is not intended to affect the use of precedent elsewhere than in this House.[30]

On a number of occasions since 1966 the House of Lords departed from[31] a previous decision, although it is not a frequent occurrence. In 1972 the Lord Chancellor, Lord Hailsham, made clear the importance of the rules of precedent, and the reluctance of the House of Lords itself to depart from its own decisions:

> The fact is, and I hope it will never be necessary to say so again, that, in the hierarchical system of courts which exists in this country, it is necessary for

---

[29] *Great Peace Shipping Ltd v Tsavliris Salvage (International) Ltd (The Great Peace)* [2002] EWCA Civ 1407, [2003] QB 679, discussed in detail below, p 172. For criticism of the decision in relation to the doctrine of precedent, see SB Midwinter, 'The Great Peace and Precedent' (2003) 119 LQR 180.

[30] Practice Statement (Judicial Precedent) [1966] 1 WLR 1234.

[31] Notice the language: a court 'departs from' an earlier decision of its own, and the later decision thereby becomes the authority. A court which overturns a decision of a lower court at an earlier stage in the same case 'reverses' the earlier decision. A court which rejects an earlier ratio of a lower court and substitutes the ratio of its own decision 'overrules' the earlier decision.

each lower tier, including the Court of Appeal, to accept loyally the decisions of the higher tiers. Where decisions manifestly conflict, the decision in *Young v Bristol Aeroplane Co Ltd*[32] offers guidance to each tier in matters affecting its own decisions. It does not entitle it to question considered decisions in the upper tiers with the same freedom. Even this House, since it has taken freedom to review its own decisions, will do so cautiously.[33]

This statement has recently been expressly approved in the House of Lords as a reminder to the lower courts of the rules of precedent.[34] The Supreme Court has taken over the same position as the House of Lords in this respect.

(d) Understanding the Case-Law in the Light of the Doctrine of Precedent

As we shall see, it can be important to bear in mind these rules of precedent in reading the cases, because it can sometimes explain the courts' attitude to the development of the law. A good example can be found in the law of contract in relation to the doctrine of privity of contract.[35] The doctrine was accepted by the House of Lords in 1915.[36] Thereafter that decision (and therefore the doctrine of privity of contract) was binding on all courts, including the House of Lords itself until the Practice Statement of 1966 when the House announced its changed view of the binding force of its own previous decisions. The doctrine of privity of contract was commonly perceived as unsatisfactory, and a proposal to reform it was made by the Law Reform Committee in 1937[37] but was not advanced because the Second World War intervened. The first signs of the willingness of the House to reconsider the earlier case-law appeared in the first case after 1966 which raised the issue,[38] although there and in the later cases there was still a reluctance to change such a fundamental doctrine judicially if Parliament could be persuaded to take action by legislation—which finally it did in 1999.[39]

---

[32] Above, n 28.
[33] *Cassell & Co Ltd v Broome* [1972] AC 1027 (HL) 1054. See also *Jones v Secretary of State for Social Services* [1972] AC 944 (HL) 966: the Practice Statement was intended to allow reconsideration of 'a comparatively small number of reported decisions of this House which were generally thought to be impeding the proper development of the law or to have led to results which were unjust or contrary to public policy' (Lord Reid), applied in *Chartbrook Ltd v Persimmon Homes Ltd* [2009] UKHL 38, [2009] 1 AC 1101 [41].
[34] *Kay v Lambeth LBC*, above, n 27, [42].
[35] Above, p 18; below, ch 10.
[36] *Dunlop Pneumatic Tyre Co Ltd v Selfridge & Co Ltd* [1915] AC 847 (HL).
[37] Law Reform Committee, Sixth Interim Report (Cmd 5449, 1937).
[38] *Beswick v Beswick* [1968] AC 58 (HL) 72 (Lord Reid). In 1962, Lord Reid had said 'Although I may regret it, I find it impossible to deny the existence of the general rule [of privity of contract]': *Scruttons Ltd v Midland Silicones Ltd* [1962] AC 446 (HL) 473.
[39] Contracts (Rights of Third Parties) Act 1999; below, ch 10.

3. The Interpretation of Legislative Texts

It is often said that in interpreting a statute the role of the judge is to ascertain the 'intention of Parliament'. However, this does not—of course—mean that the judge seeks to discover what the members of Parliament as a whole understood it to mean; nor the (subjective) intention of the member who sponsored the Bill which became enacted, nor even of the person who drafted the provision in question. Rather, the general approach is to look to the objective meaning of the words used—the intention of the legislator is inferred from the language of the legislation. There is a real reluctance in the English courts to look behind the document itself; the background documents to the legislation—the *travaux préparatoires*—and evidence from its passage through the legislative process are very sparingly used. As we shall see, this bears a striking similarity to the approach taken by the courts to the 'intention of the parties' in a contract; and in interpreting written contracts the courts take a similarly objective view.[40] The judicial attitude towards the interpretation of statutes (and contracts) is linked to the very particular style of drafting statutes (and contracts) in England.[41] In brief, one can summarise the general approach as follows.[42]

(a) *The Basic Test: Applying the Normal, Objective Meaning of the Words of the Statute*

The starting-point for the English courts is to look at the words of the statute and to give them their normal meaning. Sometimes the subject-matter of a statute makes it evident that words are being used in a particular sense; for example, if the statute is directed at a particular trade and there is an established use of certain terms in that trade. But in general the courts go beyond the normal meaning only where that interpretation gives rise to doubt about whether the legislator could really have intended such a meaning. So if there is a clear, straightforward interpretation which does not give rise to any uncertainty or absurdity, it must be given effect. This is often referred to as the 'literal' rule or the 'golden' rule of interpretation. In 1969 Lord Reid said:

> In determining the meaning of any word or phrase in a statute the first question to ask always is what is the natural or ordinary meaning of that word of phrase in its context in the statute? It is only when that meaning leads to some result which cannot reasonably be supposed to have been the intention of the legislature, that it is

---

[40] Below, p 207.
[41] Below, p 44.
[42] See generally R Cross, J Bell, G Engle, *Statutory Interpretation*, 3rd edn (London, LexisNexis, 1995); O Jones, *Bennion on Statutory Interpretation*, 6th edn (London, LexisNexis, 2013).

proper to look for some other possible meaning of the word or phrase. We have been warned again and again that it is wrong and dangerous to proceed by substituting some other words for the words of the statute.[43]

(b) Some General Principles and Presumptions of Interpretation

The courts apply a range of general 'rules' and 'presumptions' in the interpretation of statutes. Some of these are contained in Acts of Parliament—for example, statutes commonly make express provision in an 'interpretation' or 'definitions' clause[44] for the interpretation of particular terms which they use; and the Interpretation Act 1978 contains various provisions about how to interpret certain terms in statutes generally.[45] However, most of the general rules and presumptions of interpretation have been developed by the courts themselves over the years, such as:

(i) the statute is to be read as a whole; light may be cast on one part by provisions elsewhere in the statute and the same or similar words are to be given the same or similar interpretations throughout the statute;

(ii) the opening words of the statute (before the first section) can be a guide to the purpose of the statute, although UK statutes (unlike European Directives, for example) do not contain long and detailed preambles explaining the purpose of the enactment. Statutes begin with a 'long title' which is usually more explicit than the short title by which the statute is known, but the long title is usually of limited value for the purposes of interpretation;[46]

(iii) the heading, or title, of an individual section within a statute is sometimes used to assist in the interpretation of the section, but only in cases of doubt over the meaning of the words of the section itself;

(iv) the general rules of grammar are applied—such as punctuation, the '*eiusdem generis*' rule (where a statute refers to a list of things which are linked by a common theme, it is assumed that everything referred to should be interpreted by reference to the common theme) and the '*expressio unius, exclusio alterius*' rule (explicit reference to one or more things implies that other similar things are excluded);

---

[43] *Pinner v Everett* [1969] 1 WLR 1266 (HL) 1273.

[44] Eg Sale of Goods Act 1979 s 61 (as amended by later legislation) defines 19 terms 'unless the context or subject matter otherwise requires', and directs how certain phrases or legal concepts should be interpreted for the purposes of the Act.

[45] Eg s 6: 'unless the contrary intention appears, words importing the masculine gender include the feminine [and vice versa]; words in the singular include the plural [and vice versa]'; sch 1: '"month" means calendar month' and '"person" includes a body of persons corporate or unincorporate'.

[46] Eg the long title to the Contracts (Rights of Third Parties) Act 1999, set out in the Appendix: 'An Act to make provision for the enforcement of contractual terms by third parties'.

30 FINDING THE LAW

(v) if the statute is a *consolidation statute*—that is, one which draws together and re-enacts rules which have been contained in other statutes in the past—it is still interpreted afresh, as any other statute (and so clear language is given effect), but in case of doubt or ambiguity any decisions on the interpretation of the earlier statutes may be used in the interpretation of the new statute, and there is a presumption that the new statute was not intended to change the law;

(vi) there is a presumption that a statute which was intended to deal with a particular problem did not change the law more than was necessary to deal with that problem. This is sometimes called the 'mischief rule': the statute is to be interpreted so as to remedy only the 'mischief' (the particular problem). But if the statute does clearly go beyond the 'mischief', then it will be given full effect;

(vii) there are presumptions that a statute was not intended to have retroactive effect; that it was not to apply outside UK territory; and (although there is some controversy about the status or strength of such presumptions) that, in case of doubt, an interpretation should not be given which imposes criminal liability on an individual or imposes a liability to tax.

(c) Interpretation of European Law and Compliance with the European Convention on Human Rights

Particular questions have arisen in recent years about the interpretation of European Law and international treaties (and, in particular, the European Convention on Human Rights).

Where a UK statute is enacted in order to give effect to EU law or to an international treaty obligation—and this will generally be clear on the face of the statute—the courts will seek to interpret the UK enactment so as to give effect to the relevant EU or international legal rule. This can have the effect of causing a court to depart from the general approach to statutory interpretation which it would adopt in the case of a UK statute. In relation to EU law, in particular, this approach has the effect that the English courts are becoming more used to interpreting European legislative texts, which have often been drafted in a different style from UK legislation, in accordance with the interpretative techniques adopted by the European Court of Justice (now the Court of Justice of the European Union).[47]

---

[47] UK courts may refer questions of interpretation directly to the Court of Justice of the European Union under art 267 of the Treaty on the Functioning of the European Union (formerly art 234 of the EC Treaty).

Similarly, the European Convention on Human Rights (and its interpretation by the European Court of Human Rights in Strasbourg) is having an effect on the English judges' approach to the interpretation of domestic legislation. Although the convention rights do not take priority over UK statutes within the hierarchy of legislative sources,[48] section 3 of the Human Rights Act 1998 provides that, so far as it is possible to do so, legislation must be read and given effect in a way which is compatible with particular rights and freedoms set out in the Convention.

(d) The Relevance of the Context of the Statute at the Time of its Enactment

In many legal systems it is common for the courts to consider the legislative history of an enactment in order to discover its purpose and therefore to interpret it for the case in hand. There has been a marked reluctance on the part of English judges to do this. As explained above, the English courts will not normally go behind the language of the statute except in cases where in the light of the language of the provision itself there is doubt or uncertainty about its proper interpretation. However, there are certain situations in which the courts will consider the context of the statute at the time of its enactment and its background:

(i) Since a decision of the House of Lords in 1975[49] the courts have been willing to consider the background of a statute—such as a law reform proposal which contained a draft of the Bill which became the statute—in order to discover the 'mischief' which the statute was intended to address.
(ii) Until 1992 the courts had excluded Parliamentary material (such as the debates within Parliament on the Bill) in interpreting an Act. In *Pepper v Hart*[50] the House of Lords revised this strict exclusionary approach, and rejected arguments that to allow the consideration of Parliamentary material would be contrary to constitutional principle (that it would infringe article 9 of the Bill of Rights 1689 which provides that 'the Freedom of Speech, and Debates or Proceedings in Parliament, ought not to be impeached or questioned in any Court or Place out of Parliament'), or that it would confuse the respective roles of Parliament as the maker of the law and the courts as the interpreter.

---

[48] Above, n 6.
[49] *Black-Clawson International Ltd v Papierwerke Waldhof-Aschaffenburg AG* [1975] AC 591 (HL).
[50] [1993] AC 593 (HL). Lord Mackay of Clashfern LC dissented.

Nor did they regard it as an overriding objection that to allow the consideration of Parliamentary material would to some extent increase the time and expense of litigation. However, they were very cautious in their development of the law and held only that:

> [T]he exclusionary rule should be relaxed so as to permit reference to Parliamentary materials where (a) legislation is ambiguous or obscure, or leads to an absurdity; (b) the material relied upon consists of one or more statements by a Minister or other promoter of the Bill together if necessary with such other Parliamentary material as is necessary to understand such statements and their effect; (c) the statements relied upon are clear.[51]

This brings the use of Parliamentary material into line with other extra-legislative evidence: it may be used only if it is relevant, probative and necessary to resolve an uncertainty or ambiguity which arises from the language of the statute itself, by assisting the court to understand the 'mischief' at which the statute was aimed.

This power has been used very sparingly and it is still controversial.[52] The House of Lords has declined to reconsider it or to develop it further, beyond deciding that, in determining whether a statute is compatible with a convention right for the purposes of the Human Rights Act 1998, it may look at Parliamentary materials for—very limited—purposes.[53] But Lord Hobhouse warned that:

> [I]t is a fundamental error of principle to confuse what a minister or a parliamentarian may have said (or said he intended) with the will and intention of Parliament itself. Likewise, it is another fundamental principle that the verbal expression of the law be certain, whatever difficulties in interpretation the words used may cause. Once one departs from the text of the statute construed as a whole and looks for expressions of intention to be found elsewhere, one is not looking for the intention of the legislature but that of some other source with no constitutional power to make law. The process of statutory construction/interpretation is objective not subjective.... The principles are also fully familiar (mutatis mutandis) to commercial lawyers in deciding what was the bargain struck between two commercial parties by a written agreement.[54]

(iii) The context which is normally taken as appropriate to interpret a statute is that *at the time of its enactment*—and so it is relevant to consider the meaning which Parliament will have intended by its words at that

---

[51] *Ibid* 640 (Lord Browne-Wilkinson).
[52] See eg J Steyn [Lord Steyn], '*Pepper v Hart*; A Re-examination' (2001) 21 *OJLS* 59; *R (Jackson) v Attorney General* [2005] UKHL 56, [2006] 1 AC 262 (contrast [65] (Lord Nicholls of Birkenhead) with [97] (Lord Steyn)).
[53] *Wilson v First County Trust Ltd (No 2)* [2003] UKHL 40, [2004] 1 AC 816.
[54] *Ibid* [139].

time, rather than what the words mean today (if there has been a shift in the meaning of terms used in the statute). However, the courts have from time to time interpreted statutes in a dynamic way, giving them a modern equivalent meaning so as to take into account relevant changes in the subject-matter of a statute since it was passed. For example, statutes from earlier in the twentieth century which refer to members of a person's 'family' have been interpreted as including unmarried and same-sex partners, even though this would not have been a natural (or even a possible) interpretation at the time when the statute was enacted.[55]

(e) The Court Does Not Generally Reason Beyond the Statute

In reading a legislative text the court therefore starts from an objective interpretation of it, but will question the literal meaning in the circumstances which have been described above. Sometimes the court will interpret the language beyond—or even to some degree against—the literal wording if necessary to give effect to the underlying purpose of the statute or to some overriding rule, such as in order to render an interpretation which is compliant with Convention rights under the Human Rights Act 1998 and thus avoid the more drastic step of declaring the text non-compliant with the Convention.[56] But this is the exceptional case: the courts do not regard their role as to change or correct the legislative text. Nor will they generally use a legislative text as the starting-point for development beyond the text itself.[57] For example, in *Photo Production Ltd v Securicor Transport Ltd*[58] the House of Lords considered the interaction between the established rules of the common law in regulating the effectiveness of contractual exclusion and limitation clauses, and the Unfair Contract Terms 1977. Before the Act, the courts had found ways of controlling potentially unfair clauses by strict applications of the tests for incorporation of clauses in the contract, and their interpretation *contra proferentem*. The fact that Parliament had intervened to place formal legislative control on certain types of clause in certain types of contract might in another legal

---

[55] *Fitzpatrick v Sterling Housing Association Ltd* [2001] 1 AC 27 (HL). This was possible only because Parliament had not used more specific language. But in *Ghaidan v Godin-Mendoza* [2004] UKHL 30, [2004] 2 AC 557 the House of Lords held that even the words 'living with the original tenant as his or her wife or husband' should be interpreted as including same-sex couples—but only because it was necessary to do so in order to eliminate the otherwise discriminatory effect of the provision under the Human Rights Act 1998: above, section 3(c). Same-sex couples can now marry: Marriage (Same Sex Couples) Act 2013.

[56] Eg *Ghaidan v Godin-Mendoza*, above, n 55.

[57] Cf, however, J Beatson, 'The Role of Statute in the Development of Common Law Doctrine' (2001) 117 LQR 247.

[58] [1980] AC 827 (HL).

system have been seen by a court as an indication of the intention of the legislator to control such clauses, reinforcing the former judicial approach and justifying the court, in an appropriate case, in going beyond the literal meaning of the statute to an even wider control of unfair contract clauses.[59] But for the English court the reasoning is exactly the reverse. Legislative intervention places the *limit* on the control. Parliament has defined the types of contract, and the types of term, that are to be controlled. It is therefore not the role of the courts to go further.[60] Similarly, in *National Westminster Bank plc v Morgan* Lord Scarman indicated that the proper control of unfair terms in contracts more generally is for the legislature rather than for the courts:

> Parliament has undertaken the task—and it is essentially a legislative task—of enacting such restrictions upon freedom of contract as are in its judgment necessary to relieve against the mischief: for example, the hire-purchase and consumer protection legislation, of which the Supply of Goods (Implied Terms) Act 1973, Consumer Credit Act 1974, Consumer Safety Act 1978, Supply of Goods and Services Act 1982 and Insurance Companies Act 1982 are examples. I doubt whether the courts should assume the burden of formulating further restrictions.[61]

4. Reasoning from the Cases in the Common Law

Where, however, a case raises an issue governed not by a statutory provision but by the common law, the court has greater freedom to develop the law beyond the existing case-law authorities. Judicial reasoning in relation to the common law is different from reasoning in relation to the statute. In the common law, the judge is willing to look behind the rule which he finds articulated in the earlier decisions, to see the underlying principle which can be used to develop the law. But the nature of judicial law-making in the common law is of course limited.

(a) The Judge Develops the Common Law and Does Not Simply Declare it

We have already seen that the common law consists of a body of rules which have been devised and developed over the years by the courts.[62] There is

---

[59] For a good (and parallel) example in French law, see B Nicholas, *The French Law of Contract*, 2nd edn (Oxford, Clarendon Press, 1992) 143 (interpretation by the French *Cour de cassation* of a legislative text on unfair terms as providing the basis for the court to strike down a term in circumstances not literally covered by the legislation).
[60] Above, n 58, 843 (Lord Wilberforce) and 851 (Lord Diplock).
[61] [1985] AC 686 (HL) 708.
[62] Above, ch 1.

no statutory authority for many of the fundamental rules of private law; therefore they must in some sense have been devised by the courts themselves. This is not simply a matter of history. Although, for example, the common law rules governing the law of contract were established by the end of the nineteenth century, the law has not remained static and we shall see that the courts have continued to develop and sometimes radically change the common law of contract. The development in certain areas of the law of tort is even more marked; the modern tort of negligence is generally dated to the decision of the House of Lords in *Donoghue v Stevenson* in 1932; but there has been very significant judicial development of the tort since then. This will be discussed below.

It is important to realise that the courts themselves admit that they develop the common law. There was a time when judges were reluctant to make such an admission, and writers asserted that the role of the judge was only to declare the common law, not to develop it. However, this is now seen to be a fiction. There is no body of 'principles of the common law' which already exists, simply to be revealed and made concrete for particular cases by the interpretation of the judge. When a court overrules an earlier decision it might be holding that the earlier court erred at the time in its interpretation or application of the common law rule. But equally it might be holding that, although correctly decided at the time, the earlier decision no longer states the law as it should be recognised today—that is, the new decision itself changes the legal rule. This was made clear by Lord Goff in *Kleinwort Benson Ltd v Lincoln City Council*:

> Historically speaking, the declaratory theory of judicial decisions is to be found in a statement by Sir Matthew Hale over 300 years ago, viz. that the decisions of the courts do not constitute the law properly so called, but are evidence of the law and as such 'have a great weight and authority in expounding, declaring, and publishing what the law of this Kingdom is:' see *Hale's Common Law of England*, 6th ed. (1820), p. 88–90. To the like effect, *Blackstone Commentaries*, 6th ed. (1774), pp. 88–89, stated that 'the decisions of courts are the evidence of what is the common law.' In recent times, however, a more realistic approach has been adopted, as in Sir George Jessel M.R.'s celebrated statement that rules of equity, unlike rules of the common law, are not supposed to have been established since time immemorial, but have been invented, altered, improved and refined from time to time: see *In re Hallett's Estate; Knatchbull v. Hallett* (1880) 13 Ch.D. 696, 710. There can be no doubt of the truth of this statement; and we all know that in reality, in the common law as in equity, the law is the subject of development by the judges—normally, of course, by appellate judges. We describe as leading cases the decisions which mark the principal stages in this development, and we have no difficulty in identifying the judges who are primarily responsible. It is universally recognised that judicial development of the common law is inevitable. If it had never taken place, the common law would be the same now as it was in the reign of King Henry II; it is because of it that the common law is a living system of law, reacting to new events and new ideas, and so capable of providing the citizens of this country with a system of practical justice relevant to the times in which they live. The recognition that this is what

actually happens requires, however, that we should look at the declaratory theory of judicial decision with open eyes and reinterpret it in the light of the way in which all judges, common law and equity, actually decide cases today.[63]

(b) Reasoning in the Common Law

This is not to say, of course, that the power of the judge is that of a legislator. The legislator is free to lay down new general principles of law, within only those constraints which are set by the constitutional framework—such as the requirement to comply with overriding rules governing fundamental rights.[64]

The role of the judge is to decide the particular case before him. His power to develop the law is limited to relevant points of law which arise in the case; and of course the binding force of his decision, in so far as it creates a new legal rule, is limited under the doctrine of precedent to the ratio.[65] This was also made clear by Lord Goff:

> When a judge decides a case which comes before him, he does so on the basis of what he understands the law to be. This he discovers from the applicable statutes, if any, and from precedents drawn from reports of previous judicial decisions. Nowadays, he derives much assistance from academic writings in interpreting statutes and, more especially, the effect of reported cases; and he has regard, where appropriate, to decisions of judges in other jurisdictions. In the course of deciding the case before him he may, on occasion, develop the common law in the perceived interests of justice, though as a general rule he does this 'only interstitially,' to use the expression of O. W. Holmes J. in *Southern Pacific Co. v. Jensen* (1917) 244 U.S. 205, 221. This means not only that he must act within the confines of the doctrine of precedent, but that the change so made must be seen as a development, usually a very modest development, of existing principle and so can take its place as a congruent part of the common law as a whole. In this process, what Maitland has called the 'seamless web,' and I myself (*The Search for Principle*, Proc. Brit. Acad. vol. LXIX (1983) 170, 186) have called the 'mosaic,' of the common law, is kept in a constant state of adaptation and repair, the doctrine of precedent, the 'cement of legal principle,' providing the necessary stability. A similar process must take place in codified systems as in the common law, where a greater stability is provided by the code itself; though as the years pass by, and decided cases assume

---

[63] [1999] 2 AC 349 (HL) 377. In this case the House of Lords overruled a long-standing line of cases which had held that the payer could not recover a payment made under a mistake of law (rather than a mistake of fact).

[64] The (unwritten) British Constitution does not however formally constrain the UK Parliament, nor does it give the domestic courts powers of judicial review of the substantive content of legislation, in the way that some other (written) constitutions do in relation to their own legislators; above, p 36.

[65] Above, p 22.

a greater importance, codified systems tend to become more like common law systems.

> Occasionally, a judicial development of the law will be of a more radical nature, constituting a departure, even a major departure, from what has previously been considered to be established principle, and leading to a realignment of subsidiary principles within that branch of the law.[66]

Lord Goff noted here that there might be a similarity between the legal reasoning of the judge in relation to the common law, and the judicial development of a code. This analogy can be useful, although of course it is incomplete. In a codified system the code is (until amended by the legislator) a fixed legislative text, usually containing statements of general rules and principles. The courts must interpret it; and in doing so inevitably they develop the rules and principles which are stated in the text—but (in theory, at least) they are not free to overturn the rules or principles. But where the *only* authoritative statement of the law is contained in the code, the interpretative techniques of the judge in a codified system inevitably involve discovering the true meaning of the text, and if necessary developing the interpretation of the text, in order to answer the case in hand. There is no alternative source of law. In the English legal system, however, we have already seen that the judge does not view his role in interpreting statutes in this way: he need not find the law in the text. If no statute covers the point on which he must find the relevant legal rule, he can turn to the case-law of the common law. The common law, rather than legislation, is where the general, residual rules of law are to be found. And therefore the English judge's approach to the interpretation of the common law sources—the earlier decisions of the courts—has a similarity to the approach of the judge to the interpretation of the code in a fully codified system of law.

But there is a fundamental difference between the English judge's reasoning in the common law, and the judge's interpretation of a code. The code gives the judge a general statement of principle as his starting-point. He may need to consult other cases, and legal writers, to see how others have interpreted the text. But there is a text. In the case of the common law, by contrast, the judge begins not from a general statement of principle, but discovers the relevant principle by considering the particular, earlier cases. The answer to the present case is to be found in a proper analysis of its facts, to deduce the fundamental legal question which it raises; and then by a consideration of the cases in the past which have given an answer to the same or similar sets of facts, raising the same or similar legal questions, the judge can find the legal rule to apply here—unless, of course, he decides that the legal rule which is evidenced by those earlier cases should for some reason be changed or developed in the

---

[66] *Kleinwort Benson Ltd v Lincoln City Council* above, n 63, at 378.

38 FINDING THE LAW

light of other changes in the law or society. Radical changes or developments are uncommon, but (within the limits of the rules of precedent) are possible. We shall see some examples in the law of contract later in this book.[67] And in most cases the answers to questions before the courts do not hinge on a detailed analysis of earlier cases to discover the relevant legal rule—most of the rules of the law of contract, for example, are well established and set out in the form of statements of general principle in the textbooks. But in case of doubt or debate about the existing rule, how it should be interpreted and applied to a new case, and whether it should even be developed to change the old understanding of the rule, the common law judge reasons from the particular details of the earlier cases, to find the legal rule or principle which he will then apply to the present case. In *Quinn v Leathem* Lord Halsbury LC emphasised the difference between the common law and a code:

> [T]here are two observations of a general character which I wish to make, and one is to repeat what I have very often said before, that every judgment must be read as applicable to the particular facts proved, or assumed to be proved, since the generality of the expressions which may be found there are not intended to be expositions of the whole law, but governed and qualified by the particular facts of the case in which such expressions are to be found. The other is that a case is only an authority for what it actually decides. I entirely deny that it can be quoted for a proposition that may seem to follow logically from it. Such a mode of reasoning assumes that the law is necessarily a logical code, whereas every lawyer must acknowledge that the law is not always logical at all.[68]

(c) An Illustration of Common Law Reasoning: Donoghue v Stevenson *and its Aftermath*

A good illustration of the methodology of reasoning in the common law, and the potential scope of development of the common law through judicial decisions, can be found in the line of cases beginning with the decision of the House of Lords in *Donoghue v Stevenson*[69] in 1932, which is now seen as the origin of the tort of negligence in the modern law.

It should be understood first that the English law of tort is in fact a law of 'torts': there is no single rule, nor a general principle, for what constitutes a wrong actionable in the law of tort, but there is a series of wrongs which have

---

[67] Eg *Central London Property Trust v High Trees House* [1947] KB 130 (KB), below, p 145 (promissory estoppel); *The Universe Sentinel* [1983] 1 AC 366 (HL), below, p 192 (economic duress); *Solle v Butcher* [1950] 1 KB 671 (CA) and *The Great Peace* [2002] EWCA Civ 1407, [2003] QB 679, below, p 175 (mistake); *Attorney-General v Blake* [2001] 1 AC 268 (HL), below, p 293 (damages to deprive defendant of profit).
[68] [1901] 1 AC 495 (HL) 506.
[69] [1932] AC 562 (HL Sc).

their own separate rules (and, sometimes, different remedies). This structure has arisen in English law for historical reasons. From the middle ages separate forms of action were devised for separate wrongs; that is, each action required the claimant to use a particular form of claim, a 'writ'. This was changed in the mid-nineteenth century, when the separate forms of action were abolished.[70] But although there are now no longer separate actions for the torts, their rules were not merged: the separate torts retained their separate definition, although of course they have all continued to be developed by the courts since then. Some torts are designed to protect particular proprietary or personal interests—such as interests in land (the torts of nuisance and trespass to land), in personal property (the tort of conversion) or in reputation (defamation: libel and slander). Others are defined by reference to the consequences of particular types of misconduct—such as loss caused by reliance on a fraudulent (dishonest) statement (the tort of deceit). Some torts require proof of intention; a few are strict liability. But before 1932 there was no distinct tort of negligence, a tort which in its modern development can cover different types of conduct (acts, statements, even omissions) and different types of harm (physical injury to the person, damage to property and even economic loss, although there is a marked caution in the courts' extension of the tort of negligence to cover pure economic loss—that is, economic loss which is not itself consequential on damage to the person or to property).[71] In this tort a defendant is liable to pay damages to compensate the claimant's loss or damage suffered in consequence of the defendant's breach of a duty to take reasonable care. The principal limiting factor is therefore: did the defendant owe to the claimant a duty to take reasonable care in whatever he is alleged to have done (or not done)?

The question in *Donoghue v Stevenson* was quite narrow. The case was an appeal from Scotland—not, therefore, strictly a matter of English law,[72] although the House of Lords made clear that their statements were equally applicable to English law. Mrs Donoghue alleged that she suffered personal injuries from consuming ginger beer (a non-alcoholic fizzy drink), which had been manufactured by the defendant.[73] The ginger beer was supplied in a

---

[70] By, most significantly, the Common Law Procedure Act 1852, followed by the fusion of the common law and equitable jurisdictions into a single court by the Judicature Acts 1873–75; FW Maitland, 'Lectures on the Forms of Action at Common Law' in AH Chaytor and WJ Whittaker (eds), *Equity* (Cambridge, Cambridge University Press, 1909).

[71] Eg *D & F Estates Ltd v Church Commissioners for England* [1989] AC 177 (HL). A general exception was created in relation to economic loss suffered in reliance on a careless statement, by *Hedley Byrne & Co Ltd v Heller & Partners Ltd* [1964] AC 465 (HL), below, n 81.

[72] Above p 3, n 1.

[73] The 'defender' in Scots law; the claimant is the 'pursuer'. In English cases the traditional language is the 'defendant' and 'plaintiff', although since a reform of legal terminology on the introduction of new Civil Procedure Rules in 1999, the modern English usage is to refer to the 'claimant'. Other common law jurisdictions, such as the United States and Australia, still refer to the 'plaintiff'.

dark opaque glass bottle, and it was alleged that it contained a decomposed snail which remained in the bottle—and which therefore Mrs Donoghue could not see—when she drank the first glassful. She did not buy the ginger beer herself: it was paid for by a friend with whom she was having a drink in a café. The only question before the House of Lords was whether the claim was in principle valid: if the claimant could establish at trial the facts which she alleged, would her claim for damages succeed? The legal question, therefore, was whether the manufacturer owed a duty of care to her. There was no relevant statute on the matter;[74] no clear answer on the existing authorities; and not even a single view of the members of the House of Lords as to what the answer should be: two held that the manufacturer owed no duty of care to the consumer; but three held that the manufacturer did owe a duty—and therefore the ratio is to be found in the reasoning of the majority.

The difference of opinion flowed from the interpretation of the earlier cases. There were some conflicting decisions (none of them binding on the House of Lords), but it was sufficiently clearly established that a manufacturer could be liable for injury caused by an article which was: (1) dangerous in itself; or (2) in fact dangerous because of some defect known to the manufacturer. The minority in the House of Lords regarded these 'exceptional' cases of liability as showing that there was no general duty on a manufacturer: a form of reasoning *e contrario*. This outcome coincided with the view of the minority that to impose a general duty would be too wide-ranging. The majority, however, took a different approach, and had a different starting-point: that one would expect the law to impose a duty of care in such circumstances. The leading speech[75] of the majority—and the one which is generally cited in later cases—was delivered by Lord Atkin.

Lord Atkin's conclusion—and the ratio of the case—was that:

> [A] manufacturer of products, which he sells in such a form as to show that he intends them to reach the ultimate consumer in the form in which they left him with no reasonable possibility of intermediate examination, and with the knowledge that the absence of reasonable care in the preparation or putting up of the products will result in an injury to the consumer's life or property, owes a duty to the consumer to take that reasonable care.[76]

---

[74] Nowadays such a case would be covered by the Consumer Protection Act 1987 pt I (implementing Council Directive 85/374/EEC on defective products), but this Act has not removed or changed the authority of the decision in *Donoghue v Stevenson* because it is 'without prejudice to any liability arising otherwise than by virtue of' the Act: s 2(6).

[75] Notice the terminology: judges in all the courts below the House of Lords deliver 'judgments'; but members of the House of Lords when its Judicial Committee was the final court of appeal delivered 'speeches', since formally they made their speeches only as members of the Judicial Committee to recommend to the whole House the outcome of the appeal, and it was the vote of the whole House which determined the outcome. However, by convention the House simply adopted the recommendation of the Judicial Committee. Now that the appellate function has been transferred to the new Supreme Court (above p 7, n 11) this anomaly has disappeared: the judges of the Supreme Court are 'Justices', and they deliver 'judgments'.

[76] [1932] AC 562, 599.

However, in order to reach this conclusion, Lord Atkin used a process of inductive and deductive reasoning: from a detailed consideration of the earlier judgments he generalised a broad underlying principle that a duty of care is based on foreseeability of injury; and expressed the view that the existing specific cases in which a duty has been found are examples of the types of situation in which a duty can be owed; they are not a closed list of categories of duty. Lord Macmillan, also in the majority, said explicitly that the 'categories of negligence are never closed'.[77] Lord Atkin's starting-point for his general approach is indicated in the following extract:

> It is remarkable how difficult it is to find in the English authorities statements of general application defining the relations between parties that give rise to the duty. The Courts are concerned with the particular relations which come before them in actual litigation, and it is sufficient to say whether the duty exists in those circumstances. The result is that the Courts have been engaged upon an elaborate classification of duties as they exist in respect of property, whether real or personal, with further divisions as to ownership, occupation or control, and distinctions based on the particular relations of the one side or the other, whether manufacturer, salesman or landlord, customer, tenant, stranger, and so on. In this way it can be ascertained at any time whether the law recognizes a duty, but only where the case can be referred to some particular species which has been examined yet the duty which is common to all the cases where liability is and classified. And yet the duty which is common to all the cases where liability is established must logically be based upon some element common to the cases where it is found to exist. To seek a complete logical definition of the general principle is probably to go beyond the function of the judge, for the more general the definition the more likely it is to omit essentials or to introduce non-essentials ...
>
> At present I content myself with pointing out that in English law there must be, and is, some general conception of relations giving rise to a duty of care, of which the particular cases found in the books are but instances. The liability for negligence, whether you style it such or treat it as in other systems as a species of 'culpa,' is no doubt based upon a general public sentiment of moral wrongdoing for which the offender must pay. But acts or omissions which any moral code would censure cannot in a practical world be treated so as to give a right to every person injured by them to demand relief. In this way rules of law arise which limit the range of complainants and the extent of their remedy. The rule that you are to love your neighbour becomes in law, you must not injure your neighbour; and the lawyer's question, Who is my neighbour? receives a restricted reply. You must take reasonable care to avoid acts or omissions which you can reasonably foresee would be likely to injure your neighbour. Who, then, in law is my neighbour? The answer seems to be—persons who are so closely and directly affected by my act that I ought reasonably to have them in contemplation as being so affected when I am directing my mind to the acts or omissions which are called in question.[78]

---

[77] *Ibid* 619.
[78] [1932] AC 562, 579–80.

It is important to realise, however, that Lord Atkin's statement of the 'neighbour' principle is not the ratio of the case. It was part of his reasoning to explain how a new category of duty could be found—in this case, the duty of a manufacturer to an ultimate consumer of his product. But the origin of the modern tort of negligence is now traced to his generalisation of the links between the categories of duty.

There were two separate lines of development from this decision in the later cases, which illustrate the potential for judicial development of the common law.

First, the narrow context of the decision in *Donoghue v Stevenson* was extended. From 1932 the case stood as a precedent for the particular case of manufacturers' duties towards ultimate consumers of their products. But in a series of cases courts held that the principle was not limited to the *manufacturer* of products, but also extended to the *repairer* of a product,[79] or the *seller of a second-hand product*,[80] in favour of those persons whom they could foresee might be injured if the product (as repaired or sold) was defective. The reasoning here was by analogy: the underlying principles for imposing a duty on a manufacturer were equally applicable to impose a duty on a repairer or seller—he put the product into circulation when he was the person who had control over the state of the product, and could foresee that the user or a third party would be exposed to the risk of its defective state without checking the product or expecting any one else to do so.

Secondly, and much more significant, courts from the 1960s onwards took *Donoghue v Stevenson*, and in particular Lord Atkin's speech, as the starting point to develop much more generalised principles of the duty of care in negligence, beginning from the proposition, underlying Lord Atkin's reasoning, that a defendant should normally owe a duty in favour of a claimant whom he should have foreseen might suffer loss as a result of the defendant's careless words or conduct. These principles of the duty of care have been subject to much detailed development, and the scope of liability in the tort of negligence has been refined by the courts throughout each succeeding decade, at each stage building on the earlier case-law and the principles underlying the cases but without any statutory text as a guide.

The first significant extension was in *Hedley Byrne & Co Ltd v Heller & Partners Ltd*[81] where the House of Lords defined in general terms for the first time the circumstances in which a defendant could be held liable in the tort of negligence in respect of economic loss suffered by the claimant in reliance on

---

[79] *Stennett v Hancock* [1939] 2 All ER 578 (KB); *Haseldine v CA Daw & Son Ltd* [1941] 2 KB 343 (CA).
[80] *Herschtal v Stewart and Ardern Ltd* [1940] 1 KB 155 (KB); *Andrews v Hopkinson* [1957] 1 QB 229 (QB).
[81] [1964] AC 465 (HL): the issue was whether a bank owed a duty to the recipient of a credit reference on one of the bank's customers.

a statement made by the defendant. Lord Devlin made clear how this development followed on from the decision in *Donoghue v Stevenson* but within the general approach to the development of the common law:

> In his celebrated speech in that case Lord Atkin did two things. He stated what he described as a 'general conception' and from that conception he formulated a specific proposition of law. In between he gave a warning 'against the danger of stating propositions of law in wider terms than is necessary, lest essential factors be omitted in the wider survey and the inherent adaptability of English law be unduly restricted.' What Lord Atkin called a 'general conception of relations giving rise to a duty of care' is now often referred to as the principle of proximity. You must take reasonable care to avoid acts or omissions which you can reasonably foresee would be likely to injure your neighbour. In the eyes of the law your neighbour is a person who is so closely and directly affected by your act that you ought reasonably to have him in contemplation as being so affected when you are directing your mind to the acts or omissions which are called in question.
>
> The specific proposition arising out of this conception is that 'a manufacturer of products, which he sells in such a form as to show that he intends them to reach the ultimate consumer in the form in which they left him with no reasonable possibility of intermediate examination, and with the knowledge that the absence of reasonable care in the preparation or putting up of the products will result in an injury to the consumer's life or property, owes a duty to the consumer to take that reasonable care.'
>
> Now, it is not, in my opinion, a sensible application of what Lord Atkin was saying for a Judge to be invited on the facts of any particular case to say whether or not there was 'proximity' between the plaintiff and the defendant. That would be a misuse of a general conception and it is not the way in which English law develops. What Lord Atkin did was to use his general conception to open up a category of cases giving rise to a special duty. It was already clear that the law recognised the existence of such a duty in the category of articles that were dangerous in themselves.
>
> What *Donoghue v. Stevenson* did may be described either as the widening of an old category or as the creation of a new and similar one. The general conception can be used to produce other categories in the same way. An existing category grows as instances of its application multiply until the time comes when the cell divides ...
>
> In my opinion, the appellants in their argument tried to press *Donoghue v. Stevenson* too hard. They asked whether the principle of proximity should not apply as well to words as to deeds. I think it should, but as it is only a general conception it does not get them very far. Then they take the specific proposition laid down by *Donoghue v. Stevenson* and try to apply it literally to a certificate or a banker's reference. That will not do, for a general conception cannot be applied to pieces of paper in the same way as to articles of commerce or to writers in the same way as to manufacturers. An inquiry into the possibilities of intermediate examination of certificate will not be fruitful. The real value of *Donoghue v. Stevenson* to the argument in this case is that it shows how the law can be developed to solve particular problems. Is the relationship between the parties in this case such that it can be brought within a category giving rise to a special duty? As always in English law, the first step in such

an inquiry is to see how far the authorities have gone, for new categories in the law do not spring into existence overnight.[82]

As a result of this and the later developments in the tort of negligence it can now be said that there are well-defined situations in which a person can be held to owe a duty of care to another in respect of—for example—pure economic loss consequential upon the provision of information or advice;[83] damage caused by third parties over which the defendant has some definable measure of control;[84] physical damage to persons and property (but not normally the cost of repair or replacement of buildings or goods caused by defective manufacture);[85] psychiatric injury, whether suffered by a 'primary victim' of the defendant's acts—a person who is himself in the range of danger of the defendant's careless acts, or by a 'secondary victim'—a person who suffers the psychiatric injury in consequence of seeing or hearing an incident which involved another.[86] Over the years new categories of duty have been established, by analogy with particular, established duties, and by application of the general underlying principle of all the categories of duty. And new situations continue to arise in which the courts still have to consider whether to extend the duty of care in negligence to cover new situations.[87]

III. English Statutory Drafting

1. The General Style of Statutory Drafting in England

We have already described various aspects of the relationship between the legislator and the judges within the English legal system. In the hierarchy of legal sources legislation is above the common law, and the role of the judge is to interpret and implement the statutory text faithfully. But it is the task of

---

[82] *Ibid* 524–25 (fn references omitted).
[83] *Hedley Byrne & Co Ltd v Heller & Partners Ltd* above, n 81; *Caparo Industries plc v Dickman* [1990] 2 AC 605 (HL).
[84] *Home Office v Dorset Yacht Co Ltd* [1970] AC 1004 (HL).
[85] *D & F Estates Ltd v Church Commissioners for England* [1989] AC 177 (HL).
[86] *Bourhill v Young* [1943] AC 92 (HL Sc); *Alcock v Chief Constable of South Yorkshire Police* [1992] 1 AC 310 (HL); *Page v Smith* [1996] AC 155 (HL).
[87] For a discussion by the House of Lords of the methodology of extending the range of duties of care in the tort of negligence, see *Customs and Excise Commissioners v Barclays Bank plc* [2006] UKHL 28, [2007] 1 AC 181. For a detailed discussion of the development from *Donoghue v Stevenson* to the present day, see WE Peel and J Goudkamp, *Winfield & Jolowicz on Tort*, 19th edn (London, Sweet & Maxwell, 2014) ch 5.

the legislative draftsman to ensure that the legislative intention is conveyed by the language of the text when given its normal, objective meaning, since that is the basic starting-point for the judge in fulfilling the role of interpreter of the text. The judge does not see it as necessary to go beyond the language of the text, or to develop it to fill any gaps which might have been left by the drafting, because the common law—the law as developed through the cases—is the general law. Statute is there to be respected, but not as the only source of legal rules.

A consequence of this is that the drafting of statutes in England is much more detailed than in most civil law jurisdictions. Where, in a fully codified system, the totality of legal rules is required to be stated in legislative texts, two things generally follow: first, the style of legislative drafting becomes general and abstract, since the codifier can only state the full body of rules in the form of general principles, to be filled out and explained in detail by the courts in their role as interpreters of the text; and secondly, the judges see their role as not simply fleshing out the detail of the text but as using the text itself as the basis of further development of the legal rules as new circumstances demand. Neither of these things is generally true in a common law system. The English judges will give full effect to clearly-drafted legislation; but they do not generally fill gaps left by the legislator, or look for the 'spirit' behind the text if the text itself does not cover the case in hand. But, to ensure that the judges do give full effect to the legislative intention, the texts tend to be very detailed—to be 'judge-proof'.

2. An Illustration: The Contracts (Rights of Third Parties) Act 1999

It may be useful for the reader who is new to the common law to see an illustration of the English style of legislative drafting. A striking example—and one which is particularly relevant for the purposes of this book—is the Contracts (Rights of Third Parties) Act 1999.

We have already made brief mention of this Act earlier in this chapter, and we shall see the detail of it in chapter ten. For present purposes, it is sufficient to say that this is a statute which—in contrast to the common law rule of 'privity of contract'—allows a third party in certain circumstances to enforce a term in a contract made for his benefit. Most legal systems have some such provision. But codified civil law systems will generally have relatively brief provisions. In English law it is a detailed set of rules in a special statute.

The full text of the Act is reproduced in the Appendix, but it will suffice for present purposes to use one section of the Act to illustrate its detailed and complex style of drafting. Every legal system which has devised rules allowing third parties to enforce a contract has had to address the question: does this right limit the power of the contracting parties themselves to vary or rescind the contract? Codes of European legal systems deal with this question in very brief provisions. For example, the German Civil Code takes 36 words to say that if there is no express provision it is to be deduced from the circumstances and in particular from the object of the contract, whether the parties have retained the right to take away or modify the third party's right without his consent.[88] The French and Italian Civil Codes take 18 words and 23 words respectively to say that the right is irrevocable once the third party has declared that he wishes to take advantage of it.[89] This issue is addressed in 384 words in section 2 of the 1999 Act, which not only lays down the general rule (the parties' power is limited once the third party has communicated his assent to the term to the party whose obligation is in issue (the 'promisor'), or has relied on it in circumstances where the promisor knows about or ought reasonably to have foreseen the reliance); but also seeks to anticipate in minute detail the questions which might arise in the application of that rule:

> **2.**—(1) Subject to the provisions of this section, where a third party has a right under section 1 to enforce a term of the contract, the parties to the contract may not, by agreement, rescind the contract, or vary it in such a way as to extinguish or alter his entitlement under that right, without his consent if—
>
> (a) the third party has communicated his assent to the term to the promisor,
> (b) the promisor is aware that the third party has relied on the term, or
> (c) the promisor can reasonably be expected to have foreseen that the third party would rely on the term and the third party has in fact relied on it.
>
> (2) The assent referred to in subsection (1)(a)—
>
> (a) may be by words or conduct, and
> (b) if sent to the promisor by post or other means, shall not be regarded as communicated to the promisor until received by him.
>
> (3) Subsection (1) is subject to any express term of the contract under which—
>
> (a) the parties to the contract may by agreement rescind or vary the contract without the consent of the third party, or
> (b) the consent of the third party is required in circumstances specified in the contract instead of those set out in subsection (1)(a) to (c).
>
> (4) Where the consent of a third party is required under subsection (1) or (3), the court or arbitral tribunal may, on the application of the parties to the contract, dispense with his consent if satisfied—

---

[88] BGB §328(2): 'In Ermangelung einer besonderen Bestimmung ist aus den Umständen, insbesondere aus dem Zwecke des Vertrags, zu entnehmen, ... ob den Vertragschließenden die Befugnis vorbehalten sein soll, das Recht des Dritten ohne dessen Zustimmung aufzuheben oder zu ändern.'

[89] *Code Civil* art 1121: 'Celui qui a fait cette stipulation ne peut la révoquer, si le tiers a déclaré vouloir en profiter'; *Codice civile* art 1411: 'Questa però può essere revocata o modificata dallo stipulante, finché il terzo non abbia dichiarato, anche in confronto del promittente, di volerne profittare.'

(a) that his consent cannot be obtained because his whereabouts cannot reasonably be ascertained, or
(b) that he is mentally incapable of giving his consent.

(5) The court or arbitral tribunal may, on the application of the parties to a contract, dispense with any consent that may be required under subsection (1)(c) if satisfied that it cannot reasonably be ascertained whether or not the third party has in fact relied on the term.

(6) If the court or arbitral tribunal dispenses with a third party's consent, it may impose such conditions as it thinks fit, including a condition requiring the payment of compensation to the third party.

(7) The jurisdiction conferred on the court by subsections (4) to (6) is exercisable in England and Wales by both the High Court and the county court and in Northern Ireland by both the High Court and a county court.

Part II

The Law of Contract

In this Part we consider the English law of contract. The first Part of the book gave an introduction to the common law in general, and to English law in particular, in order to give the context for the substantive discussion of the law of contract.

In chapter three we give a general introduction to the law of contract in the common law—both to show where contract fits within the structure of private law in the common law system and its relationship to other areas such as the law of tort; and to give an outline of some of the key features of the common law approach to analysing a contract and some of the points which mark a contrast between the common law and civil law in this area. These matters will all be relevant later in the book, in relation to particular topics within the law of contract, but it is necessary to set them out at the very beginning so that the reader who is familiar with the law of contract in another system may approach the particular rules within the English law of contract with an understanding of their essential starting-point.

In chapters four to twelve we then consider the rules of the English law of contract, largely following the traditional topics which are found in most legal systems in the exposition of the law of contract, and taking the life of the contract through from its formation to remedies for breach (that is, non-performance or defective performance). Some of these topics are however treated in a slightly different way from the traditional English contract law textbooks, because it is necessary for the civil lawyer to see them through a discussion of certain questions which would commonly arise in the civil law. Most notably, one chapter (chapter four) is devoted to a topic which does not normally appear as a distinct chapter in an English contract law textbook, the negotiations for a contract. It is in this topic that the civil lawyer will see some very significant differences between English law and his or her own system.

3

Introduction to the English Law of Contract

There are certain features of the law of contract in the common law—and, in particular, English law—which need to be seen at the outset. The lawyer who comes to this subject with knowledge of the law of contract in another system may have assumptions and preconceptions about the place of contract (in relation to, for example, the law of tort or property), the role of 'special' types of contract, and the appropriate use of standards such as 'good faith' in the formation and performance of contracts. These are matters on which there are some significant differences between English law and certain other jurisdictions. Whilst not seeking to draw direct comparisons with the law in any other particular jurisdiction, this chapter will set out a general account of these matters from the point of view of English law, by way of an introduction to the chapters which follow and which give a more detailed and specific account of the English rules of contract law.

I. The Place of Contract in Private Law

1. Contract within the Law of Obligations

In general terms, contract in English law sits in the same place as in other western legal systems: it is part of the law of obligations. A legacy of Roman law in those systems which received it more directly than did English law[1] is a structure of private law which divides a person's wealth into his property rights, and the rights he has (or duties he owes) under obligations; and within the

---

[1] Above, pp 7–8.

law of obligations are distinguished contractual and tortious (or 'delictual') obligations as well as obligations which do not depend on contract or tort but are often grouped under a third heading of obligations which arise so as to prevent or reverse an unjust enrichment. This last category (unjust enrichment) is the least well settled as a common element of the structure of the law of obligations, but there is no doubt about the significance of both contract and tort as sources of obligations in all western systems.

English law follows a broadly similar structure. The place of the law of unjust enrichment (for which *restitution* is due) has been worked out only relatively recently.[2] But the law of contract and the law of tort each have their established place. And, as in other systems, contracts and torts give rise to obligations. But this is not a result of a general, systematic view of a 'law of obligations' which is subdivided into contract, tort and unjust enrichment. Books have not traditionally been written, nor have university law courses traditionally been taught, on the 'law of obligations' in England: contract and tort have their own separate place in the law library and in the law curriculum.[3]

This may be a result of the lack of generalisation of legal principles in English law, which results in a lack of generalisation of the overall structures of private law, by contrast with civilian systems whose codes necessarily present a framework within which places for the law of contract and the law of tort have to be found—and which are often found in a unified law of obligations following some form of inheritance of the Roman model. English law developed contractual actions and a range of actions for torts as a result of particular cases which have arisen over the years in the traditional manner of the common law—and it was the forms of action which were available from time to time for the litigation of such cases which gave us the modern rules of contract and tort and the relationship between contract and tort, rather than any overall view of the system within which they were to be developed.[4]

---

[2] Until recently restitution, or 'quasi-contract', was treated within the contract books (often rather uncomfortably as a final chapter). The first edition of the leading English text by R Goff and G Jones, *The Law of Restitution* (London, Sweet & Maxwell), was published in 1966; the subject has developed significantly and the latest edition of Goff & Jones was published in 2011 under the name *The Law of Unjust Enrichment*.

[3] There are, however, some modern attempts to unify contract and tort within a general theory of obligations: eg A Burrows (ed), *English Private Law* 3rd edn (Oxford, Oxford University Press, 2013) attempts to restate English law in a structure which follows the classical Roman model: I Sources of Law; II The Law of Persons; III The Law of Property; IV The Law of Obligations; V Litigation. Within the Law of Obligations are chapters on contract (general rules and certain special contracts: agency, sale of goods, carriage of goods by sea, air and land, insurance, banking and employment); bailment; torts and equitable wrongs; and unjust enrichment.

[4] Above, p 38; D Ibbetson, *A Historical Introduction to the Law of Obligations* (Oxford, Oxford University Press, 1999); JH Baker, *An Introduction to English Legal History*, 4th edn (London, Butterworths LexisNexis, 2002) chs 18–26.

2. Contract and Tort

In any study of the law of contract it is important to understand the relationship between contract and tort. It is from the borderlines of a topic that we often learn much about its fundamental characteristics: what really distinguishes it from its neighbours, and how the lawyers within the legal system will characterise issues as belonging to one category rather than the other. In the context of the relationship between contract and tort there are various relevant issues.

First, there is a question whether the line between contract and tort is a sharp division where a case must fall on one side or the other. In English law, after some hesitations, the courts have settled into a firm acceptance of the overlap between contract and tort.[5] Where a claim in tort is brought the question is whether, on the facts, the tort can be established—and the existence of a contract between the same parties may be relevant to whether a tort is in fact committed; but there is nothing inherently inconsistent in the co-existence of contractual and tortious liability between the same parties in relation to the same act by a defendant. In consequence, a claimant may often choose to pursue either a tort claim or a contract claim depending on which of the two is the more advantageous: the contract claim may have become barred by the expiry of a limitation period, leaving the tort claim still available;[6] or the remedy in tort may be more advantageous to the claimant than the remedy in contract, or vice versa, given that the quantification of recoverable loss proceeds on different bases in the two separate regimes.[7] The dynamics of the borderline between contract and tort will have some effect on the way in which parties argue their cases, and therefore have an indirect effect on the development of both areas of law.

Secondly, one system might naturally identify the legal responsibility in a particular set of facts on the basis of contract, whereas another system would classify it as tortious. The very scope of contract may well differ between legal systems, and so at first sight a claim which the lawyer from one system would expect to succeed on the basis of the law of contract will fail—but before criticising the law it is important to see whether what is left out of contract is in fact being dealt with elsewhere in the system. The lack of contractual remedy may reflect a difference in the underlying values of the two systems: there is no liability in contract *or on any other basis* because the legal system does not attribute legal consequences (liability) to the particular conduct in question.

---

[5] *Henderson v Merrett Syndicates Ltd* [1995] 2 AC 145 (HL).
[6] *Ibid.*
[7] For the concurrence of liability in relation to precontractual misrepresentations, and the choices between tort and contract remedies in this context, see below, p 184.

But a solution which is apparently lacking in the law of contract might in fact be found elsewhere.[8]

Certain types of contract which might be common in other legal systems will not (or not fully) fall within the law of contract in England. The obligations arising from the delivery of a chattel are in many systems categorised as contracts—sometimes even expressly referred to as 'real contracts' following the Roman model.[9] However, although such transactions are equally common in England, they are not always seen as contractual—and if the delivery of a chattel is not in return for some form of reward, it will not fall within the general rules of contract (lacking the necessary 'consideration').[10] This is, in fact, one area in which the common law borrowed concepts from Roman law, but did not place its transplant within the English law of contract but created a separate notion—bailment.[11] This is a relationship under which a person (the 'bailor') transfers possession of a chattel to another (the 'bailee'). If the possession is transferred under a contract (such as the hire of a chattel) the contract will determine the parties' rights and obligations by its express or implied terms. But if there is no contract, such as where the bailment is gratuitous, or if the contract is silent about the duties in question, the parties' rights will be determined by general rules of the law of tort, or of the rules of bailment as an independent source of obligation.[12]

There is also a temporal context. Allowing a particular circumstance to be covered within the law of contract might be an indirect response to the lack of alternative solutions elsewhere in the legal system, but this can change over time as the other areas also develop. For example, judges might be tempted to find a contract in order to give rise to a liability where there is no alternative remedy in tort: but as the law of tort develops and opens up new remedies the courts might become less willing to 'distort' the law of contract in order to 'imply' contractual promises. The English law of tort has undergone very significant developments in the last 80 years—and even more so in the last 50 years[13]—in areas which relate closely to the law of contract. It will

---

[8] The English approach to precontractual liability illustrates these issues in various measures. There is a reluctance as a matter of principle to impose any form of liability in the negotiations— a value judgment about the relationship between negotiating parties. But sometimes English law does impose particular liabilities on negotiating parties where the conduct falls within a tort (such as fraudulent misrepresentations giving rise to liability in the tort of deceit). See generally below, ch 4.

[9] B Nicholas, *The French Law of Contract*, 2nd edn (Oxford, Clarendon Press, 1992) 40–42.

[10] Below, ch 6.

[11] *Coggs v Bernard* (1703) 2 Lord Raym 909, 92 ER 107; D Ibbetson, '"The Law of Business Rome": Foundations of the Anglo-American Tort of Negligence' [1999] *CLP* 74, 80–83. See generally H Beale (ed), *Chitty on Contracts*, 32nd edn (London, Sweet & Maxwell, 2015) ch 33.

[12] NE Palmer, *Palmer on Bailment*, 3rd edn (London, Sweet & Maxwell, 2009) para 1–047.

[13] *Hedley Byrne & Co Ltd v Heller & Partners Ltd* [1964] AC 465 (HL), building on the decision in *Donoghue v Stevenson* [1932] AC 562 (HL), above, p 39, to define a general test for liability in respect of economic loss suffered through the reliance on the defendant's careless statement in 'relationships which ... are "equivalent to contract," that is, where there is an assumption of

therefore be important on occasion to consider not only the actual result (and reasoning) of a particular decision on the law of contract but also, in order fully to understand the context of the decision, to bear in mind any other influences which might explain the decision at the particular time at which it was made—and this includes not only other related areas of the law of contract, but also the then-current state of development of other areas, such as the law of tort.

3. Contract and Property

Another borderline which should be kept in mind is that between contract and property.

In some respects the issues which arise in relation to property are obvious. For example, where the contract contains an obligation to transfer specific property, every legal system has to determine whether the contract itself transfers the property rights[14] or whether a separate transfer is necessary.[15] In principle, English law separates the contract and the transfer of property: a contract for the sale of goods does not of itself automatically transfer the property in the goods. Rather, the passing of the property depends upon the parties' *intentions* as to when it should pass; and the approach taken here is typical of the general approach to the significance of the intention of the parties in contract law generally. An objective test is applied;[16] 'for the purpose of ascertaining the intention of the parties regard shall be had to the terms of the contract, the conduct of the parties and the circumstances of the case'; and there are statutory 'rules'[17] to ascertain the intention where there is no other indication—including the general rule that in the case of an unconditional contract for the sale of specific goods in a deliverable state the property passes to the buyer when the contract is made. So in many cases the contract will transfer the property, although this is attributed to the intention of the parties rather than to a rule of law.

The link between the contract and the passing of property is significant in the context of the approach of English law to one particular rule: that

responsibility in circumstances in which, but for the absence of consideration, there would be a contract' (Lord Devlin at 529). At 528 Lord Devlin identified cases which had been decided on the basis of contract by artificially finding consideration; this showed 'that in one way or another the law has ensured that in this type of case a just result has been reached. But I think that today the result can and should be achieved by the application of the law of negligence and that it is unnecessary and undesirable to construct an artificial consideration'.

[14] As in French law: art 1138 C Civ; Nicholas, *The French Law of Contract*, above, n 9, 155.
[15] As in German law: BS Markesinis, H Unberath and A Johnston, *The German Law of Contract, A Comparative Treatise*, 2nd edn (Oxford, Hart Publishing, 2006) 496–97.
[16] Sale of Goods Act 1979 s 17(2).
[17] *Ibid* s 18.

one cannot pass a greater title than one has (*nemo dat quod non habet*). If I purport to transfer property to you under a contract which is in fact void (and not just voidable)[18] there is no transfer of the property rights even if I deliver the goods to you; and so you have no property rights to transfer on to a third party. The defect in the first contract prevents the second contract being effective to transfer the property for the simple reason that the intended transferee under the first contract received nothing and therefore had nothing to transfer on. English law does not have a general rule within the law of property to the effect that a transfer of movable property by a non-owner in possession is effective to give title to the person who receives it in good faith.[19] We shall see that this means that where a person who delivered movable property to another under an intended contract seeks to recover the property from a third party, the validity of the initial contract will become critical: the validity of the contracts in the chain is often a central issue in the claim to determine property rights.[20]

One particular feature of the passing of property should be understood regarding contracts relating to land. As in many legal systems, contracts for the sale or other disposition of an interest in land are subject to special rules of formality.[21] However, where a contract fulfils those rules, English law gives it a limited but significant proprietary effect. Although the transfer of the interest in land requires a separate formality and, in most cases, registration of the transfer in a public register before it is fully effective as against third parties, the contract is treated as itself giving rise to equitable property rights equivalent to the legal property rights that will be created when the transfer and registration are completed.[22]

The relationship between contract and property is also different in other respects in English law from that in other legal systems. For example, English law will treat as within the law of property certain relationships which are

---

[18] Below, p 160.
[19] The difference between English law and German law was criticised by Lord Millett in *Shogun Finance Ltd v Hudson* [2003] UKHL 62, [2004] 1 AC 919 [84]–[86], on the basis that English law gives inadequate protection against the third party: below, p 170. In fact, the original title will be extinguished (and therefore third parties protected) after the expiry of the limitation period for the claim against the third party: six years from the first wrongful interference with the property; Limitation Act 1980 s 3. In the case of stolen property the thief can be sued in tort without any limitation period; but the claim against a third party is barred—and the claimant's title to the chattel is extinguished—six years after the first sale of the chattel to a purchaser in good faith: s 4.
[20] Below, pp 161–62.
[21] Below, p 126.
[22] This is the doctrine of *Walsh v Lonsdale* (1882) 21 ChD 9 (CA) under which the courts regard a contract to convey an interest in land as already having the same effect as a conveyance as long as the contract is one of which the court could order specific performance, on the basis that 'equity looks on that as done which ought to be done': EH Burn and J Cartwright, *Cheshire & Burn's Modern Law of Real Property*, 18th edn (Oxford, Oxford University Press, 2011) 978–82. For specific performance of contracts relating to land, see below, p 280.

created by contract and which in other systems might remain only within the law of contract. Perhaps the most obvious example is the lease of land, which is not only a contract (which therefore regulates the relationship between the parties) but also normally creates an estate in the land itself which gives it proprietary effect as against third parties.[23]

II. A General Law of Contract: The Place of 'Special' Contracts

1. 'General' and 'Special': A Different Starting-Point

Modern legal systems adopt a general law of contract: a set of general rules to determine such questions as what a contract is—that is, what is necessary to give a promise or an agreement contractual (legal) binding effect rather than just moral (social) binding effect; the contents of the contract; and the legal consequences of a failure to comply with the contractual obligations. English law adopts this general approach. In one respect, however, the approach in English law is different from that taken in many other systems which organise their law of contract not only as a general law, but also within categories of 'special' contracts. Such categorisation is an inheritance of the classical Roman system of contract, where an agreement could be a contract only if it fitted the model of one of the particular nominate contracts—some contracts being defined by their form, others by their content, but each having their own special rules for formation as well as separate (or, at least, not uniform) rules as regards their contents and the remedies for non-performance, including the procedural actions available. Modern systems which have received Roman ideas of contract[24] have moved beyond this, and accept a general concept of contract; but have also retained—at a secondary level—the idea that there are special principles and special rules which apply to particular types of contract. English law has not developed its law of contract based on the reception of Roman law through the *ius commune*, and so has not received this idea of special contracts in the same way. That is not to say that English law does not distinguish between different types of contract—sale, hire, partnership, and so on; of course it does. But the categorisation of contracts can be significant

---

[23] Burn and Cartwright, *Cheshire & Burn's Modern Law of Real Property*, above, n 22, 180–84.
[24] Above, pp 7–8.

to the civil lawyer in a way which is rather different from the way in which the English lawyer sees things. It can affect how the civil lawyer approaches the negotiation of a contract, or the analysis of a contract which has already been formed. There can be similarity of result between the common law and the civil law on the same point—for example, the formation, content and remedies relating to a contract of sale. But the results may not always be the same, and—more important for the point of view of the civil lawyer who is reading the English law of contract for the first time—the reasoning is substantially different.

2. The (Limited) Role of 'Special Contracts' in English Law

The general principle in English law is that all contracts are governed by the same principles; and that the rules for the formation, contents and remedies apply equally to all contracts. The starting-point here is the same as generally in the common law: since the body of rules governing the law of contract have been developed by the courts (the common law) and are not contained in any comprehensive statutory provisions, the same general principles apply to all contracts *except* to the extent that legislation has intervened to override the common law; and such intervention is relatively limited. The courts did not themselves develop a formal separation into 'special' contracts; therefore 'general' is the rule and 'special' is the exception.

(a) Formation of the Contract

English law does occasionally provide for special rules relating to the formation of the contract for particular reasons of policy. For example, there are special rules, imposed by statute, for the execution of certain consumer credit agreements requiring specific forms of agreement to be signed by the parties and giving the debtor notice of his statutory cancellation rights: an improperly-executed agreement is enforceable against the debtor only on the order of the court.[25] A contract for the sale or other disposition of an interest in land must be in writing, and the writing must be in the form of a single document signed by both parties (or identical documents, each signed by one party and exchanged), incorporating all the expressly agreed terms.[26] This formal condition of writing for the existence of a land contract was introduced in 1989; until then there had been a rule that such a contract could be made orally, but could not be enforced against a party who had not (either personally

---

[25] Consumer Credit Act 1974 pt V.
[26] Law of Property (Miscellaneous Provisions) Act 1989 s 2.

or through his agent) signed at least a written memorandum or note of the contract.[27] That is, there was a rule requiring written and signed *evidence* of a contract as a condition of its enforceability, although not of its existence. This originated in the Statute of Frauds 1677, which was itself a reaction to the general problem of finding reliable evidence of contracts at a time when English law had settled on a general principle that an oral agreement was sufficient to constitute a contract, and when litigation to enforce contracts was generally based on oral testimony. The Statute contained a range of rules requiring writing by way of evidence for particular types of contract.[28] Most of these provisions of the Statute of Frauds were finally repealed in 1954;[29] all that now remains is the (now even tougher) rule relating to writing as a condition of formation of a land contract; and one unrepealed provision which still requires writing as evidence of a contract of guarantee.[30] Other common law jurisdictions adopted similar provisions by way of their own Statutes of Frauds; and changes to them have proceeded differently in different jurisdictions. Even today, much more of the Statute of Frauds remains in many states within the United States than in England.[31]

(b) The Terms of the Contract

In finding the terms of the contract, in principle the common lawyer asks what the parties have agreed. The express terms of the contract are to be found in the express agreement (the offer, as accepted; or the written document which the parties have agreed constitutes their contract). The search for implied terms[32] is in theory, at least, also a search for the (implied) intentions of the parties. The court, by finding implied terms, is filling out the intentions of the parties.

Of course, it is not quite as simple as this. In the first place, in determining or interpreting the 'intention' of the parties the English court is looking

---

[27] Law of Property Act 1925 s 40, which replaced earlier provisions of the Statute of Frauds 1677 (below).

[28] Baker, *An Introduction to English Legal History*, above, n 4, 348–49, noting that in its first draft (which was later changed) the draftsmen were inspired by earlier Continental legislation which had recently been re-enacted in France. Under Statute of Frauds s 4 written evidence was required in cases of promises by executors to answer for damages out of their own estate; promises 'to answer for the debt, default or miscarriages of another person' (that is, a guarantee) or to enforce an agreement in consideration of marriage; contracts for the sale of land or an interest in land; and any agreement which is not to be performed within a year. And under s 17 a contract for the sale of goods for £10 or more, if not partly performed nor secured by a deposit, required writing signed by or on behalf of both parties.

[29] Law Reform (Enforcement of Contracts) Act 1954.

[30] Discussed and applied by the House of Lords in *Actionstrength Ltd v International Glass Engineering IN.GL.EN SpA* [2003] UKHL 17, [2003] 2 AC 541.

[31] EA Farnsworth, *Contracts*, 4th edn (New York, Aspen, 2006) ch 6.

[32] For more detail see below, ch 8.

for an objective, rather than a subjective, intention. This is discussed later in this chapter. Secondly, filling out the intentions of the parties can become a very fictitious exercise, because the courts often have to insert terms which are not those which the parties did in fact intend (and just failed to express), but which are necessary to make sense of the overall contract where the parties have left a gap even though one or other of them would probably have resisted it or otherwise negotiated the detail of the term if it had been put to him. Some implied terms depend simply on the particular circumstances of the case, and the detail of the express terms of the contract. That is not an issue for us here. However, certain terms are generally implied into certain types of contract. For example, a person who contracts to sell or otherwise transfer goods in the course of a business impliedly promises that the goods are of satisfactory quality.[33] And a person who contracts to supply a service in the course of a business impliedly promises that he will carry out the service with reasonable care and skill.[34] These are both the statutory enactment of approaches which (before their first enactment) had already been reached by the courts in relation to contracts of sale and supply of goods and contracts of supply of services, although their enactment crystallises the contract term and clarifies its scope. There are other standard terms which are implied into other contracts by statute for policy reasons—such as obligations as to the state of property, and obligations to repair, which are implied into certain leases where the tenant is deemed to need such protection.[35] And, without the intervention of statute, the courts continue on occasion to identify typical implied terms in particular types of contract, such as the landlord's obligation to maintain the common parts of a building in multiple occupation.[36]

These examples of the implication of terms into contracts by reference to their type can look rather like the civil lawyer's approach to 'special contracts'. But there is a subtle difference. In many civil law jurisdictions, the lawyer asks first whether there is a contract (applying the general principle); but then asks as a matter of some routine *what kind* of contract it is. Civil codes tend to have detailed provisions covering a range of different types of contract; and so the proper classification of the contract is seen as an inherent part of the proper analysis of the contract and its terms. For the common lawyer, the reverse is

---

[33] Non-consumer contracts of sale: Sale of Goods Act 1979 s 14(2), replacing the first enactment in Sale of Goods Act 1893 s 14(2); and transfer of goods: Supply of Goods and Services Act 1982 s 4. The original language was 'merchantable' quality, but this was changed to 'satisfactory' quality in 1994. Until 1 October 2015, these provisions applied also to consumer contracts, but contracts for the supply of goods by a trader to a consumer are now covered by similar provisions in the Consumer Rights Act 2015 s 9: see below, p 214.

[34] Non-consumer contracts: Supply of Goods and Services Act 1982 s 13. Until 1 October 2015, this provision also applied to consumer contracts, but contracts for the supply of a service by a trader to a consumer are now covered by similar provisions in the Consumer Rights Act 2015 s 49: see below, p 215.

[35] Eg Landlord and Tenant Act 1985 ss 8 (contract for letting a house for human habitation: house is, and will be kept, fit for habitation), 11 (repairing obligations in lease of dwelling-house for less than 7 years).

[36] *Liverpool City Council v Irwin* [1977] AC 239 (HL).

true. The contract is formed by the parties' agreement, and there is no automatic second question based on the 'type' of the contract. In determining what the parties have (or are deemed in law to have) agreed some assistance can be found in the general rules which apply to particular contracts. But the range of such special provisions for special contracts is much more limited in practice. And it is not really part of the common lawyer's routine analysis.

There are, however, certain particular contexts in which the lawyer will need to check whether the parties' agreement falls within one type of contract or another, because it impacts on the validity of some of the terms of the agreement, either under common law rules or under statute. For example, if the contract is a mortgage of land, it must not contain an option for the mortgagee (the lender) to purchase the mortgaged property, because such a term is inherently inconsistent with the nature of a mortgage transaction under which the borrower must have the right to recover the mortgaged property on payment of the sums due under the mortgage; the option would therefore be struck out by the courts.[37] And if the contract is one of employment, it will be regulated by various statutes which give the employee rights which the contract cannot take away.[38] The categorisation of contracts for such purposes is still the exception rather than the rule, however; and it is done with a view to protecting one of the parties to a particular type of transaction where the court or the legislature has identified the type of relationship as deserving of special treatment.[39] The most significant categories of contracts are now *consumer* contracts for the supply of goods, digital content and services, which have been brought together in, and in some respects reformed by, the Consumer Rights Act 2015. This Act may look to the civil lawyer rather like a codification of the rules for consumer contracts, but it is not a complete set of rules for these types of contract; it contains only some particular—although very significant—rules relating to the terms which are 'treated as' being included in the contracts and the remedies for the consumer which flow from their breach.[40]

(c) Remedies

English law starts from the position that there is a single remedial regime for all contracts, of whatever type.[41] However, one can then identify certain

---

[37] *Samuel v Jarrah Timber and Wood Paving Corp Ltd* [1904] AC 323 (HL). This is part of the control devised by the old equity courts to protect the mortgagor, and which is still applied today, although the strictness of some of the old equitable rules was mitigated during the twentieth century: Burn and Cartwright, *Cheshire & Burn's Modern Law of Real Property*, above, n 22, 814–25.
[38] Eg Employment Rights Act 1996 s 203.
[39] For control over contract terms generally see below, ch 9.
[40] Below, pp 214–15, 297–99.
[41] Below, ch 12.

contracts where the remedy will generally be of a particular kind: for example, although specific performance is rarely awarded, a contract for the sale of land will be normally be specifically enforceable.[42] And there have been legislative interventions in relation to the remedies available for breach of particular types of contract: for example, the introduction of the remedies of repair, replacement or reduction in price of non-conforming goods in favour of consumers, which has recently been reformed and extended to cover replacement or reduction in price in consumer contracts for digital content and the right to repeat performance or reduction in price for consumer services contracts;[43] and statutory remedies available to an employee for unfair dismissal separately from the claim for breach of contract at common law for wrongful dismissal.[44]

(d) Significance of the Adoption of a General Rule Rather than 'Special' Contracts in English Law

In many cases there may be little practical difference between a theory of contracts based on a general rule, and one which considers in addition the 'type' of contract to be significant. For example, most legal systems will have provisions imposing on the seller of goods an obligation relating to the quality of the goods. However, it may be that a system which regulates contracts by type will at the same time take a stronger line in limiting the parties' ability to contract out of the particular obligations which that regulatory regime imposes. In English law, as we shall see,[45] the general rule is that all terms are negotiable unless there is a specific prohibition to the contrary. So the terms which are implied by reference to the type of contract will also be in principle negotiable—since, in theory, the term is generally being implied by reference to the intentions of the parties—although in the modern law there are some specific limitations on the freedom to avoid particular implied terms within particular types of contract, the strictest limitations being in the case of consumer contracts.[46]

---

[42] Below, p 280.
[43] See the original provisions of the Sale and Supply of Goods to Consumers Regulations 2002 SI 2002/3045; now Consumer Rights Act 2015 pt 1: below, p 297.
[44] Employment Rights Act 1996 pt X.
[45] Below, ch 9.
[46] Since 1977 the implied terms of quality in contracts for the sale or transfer of goods cannot be excluded or restricted as against consumers, and as against non-consumers can be excluded or restricted only by a term which satisfies the requirement of reasonableness: Unfair Contract Terms Act 1977 ss 6, 7, 11; the rules for consumer goods contracts are now found in the Consumer Rights Act 2015 s 31, and see also ss 47 (digital content) and 57 (services).The Landlord and Tenant Act 1985 (in ss 8 and 12, respectively) prohibits the exclusion by the contract of the terms it implies by ss 8 and 11, above, n 35.

This difference of approach between the common law and the civil law to the standardisation of contract types may, however, sometimes have a practical consequence in the form of contract drafting. It is well known that contracts in common law jurisdictions can be significantly longer and more detailed than similar contracts in civil law jurisdictions. One reason—there are others, too[47]—is the approach taken to finding the terms of the contract. Civil lawyers may take the view that, since the contract which they are negotiating is of a type which will automatically contain particular obligations, there is no need to draft those obligations into it. By entering into a contract of sale or hire, for example, the parties are contracting into those provisions which the code sets out for them. The standardisation of contract terms by reference to contract type can be an efficient way of filling out the obligations required for the contract. The common lawyer, however, is not content to leave the detail of the contract to the courts' implication of terms—even where there is good authority that certain standard terms are normally to be implied into a contract of the kind under negotiation. Since the general rule is that the contract is what the parties have agreed that it is—and any implication of terms is only to support the application of that general rule—the common lawyer's instinct is to make express provision, wherever possible, for the intended terms. Without a fully developed theory of special contracts, there would be significant uncertainty about the scope of obligations to be implied into contracts. And so express drafting helps to make the contract 'judge-proof': to anticipate and provide for possible conflicts in advance.

III. Some General Features and Some Fundamental Starting-Points

Before we move on to consider the detail of the rules of the English law of contract, it is worth mentioning some general features which we shall encounter throughout the rest of the book. These are highlighted here, first, because they are pervasive issues, and it is as well to have them in mind in relation to all topics as we come to them. But, secondly, these features are in some sense or to some degree different from those which a lawyer familiar with the law of contract in a civil law jurisdiction might expect.

---

[47] Below, p 71.

1. The Role of 'Good Faith'

The first—and, perhaps, most significant—issue is one which must be put negatively. There is no general principle of good faith in the English law of contract. This has to be understood from the very beginning, because there is a danger that a reader from a system which does acknowledge a significant role for good faith will otherwise assume that it is an underlying principle. In this respect, there is a difference between English law and some other common law systems: most notably, the courts in the United States and Australia have gone much further than the English courts in accepting a significant role for the requirement of good faith between contracting parties in particular contexts, and especially a duty of good faith in the performance of a contract.[48] So far, English law has resisted this although we shall see that the resistance may be softening in certain contexts.

In saying that there is no duty of good faith in this context, we are saying that there is no general duty to negotiate a contract in good faith; nor any general duty to perform the contract in good faith, nor to renegotiate in good faith in the event of a significant change of circumstances affecting the balance of the contract; nor any general duty on contracting parties to exercise in good faith their rights arising under the contract. Some legal systems will use the language of good faith in imposing duties in these contexts; others will use the language of 'abuse of right'. But neither of these terms is in common usage in the English law of contract, largely because English law rejects the notion of duties of good faith in the formation and performance of contracts, and does not limit the enforceability of contractual rights by any doctrine based on their potential 'abuse'. Even though English law sometimes uses language which might appear to be similar to the concept of good faith in the eyes of a lawyer from a civil law jurisdictions, such as a test of 'fairness and reasonableness', it does so only in particular contexts, and there is no general duty of fairness, or to act reasonably, in forming and performing contracts. We shall see the significance of this approach in particular contexts later in this book. For the moment it is sufficient to note that the resistance to a general duty of good faith can be attributed to various reasons.

In the first place, we saw in chapter two that there is a general reluctance on the part of the English courts to generalise abstract principles. Within the common law—as opposed to rules whose authority rests on a statutory text—the courts prefer to work with particular instances of duty which can be identified in particular cases. In consequence, one might expect that the

---

[48] In the US: Farnsworth, *Contracts* (above, n 31) para 7.17 (implication of duty of good faith in performance); Uniform Commercial Code para 1–304 (obligation of good faith in performance and enforcement). In Australia: JW Carter, *Contract Law in Australia*, 6th edn (Chatswood, LexisNexis, 2013) ch 2; and see *Yam Seng Pte Ltd v International Trade Corp Ltd* [2013] EWHC 111 (QB), [2013] 1 Lloyd's Rep 526 [127]–[128].

SOME GENERAL FEATURES AND STARTING-POINTS 65

English approach will be inherently more particular and less generalised; and this point was made by Bingham LJ in the context of good faith:

> In many civil law systems, and perhaps in most legal systems outside the common law world, the law of obligations recognises and enforces an overriding principle that in making and carrying out contracts parties should act in good faith. This does not simply mean that they should not deceive each other, a principle which any legal system must recognise its effect is perhaps most aptly conveyed by such metaphorical colloquialisms as 'playing fair', 'coming clean' or 'putting one's cards face upwards on the table'. It is in essence a principle of fair and open dealing ...
>
> English law has, characteristically, committed itself to no such overriding principle but has developed piecemeal solutions in response to demonstrated problems of unfairness. Many examples could be given. Thus equity has intervened to strike down unconscionable bargains. Parliament has stepped in to regulate the imposition of exemption clauses and the form of certain hire-purchase agreements. The common law also has made its contribution, by holding that certain classes of contract require the utmost good faith, by treating as irrecoverable what purport to be agreed estimates of damage but are in truth a disguised penalty for breach, and in many other ways.[49]

There are therefore circumstances where English law will use more particular doctrines in order to respond to problems which might be solved in other legal systems by using a general principle of good faith. However, this does not mean that it is simply a question of technique and classification of solutions, rather than a question of substantive difference in approach to the law of contract. English law will reach solutions in certain types of case which may surprise some civil lawyers.[50]

A second difficulty with the notion of 'good faith' is that the English judges have expressed concern about the lack of certainty in defining the content of a duty of good faith in the context of the relationship between contracting parties. This has arisen most commonly in claims in relation to the precontractual period, where many legal systems would say that there is a duty to negotiate in good faith. But the English courts have held not only that there is no implied duty to negotiate in good faith, but that even an *express* agreement to negotiate in good faith is lacking in certainty: an agreement to negotiate is uncertain; and adding 'in good faith' makes it no more certain.[51] In another context, the English and Scottish Law Commissions have said that it is better

---

[49] *Interfoto Picture Library Ltd v Stiletto Visual Programmes Ltd* [1989] QB 433 (CA) 439.
[50] Eg the limited scope of liability for breaking off negotiations (there being no duty to negotiate in good faith): below, ch 4; the freedom for a party to exercise an express termination clause for a very trivial breach of contract (there being no duty to exercise one's contractual rights in good faith): below, pp 285–86.
[51] *Walford v Miles* [1992] 2 AC 128 (HL) 138; *Courtney & Fairbairn Ltd v Tolaini Brothers (Hotels) Ltd* [1975] 1 WLR 297 (CA) 301. See further below, pp 76–78.

to avoid the use of the language of 'good faith'—even when implementing a European Directive which itself uses that language as a core element of the test which it applies—on the ground that it is not sufficiently clear to a lawyer in the United Kingdom, and in the context in question (the control of unfair contract terms) it is adequately represented by the test of 'fairness and reasonableness' which is already established under domestic legislation.[52] However, this objection to the language of 'good faith', based on an alleged lack of certainty, has been challenged. The Law Commissions changed their view and concluded that there is a growing body of case-law in the UK and Europe interpreting the European terminology, and that in the re-implementation of the Directive on Unfair Terms in Consumer Contracts the language of 'good faith', which is used in the Directive in the test of the 'fairness' of contract terms, should be retained and should even be used in certain circumstances in place of the existing domestic test of 'fairness and reasonableness'.[53] This has now been done in Part 2 of the Consumer Rights Act 2015.[54] Moreover, in a very significant recent decision at first instance, *Yam Seng Pte Ltd v International Trade Corp Ltd*,[55] Leggatt J has rejected the argument that a duty to perform a contract in good faith is too uncertain, saying that it would be based on an express or implied term of the contract, which is subject to the normal processes of contractual interpretation, and that the test of good faith is objective, sensitive in its meaning to the factual context, but giving effect to the standards of conduct which would be expected by reasonable and honest people in the parties' position.

Another substantive reason for the rejection of a general principle of good faith in English contract law is linked particularly to the context of contractual negotiations. As we shall see, English law rejects a duty to *negotiate* in good faith because it would be inconsistent with the nature of the relationship which the law attributes to negotiating parties: 'the concept of a duty to carry on negotiations in good faith is inherently repugnant to the adversarial position of the parties when involved in negotiations'.[56] In certain specific contracts, such as partnerships, where the relationship between the parties is essentially cooperative rather than arm's length and adversarial, the courts have accepted both implied and express duties of good faith between the parties in both the formation and the performance of the contract. There is no question, however, of a general duty to negotiate.

---

[52] Law Commission, 'Unfair Terms in Contracts' (Law Com No 292, Cm 6464, 2005) para 3.89: 'It will be easier for UK lawyers to apply than a more "European" test which makes express reference to good faith'. The test of 'fairness and reasonableness' is set by the Unfair Contract Terms Act 1977 s 11. See further below, ch 9.
[53] Law Commission, 'Unfair Terms in Consumer Contracts: Advice to the Department for Business, Innovation and Skills' (March 2013) pt 6.
[54] Below, p 230.
[55] Above, n 48, [144], [152].
[56] *Walford v Miles*, above, n 51, 138. See further below, p 78.

Even if we characterise the parties' relationship during the negotiations for a contract as adversarial, it is much less obvious that, once the contracts has been formed, the parties' positions vis-à-vis each other should remain so individual. Yet in English law there is no general duty of good faith in performance in all contracts; nor a general rule that contractual rights should be exercised in good faith. Particular exceptions have been developed.[57] But traditionally the emphasis is on certainty for the contracting parties; reluctance to go beyond the terms of the contract itself except where that is necessary in order to make sense of the contract for the parties; and therefore reluctance to use a general principle to override the apparent rights and duties which are set out in the contract. This is a model of contract based on the paradigm of a negotiated, arm's length, written contract between commercial parties—by no means the most common contract. But the fundamental approach to securing certainty for the parties, based on that paradigm, runs deep in English law and a general principle of 'good faith' in formation or performance would run counter to it. This not to say, however, that there is no scope for further development which might even move towards an eventual broader recognition of duties of good faith in the performance of contracts. Leggatt J, in *Yam Seng*, whilst accepting that English law has not yet reached the stage where it is ready to recognise a requirement of good faith as a duty implied by law (even as only a default rule) into all commercial contracts, has none the less opened the door to a more ready implication of duties of good faith in performance as a matter of fact, depending on the context of the parties and subject always to the express terms of the contract.[58] Whether this door is opened further in future cases remains to be seen: the decision in *Yam Seng* has been applied in some cases at first instance[59] but in other cases the judges have been reluctant to apply it and it is clear that the courts will not allow a general principle, or an implied term, of 'good faith' to undermine the terms expressly agreed by the parties.[60]

2. Objectivity, Reasonableness and Reliance

The common starting-point of modern legal systems is to say that a contract is in some sense an agreement between the parties. But many systems will

---

[57] Eg relief against forfeiture: below, p 286; the use of implied terms to allow a party to escape the literal terms of a contract where it is no longer appropriate: below, p 264; and the doctrine of frustration: below, ch 11.
[58] *Yam Seng Pte Ltd v International Trade Corp Ltd*, above, n 48, [131].
[59] *British Groundschool Ltd v Intelligent Data Capture Ltd* [2014] EWHC 2145 (Ch); *G&G Cars Ltd v Essex Police Authority* [2015] EWHC 226 (QB) [175].
[60] Eg *Mid Essex Hospital Services NHS Trust v Compass Group UK & Ireland Ltd* [2013] EWCA Civ 200, [105], [154]; *TSG Building Services plc v South Anglia Housing Ltd* [2013] EWHC 1151 (TCC), [2013] BLR 484 [46]; *Carewatch Care Services Ltd v Focus Caring Services Ltd* [2014] EWHC 2313 (Ch) [108]–[112].

interpret this as injecting an inherently subjective notion into contract, both as to whether the contract is formed at all, and as to what its terms are. A general feature of the common law, however, is an *objective* approach: a significant emphasis is laid on whether, when the facts are tested objectively, the parties can be said to have come to an agreement;[61] and an objective assessment is made of the content of their agreement, and the interpretation to be put on the language by which it was constituted—whether through an objective interpretation of the communications between the parties which constituted the offer and its acceptance;[62] or an objective interpretation of the language of the document in the case of a written contract.[63] Objectivity inevitably involves taking the view which a reasonable person would take; and so we shall see that the language of reasonableness appears from time to time in certain areas of contract law.

There is more, however, to this than simply taking an external, objective approach to the analysis of the contract. Indeed, in taking an objective interpretation English law is often doing so with a view to protecting one of the parties: to allow one party's (reasonable) understanding to prevail over the (mis)understanding of the other party—and so placing the 'reasonable person' in the shoes of one the parties themselves rather than as a neutral observer.[64]

This can then be linked to another theme: the protection of one party's reasonable reliance on the other. A number of the rules for the formation of contracts can be said to be based on this general approach,[65] although we shall see that the more general role of 'reliance' as a trigger for the creation of contractual obligations,[66] or in relation to the remedies for breach,[67] is more problematic, and it is certainly not the case that English law has elevated 'reliance' to a general principle of the law of contract.

3. The Significance of the 'Intentions of the Parties'

The emphasis on objectivity inevitably has an impact on the significance of the 'intentions of the parties' within the English law of contract. 'Intention' is to be determined principally by objective criteria, rather than by subjective criteria. But also, beyond this—and as a consequence of the emphasis given to each party's reasonable reliance on what the other appears (objectively) to be agreeing—English law gives only a limited place to mistake within contract. The focus is much more on what parties have done (and so,

---

[61] Below, p 100.
[62] Below, p 205.
[63] Below, p 207.
[64] Below, p 100.
[65] Below, p 103.
[66] Promissory estoppel: see below, p 143.
[67] So-called 'reliance measure damages': see below, p 289.

for example, misrepresentation is a much more significant source of remedies than mistake); or on the failure to comply with terms of the contract.

English law does, however, attribute the existence and content of the contractual obligations to the parties' intentions: as we have already seen, the theoretical basis of the obligations is the express or implied intentions of the parties, rather than the idea that the law fills out the contents of the contract for them. The fact that the 'intentions' are interpreted objectively can give the impression that in effect the law is filling the gaps in the contract, although this is not the way in which a common lawyer would traditionally see it.[68]

There are however some recent signs of a new emphasis on the intention of the parties in certain contexts. Although the parties' intention to be bound is not the test for the existence of a contract—the test being rather whether the parties have (objectively) agreed to a transaction which constitutes a bargain: the doctrine of consideration[69]—the courts are reluctant to come to the conclusion that there is no consideration, and therefore no contract, where there was a clear intention to be bound to an agreement, particularly as between commercial parties of equal bargaining strength. We shall see that there have been some developments in the doctrine of consideration which point towards an increased emphasis on finding a contract where the parties did intend to be bound;[70] and that, in the related area of the enforceability of third-party rights (the doctrine of 'privity of contract') the recent reform in the Contracts (Rights of Third Parties) Act 1999 has also placed the parties' intentions into the spotlight.[71]

4. Contract as an Economic Instrument: Contractual Freedom, Certainty and the Commercial Model of Contracting

One theme which runs throughout the English law of contract is the significance of a contract as an economic instrument for the parties. The very notion of contract is based on the model of a bargain between the parties— the doctrine of consideration.[72] The relationship between the parties in the negotiations is analysed by reference to this same model: each party is entitled to seek the best bargain with only precise limitations on the freedom of contract. The court will be very reluctant to interfere in the substance of the contract,[73] and will not adjust the contract even in cases where supervening circumstances have caused the original balance of the parties' bargain to be very severely upset.[74]

---

[68] Above, p 60; below, p 210.
[69] Below, ch 6.
[70] Below, p 141.
[71] Below, p 251.
[72] Below, ch 6.
[73] Below, ch 9.
[74] Below, ch 11.

70   INTRODUCTION TO THE ENGLISH LAW OF CONTRACT

Certainty is an important value to be respected—and this generally means holding the parties to the contract as agreed, not allowing the contract to be too easily undermined. But breach of contract is not necessarily seen as a wicked thing—each party is normally free to break the contract as long as he pays damages to compensate the other—and this means using money as the primary remedy for breach, calculated so as to remedy in economic terms the other party's loss of the contracted-for performance. The scope of damages to be awarded is assessed by reference to the (economic) risk allocation between the parties in the terms of the contract itself.[75]

There are, of course, exceptions to all this: there are cases where the courts will intervene in harsh bargains—most commonly by using statutory controls which have been created in the last fifty years, although the courts are not oblivious to the harshness of bargains in operating the common law of contract.[76] They may also use the implication of terms (at least notionally, by appealing to the imputed intentions of the parties) as a tool to mitigate the strictness of the rules about judicial intervention; and specific performance (rather than just damages) is sometimes available. But the thrust of the courts' approach and—certainly their rhetoric—is in terms of respecting the individual parties' freedom, the absence of judicial intervention in the contract, the importance of certainty for the parties, and the protection of the bargain.

This approach flows—at least in part—from the fact that many core doctrines in the modern English law of contract are a product of the second half of the nineteenth century. We still refer to cases from that period as the foundation of the rules for such things as the formation of a contract,[77] the doctrine of consideration,[78] the doctrines of mistake[79] and frustration (supervening circumstances),[80] and the purposes of the remedy of damages for breach of contract.[81] These doctrines have been subject to development during the twentieth century. And there have been some significant statutory interventions, either to change particular common law rules,[82] or to introduce new rules, often in the name of consumer protection which has been a preoccupation of the later twentieth century.[83] But the underlying thinking of much of the *common law* of contract is rooted in the earlier cases.

---

[75] Below, ch 12.
[76] Below, pp 224–26.
[77] *Smith v Hughes* (1871) LR 6 QB 597, below, p 100 (objective test for formation).
[78] *Currie v Misa* (1875) 10 Exch 153, below p 133; *Tweddle v Atkinson* (1861) 1 B & S 393, 121 ER 762, below, p 237 (consideration as the basis of the common law rejection of third-party rights).
[79] *Smith v Hughes*, above, n 77; below, p 171.
[80] *Taylor v Caldwell* (1863) 3 B & S 826, 122 ER 309, below, p 262.
[81] *Robinson v Harman* (1848) 1 Ex 850, 154 ER 363, below, p 288; *Hadley v Baxendale* (1854) 9 Ex 341, 156 ER 145, below, p 294.
[82] Eg Contracts (Rights of Third Parties) Act 1999, creating a significant general exception to the doctrine of privity of contract; below, p 250.
[83] Eg Consumer Credit Act 1974; Unfair Contract Terms Act 1977. Much of the recent change in the protection of consumers has followed from the implementation of European Directives; eg Unfair Terms in Consumer Contracts Regulations 1999 (now replaced by the Consumer

5. Contract Drafting in the Common Law

One well-known practical matter in relation to contracts in the common law, and in particular in relation to negotiated commercial contracts, is the custom of drafting lengthy, detailed documents. Some of the reasons for this will be evident from this rather brief overview of the features of the common law of contract. The absence of a principle of 'special contracts' in the common law,[84] and the ascription of the terms of the contract (in theory, at least) to the intentions[85] of the parties naturally leads the parties to draft their agreement in as much detail as possible, to limit the scope of judicial interpretation. The absence of general principles of good faith or co-operation means that the content of the bargain should be set out explicitly as far as possible, in the interests of certainty.[86] The absence of general duties of disclosure during the negotiations, and the fact that liability for what went on during the negotiations will normally arise only where there was a misrepresentation or a breach of contract means that the parties will conduct due diligence exercises, and will tend to insist on clauses confirming precontractual statements which are critical to the bargain, and guaranteeing the subject-matter of the contract (clauses of 'representation' and 'warranty', as they are often known).[87] The limited role for the court in the case of serious supervening circumstances (and the generally unsatisfactory doctrine of frustration) leads parties to allocate risks as far as possible in the contract itself.[88]

IV. English Contract Law in a European Context

There is a European context to the English law of contract. England and Ireland are the two common law jurisdictions which receive direct influences through their membership of the European Union, and therefore the development of their domestic contract law is influenced by developments in the European Union in a way which may not be matched in other common

---

Rights Act 2015 pt 2), below, p 230; amendments to the Sale of Goods Act 1979 by the Sale and Supply of Goods to Consumers Regulations 2002 (now replaced by the Consumer Rights Act 2015 pt 1), below, p 297.

[84] Above, p 58.
[85] Below, ch 8.
[86] Below, ch 4.
[87] Below, ch 7.
[88] Below, ch 11.

law jurisdictions around the world.[89] A number of Directives have required Member States to reform particular aspects of their contract law, most notably in the field of consumer contracts, such as the Directives on unfair terms in consumer contracts,[90] on the sale of consumer goods and associated guarantees,[91] and on consumer rights.[92] In so far as English law becomes more distant from other common law jurisdictions through such ever-increasing European developments, it becomes closer to its continental European neighbours, although this can then itself throw up sharp contrasts between the common law methodology and the substantive rules of the common law of contract, and the methodology and substantive rules of the continental systems which are all based on the civil law. This is not the place to undertake a general comparison of the English law of contract and the contract law of the civil law legal systems in Europe,[93] but it should be noted that there has been a certain impetus in recent years towards an increasing convergence between the domestic contract laws of Member States, although this has now stalled. The most significant project has been towards the production of a 'Common Frame of Reference' for European contract law. Building on earlier academic work of the Commission on European Contract Law which produced the *Principles of European Contract Law*,[94] followed by the work of the Study Group on a European Civil Code and the Research Group on EC Private Law (Acquis Group) which produced the *Draft Common Frame of Reference*[95] and the *Principles of the Existing EC Contract Law (Acquis Principles)*,[96] the European Commission published in 2011 a proposal for a Regulation on a Common European Sales Law ('CESL'),[97] which would

---

[89] Above, pp 9–12.

[90] Council Directive 93/13, implemented now by the Consumer Rights Act 2015 pt 2; see below, p 230.

[91] Directive 1999/44/EC, implemented now by the Consumer Rights Act 2015 pt 1; see below, p 297.

[92] Directive 2011/83/EU, implemented by (inter alia) the Consumer Contracts (Information, Cancellation and Additional Charges) Regulations 2013 SI 2013/3134; see below, p 187.

[93] See, eg, H Beale, B Fauvarque-Cosson, J Rutgers, D Tallon and S Vogenauer, *Cases, Materials and Text on Contract Law*, 2nd edn (Oxford, Hart Publishing, 2010); H Kötz and A Flessner, *European Contract Law* vol 1(trans T Weir) (Oxford, Clarendon Press, 1997); and books in the *Common Core of European Private Law* series, such as J Cartwright and M Hesselink, *Precontractual Liability in European Private Law* (2008); J Gordley, *The Enforceability of Promises in European Contact Law* (2001); R Sefton-Green, *Mistake, Fraud and Duties to Inform in European Contract Law* (2005); E Hondius and HC Grigoleit, *Unexpected Circumstances in European Contract Law* (2011) and R Zimmermann and S Whittaker, *Good Faith in European Contract Law* (2000) (all published by Cambridge University Press).

[94] O Lando and H Beale, *Principles of European Contract Law*, Pts I and II (2000), Pt III (2003) (The Hague, Kluwer Law International).

[95] C von Bar and E Clive (eds), *Principles, Definitions and Model Rules of European Private Law: Draft Common Frame of Reference (DCFR)* (Munich, Sellier, 2009).

[96] Research Group on the Existing EC Private Law (Acquis Group), *Principles of the Existing EC Contract Law (Acquis Principles), Contract I* (Munich, Sellier, 2007).

[97] COM(2011) 635.

constitute an 'optional instrument': a self-standing set of contract law rules, common to all Member States and constituting a second regime of domestic contract law in each Member State, which could be chosen by parties in cross-border transactions for the sale of goods, for the supply of digital content, and for related services. The rules contained in the CESL were drafted in the rather brief style of a continental civil code, rather than a (lengthier, and detailed)[98] English statute; and many of the proposed rules were closer in substance to the existing domestic contract law rules of civil law jurisdictions than to English law, although no single European civil jurisdiction was favoured and some aspects of the rules followed the position taken by English law.[99] However, the proposed Regulation was subjected to significant criticism,[100] and it was finally withdrawn at the end of 2014. It was replaced by a much narrower project to provide contract rules for online purchases of digital content and tangible goods (ie internet and e-commerce transactions), on which the European Commission opened a new consultation in 2015, and published in December 2015 a proposal for a Directive on contracts for the supply of digital content.[101] For the moment, therefore, the European aim for the harmonisation of contract law remains directed at particular types of transaction where intervention is required and justified at the EU level, rather than at any general harmonisation of the principles of contract law amongst Member States. Subject only to particular interventions by EU law, as has been the case in the past, each jurisdiction will retain—and will develop in its own way—its own approach to the law of contract. The purpose of this book is to highlight the approach taken in English law.

---

[98] Above, p 45.
[99] For a comparative discussion of the provisions of the CESL in the light of English law and German law, see G Dannemann and S Vogenauer (ed), *The Common European Sales Law in Context: Interactions with English and German Law* (Oxford, Oxford University Press, 2013).
[100] The English Law Commission criticised the proposal in advice to the UK Government: 'An Optional Common European Sales Law: Advantages and Problems' (November 2011). In February 2013 the Committee on Legal Affairs of the European Parliament published a draft report suggesting (inter alia) that the CESL be limited to distance contracts, including online contracts.
[101] COM(2015) 634 (final).

4

The Negotiations for a Contract

Textbooks on the English law of contract do not generally contain a separate chapter on the precontractual stage—the negotiations. However, this is logically the place to begin in a book which considers the whole life of the contract, from its creation to its fulfilment or termination. In this book it is particularly appropriate to begin with a chapter devoted to the precontractual stage because it is here that we can see a very significant difference between the common law and the civil law. Put very briefly: English law is reluctant to characterise the negotiations as constituting a legally-protected relationship, and so there is no general principle of precontractual liability. One party's (mis)conduct during the negotiations may affect the validity of the contract if it has been concluded, and sometimes it may also be possible to obtain an award of damages for loss suffered as a result of entering into the contract in such circumstances. The 'vitiating factors' which can be relied on to obtain such remedies are considered in chapter seven. But there is no general norm of conduct between parties negotiating for a contract—and so, for example, no general duty to negotiate in good faith, and no recognition of a principle of *culpa in contrahendo*—to give rise to liability during the negotiations themselves.[1]

The common law systems are not entirely united in their approach to this question. American law and Australian law, in particular, have developed some different approaches to the precontractual stage and to the imposition of liability. This chapter will focus on the approach taken by English law—which is in this area the most conservative of the common law systems—but

---

[1] For an overview of the approach of European legal systems, see J Cartwright and M Hesselink, *Precontractual Liability in European Private Law* (Cambridge, Cambridge University Press, 2008).

will mention different approaches in other common law systems from time to time where appropriate.

I. The Starting Point: No General Duty between Negotiating Parties

1. The General Approach

The approach of English law to the duty between negotiating parties is very restrictive. One can put this in various (negative) propositions. During negotiations the parties do not owe each other any general duties which arise by virtue of the negotiations themselves—whether at the outset or even when the negotiations have lasted for a protracted time or have apparently almost reached their conclusion. There is no inherent (implied) duty of good faith, loyalty or co-operation between negotiating parties. Negotiating parties do not owe each other any general duty of disclosure—and this even extends to the case where one party realises that the other is making a serious mistake about the subject-matter of the contract. There is no implied duty to continue to negotiate, and the courts have even rejected the validity of an express agreement to negotiate. Breaking-off negotiations does not constitute a wrong—does not as such constitute a tort. Even the malicious breaking-off of negotiations is not in law wrongful, since in principle breaking-off negotiations is a right, and the malicious exercise of a right does not automatically turn it into a wrong.

There are, however, exceptions to this: there are circumstances in which English law will impose liability on one negotiating party in favour of the other. These will be explained in a little more detail in the following sections of this chapter. But first it is worth exploring the reasons for the general approach.

2. No General Duty Because of a Reluctance to Use General Principles?

One reason for the reluctance of English law to impose a general duty on each party in favour of the other during the negotiations may be the reluctance of English law to work from general principles. This being an area of common law, rather than statute, it develops from the particular cases, the particular problems which have arisen and for which remedies have been found (or refused) within the existing law. We have seen that this is a general approach in the common law.[2] The English judges are able in some contexts to derive a general test, or a general principle, from particular cases by a process of inductive and deductive reasoning.[3] But they generally prefer to work from case to case, rather than through the derivation of broad general principles. In consequence, where one party seeks a remedy against the other for what has gone on during the negotiations, the search is focused on the question whether the defendant has committed a breach of a contractual obligation or a tort, or a claim has arisen for the reversal of an unjust enrichment. The negotiations are not a relationship which gives rise to obligations *sui generis*. By definition, they are not inherently contractual; and the difficulty in fitting them within the law of tort or unjust enrichment is the particular nature of those sources of obligation.

3. Difficulties in Defining the Duty?

One reason which has been given by the courts in rejecting a general duty is the difficulty in defining its content—that is, an argument based on a lack of *certainty*. If the obligation cannot be defined, then the court could not properly police the parties' compliance with it—it could not determine whether the obligation has been complied with, and so it could not make orders consequent upon a breach of such an obligation.

The strength of the argument based on 'certainty' depends on the nature of the alleged duty between negotiating parties. The English courts have long held that an agreement simply 'to agree', or 'to negotiate' is not of sufficiently certain content, since the court cannot assess what agreement the parties would or should have come to;[4] and, in consequence, even in the clearest case of failure to fulfil the agreement to negotiate (such as a flat refusal to engage in the negotiations) the court would not be able to assess the remedy because it could not assess the value of the lost opportunity to achieve a negotiated result. In *Courtney & Fairbairn Ltd v Tolaini Brothers (Hotels) Ltd* Lord Denning MR said:

> If the law does not recognise a contract to enter into a contract (when there is a fundamental term yet to be agreed) it seems to me it cannot recognise a contract to negotiate. The reason is because it is too uncertain to have any binding force. No court could estimate the damages because no one can tell whether the negotiations would be successful or would fall through: or if successful, what the result would be.

---

[2] Above, ch 2; *Interfoto Picture Library Ltd v Stiletto Visual Programmes Ltd* [1989] QB 433 (CA) 439 (Bingham LJ, quoted above, p 65).

[3] A clear case of this is the generalisation of a concept of a duty of care in the tort of negligence, in *Donoghue v Stevenson* [1932] AC 562 (HL Sc), above, p 38.

[4] Below, p 122.

It seems to me that a contract to negotiate, like a contract to enter into a contract, is not a contract known to the law.[5]

The civil lawyer may reasonably say: the lack of content in the duty to negotiate can be remedied by formulating it in terms of a duty to negotiate *in good faith*. But this has been expressly rejected by the House of Lords. There are certain standards of conduct which the parties may contract to achieve, and to which the law will then give effect—such as the duty to use 'reasonable endeavours' or 'best endeavours'. These are undertakings to engage in a course of conduct towards achieving a particular result; 'best endeavours', as one might expect, being a higher standard than 'reasonable endeavours'.[6] But if the result which is to be achieved is not itself capable of definition with sufficient certainty, it does not make it any more certain to add the words 'will use best endeavours to ...'. Therefore, an agreement 'to use best endeavours to agree' is no more certain than an agreement simply 'to agree'.[7] Similarly, adding the words 'in good faith' do not make an agreement 'to negotiate' any more certain. Indeed, this is even less certain—since the very content of the duty to negotiate 'in good faith' has been held to be uncertain. In *Walford v Miles* Lord Ackner said:

> The reason why an agreement to negotiate, like an agreement to agree, is unenforceable, is simply because it lacks the necessary certainty. The same does not apply to an agreement to use best endeavours. This uncertainty is demonstrated in the instant case by the provision which it is said has to be implied in the agreement for the determination of the negotiations. How can a court be expected to decide whether, subjectively, a proper reason existed for the termination of negotiations?[8] The answer suggested depends upon whether the negotiations have been determined 'in good faith.' However the concept of a duty to carry on negotiations in good faith is inherently repugnant to the adversarial position of the parties when involved in negotiations. Each party to the negotiations is entitled to pursue his (or her) own interest, so long as he avoids making misrepresentations. To advance that interest he must be entitled, if he thinks it appropriate, to threaten to withdraw from further negotiations or to withdraw in fact, in the hope that the opposite party may seek to reopen the negotiations by offering him improved terms. [Counsel for the claimant], of course, accepts that the agreement upon which he relies does not contain a duty to complete the negotiations. But that still leaves the vital question—how is a vendor ever to know that he is entitled to withdraw from further negotiations? How is the court to police such an 'agreement?' A duty to negotiate in good faith

---

[5] [1975] 1 WLR 297 (CA) 301.
[6] *Malik Co v Central European Trading Agency Ltd* [1974] 2 Lloyd's Rep 279 (QB) 284.
[7] *Little v Courage* (1994) 70 P & CR 469 (CA) 476.
[8] The insistence by Leggatt J in *Yam Seng Pte Ltd v International Trade Corp Ltd* [2013] EWHC 111 (QB), [2013] 1 Lloyd's Rep 526, above, p 66, that the duty of good faith is to be tested objectively, and is not necessarily uncertain, was directed at the implied term of the contract imposing the duty to *perform* in good faith, not the duty to negotiate in good faith.

is as unworkable in practice as it is inherently inconsistent with the position of a negotiating party. It is here that the uncertainty lies. In my judgment, while negotiations are in existence either party is entitled to withdraw from those negotiations, at any time and for any reason. There can be thus no obligation to continue to negotiate until there is a 'proper reason' to withdraw. Accordingly a bare agreement to negotiate has no legal content.[9]

In order for a 'negotiation contract' to be effective, therefore, it must contain criteria for resolution of the differences between the parties which are sufficiently certain for the court to be able to give effect to them—such as providing that the price shall be 'reasonable' (which the court can determine objectively, as long as the applicable criteria are sufficiently ascertainable);[10] or a mechanism for resolution of the differences which is objectively capable of operation without the co-operation of the parties themselves, such as a recognised form of dispute resolution.[11] However, although the question is always whether the contractual provision is sufficiently certain, the courts will try to find a construction which gives effect to the contract rather than to defeat the parties' intentions.[12]

4. The Relationship between Negotiating Parties is Adversarial; The Allocation of Risk in Negotiations

The reluctance to recognise general duties between negotiating parties is not simply a reluctance to use general principles. The extract from Lord Ackner's speech in *Walford v Miles*, quoted above, intertwines two separate strands of reasoning. The first is the uncertainty inherent in a duty to negotiate 'in good faith'. The second is a more fundamental point of principle: that the very nature of the relationship between the parties during the negotiations is inconsistent with such a general duty. Lord Ackner described it as 'inherently repugnant to the adversarial position of the parties when involved in negotiations'. These are strong words; and the decision in *Walford v Miles* even goes so far as to reject the notion of an *express* agreement to negotiate in good faith. This latter point may be the subject of challenge in the courts

---

[9] [1992] 2 AC 128 (HL) 138; the other members of the House agreed.
[10] *Sudbrook Trading Estate Ltd v Eggleton* [1983] 1 AC 444 (HL).
[11] *Cable & Wireless plc v IBM United Kingdom Ltd* [2002] EWHC 2059 (Comm), [2002] 2 All ER (Comm) 1041 (provision that parties shall 'attempt in good faith to resolve any dispute or claim' arising out of the contract was saved by a provision that if the negotiations failed the differences would be settled by alternative dispute resolution).
[12] *Tang v Grant Thornton International Ltd* [2012] EWHC 3198 (Ch), [2014] 2 CLC 663 at [56]–[61]. See also *Foley v Classique Coaches Ltd* [1934] 2 KB 1 (CA) 10 (sale of petrol 'at a price to be agreed by the parties in writing and from time to time' with an arbitration clause to resolve disputes over price: term implied into the contract that the petrol should be supplied at a reasonable price).

in the coming years: there have been calls to reconsider the absolute rejection of a duty to negotiate in good faith,[13] and in a different context (supervening circumstances during the performance of the contract) there has been an indication from the Court of Appeal that it is not acceptable to refuse to give effect to an express agreement to *re*-negotiate a contract since such a refusal would frustrate the intentions of the parties.[14] However, the rejection of an *implied* duty to negotiate in good faith is a reflection of a general view of the position of the negotiating parties under which each retains the freedom to withdraw, and the freedom to act in his own interests as he sees fit, until the moment at which the contract is concluded. Until then, each party bears the risk that the contract may not be concluded and that he will have no recourse to the other for expenditure incurred during the negotiations. The formation of the contract is the moment at which the risk normally shifts.[15]

5. Negotiations 'Subject to Contract'

One way in which the parties may seek to put beyond doubt the absence of liability during the negotiations is to identify the negotiations as being conducted 'subject to contract' or by other words to similar effect.[16] Once one of the parties has made this clear during the negotiations, it carries through the following communications until the parties make clear that it is no longer to apply. It protects the parties not only against liability during the negotiations, but also from being bound by contract once the agreement is concluded but before the parties have taken the final steps which they have defined as necessary—for example, to formalise the agreement in a written contract.[17] It has traditionally been used in the negotiations for contracts for the sale of land, but can equally apply to any negotiations, since in effect it is simply an

---

[13] J Steyn (Lord Steyn), 'Contract Law: Fulfilling the Reasonable Expectations of Honest Men' (1997) 113 LQR 433, 438–39, noting that European jurisdictions, as well as the Principles of International Commercial Contracts, published by Unidroit, and the Uniform Commercial Code in the United States, accept duties of good faith.

[14] *Petromec Inc v Petroleo Brasilieiro SA* [2005] EWCA Civ 891, [2006] 1 Lloyd's Rep 121, [121]; below, pp 270–71.

[15] Precontractual expenditure is not normally recoverable as such in the event of breach of contract, since the remedy for breach is damages on the expectation measure, rather than calculated to compensate the claimant for wasted expenses: below, ch 12. However, in a case where damages are to be calculated on the basis of wasted expenditure rather than lost profits, damages for breach of contract can include precontractual expenses: *Anglia Television Ltd v Reed* [1972] 1 QB 60 (CA).

[16] *RTS Flexible Systems Ltd v Molkerei Alois Müller GmbH & Co KG* [2010] UKSC 14, [2010] 1 WLR 753 (contract would 'not become effective until each party has executed a counterpart and exchanged it with the other').

[17] If the parties not only reach agreement but in fact begin performance of the contract, then they may implicitly become bound by their conduct in performing: *Rugby Group Ltd v ProForce Recruit Ltd* [2005] EWHC 70 (QB) [16].

indication that a party has no intention to create legal relations[18]—no intention to be bound by contract—until a later stage. Rattee J has said:

> [In a case such as the present case] however much the parties expect a contract between them to materialise, both enter negotiations expressly (whether by use of the words 'subject to contract' or otherwise) on terms that each party is free to withdraw from the negotiations at any time. Each party to such negotiations must be taken to know ... that pending the conclusion of a binding contract any cost incurred by him in preparation for the intended contract will be incurred at his own risk, in the sense that he will have no recompense for those costs if no contract results.[19]

6. No General Duty of Disclosure

The adversarial character of the relationship between negotiating parties is also reflected in the refusal of the English courts to impose general duties of disclosure of information during the negotiations. It would be contrary to the nature of negotiations to require both parties as a matter of course to disclose all information relevant to their own bargaining position. No legal system will start from a general duty of disclosure for all contractual negotiations. However—whether or not they base this on the duty to negotiate in good faith—many systems will say that the failure to disclose information should be sanctioned in certain types of case: for example, where one party is a professional, and is aware that the other (non-professional) party lacks information which would be of importance in deciding whether to contract or on what terms to contract; or where one party knows that the other party is making a serious mistake about the facts surrounding the contract, which would affect his decision to contract. English law, however, is much more reticent than most civil law systems in this respect. We shall see this in more detail when we consider the relationship in English law between mistake, misrepresentation and non-disclosure in chapter seven, and we shall see there that there are certain particular circumstances in which English law admits a duty of disclosure or creates incentives on parties to disclose information, and that some significant duties of disclosure are imposed by statute, particularly statutory duties on traders to provide information to consumers.[20] But the flavour of the general approach of the common law can be seen in the judgment of Cockburn CJ in *Smith v Hughes*:

> Here the defendant agreed to buy a specific parcel of oats. The oats were what they were sold as, namely, good oats according to the sample. The buyer persuaded

---

[18] Below, pp 156–57.
[19] *Regalian Properties plc v London Docklands Development Corp* [1995] 1 WLR 212 (Ch) 231.
[20] Below, pp 187–88.

himself they were old oats, when they were not so; but the seller neither said nor did anything to contribute to his deception. He has himself to blame. The question is not what a man of scrupulous morality or nice honour would do under such circumstances. The case put of the purchase of an estate, in which there is a mine under the surface, but the fact is unknown to the seller, is one in which a man of tender conscience or high honour would be unwilling to take advantage of the ignorance of the seller; but there can be no doubt that the contract for the sale of the estate would be binding.[21]

The same approach appears in the judgment of Blackburn J in the same case:

[E]ven if the vendor was aware that the purchaser thought that the article possessed that quality, and would not have entered into the contract unless he had so thought, still the purchaser is bound, unless the vendor was guilty of some fraud or deceit upon him, and that a mere abstinence from disabusing the purchaser of that impression is not fraud or deceit; for, whatever may be the case in a court of morals, there is no legal obligation on the vendor to inform the purchaser that he is under a mistake, not induced by the act of the vendor.[22]

7. Breaking off Negotiations is Not a Tort

As we shall see in the next section, the law of tort can sometimes be invoked to remedy misconduct during the negotiations. But in substance it is a law of *torts*, made up of a set of compartmentalised wrongs, designed to protect different interests and in different circumstances. Precontractual negotiations are not in themselves a protected interest within the law of tort. Even the deliberate breaking-off of negotiations with the knowledge that loss will be inflicted on the other party does not fall within one of the torts in English law. And although the law of tort can provide protection against loss caused by reliance on a false statement (a misrepresentation), deliberate silence does not normally constitute an actionable wrong in English law.[23] Similarly, although English law has a tort of *negligence*—the most general and pervasive of the torts—which imposes liability on a party who fails to fulfil his duty to take reasonable care in favour of a party to whom the duty was owed and who suffers loss in consequence of the breach of duty, the courts have not taken the view that, except in the case of misrepresentations, the relationship between negotiating parties itself gives rise to mutual duties of care within the law of tort.

Indeed, in the context of a claim for failure to disclose information, the Supreme Court of Canada has rejected a general extension of the tort of

---

[21] (1871) LR 6 QB 597, 603–04.
[22] *Ibid* 607.
[23] *Peek v Gurney* (1873) LR 6 HL 377, 391, 403; below, p 188. Where there is a duty of disclosure, fraudulent non-disclosure may be actionable in tort: *Conlon v Simms* [2006] EWCA Civ 1749, [2008] 1 WLR 484; below, p 188.

82   THE NEGOTIATIONS FOR A CONTRACT

negligence to contractual negotiations, again based on the nature of the negotiations and the adversarial relationship between the parties:

> It would defeat the essence of negotiation and hobble the marketplace to extend a duty of care to the conduct of negotiations, and to label a party's failure to disclose its bottom line, its motives or its final position as negligent. Such a conclusion would of necessity force the disclosure of privately acquired information and the dissipation of any competitive advantage derived from it, all of which is incompatible with the activity of negotiating and bargaining.
>
> ... [T]o impose a duty in the circumstances of this appeal could interject tort law as after-the-fact insurance against failures to act with due diligence or to hedge the risk of failed negotiations through the pursuit of alternative strategies or opportunities.[24]

8. No General Liability Based on Estoppel

The doctrine of estoppel will be explained later in more detail,[25] but for the moment it can be said that there are certain circumstances in which a person who has made a representation to another may be 'estopped' from denying that he must give effect to the representation where the other has relied on the representation to his detriment. That is, the representee's detrimental reliance can be a source of obligation on the representor. However, this doctrine is very limited in the context with which we are concerned. Except in the case of proprietary estoppel (which is limited to cases where, broadly, the defendant owner of land leads the claimant to believe that he has or will acquire an interest in the land, and the claimant relies on this to his detriment), English law does not recognise a claimant's reliance on the defendant's representation as creating new positive rights. The High Court of Australia has extended the doctrine of promissory estoppel to impose liability in damages on the party seeking to withdraw from negotiations. In *Waltons Stores (Interstate) Ltd v Maher*[26] there was not yet a concluded contract to grant the lease of property but the prospective tenant had encouraged the landowner to continue to build the property when he had already decided not to take the lease. The court held that the tenant was estopped from denying that he was bound to complete the lease, because it would be unconscionable for him to retreat from his implied promise to complete the contract. The remedy was not enforcement of the contract, but damages in place of specific performance,[27] but the use of estoppel here had the effect of imposing a liability on one party for his

---

[24] *Martel Building Ltd v Canada* (2000) 193 DLR (4th) 1, [67]–[68]. This decision has been followed, and for similar reasons, by the High Court in New Zealand: *Onyx Group Ltd v Auckland City Council* (2003) 11 TCLR 40 in the context of tenders.
[25] Below, pp 143–55.
[26] (1988) 164 CLR 387; below, p 153.
[27] Below, p 281.

failure properly to conduct himself during the negotiations. The language of 'unconscionability' used by the High Court of Australia may not seem so very far removed from the principle of 'good faith' which many civil law systems would apply in such a case to achieve, no doubt, a rather similar result.

The use of promissory estoppel in such a context is even better established within the United States. In *Hoffman v Red Owl Stores Inc*[28] negotiations for the terms for the grant of a franchise of a grocery store failed at a late stage after Red Owl, the intended franchisor, had induced Hoffman, the intended franchisee, to sell his existing business in order to finance the new franchise contract by telling him 'everything is ready to go. Get your money together and we are set'. There was no concluded contract of franchise, but Red Owl was liable to compensate Hoffman for his reliance under the doctrine of promissory estoppel.

Such an analysis is not, however, yet possible in England below the level of the Supreme Court because of a decision of the Court of Appeal in 1951[29] to the effect that promissory estoppel cannot be used to create new obligations; the doctrine generally applies only to prevent one party to a contract from going back on a promise to the other party that he will not enforce his existing rights under the contract. The Court of Appeal[30] has made clear that, on the basis of this authority, it is bound to hold that promissory estoppel does not create a new cause of action, although it is not out of the question that the Supreme Court might be persuaded to take such a step.

II. Particular Liabilities Arising During the Negotiations

1. Particular Liabilities Rather than General Duties

The rejection by English law of general duties between negotiating parties does not mean that one party cannot incur liability to the other by virtue of

---

[28] 133 NW 2d 267 (Wisconsin, 1965), adopting the American Law Institute's Restatement of the Law, 1, Contracts (1933) para 90. For the current provision in Restatement 2d, Contracts (1981), see below, p 153.

[29] *Combe v Combe* [1951] 2 KB 215 (CA).

[30] *Baird Textile Holdings Ltd v Marks & Spencer plc* [2001] EWCA Civ 274, [2002] 1 All ER (Comm) 737 [55]: 'there is no real prospect of the claim succeeding unless and until the law is developed, or corrected, by the House of Lords' (Judge LJ). The Court of Appeal is bound by its own previous decisions: above, p 25.

what is done during the negotiations. However, English law looks to find a particular reason for imposing liability: in tort, contract, unjust enrichment or some other source of obligation.

2. Misrepresentation: Remedies in Tort

English law distinguishes separate torts, which protect different interests and have their own separate rules.[31] The precontractual context in which tortious liability can most easily arise is where one party has made a false statement—a misrepresentation—on which the other party has relied. In chapter seven we shall see the general approach to misrepresentation in English law, including the remedies in tort, in a case where a party to a contract seeks a remedy for loss which flows from having entered into the contract in reliance on the misrepresentation. Here we consider more briefly the two particular torts which can be invoked during the negotiations themselves—that is, to cover the case where the negotiations fail and no contract is concluded. These are the torts of *deceit* and *negligence*.

Under the tort of deceit a person who makes a fraudulent misrepresentation to another, intending that other to act upon it, must compensate the other for the loss he suffers in consequence of acting upon it. This is not limited to parties negotiating a contract; it is a general tort, but it can apply during negotiations, and the recoverable loss could be the expenditure incurred by one party during the negotiations in reliance on the other's fraudulent misrepresentation about, for example, his intention to proceed with the contract. 'Misrepresentation' here means any words or conduct which communicate false information. But the defendant is liable only if the claimant can establish fraud: that the defendant knew that his statement was false, or that he did not believe it to be true or was reckless about its truth—that is, he did not have a positive, honest belief in its truth.[32] However, there is a wide scope for this tort in the context of precontractual negotiations. Liability can arise in the case of one party's actions which lead the other to begin or to continue negotiations and so to incur expenditure which is wasted—for example, where the defendant has no serious intention to contract but gives the impression that he does; or where he conducts parallel negotiations with another potential contracting party whilst pretending that he is not doing so; or where he comes to a decision during the negotiations that they are doomed to fail but does not tell the other party but by his words or conduct gives the other party the idea that all is well. In such cases liability is not imposed because of a rule that a party must begin or conduct negotiations in good faith; or that he must disclose the

---

[31] Above, p 38.
[32] *Derry v Peek* (1889) 14 App Cas 337 (HL) 374.

fact of parallel negotiations or of his change of decision as regards the contract. English law does not recognise such general propositions—nor would an English lawyer even say that there is a general duty to be honest in the negotiations. Rather, the question is whether there is evidence of dishonesty; and whether the defendant said or did something which could be taken by (and was taken by) the claimant as giving false information about the current state of the negotiations or his willingness to pursue them. It should be noted that if a claim is brought on this basis, the claimant can recover only those losses which flowed from the fraudulent misrepresentation—that is, there must be a causal link between the fraudulent statement and the losses claimed. In practice, this means that only losses incurred after the misrepresentation was made are recoverable—losses which were suffered in reliance on the misrepresentation.

The tort of negligence can cover misrepresentations where there is no evidence of fraud. A defendant is liable in negligence where he owed to the claimant a duty to take reasonable care, and failed to fulfil his duty of care, causing loss to the claimant. In 1963 it was established that a person can owe a duty to take care in the provision of information or advice, in favour of a person who relies on it for a foreseeable purpose.[33] In theory this can apply in the context of precontractual negotiations, such as where one party gives inaccurate information to the other during the negotiations, on which the other is (in the circumstances) entitled to rely and does in fact rely. But it is not a common claim. The duty only arises where the relative positions held by the claimant and defendant are such that the claimant is *entitled* to rely on what the other party says, without checking the accuracy of the information. In the context of negotiations, much of what passes between the parties will not fall within this, although where one party makes statements which are within his sphere of specialist knowledge or skill, and which reasonably induce the other party to trust him and to act on the basis of the statements, a duty can indeed arise. For example, in *Esso Petroleum Co Ltd v Mardon*,[34] Esso, which owned a petrol station, gave an inaccurate estimate of the likely profitability of the petrol station to Mr Mardon, who was considering taking a lease of it. The Court of Appeal held that, in providing that opinion, Esso owed a duty to Mr Mardon to take care given that it held itself out as having specialist knowledge and skill in the matter. Esso breached that duty; Mr Mardon took the lease and recovered damages based on his losses in entering into the lease and the associated business. The context in which claims under this head generally arise is, as in the *Esso* case, where the claimant is induced to enter into a contract by the misrepresentation, but in theory it would be possible for a person to whom inaccurate information was supplied, and who was thereby induced to

---

[33] *Hedley Byrne & Co Ltd v Heller & Partners Ltd* [1964] AC 465 (HL).
[34] [1976] QB 801 (CA).

refuse to conclude a contract, to bring a claim similarly in negligence, as long as he suffered losses of a kind as are compensated by the law of tort—that is, the out-of-pocket losses suffered as a result relying on the misrepresentation.

However, if fraud can be proved, the tort of deceit may be more useful in order to provide a remedy in the precontractual stage where no contract is concluded. It may be possible to show that the defendant had decided not to proceed with the negotiations to their completion, but allowed the defendant to continue to incur costs and losses. This will not be covered by the tort of negligence, which covers only false or inaccurate information or advice. But it can fall within deceit because a fraudulent misrepresentation of one's own intention is actionable in deceit.[35]

It should be remembered that the tort of deceit generally requires a misrepresentation—by words or conduct, but not simply by silence. English law has not developed a general notion of 'fraudulent silence'; the omission to disclose information is a fundamentally different issue, and even a deliberate withholding of information, or a deliberate failure to inform the other party of one's decision not to go ahead with the contract, is normally not deceit.[36]

3. Contractual Liability in the Precontractual Phase

It is possible for one party to become liable to the other *in contract* during the precontractual phase. That is, even if the negotiations for the principal contract fail, there are circumstances in which there may be a subsidiary contract under which liability arises. This will normally be an express contract, but may sometimes be implied.

(a) Express Contracts: Options, Rights of Pre-emption, Lock-out Agreements and 'Letters of Intent'

The parties may enter into a form of preliminary contract—in advance of the main contract which they are negotiating—where they wish to provide for some aspect of their negotiations to be regulated by contract. It is for the parties to determine whether to enter into such a preliminary contract, and to define its scope and terms; but common forms are option contracts, rights of pre-emption, 'lock-out' agreements and 'letters of intent'.

An *option contract* is a contract under which one party is given the right to enter into the main contract if he so chooses—if he 'opts' to do so.

---

[35] *Edgington v Fitzmaurice* (1885) 29 ChD 459 (CA) 483.
[36] *Peek v Gurney* (1873) LR 6 HL 377, 391, 403; below, p 188. Cf, however, *Conlon v Simms* [2006] EWCA Civ 1749, [2008] 1 WLR 484; below, p 188.

The option contract will define what he has to do in order to 'exercise the option'—typically, he must give notice to the other party. One common way of viewing an option contract is as a contractually binding (that is, irrevocable) offer by one party to enter into the contract if the offeree so requires[37]—and it is certainly possible for an offeror to enter into a contractually binding commitment not to revoke his offer. Such a form of contract is necessary if one party requires the certainty that the offer of the contract will be kept open, since there is no principle in English law that an offer must be kept open for a reasonable period (or, indeed, any period): the offeror is free to withdraw it at any time, up to the instant before the offeree was minded to accept it, and even if the offeree has in the mean time been incurring significant expenditure to prepare himself to be able to accept the offer. However, it is important to remember that an option contract is *a contract*—and therefore must fulfil the requirements of any contract: it must be sufficiently certain in its terms,[38] and (if not executed as a deed) must be supported by consideration.[39] The requirement of certainty means that the terms of the main contract must themselves be sufficiently certain already, so that the unilateral exercise of the option by the party holding the option can create the main contract with a complete and sufficiently certain set of terms. The requirement of consideration (or a deed) shows that a 'firm offer'—an express promise to keep open the offer—even if accepted by the offeree, is not of itself binding.[40] In fact, the courts will look quite carefully to attempt to find consideration to support a firm offer, since they are generally keen to hold a party to his undertaking to maintain his offer; but in the final analysis, they must find consideration.[41]

A *right of pre-emption* is a contractual right of first refusal—the right for a party to be given an opportunity to enter into negotiations, or even to enter into an already-identified contract, but only if the other party decides to proceed with the transaction. For example, the owner of land may give a person the right to buy the land *if* he decides to sell it, but without at this stage committing himself to sell it at all. In a sense, a right of pre-emption is one stage further removed from the main contract itself than an option

---

[37] *Helby v Matthews* [1895] AC 471 (HL) 477, 479–80. On the other hand, it is sometimes characterised as a conditional contract—and for reasons connected particularly to the requirements of formality for land contracts it has been held that where the option relates to land it is the option contract, rather than the exercise of the option, which constitutes the 'contract for the sale or other disposition of an interest in land' and must therefore be in writing to comply with Law of Property (Miscellaneous Provisions) Act 1989 s 2(1): *Spiro v Glencrown Properties Ltd* [1991] Ch 537 (Ch).

[38] Below, p 122.

[39] Below, ch 6.

[40] In 1975 the Law Commission identified this as a problem for business practice, and recommended reform to allow firm offers to be binding: Law Commission Working Paper No 60, 'Firm Offers' (1975). But this has not been taken further.

[41] *Pitt v PHH Asset Management Ltd* [1994] 1 WLR 327 (CA); below, p 137 n 45.

contract, since in an option the offeror has already committed himself to enter into the contract if the offeree exercises the option, but in a pre-emption the party granting the right of pre-emption is not yet bound at all. He has, as it were, bound himself only to make an offer to the beneficiary of the pre-emption first, if he decides to enter into the main contract. But, in order to be enforceable, the right of pre-emption must (like the option contract) be a contract—supported by consideration or contained in a deed. However, unlike an option contract, in the case of a right of pre-emption the terms of the final contract need not yet be defined, since the obligation is only to make an offer. It has been said that the duty on the seller is to act in good faith in making the offer on terms on which he would be prepared to sell. He cannot avoid entering into a contract to sell to the beneficiary of the right of pre-emption by making an offer at an unreasonably high price which will be rejected, so as to be able instead to sell at a lower price to a third party. A challenge to the seller's good faith may not be easy to establish, but in practice in the case of a right of pre-emption over land, the price at which the beneficiary of the pre-emption must be allowed to buy is the reserve price if the property is to be auctioned or, if it is to be sold by private treaty, the price to be specified in the estate agent's particulars or any lower price to which the seller would in fact be prepared to reduce the asking price.[42]

A *'lock-out' contract* is a contractually binding agreement under which one or both parties agree not to enter into a contract with any third party, or even not to negotiate with third parties: they 'lock' themselves 'out' of a competing contract or parallel negotiations. Such a contract is necessary for a party who is concerned to obtain legally enforceable exclusive negotiating rights, since there is no implied obligation not to negotiate with others. But the 'lock-out' agreement must be for a defined or definable period of time (otherwise it does not satisfy the requirements of contractual certainty); and it must be a 'lock-*out*' and not a 'lock-*in*' since, as we have already seen, English law does not accept a contract to negotiate.[43] A 'lock-out' contract must also be supported by consideration (if not in a deed), although again the courts will attempt to find consideration in order to render such an agreement binding.[44]

The precise scope of a 'lock-out' contract will depend on its language. Indeed, it must be drafted carefully if it is to be commercially useful, because even if the scope of the 'lock-out' is clear, there can still be a question over the remedy for breach. The contract only restricts a party from entering into a contract with a third party, or negotiating with third parties, for a definite period, and so the party can simply wait until the end of the period and then enter into the competing contract, or begin the competing negotiations. There

---

[42] *Smith v Morgan* [1971] 1 WLR 803 (Ch) 808.
[43] *Walford v Miles* [1992] 2 AC 128 (HL) 139; above, p 77.
[44] *Pitt v PHH Asset Management Ltd* above, n 41.

is no duty during the 'lock- out' period to negotiate in good faith (or at all), so unless it can be shown that there is some other ground of remedy (such as a fraudulent misrepresentation at the outset as to the party's intention to conduct the negotiations)[45] the party can evade the spirit of the 'lock-out' contract. Indeed, even if the party breaks the 'lock-out' agreement and begins negotiations with a third party, it is not clear that there is a very satisfactory remedy. The courts are reluctant to award injunctions in such cases, but will normally leave the claimant to his remedy in damages[46]—and it may be difficult to show that any quantifiable loss flowed from the breach of contract because there is no certainty that the beneficiary of the 'lock-out' contract would have obtained a contract: damages can be awarded only if the claimant can establish that he lost a real or substantial chance of the contract.[47] One drafting technique sometimes used in civil law legal systems to reinforce a 'lock-out' agreement is to include a clause providing for a penalty to be payable on breach. However, this is not possible in English law, since penalty clauses are struck out.[48] But a 'liquidated damages' clause is permissible: a clause which provides for an agreed sum to be payable (and enforceable as a debt) in the event of breach, but which is calculated as a genuine estimate of the likely loss in the event of breach—such as the wasted expenditure in the event of the negotiations failing by virtue of the breach of the 'lock-out'.[49]

Letters of intent are commonly used in practice, but their scope is less clearly definable than the other forms of preliminary contract discussed in this section. 'Letter of intent' is not a term of art; it is a label attached by negotiating parties and their lawyers to describe a preliminary agreement or intention to enter into a contract, but where the details have not yet been finalised. Other terms used for such a document include 'memorandum of understanding', or 'comfort letter'. It is generally some form of assurance, or 'comfort' for one or both parties that their negotiations are still on track. As such, it may well have no binding force, either because its does not contain any sufficiently certain undertakings to form a contract or because (as is often the case) it is expressed to be only for the 'comfort' of the other party and to be not binding. However, the parties may decide to enter into an agreement which is contractually binding, where they are still negotiating for the main contract, under which one party agrees to pay for particular pre-contract work, or to reimburse the other for expenses which he incurs if the main contract should not in fact be concluded. This form of contract (often unhelpfully referred to as a 'letter of intent') is designed to protect one party

---

[45] Above, p 84.
[46] *Tye v House* (1998) 79 P & CR 188 (Ch).
[47] *Dandara Holdings Ltd v Co-operative Retail Services Ltd* [2004] EWHC 1476 (Ch), [2004] 2 EGLR 163.
[48] Below, p 224.
[49] Such a clause was used successfully in *Dandara Holdings Ltd v Co-operative Retail Services Ltd* above, n 47.

against the risk of wasting expenditure incurred during the negotiations; and is commonly used where it is in the interests of the parties that some work be done, or some expenditure be incurred, in advance of the final details of the contract being agreed, in order to avoid delay to the eventual performance of the contract. It reverses by contract[50] the normal allocation of risk during the negotiations—under which each party takes the risk of loss in respect of expenditure incurred in anticipation of a concluded contract.[51]

(b) Implied Contracts: Duties to Consider Tenders

Invitations to tender can sometimes present particular problems. As a general rule an invitation to tender is not a contractual offer: it is the tenderer (bidder) who makes an offer which the person inviting tenders is free to consider and to decide which (if any) bid to accept.[52] However, if the invitation to tender goes further, and provides that the contract will be given to the bidder who submits the tender that is the lowest (or fulfils some other, objectively definable, criterion for acceptance), the general rule is displaced and the invitation forms an offer which will be accepted by the submission of the conforming tender.[53]

Even if the bidder cannot establish that he had a contractual entitlement to have his bid accepted, he might still sometimes technically have a claim for breach of contract if his bid was not properly considered in accordance with the published bidding procedures. In *Blackpool and Fylde Aero Club Ltd v Blackpool Borough Council*[54] it was held that, where tenders had been solicited from selected parties, all of them known to the invitor, and where the invitation to tender prescribed a clear, orderly and familiar procedure, the invitation to tender was as an offer to the extent that it promised to each tenderer that if he submitted a conforming tender it would be considered, or at least would be considered if other tenders were. This is quite a narrow decision; the judges emphasised the small class of intended bidders, selected by the invitor, as a significant feature in implying the offer to consider the bids. There is also case-law in New Zealand which accepts that an invitation to tender can, by its language, give rise to a preliminary contract requiring compliance with certain procedural obligations, including an implied duty to act fairly and in good faith in considering the tenders.[55] However, the Privy

---

[50] The risk may similarly be reversed by a non-contractual request to take steps beyond those normally expected of a negotiating party: see p 92, below.
[51] Above, pp 78–79.
[52] *Spencer v Harding* (1870) LR 5 CP 561; below, p 110.
[53] *Harvela Investments Ltd v Royal Trust Co of Canada (CI) Ltd* [1986] AC 207 (HL).
[54] [1990] 1 WLR 1195 (CA).
[55] *Pratt Contractors Ltd v Transit New Zealand* [2003] UKPC 83, [2004] BLR 143.

Council has made clear that the duty (which, it should be noted, is a *contractual* duty to *act* in good faith, and not a *precontractual* duty to *negotiate* in good faith) was quite limited:

> It is ... necessary to identify exactly what standard of conduct was required of the TET [tender evaluation team] in making its assessment. In their Lordships' opinion, the duty of good faith and fair dealing as applied to that particular function required that the evaluation ought to express the views honestly held by the members of the TET. The duty to act fairly meant that all the tenderers had to be treated equally. One tenderer could not be given a higher mark than another if their attributes were the same. But Transit was not obliged to give tenderers the same mark if it honestly thought that their attributes were different ... The obligation of good faith and fair dealing also did not mean that the TET had to act judicially. It did not have to accord Mr Pratt a hearing or enter into debate with him about the rights and wrongs of, for example, the Pipiriki contract [an earlier contract with another party which was known to be the subject of a dispute]. It would no doubt have been bad faith for a member of the TET to take steps to avoid receiving information because he strongly suspected that it might show that his opinion on some point was wrong. But that is all.[56]

The Canadian courts appear to have become even more open in recent years to accepting that an invitation to tender may give rise to a contractual duty to consider conforming tenders.[57] This goes beyond the more restricted view presently taken in the English courts. But in any case the utility of the duty to consider the tenders is rather doubtful, since the damages claim may be limited to nominal damages: if the tender that was submitted was not one which should have been accepted according to the bidding rules, the bidder suffers no substantial loss.

(c) Implied Duty to Maintain Offer of Unilateral Contract

A 'unilateral contract' is one in which only one party undertakes obligations, but the other party performs a service or fulfils some other condition requested by the offeror as the consideration for the offeror's obligations. A typical example of such a contract is where a person satisfies the conditions set by a public offer of a reward,[58] but it may also arise where the offer is made to a defined group, or even a single person.[59] The 'reward' is earned only when the requested performance is complete, but the offeror may not revoke the

---

[56] *Ibid* [47].
[57] Eg *Martel Building Ltd v Canada* above, n 24.
[58] *Carlill v Carbolic Smoke Ball Co* [1893] 1 QB 256 (CA) (£100 to be paid to anyone catching influenza after using defendant's 'smoke ball').
[59] *Errington v Errington* [1952] 1 KB 290 (CA) (father promised to transfer title to house to son and daughter-in-law if they occupied the house and paid all the instalments due under the mortgage).

offer once the offeree has begun performance.[60] This is based on an implied obligation on the part of the offeror not to prevent the offeree from satisfying the condition set by the offer, an obligation which arises as soon as the offeree starts to perform.[61]

4. Unjust Enrichment

We have already noted that the starting point is that pre-contract expenditure is at the risk of the spending party. If the other party has not requested that the expenditure be incurred, and has not encouraged it, it would be contrary to the general approach to the precontractual phase for him to be held liable to pay for it—even if he has stood by and watched the other party incur the expenditure. However, it will be different if one party has contracted to reimburse the other for pre-contract work or for expenses which he incurs if the main contract should not be concluded.[62] But even if no such contract is entered into, one party may still have an obligation to make a payment in respect of work done or other benefits conferred, under the law of unjust enrichment.

Where there is no promise to pay for pre-contract work, but one party has requested the other to undertake the work, the request may trigger the obligation to pay for the work. Sometimes a request may give rise to a contract for the work, even though there is no express promise to pay for it. If A asks B to perform a service for him, a contract can come into existence for the performance of the service, as long as all the requirements of a valid contract are present. If there is no express promise to pay, then such a request may often not give rise to a contract, because there may be no sufficient agreement on the price. But if the parties are silent as to price, and it is clear that the service was intended to be paid for, the law may sometimes imply a reasonable price.[63] This is then a contract for a reasonable price, not a claim in unjust enrichment.[64] However, where there is no contract (either express or implied) covering the payment for the pre-contract work, there may be a claim on the basis that the defendant would otherwise be unjustly enriched at the claimant's expense, having requested the work to be done.

---

[60] *Ibid* 295.
[61] *Daulia Ltd v Four Millbank Nominees Ltd* [1978] Ch 231, 239.
[62] Above, p 89 ('letters of intent').
[63] Supply of Goods and Services Act 1982 s 15.
[64] Eg *Brewer Street Investments Ltd v Barclay Woollen Co Ltd* [1954] 1 QB 428 (CA): prospective tenants asked for alterations to be done to the premises they were negotiating to lease; landlords paid for the alterations, but the lease negotiations finally broke down and no lease was granted. The majority held that there was a contract for the alterations, so the tenants must pay the costs incurred by the landlords.

The case-law is not entirely settled. Where the pre-contract work has conferred a *benefit* on the defendant it is within the normal principles of unjust enrichment that the defendant can be required to pay the value of that benefit ('*quantum meruit*' or '*quantum valebat*') since, having requested the work to be performed in circumstances where it was not intended to be gratuitous but is not covered by a contractual obligation of payment, he cannot retain the benefit but must make restitution. However, there are cases where the courts have not required an objective benefit to have been conferred on the defendant by the claimant's work: they have sometimes held that the mere fact that the claimant performed services at the defendant's request was itself a benefit for which the defendant must pay. Such a claim looks much more like an implied contractual claim than a restitutionary claim, since the analysis does not require proof of the receipt by the defendant of a benefit valuable in money terms, and the claim is sometimes calculated by reference to the cost to the claimant of performing such work (that is, it looks more like a claim for the claimant's losses than for restitution of the defendant's benefit).

In *William Lacey (Hounslow) Ltd v Davis* Barry J held that a builder could recover for work done after he had been told that his tender was the lowest and that he could expect to receive the contract. But the claim was not in contract but implied or quasi-contract (or, in modern terms, restitution for unjust enrichment):

> I am unable to see any valid distinction between work done which was to be paid for under the terms of a contract erroneously believed to be in existence, and work done which was to be paid for out of the proceeds of a contract which both parties erroneously believed was about to be made. In neither case was the work to be done gratuitously, and in both cases the party from whom payment was sought requested the work and obtained the benefit of it. In neither case did the parties actually intend to pay for the work otherwise than under the supposed contract, or as part of the total price which would become payable when the expected contract was made. In both cases, when the beliefs of the parties were falsified, the law implied an obligation—and in this case I think the law should imply an obligation—to pay a reasonable price for the services which had been obtained. I am, of course, fully aware that in different circumstances it might be held that work was done gratuitously merely in the hope that the building scheme would be carried out and that the person who did the work would obtain the contract. That, I am satisfied, is not the position here. In my judgment, the proper inference from the facts proved in this case is not that the work was done in the hope that the building might possibly be reconstructed and that the plaintiffs might obtain the contract, but that it was done under a mutual belief and understanding that the building was being reconstructed and that the plaintiffs were obtaining the contract.[65]

---

[65] [1957] 1 WLR 932 (QB) 939. In *Brewer Street Investments Ltd v Barclay Woollen Co Ltd* above, n 64, Denning LJ held that there was no contract for the alterations, but the landlords could recover in restitution for the costs they had incurred. See also *British Steel Corp v Cleveland Bridge and Engineering Co Ltd* [1984] 1 All ER 504 (QB).

The courts sometimes use the evidence of the contract negotiations to assist in the valuation of the benefit that has been conferred, and is therefore to be paid for. Lord Atkin said in *Way v Latilla:*

> [I]t appears to me clear that the court may take into account the bargainings between the parties, not with a view to completing the bargain for them, but as evidence of the value which each of them puts upon the services.[66]

There is no obligation to pay, however, where the work done does not confer a benefit on the requesting party, and does not involve the accelerated performance of obligations which are expected to be imposed by the (future) contract, but only involves the claimant putting himself into the position to obtain and then perform the contract.[67] That is simply the normal risk allocation in negotiations.

5. Breach of Confidence

All legal systems will start from the position that each party is entitled to confidentiality as regards his own information during the negotiations. This is a separate question from duties of disclosure, which determine whether one party ought to disclose certain information to the other. Here, the question is what obligations are owed in relation to respecting the confidentiality of information which is in fact disclosed. In English law there are well-established rules relating to confidential information, which can apply to information disclosed by one negotiating party to the other. Again, this is an example of a particular form of liability, which arises where a party makes unauthorised use or disclosure of information which is confidential, where he received it in circumstances which imported the obligation of confidence.[68] It is not seen as part of a broader principle of good faith or fair dealing between negotiating parties. It is not a tort, but was developed by the courts of equity—and so is an 'equitable duty' and its breach is an 'equitable wrong', remedied by an injunction to restrain future breaches, or damages, or an account of profits made from the improper use of the information.[69]

---

[66] [1937] 3 All ER 759 (HL) 764; see also *Benedetti v Sawiris* [2013] UKSC 50, [2014] AC 938 [168].

[67] *Regalian Properties plc v London Docklands Development Corp* [1995] 1 WLR 212 (Ch), where the negotiations were 'subject to contract': above, p 79.

[68] *Saltman Engineering Co Ltd v Campbell Engineering Co Ltd* (1948) 65 RPC 203 (CA).

[69] *Peter Pan Manufacturing Corporation v Corsets Silhouette Ltd* [1967] 1 WLR 923 (CA); *Seager v Copydex Ltd (No 2)* [1969] 1 WLR 809 (CA).

5

Formation of the Contract: Contract as 'Agreement'

All modern legal systems would say that a contract is in some sense an agreement, and the parties to the contract are those who are parties to the agreement. English law is no exception. This is not to say that an agreement is sufficient to form a contract; there will be further requirements, and we shall consider the approach taken by English law to that question (and, in particular, the doctrine of 'consideration') in chapter six. But at its core, a contract necessarily embodies an agreement between the parties, and this is the subject of this chapter.

However, in analysing the formation of a contract in English law, it is important to bear in mind two separate but related issues: first, what the courts mean by saying that they are looking for an 'agreement' (using an 'objective' test); and, secondly, the mechanisms which are regarded by the law as sufficient to form a contract (the rules of offer and acceptance). In addition, there are questions of how full the parties' 'agreement' must be in order for a contract to be formed—that is, what the law sets as the minimum content for a valid contract, and the corresponding rules relating to certainty of content.

I. The Meaning of 'Agreement': The 'Objective Test'

1. An 'Agreement' Requires Communication between the Parties

It is important to note at the outset that an agreement is more than a coincidence of intentions. Before there can be an agreement (and therefore before there can be a contract) there must be some communication between the parties of the common intention to contract. Therefore anything in the mind of one party which is not disclosed to the other cannot in principle be part of the contract. Terms may be *implied* into contracts.[1] But the unexpressed intentions of one party are in themselves irrelevant: and if one party communicates a proposed term to his own agent who is conducting the negotiations for him, it cannot become part of the contract if the agent does not pass it on to the other party.[2] Even if the two parties have a desire to contract with each other on similar terms, and each has communicated that desire to the other, there is not necessarily a contract, since one party's communication must be referable to the other's: cross-offers do not make a contract:

> [T]here must be an offer which the person accepting has had an opportunity of considering, and which when he accepts he knows will form a binding contract.[3]

We shall consider in the next section the way in which the courts analyse the formation of the agreement into offer and acceptance. Here we concentrate on the interpretation of the communications between the parties which are alleged to have given rise to their agreement—and whether the 'agreement' is tested objectively or subjectively.

2. 'Objectivity' and 'Subjectivity'

To say that we are looking for the parties 'agreement' in order to find a contract might suggest that the test is subjective; that is, there is only an 'agreement' if the parties both in fact intend to enter into a contract with each other, and on the same terms. However, this is misleading. Some legal systems adopt a theory of contract which requires a meeting of the subjective wills of the parties. But others consider that the parties' intentions are to be determined by reference to their external manifestation: it is the *declared* intention, rather than the internal, subjective intention, which counts. As we shall see, there are various arguments to be made in relation to the choice between a subjective test and an objective test for the formation of a contract. Ultimately, however, the choice of the test will depend on the reason for using the test—in this context, what the legal system sees as the essential nature of the contract, and the 'agreement' contained within it. In broad terms, English law adopts an objective test to ascertain the agreement, rather than a subjective test, although it will be important to understand the particularity of the English test and to see its rationale in the eyes of the English judges and the links which can be made between the use of objectivity in this context and other contractual doctrines.

---

[1] Below, pp 210–17.
[2] *Wood v Scarth* (1858) 1 F & F 293, 175 ER 733.
[3] *Tinn v Hoffman & Co* (1873) 29 LT 271, 277 (Grove J, obiter).

3. Arguments in Relation to the Different Approaches

The most obvious argument in favour of subjectivity is that the contract is an expression of the wills of the parties, and this necessarily involves the parties being bound if, but only if, they both so intend. As a corollary, the disadvantage of an objective test is that it envisages a party being bound in spite of his intention not to be—since it is his external, declared intention that will be taken into account, even if it does not coincide with his actual intention. A subjective theory of contract focuses on the parties' actual intentions.

One might immediately object that the parties' actual intentions cannot be ascertained—the subjective intention of each party depends on what was in his mind at the moment when the contract was alleged to have been formed, and (as it was put by Bryan CJ in rather picturesque language in 1477) 'the Devil himself knows not the intent of man'.[4] There is an inevitable problem of proof in a subjective test. And because the court cannot easily prove a subjective state of mind, it would be too easy for a person who apparently agreed to a contract to say that, in fact, he did not do so: there is a risk of parties fraudulently claiming that there was no subjective agreement. This objection has been made in some English cases. For example, where a person claimed that he had not agreed to buy a plot of land because he misunderstood the extent of the property, James LJ said:

> It is not enough for a purchaser to swear, 'I thought the farm sold contained twelve fields which I knew, and I find it does not include them all,' or, 'I thought it contained 100 acres and it only contains eighty'. It would open the door to fraud if such a defence was to be allowed.[5]

But it is certainly possible for the law to adopt a subjective test:

> [T]he state of a man's mind is as much a fact as the state of his digestion. It is true that it is very difficult to prove what the state of a man's mind at a particular time is, but if it can be ascertained it is as much a fact as anything else.[6]

If a subjective test is used, it becomes inevitable that a court will use external, objective evidence in order to prove the subjective intention; they will consider whether the external signs of the party's intention—his words and conduct—corroborate his claim about his subjective intention. So a subjective test inevitably begins to take on some form of objectivity in the matter of its proof. However, even if such objective proof is employed, it is only *evidence*; the contract still depends in principle on the actual intentions of the parties, and so if there is in fact no coincidence of intentions on the existence

---

[4] Year Book 17 Edw IV Pasch fo 2, pl 2: 'le Diable n'ad conusance de l'entent de home'.
[5] *Tamplin v James* (1880) 15 ChD 215, 221.
[6] *Edgington v Fitzmaurice* (1885) 29 ChD 459 (CA) 483 (Bowen LJ, discussing misrepresentation of intention; below, p 178).

of the contract and on those terms which are necessary for the contract to come into existence,[7] there is no contract.

One might then prefer not simply objective evidence, but an objective *test* for the formation of a contract. This would avoid the problems of proof; the question becomes how a (reasonable) observer would interpret the parties' intentions based on what they said and did, rather that on what the parties intended their words and actions to communicate. And—if this is seen as a virtue—an objective test is more likely to find a contract than no contract. One risk of a subjective test is that a misunderstanding between the parties— however unreasonable on the part of either of the parties—will prevent the formation of a contract. An interest in upholding contracts is therefore furthered by an objective test. However, an objective approach appears to risk the court constructing a contract for the parties—and that is not (one might think) what contract is about. If the aim of the law of contract is to facilitate the parties' own creation of legally enforceable obligations—their own 'local law'—then for the court to impose on them a contract which they did not intend is to frustrate this aim. The very fact that an objective test is employed carries this risk, at least to some extent; but to what extent depends on how the 'objective test' is formulated.

A wholly objective test would ignore the subjective intentions of the parties altogether, and simply ask whether a detached observer, with access to all information that such an observer might know, would conclude that the parties have agreed on the same terms. This would involve a consideration of the communications between the parties and their conduct, and anything else that an external observer might be able to draw upon to interpret the communications and conduct. But it would ignore how each party intended his communications or conduct to be interpreted, and how each party in fact understood the other. It could even in theory result in a contract which neither party intended. There has been some support for this approach in English law. We shall see that it is the approach generally adopted by the courts in interpreting a written contract.[8] That, however, raises different issues. In such a case the court is faced with a document which both parties have agreed constitutes their contract; and as long as there is no challenge to the validity of the document itself, and the only question is how to interpret and give effect to its language, it is seen as quite natural to the courts that they should use an objective test. Just as the courts interpret the text of an Act of Parliament objectively,[9] so they interpret the text of a contract objectively. It is the responsibility of the draftsman of a contract, as much as the draftsman of a statutory text, to ensure that the language properly conveys the intended meaning.

---

[7] Below, section III.
[8] Below, pp 207–10.
[9] Above, pp 28–29.

Where, however, the question is how to determine whether the parties have come to a sufficient agreement by means of their communications during the negotiations, it is not evident that such an external, wholly objective analysis is appropriate. The communications, whether oral or in writing, made face-to-face or at a distance, are made between the parties themselves as they are trying to come to an agreement. The more natural perspective for the interpretation of the language would therefore be the position of the parties themselves. Some writers[10] and judges have preferred to use a wholly objective test even in this situation. The strongest judicial proponent was Lord Denning, who said:

> [O]nce a contract has been made, that is to say, once the parties, whatever their inmost states of mind, have to all outward appearances agreed with sufficient certainty in the same terms on the same subject matter, then the contract is good unless and until it is set aside for failure of some condition on which the existence of the contract depends, or for fraud, or on some equitable ground.[11]

Lord Denning also rejected the rules of offer and acceptance as the appropriate test in order to find a contract,[12] instead preferring a broad test based on the objective interpretation by the court of all the evidence in order to decide whether there is an agreement:

> The better way is to look at all the documents passing between the parties—and glean from them, or from the conduct of the parties, whether they have reached agreement on all material points.[13]

But this is not the approach generally used by the cases in English law.[14] Rather, we shall see that the courts adopt an objective test which asks how a reasonable person, *placed in the position of the parties themselves*, would have interpreted their communications; but that the subjective understandings of the parties are not wholly excluded.

---

[10] W Howarth, 'The Meaning of Objectivity in Contract' (1984) 100 LQR 265, criticised by JP Vorster, 'A Comment on the Meaning of Objectivity in Contract' (1987) 104 LQR 274; reply by Howarth at (1987) 103 LQR 527.

[11] *Solle v Butcher* [1950] 1 KB 671 (CA) 691 (Denning LJ); see also *Frederick E Rose (London) Ltd v William H Pim Jnr & Co Ltd* [1953] 2 QB 450 (CA) 460; *Oscar Chess Ltd v Williams* [1957] 1 WLR 370 (CA) 373–74. The actual decision in *Solle v Butcher* (on common mistake) was departed from by CA in *Great Peace Shipping Ltd v Tsavliris Salvage (International) Ltd (The Great Peace)* [2002] EWCA Civ 1407, [2003] QB 679, below, pp 175–76.

[12] Below, p 107.

[13] *Butler Machine Tool Co Ltd v Ex-Cell-O Corporation (England) Ltd* [1979] 1 WLR 401 (CA) 404. Lord Denning repeated this in *Gibson v Manchester City Council* [1978] 1 WLR 520 (CA) 523–24, but it was rejected by HL: [1979] 1 WLR 294 (HL) 296–97 (Lord Diplock); below, p 108.

[14] The High Court of Australia has followed the wholly objective approach of Lord Denning in the case of a formal written contract, although the court 'left to another day' the question whether it should properly be accepted as applying in the case of an informal contract: *Taylor v Johnson* (1982–1983) 151 CLR 422, 430–31. In American law the interpretation of an offer is (as in England) not wholly objective but depends on the reasonable perspective of the offeree: EA Farnsworth, Contracts, 4th edn (New York, Aspen, 2006) paras 3.10, 3.13.

4. The 'Objective' Test in English Law

In *Centrovincial Estates plc v Merchant Investors Assurance Co* Slade LJ made clear that the interpretation of communications between the parties is tested objectively, but from the position of the parties:

> It is a well-established principle of the English law of contract that an offer falls to be interpreted not subjectively by reference to what has actually passed through the mind of the offeror, but objectively, by reference to the interpretation which a reasonable man in the shoes of the offeree would place on the offer.[15]

Later in this chapter we shall see the significance of the analysis of the agreement through 'offer' and 'acceptance'. But Slade LJ's statement makes clear that, in determining whether the offer and acceptance have formed an 'agreement' and therefore a contract, what a party is in law to be taken as intending is what a reasonable person in the position of the other party—the recipient of his communication—would interpret him to have intended, rather than what he in fact intended.

This approach can be traced back to the nineteenth century. In *Smith v Hughes* Blackburn J said:

> [I]f one of the parties intends to make a contract on one set of terms, and the other intends to make a contract on another set of terms, or, as it is sometimes expressed, if the parties are not ad idem, there is no contract, unless the circumstances are such as to preclude one of the parties from denying that he has agreed to the terms of the other. The rule of law is that stated in *Freeman v. Cooke*.[16] If, whatever a man's real intention may be, he so conducts himself that a reasonable man would believe that he was assenting to the terms proposed by the other party, and that other party upon that belief enters into the contract with him, the man thus conducting himself would be equally bound as if he had intended to agree to the other party's terms.[17]

This statement deserves to be read very carefully, because it says a good deal about the approach to the formation of a contract in English law.

In the first place, Blackburn J appeared to assume that his test is to be invoked only if the parties are not, in fact, in agreement about the terms of the contract—that is, he would first ask whether the parties were subjectively in agreement about the terms, and (if so) he would presumably simply give effect to that agreement. And this is a sensible starting-point. If the parties in fact understood each other, even though an external observer would have interpreted their intentions differently, that should still lead to a contract on

---

[15] [1983] Com LR 158 (CA) 158. See also *RTS Flexible Systems Ltd v Molkerei Alois Müller GmbH & Co KG* [2010] UKSC 14, [2010] 1 WLR 753 [45], [86], [87].
[16] (1848) 2 Exch 654 at 663, 154 ER 652 at 656; below, n 18.
[17] (1871) LR 6 QB 597, 607.

the (subjectively) agreed terms. The need for the objective test arises where one party is seeking to deny being bound on the basis that he did not in fact agree with the other party. To override a subjective agreement by an external objective interpretation of the communications involves the imposition of a different contract on both parties.

But if there is in fact no subjective agreement between the parties, Blackburn J made clear that one party can be held to the terms intended by the other party, where 'the circumstances are such as to preclude one of the parties from denying that he has agreed to the terms of the other'. And those 'circumstances' are where the first party 'so conducts himself that a reasonable man would believe that he was assenting to the terms proposed by the other party, and that other party upon that belief enters into the contract with him'—that is, he intends one set of terms, but conducts himself in his dealings with the other party in such a way that the latter reasonably misunderstands him. This test prevents one party from insisting on his own subjective terms (or on their being no contract at all) where he has acted in such a way as to mislead the other party about his intentions. In *Smith v Hughes* Hannen J made the same point:

> It is essential to the creation of a contract that both parties should agree to the same thing in the same sense ... But one of the parties to an apparent contract may, by his own fault, be precluded from setting up that he had entered into it in a different sense to that in which it was understood by the other party.[18]

It is important to note, however, that this test allows the party whose understanding of the terms prevails to insist on the contract only where he in fact believed that this was what the other intended: '*upon that belief* enters into the contract with him'. If he knew that the other party was not expressing his real intentions, he cannot hold him to the objectively expressed intentions.

In substance the same approach—the same version of the 'objective test'—was used by the House of Lords in *The Hannah Blumenthal*.[19] Lord Diplock made clear that the notion of 'agreement' in English law is objective, rather than subjective:

> To create a contract by exchange of promises between two parties where the promise of each party constitutes the consideration for the promise of the other, what is necessary is that the intention of each *as it has been communicated to and understood by the other* (even though that which has been communicated does not represent the actual state of mind of the communicator) should coincide. That is what English lawyers mean when they resort to the Latin phrase consensus ad idem and the words

---

[18] *Ibid* 609. This is reinforced by the fact that the case to which Blackburn J referred, *Freeman v Cooke*, is a case dealing with estoppel, where one party is estopped from denying that he must give effect to his statement where the person to whom it was made has relied on it.
[19] *Paal Wilson & Co A/S v Partenreederei Hannah Blumenthal* (*The Hannah Blumenthal*) [1983] 1 AC 854 (HL).

that I have italicised are essential to the concept of consensus ad idem, the lack of which prevents the formation of a binding contract in English law.[20]

Lord Brightman also emphasised that the test is not wholly objective—it depends on the party who seeks to rely on the contract being able to show that he in fact (subjectively) so understood it:

> The test in my opinion is not wholly objective ...
>
> To entitle the sellers to rely on abandonment, they must show that the buyers so conducted themselves as to entitle the sellers to assume, *and that the sellers did assume*, that the contract was agreed to be abandoned sub silentio.[21]

One should add that, if *both* parties' subjective understandings are (from their individual perspectives) reasonable but contradictory, there can be no contract. The ambiguity cannot be resolved. This shows that the approach in English law is, broadly, to prefer one party who was reasonable in his belief about the existence and terms of the contract, over the other party who was not reasonable in his own belief and whose words or conduct were the source of the first party's misunderstanding.

In summary, the test which is applied in English law in a case where there is doubt about whether the parties reached an 'agreement' and therefore a contract, can be set out in the following propositions:

1. The first question is whether the parties were in fact (subjectively) in agreement on the existence and terms of the contract. If they were, that should be determinative.
2. If the parties were not, in fact, in agreement, then—in the case where the claimant is seeking to rely on there being a contract on terms [x], and the defendant is either denying that there is a contract at all, or is asserting that there is a contract on terms [y]—the question becomes whether the claimant can in law hold the defendant to have agreed to a contract on terms [x]. He may do so if:
   (a) the defendant's words, conduct or (exceptionally) silence would have led a reasonable person in the claimant's position to believe that the defendant was agreeing to [x]; and
   (b) the claimant in fact believed that the defendant was agreeing to [x].
3. If the claimant succeeds in showing that he can hold the defendant to a contract on terms [x] in accordance with proposition 2, he has established a contract on terms [x] *unless* the defendant can rebut this by showing that the claimant's conduct, words or (exceptionally) silence would have led a reasonable person in his position to believe that the claimant was agreeing to [y], and that the defendant in fact believed that the claimant was agreeing to [y]. In such a case, there is no contract.[22]

---

[20] *Ibid* 915.
[21] *Ibid* 924. The case involved an alleged contract to abandon an arbitration.
[22] J Cartwright, *Misrepresentation, Mistake and Non-Disclosure*, 3rd edn (London, Sweet & Maxwell Ltd, 2012) para 13-19 (fns removed). See also paras 13-08 to 13-26 for a fuller discussion of the cases from which these propositions are drawn and illustrations of the application of the 'objective test'.

5. The Objective Test in Context in the English Law of Contract

The use of the 'objective test' to find the agreement in the formation of a contract is consistent with other areas of law which display similar underlying policies.

One purpose of using an objective test is to protect the party who reasonably believes what he sees and hears from the other party. Steyn LJ said:

> English law generally adopts an objective theory of contract formation. That means that in practice our law generally ignores the subjective expectations and the unexpressed mental reservations of the parties. Instead the governing criterion is the reasonable expectations of honest men.[23]

We shall see that the idea of protecting one party against the other, so as to find an enforceable contract in favour of the party who is not at fault in relation to alleged defects in its formation, is also found in various aspects of the rules relating to the vitiating factors.[24] Some of the particular rules relating to offer and acceptance are also consistent with this general approach, as we shall see in the next section of this chapter.[25]

The preference of objectivity over subjectivity can also be seen in the use of an objective approach in the interpretation of a written contract;[26] and in the identification of implied terms.[27] And the rejection of subjectivity gives a greatly reduced place for doctrines of mistake in English law: a subjective theory of agreement would give a wide scope for a mistake to negative the formation of a contract, but English law is very reluctant to allow a contract to be void for mistake.[28]

II. The Mechanisms of Contract Formation: The Rules of Offer and Acceptance

1. 'Offer and Acceptance' as a *Rule*

Since an agreement is based on the communicated (shared) intentions of the parties,[29] it is natural to analyse the formation of a contract through an

---

[23] *G Percy Trentham Ltd v Archital Luxfer Ltd* [1993] 1 Lloyd's Rep 25 (CA) 27.
[24] Below, ch 7; see esp pp 159–60.
[25] Below, pp 113, 118–19.
[26] Below, p 207.
[27] Below, p 210.
[28] Below, p 159.
[29] Above, p 95.

analysis of the communications which passed between the parties. Legal systems commonly look for an 'offer' made by one party, followed by an 'acceptance' of the offer by the other party. An unqualified acceptance of an offer shows an agreement between the parties—which is what we are looking for in a contract. An initial question is whether the 'offer and acceptance' analysis is simply a convenient method of establishing the agreement—one tool in the lawyer's toolbox of analysis in the formation of a contract. Or is it more than just a tool: a *rule* that the only way in which a contract can be sufficiently established in law is if the formation of the parties' agreement can be analysed through the acceptance by one party of an offer made by the other. The English courts have explored this and have come down decisively in favour of regarding 'offer and acceptance' as normally a rule.

(a) Problems and Benefits of the 'Offer and Acceptance' Analysis

One problem with a strict analysis of the formation through 'offer and acceptance' is that it is often very artificial. Many day-to-day contracts can be analysed in this way only if we impute to the parties the intention to make an offer. It is not difficult to see that an agreement has been formed between the customer and the supermarket when the customer has passed through the check-out or between the passenger and the bus company when the passenger has boarded the bus and paid his fare, but it is not self-evident that the parties would themselves have identified their transaction as being formed by the offer by one party being accepted by the other—nor, indeed, which of them was making the offer and which was accepting it. Where an agreement is reached at the end of negotiations between the parties, one of the parties may make a firm proposal to the other to settle their differences in a particular way, and if the other party assents to that, he might say that he is accepting the offer. But even in the case of a negotiated commercial contract it is by no means always as simple as this to find an explicit offer and an acceptance. The difficult of such an analysis was noted by Lord Wilberforce:

> It is only the precise analysis of this complex of relations into the classical offer and acceptance, with identifiable consideration, that seems to present difficulty, but this same difficulty exists in many situations of daily life, e.g., sales at auction; supermarket purchases; boarding an omnibus; purchasing a train ticket; tenders for the supply of goods; offers of rewards; acceptance by post; warranties of authority by agents; manufacturers' guarantees; gratuitous bailments; bankers' commercial credits. These are all examples which show that English law, having committed itself to a rather technical and schematic doctrine of contract, in application takes a practical approach, often at the cost of forcing the facts to fit uneasily into the marked slots of offer, acceptance and consideration.[30]

---

[30] *New Zealand Shipping Co Ltd v AM Satterthwaite & Co Ltd* [1975] AC 154 (PC) 167.

It must also be added that there are cases in which an 'offer and acceptance' analysis may become fictitious to the point of being impossible, if the law is to accept that there can be a contract between parties who never communicated with each other either directly or through their agents. For example, it has been held that the relationship between members of a club is governed by contract on the terms of the club's rules—and so there is a multi-party contract, or even a web of separate contracts between each of the members of the club, based on each party's expression of willingness to be bound by the rules on joining the club. But it can be so artificial to try to establish any offer and acceptance between each of the parties that the courts have simply ignored it. In holding that there was a contract between the participants in a yacht race, Lord Herschell said:

> I cannot entertain any doubt that there was a contractual relation between the parties to this litigation. The effect of their entering for the race, and undertaking to be bound by these rules to the knowledge of each other, is sufficient, I think, where those rules indicate a liability on the part of the one to the other, to create a contractual obligation to discharge that liability.[31]

However, there are certain advantages in using a formal analysis of the formation of the contract. It may be that the law has to take a position on what constitutes the offer and the acceptance in certain typical situations—such as contracts formed through answering newspaper advertisements; in supermarkets; at auctions; and following invitations to tender. The decision on the detail of such an analysis (where is the offer? and what is sufficient to constitute acceptance?) might be rather arbitrary, and not reflective of how the parties themselves would have thought of it—but at least having a clear rule for such cases facilitates the analysis. It provides a greater certainty for parties who know the rules, or have legal advice, and who wish to arrange their transactions so as to have control over when they become contractually bound: it allows them to plan in the knowledge of how their communications will be interpreted by a court. And having a clear set of rules also assists the parties who negotiate a dispute about the formation of their contract to be able to predict the court's approach to the analysis and therefore encourages out-of-court settlements. As long as the rules which the courts devise for what constitutes an 'offer' and an 'acceptance' do not run directly contrary to the parties' own expectations, then the price of assisting those who know the rules, and

---

[31] *Clarke v Earl of Dunraven (The Satanita)* [1897] AC 59 (HL) 63. It is well established that the relationship between members of an unincorporated association, such as a members' club, can be governed by contract: *Re Recher's Will Trusts* [1972] Ch 526 (Ch) 538–39 (Brightman J). The relationship between a company and its members (shareholders, in the case of a company with a share capital) is based on a statutory contract—the provisions of the company's constitution bind them to the same extent as if there were covenants on the part of the company and of each member to observe them: Companies Act 2006 s 33.

can plan accordingly, may be acceptable. It will doubtless be so in commercial cases, where the courts regularly emphasise the importance of providing clear and certain rules to facilitate trade[32]—although the problem here is that the emphasis on commercial certainty, and the assumption that parties know the rules or have legal advice, may play too significant a part in the rules given that the law needs also to cover non-commercial contracts.

It can be very useful—particularly, but not exclusively, in commercial contexts—to have an overriding rule that there must generally be an offer and an acceptance before a contract can be formed, together with a clear set of rules about what constitutes an offer and an acceptance. Put simply, if a contract is formed by offer and acceptance, then identifying the acceptance is fundamental because that shows a range of things:

(i) that there is a contract—the most obvious issue;
(ii) who the parties are to the contract—those between whom the offer and the acceptance take effect;[33]
(iii) the express terms of the contract—since these will be contained or referred to in the offer which was accepted;[34]
(iv) the time at which the contract comes into being—the time at which in law the acceptance takes effect;[35]
(v) the place at which the contract comes into being—the place at which in law the acceptance takes effect.[36]

It should not, however, be assumed that the rules which the courts have devised are simply arbitrary—certainty for certainty's sake. Rather, they are often based on assumptions about how particular transactions are (or should) normally be effected, and which party needs to be protected. They also often allow for the parties to vary them—and so the particular 'rules' of offer and acceptance are generally default rules as to how the courts will interpret the communications between the parties in the absence of contrary indications, rather than mandatory rules. The detail of the particular rules will be considered later in this chapter.

---

[32] Eg *Tekdata Interconnections Ltd v Amphenol Ltd* [2009] EWCA Civ 1209, [2010] 1 Lloyd's Rep 357, [25] (Dyson LJ); below, n 104.

[33] This can be relevant not only for deciding who is a party as opposed to who is a third party (below, ch 10), but also sometimes for deciding whether there is a contract at all, if the intended offeree is not the person who actually accepted it—as in cases of mistaken identity: below, p 168.

[34] For further discussion of how the courts ascertain the terms of a contract see below, ch 8.

[35] This can be relevant for many reasons, eg if there is a time period built into the contractual obligations, and so the date of commencement becomes critical; or if the contract is one pursuant to which the risk passes at the moment of the contract (eg with the passing of title on sale) and so the question is which party runs the risk of loss, and so should insure.

[36] Typically for questions of jurisdiction in relation to contractual disputes; see eg *Brinkibon Ltd v Stahag Stahl und Stahlwarenhandelsgesellschaft mbH* [1983] 2 AC 34 (HL).

(b) Rejection of the 'Offer and Acceptance' Analysis by Lord Denning

Lord Denning was a particular critic of the traditional approach which requires the acceptance of an offer before a contract can be found. He said this explicitly in *Butler Machine Tool Co Ltd v Ex-Cell-O Corporation (England) Ltd*:

> In many of these cases our traditional analysis of offer, counter-offer, rejection, acceptance and so forth is out of date. This was observed by Lord Wilberforce in *New Zealand Shipping Co. Ltd. v. A. M. Satterthwaite & Co. Ltd.*[37] The better way is to look at all the documents passing between the parties—and glean from them, or from the conduct of the parties, whether they have reached agreement on all material points.[38]

This case involved a particular problem of a 'battle of forms'—that is, where each party was seeking to obtain a contract on the basis of its own standard terms of business.[39] In that case, all members of the Court of Appeal came to the same conclusion—that a contract was concluded on the buyer's terms, and therefore did not include a clause which was in the seller's standard form and which in the circumstances would have allowed a price increase. The majority came to this conclusion by an application of the traditional approach, identifying the offer and the acceptance on the facts of the case. But Lord Denning—who would also have come to the same conclusion if he had applied the 'traditional analysis'—preferred to use the more general test of looking for the agreement of the parties based on all the evidence of the documents passing between them, and their conduct.

Although the result of the two tests—the 'traditional analysis' and Lord Denning's broader approach—gave the same result in the *Butler* case, it certainly need not do so. Lord Denning preferred a more external, objective analysis. Under his test, the existence and terms of the contract are to be deduced from the judge's view of the documents, words and conduct of the parties. And we have already seen that a potential problem of the external objective test is that it can impose on the parties a different contract from that which either of them intended.[40]

(c) Insistence on the 'Offer and Acceptance' Analysis by the House of Lords

The broader approach was later applied by Lord Denning again in *Gibson v Manchester City Council*[41]—a quite different case, in which the question was

---

[37] [1975] AC 154, 167 (above, n 30).
[38] [1979] 1 WLR 401 (CA) 404.
[39] For difficulties created by battles of forms, see below, p 120.
[40] Above, p 98.
[41] [1978] 1 WLR 520 (CA). *Butler* was decided in April 1977 but not reported until 1979, alongside the decision of the House of Lords in *Gibson*: below, n 44.

whether the Council was contractually bound to sell to Mr Gibson the house in which he was living as a tenant, where it had sent him a letter stating that it 'may be prepared to sell' the house, and he had filled in a 'formal application to buy' it. On these facts, there was no sufficient offer and acceptance. But Lord Denning looked at other facts—such as that the Council had placed the house on its list of owner-occupied houses, and that Mr Gibson began to spend money on improvements—to show that both parties in fact agreed that the sale was going ahead.[42] On this occasion a second member of the Court, Ormrod LJ, agreed with this broader approach, although he was also able to reach the same conclusion by interpreting the Council's letter as an offer.[43] The third member, Geoffrey Lane LJ dissented on the basis that there was no offer and acceptance.

In the House of Lords, Geoffrey Lane LJ's approach was preferred. Lord Diplock, giving the leading speech, rejected Lord Denning's alternative broader test and insisted on the traditional 'offer and acceptance' analysis as the normal rule:

> My Lords, there may be certain types of contract, though I think they are exceptional, which do not fit easily into the normal analysis of a contract as being constituted by offer and acceptance; but a contract alleged to have been made by an exchange of correspondence between the parties in which the successive communications other than the first are in reply to one another, is not one of these. I can see no reason in the instant case for departing from the conventional approach of looking at the handful of documents relied upon as constituting the contract sued upon and seeing whether upon their true construction there is to be found in them a contractual offer by the corporation to sell the house to Mr. Gibson and an acceptance of that offer by Mr. Gibson. I venture to think that it was by departing from this conventional approach that the majority of the Court of Appeal was led into error.[44]

This makes clear that, apart from 'exceptional' cases, a contract can be found only if there is an acceptance of an offer. 'Offer and acceptance' is therefore a rule, and not simply a convenient tool by which a court can find the agreement necessary for a validly formed contract. Lord Diplock did not make clear what might count as an exceptional case; but he did make clear that a contract formed between two parties negotiating by correspondence is *not* an exceptional case. At least in such cases formation of the contract necessarily requires the acceptance by one party of an offer by the other. Presumably cases such as multipartite agreements (members clubs and so on) will be exceptional cases—they are cases where the courts have in any event not sought to squeeze the facts into finding an offer and an acceptance.[45]

---

[42] *Ibid* 524.
[43] *Ibid* 527 ('may be prepared to sell' to be read as 'are prepared to sell').
[44] [1979] 1 WLR 294 (HL) 297.
[45] *Clarke v Earl of Dunraven (The Satanita)* above, n 31.

(d) 'Offer and Acceptance' is Normally a Rule

The highest authority on this issue is the decision of the House of Lords in *Gibson v Manchester City Council*; and since the House decided that on the facts there was no contract *for the reason that* there was no offer and acceptance, the proposition by Lord Diplock quoted above can be identified as part of the *ratio* of the case.[46]

The idea of elevating the practice of offer and acceptance into a general rule requiring that there be offer and acceptance, as well as developing particular rules as to what constitutes an offer and an acceptance, is not strange to the English lawyer. Since English law derives common law rules from the cases, rather than starting from a broad, general principle,[47] there is inevitably a focus on the cases, and their particular facts, in order to deduce why in a particular earlier case there was (or was not) a contract, so as to apply that reasoning in factually similar cases. The repetition of fact-types in the case-law has a tendency to crystallise into particular rules for similar facts. Added to the tendency of the common law courts to favour rules which further the policy of certainty in contracting,[48] this development of rules is what one might expect of the English judges.

2. The Particular Rules of 'Offer and Acceptance'

In many cases over the years the courts have discussed what constitutes an offer and an acceptance. There are now well-established rules about many typical situations in which contracts are formed. However, new situations can still arise—for example, contracts can be formed through the use of new technologies—and so the courts need to be able to develop the existing rules to cover new cases.

Much of what follows in this section will be familiar to the lawyer trained in another legal system, since most systems have to respond to similar types of problem, and to answer similar questions—such as how a contract is formed in a supermarket or following a public advertisement; when a contract is formed where the parties communicate by post or through other long-distance methods; whether an offeror is free to revoke his offer; and whether silence can constitute acceptance. But the particular answers to these questions which are given by the English courts may well differ from those which are familiar to the civil lawyer, not only because they are regarded as rules, based on precedents in the cases which are to be followed in future

---

[46] Above, p 22.
[47] Above, p 16.
[48] Above, p 69.

cases, but also because the particular rules will often be based on a particular analysis of the nature of a contract, or the policies underlying the contract and its formation, in the view of the English courts. A brief account of some of the particular rules of offer and acceptance, and the reasons given by the courts for their adoption, will therefore be given here.

(a) Offer

Although there is no established definition of an 'offer', the cases in general show that an offer is an expression of willingness by the person making it— the offeror—to enter into a contract on the terms set out in it. For there to be an 'offer' there must therefore be a proposition which is sufficiently full and clear that it could become a contract simply by being accepted,[49] and it must be made in circumstances where the person to whom it is addressed— the offeree[50]—is entitled to take it as capable of giving rise to a contract by his simple acceptance. We have already seen that the offeror's intention, and the terms of the proposal he is to be taken as making, are tested objectively from the perspective of the offeree.[51]

Preliminary discussions and proposals to enter into negotiations are not offers, but are often called 'invitations to treat'. In a range of particular types of case the courts have drawn the distinction between offers and invitations to treat. For example, they have held that newspaper advertisements,[52] displays in shop windows[53] and on supermarket shelves,[54] the announcement of items for sale at an auction[55] and invitations to submit tenders[56] are normally

---

[49] On the minimum content of a contract and the rules of certainty, see below, pp 122–24.

[50] There may be more than one person to whom the offer is addressed; and there can even be an offer to an indeterminate number of persons, such as a general offer to the public: *Carlill v Carbolic Smoke Ball Co*, below, n 64.

[51] Above, pp 100–02.

[52] *Partridge v Crittenden* [1968] 1 WLR 1204 (QB).

[53] *Timothy v Simpson* (1834) 6 C & P 499, 172 ER 1337 (shopkeeper entitled to refuse to sell at marked price; customer who refuses to leave then becomes a trespasser); *Fisher v Bell* [1961] 1 WLR 394 (DC). In the modern law there may be other limitations on the shopkeeper's freedom to refuse to deal with the customer who offers the marked price: eg Equality Act 2010 prohibits discrimination on the basis of a range of protected characteristics (age, disability, gender reassignment, marriage and civil partnership, pregnancy and maternity, race, religion or belief, sex and sexual orientation); and Consumer Protection from Unfair Trading Regulations 2008 SI 2008/1277 (implementing Directive 2005/29/EC) prohibits unfair commercial practices, and provides for criminal sanctions.

[54] *Pharmaceutical Society of Great Britain v Boots Cash Chemists (Southern) Ltd* [1953] 1 QB 401 (CA).

[55] *British Car Auctions Ltd v Wright* [1972] 1 WLR 1519 (QB).

[56] *Spencer v Harding* (1870) LR 5 CP 561.

only invitations to treat. The reasons for developing the rule that there is normally no offer in such circumstances are commonly that it is a 'sensible' or 'commercial' view of the nature of such communications—and so, in effect, the recipient is not normally entitled to take such communications as being sufficiently definite and serious to be an offer rather than simply an invitation to negotiate. For example, Lord Parker CJ said in *Partridge v Crittenden*:

> [W]hen one is dealing with advertisements and circulars, unless they indeed come from manufacturers, there is business sense in their being construed as invitations to treat and not offers for sale. In a very different context in *Grainger & Son v Gough*[57] Lord Herschell said dealing with a price-list:[58]
>
> 'The transmission of such a price-list does not amount to an offer to supply an unlimited quantity of the wine described at the price named, so that as soon as an order is given there is a binding contract to supply that quantity. If it were so, the merchant might find himself involved in any number of contractual obligations to supply wine of a particular description which he would be quite unable to carry out, his stock of wine of that description being necessarily limited'.
>
> It seems to me accordingly that not only is it the law but common sense supports it.[59]

And in *Pharmaceutical Society of Great Britain v Boots Cash Chemists (Southern) Ltd* Lord Goddard CJ said:

> Ordinary principles of common sense and of commerce must be applied in this matter, and to hold that in the case of self-service shops the exposure of an article is an offer to sell, and that a person can accept the offer by picking up the article, would be contrary to those principles and might entail serious results. On the customer picking up the article the property would forthwith pass to him and he would be able to insist upon the shopkeeper allowing him to take it away, though in some particular cases the shopkeeper might think that very undesirable. On the other hand, if a customer had picked up an article, he would never be able to change his mind and to put it back; the shopkeeper could say, 'Oh no, the property has passed and you must pay the price.'[60]

This case involved a new situation—a self-service shop—and the court had to decide whether the display of goods in such a context is different from any other shop display. Lord Goddard held that there was no difference—and therefore the case stands as authority for a new rule, or for a widening of the existing rule relating to shop displays:

> It seems to me, therefore, that the transaction is in no way different from the normal transaction in a shop in which there is no self-service scheme. I am quite satisfied it

---

[57] [1896] AC 325 (HL) (whether foreign merchant is exercising trade in UK for tax purposes).
[58] *Ibid* 334.
[59] Above, n 52, 1209–10.
[60] [1952] 2 QB 795 (QB) 802; Lord Goddard was sitting as the trial judge. In CA (above, n 54) all three judges agreed with Lord Goddard's reasoning.

would be wrong to say that the shopkeeper is making an offer to sell every article in the shop to any person who might come in and that that person can insist on buying any article by saying 'I accept your offer.' I agree with the illustration put forward during the case of a person who might go into a shop where books are displayed. In most bookshops customers are invited to go in and pick up books and look at them even if they do not actually buy them. There is no contract by the shopkeeper to sell until the customer has taken the book to the shopkeeper or his assistant and said 'I want to buy this book' and the shopkeeper says 'Yes.'[61]

That was a response to what was then a relatively new form of shop display. It would equally be open for the courts to develop this further in the context of new styles of shop—for example, they may be called upon to decide whether the customer's request for meat to be cut at the delicatessen counter in a supermarket is in fact an offer and acceptance there rather than (for the rest of the shopping in the basket) at the check-out (is it really possible for the customer to change his mind once he has been given the cut meat?); or whether the growing use of 'scanning' of products by customers either as they proceed around the supermarket or at an unmanned check-out is different (probably not: as long as there is the facility to 'un-scan' products during their shopping; and the scanner at the check-out may be just a mechanical equivalent of the cashier?). As new situations arise, the courts will develop new rules based on a consideration of analogous cases on which they have already ruled. This is the way in which the common law develops.[62]

It is important to realise that the rules which have been developed are only *default* rules. They are based on standard types of situation where standard solutions have been adopted based either on the approach which parties would normally expect to be taken to the question of whether a communication is an offer, or on the approach which the courts decide that the parties should normally expect in those circumstances, often taking such a decision based on what they perceive to be commercially sensible grounds. But the interpretation of the communication as either an offer or an invitation to treat should in the last analysis be based on how its recipient does and reasonably should interpret it. So a negotiating party can always make clear that he is only putting forward a proposal for negotiation, and that it is not an offer, even if it might otherwise be thought to be an offer.[63] Or (conversely) he may make clear that he is going beyond an invitation to treat and is in fact making an offer in a context where the communication might otherwise be covered by the default rule in favour of it being only an invitation to treat—for example, a newspaper advertisement offering a reward may make clear that the finder will be entitled to the reward;[64] or an invitation to submit tenders may

---

[61] *Ibid* 802.
[62] Above, p 42.
[63] Eg he may label it 'subject to contract': above, p 79.
[64] *Carlill v Carbolic Smoke Ball Co* [1893] 1 QB 256 (CA) (£100 to be paid to anyone catching influenza after using defendant's 'smoke ball'; advertisement stated that £1000 had been

make clear that the tender which best satisfies some objectively ascertainable criteria will be accepted.[65]

(b) Termination of Offer by the Offeror or the Offeree

Unless the offeror has bound himself by contract to maintain the offer for a particular period—for example, by granting the offeree an 'option' to enter into the contract[66]—he is free to withdraw it at any time until the moment when it is accepted, even if the offer was expressed to be open for a particular period of time.[67] We have already seen that negotiating parties do not owe each other general duties (such as a duty to negotiate in good faith), and that the party who withdraws an offer even at a very late stage in the negotiations does not incur liability unless there is some other ground for it, such as a misrepresentation giving rise to a claim in tort.[68] On the other hand, an offer may lapse by its own terms, such as where it contains a time-limit for acceptance. And the courts have held that in the absence of express provision, an offer will contain an implied provision that it will lapse if it is not accepted within a reasonable time.[69]

However until he receives *actual* notice of the offeror's decision to withdraw, the offeree is entitled to believe that the offer is still open, and therefore to accept it.[70] This is what one would expect, given the objective approach of the English law of contract. Having been led reasonably to believe that there is an offer available to be accepted, and there being nothing in the language of the offer which contradicts that belief, the offeree is entitled to act on it by acceptance unless and until he hears that it has been withdrawn. So the offeror's change of mind, or a failed attempt to communicate his change of mind—at least if it is not the fault of the offeree that he fails to receive the information[71]—is not sufficient to prevent the offeree from taking steps to finalise the contract by accepting the offer. On the other hand, once the offeree in fact knows of the offeror's decision to withdraw he can no longer

---

deposited in a bank 'shewing our sincerity in the matter': this was an offer to pay. 'It was intended to be issued to the public and to be read by the public. How would an ordinary person reading this document construe it?': Bowen LJ at 266).

[65] *Spencer v Harding*, above, n 56, 563; *Harvela Investments Ltd v Royal Trust Company of Canada (CI) Ltd* [1986] AC 207 (HL).

[66] Above, p 86. The option must be either executed as a deed, or supported by consideration: below, ch 6. An offer of a 'unilateral contract' may be irrevocable by the offeror once the offeree has begun to perform in accordance with the offeror's request: above, p 91.

[67] *Routledge v Grant* (1828) 4 Bing 653, 130 ER 920.

[68] Above, ch 4.

[69] *Ramsgate Victoria Hotel Co Ltd v Montefiore* (1866) 1 LR 1 Exch 109.

[70] *Byrne & Co v Van Tienhoven & Co* (1880) 5 CPD 344.

[71] On the relevance of fault as reversing the normal position in such cases, see below, p 119.

accept the offer—and again this is consistent with the general objective test for the formation of a contract which allows a party to insist on a contract, or on particular terms of the contract, only if he in fact believed that the other party was so agreeing.[72]

It has been held that it is sufficient if the offeree knows from a third-party source about the offeror's withdrawal—such as where the offer is for the sale of property and the offeree discovers that the offeror has in the mean time sold it to someone else.[73] Whether such third-party information is sufficiently reliable to lead the offeree reasonably to believe that there is no longer an offer to be accepted will depend on the facts, including the reliability of the third party who provides the information. Similarly, although the authorities are not clear on this question, it is likely that an offeree can still accept an offer after the death of the offeror (and so create a contract which must be fulfilled by the offeror's personal representatives after his death) unless he knows about the death, and as long as there is nothing in the terms of the offer that indicates that it is personal to the offeror.

On the other hand, if the offeree rejects the offer, it is gone for good. This is the case with a simple rejection—and so the offeree who later regrets his rejection must himself make a new offer if he wishes to resurrect the rejected proposal: he cannot simply withdraw his rejection and accept the original offer. It is also the case with a *counter-offer*—a response to the offer which fails to constitute an unequivocal acceptance of it, but which in turn puts new (or varied) proposals to the offeree which are capable of being themselves accepted.[74] There is no mixing of the terms of the old offer and the new (counter-)offer; the counter-offer becomes in all respects the offer which is open for acceptance and the old offer has been irrevocably terminated.

(c) Acceptance

It follows from what has been said already that an acceptance is the offeree's unequivocal assent to the offer with a view to concluding the contract. If it is not clear and unequivocal but, say, contains new terms or otherwise varies the deal, it is not an acceptance, but a counter-offer.

Anything that shows to the offeror the offeree's unequivocal assent is sufficient: it can be by words or conduct, including starting to perform the

---

[72] Above, p 101.

[73] *Dickinson v Dodds* [1876] 2 ChD 463 (CA). There are suggestions in this case that the mere sale of the property to a third party would be sufficient to revoke the offer even if the offeree had not yet discovered it; but this is contrary to principle and inconsistent with *Byrne & Co v Van Tienhoven & Co*, above, n 70.

[74] *Hyde v Wrench* (1840) 3 Beav 334, 49 ER 132. If the offeree does not reject the offer but merely makes an enquiry about its terms or the offeror's willingness to discuss aspects of it, the offer remains open: *Stevenson, Jaques & Co v McLean* (1880) 5 QBD 346 (QB).

contract in circumstances where the offeror can reasonably infer that it is on the basis of the proposed terms. Indeed, there are situations in which the courts can infer from the mutual dealings between the parties that they have agreed to enter into a contract—and such conduct can form both the offer (by one party) and the acceptance (by the other) to the contract, as long as the terms of the contract are sufficiently ascertainable.[75] But the courts will not generally infer acceptance from silence, nor from words or conduct of the offeree which are not communicated to the offeror. This follows from the general approach to contract formation: before there is an agreement sufficient to form a contract there must be some communication between the parties and each must be in a position reasonably to understand the other's intentions. There are well-established situations in which the courts are willing to hold that an offeree has accepted an offer where he has done something at the request of the offeror and the offeror has expressly or impliedly dispensed him from the additional requirement to communicate his acceptance.[76] But where there is neither an overt act as requested by the offeror nor any actual communication, it is a different matter:

> [S]ilence and inaction are of their nature equivocal, for the simple reason that there can be more than one reason why the person concerned has been silent and inactive.[77]

Unless, therefore, the silence can in context communicate meaning sufficiently clearly to the other party, it cannot be treated as part of the communications by which their agreement was formed. Even if the offeror expressly invites the offeree to accept by silence, the offeree's silence is not sufficient. In *Felthouse v Bindley*[78] negotiations for the sale of a horse by a nephew in favour of his uncle ended by the uncle offering a price mid-way between their respective proposals and saying, 'If I hear no more about him, I consider the horse is mine at £30 15s.' The nephew decided to proceed with the sale, and told the auctioneer who was about to sell it for him. But it was held that there was no contract between the nephew and the uncle:

> [T]he nephew in his own mind intended his uncle to have the horse at the price which he (the uncle) had named—£30 15s.: but he had not communicated such his intention to his uncle, or done anything to bind himself.[79]

---

[75] *Brogden v Metropolitan Railway Co* (1876) 2 App Cas 666 (both parties began to act on basis of unexecuted (but, in its terms, finalised) draft).

[76] *Carlill v Carbolic Smoke Ball Co* above, n 64 (offer implied that satisfaction of conditions—by buying and using the smoke ball and catching influenza—was sufficient to give rise to the right to receive payment without separate notification of acceptance of the offer). This is an example of a 'unilateral contract', above, p 91.

[77] *Allied Marine Transport Ltd v Vale do Rio Doce Navagacao SA (The Leonidas D)* [1985] 1WLR 925 (CA) 941 (Robert Goff LJ).

[78] (1862) 11 CB NS 869, 142 ER 1037.

[79] *Ibid* 876, 1040. The auctioneer by mistake included the horse in the auction; the case turned on whether there was a valid contract for the uncle to buy the horse, in order to found the uncle's claim against the auctioneer for the tort of conversion of the horse.

This does not mean that silence can never operate to create a contract. In rare cases the courts have held that silence can communicate a party's intentions—indeed, that silence can even constitute both offer and acceptance. But this is in the very particular situation (and only rarely) where the claim is that the parties to an arbitration have agreed to abandon it; and it is the lengthy period of silence on both sides that can lead to an inference of an intention to abandon because silence and inactivity are contrary to the otherwise-expected activity in pursuing the arbitration.[80] Furthermore, although there is no clear case-law authority in favour of this, academic writers have suggested that where the offeror waives the requirement of communication of acceptance, then although the silence of the offeree cannot bind him to the contract, the *offeror* can nevertheless be bound. This might be put on the analogy of the cases where the courts accept that an offeror can waive communication of acceptance but require the performance of some condition;[81] or on the basis that the rule against silence constituting acceptance is designed to protect the offeree against being bound against his will if he does not take the trouble to reject the offer, but in a case where the offeree wishes to hold the offeror to the contract he can waive the benefit of that protection;[82] or perhaps on the basis of estoppel—that the offeror is estopped from denying that the offeree has properly accepted the offer when the offeree has acted in reliance on not having to communicate his acceptance.[83]

Of course the acceptance, to be valid, must in principle comply with any conditions set by the offer. The offeror can require the acceptance to be made in a particular form: only an acceptance which complies with this requirement will then be sufficient, although it is for the offeror to make this clear. If he prescribes a particular method of acceptance but does not also make clear that it is the only permissible method of acceptance, it may be held that an acceptance in fact communicated to the offeror by any other method which is no less advantageous to him will conclude the contract—for example, if a reply by return of post is required, but the offeree in fact replies by fax earlier than the post could have arrived.[84]

---

[80] Eg *André et Compagnie SA v Marine Transocean Ltd (The Splendid Sun)* [1981] QB 694 (CA). But silence did not constitute agreement in similar claims in *Paal Wilson & Co A/S v Partenreederei Hannah Blumenthal (The Hannah Blumenthal)* [1983] 1 AC 854 (HL) or *Allied Marine Transport Ltd v Vale do Rio Doce Navagacao SA (The Leonidas D)* above, n 77.

[81] CJ Miller, '*Felthouse v Bindley Revisited*' (1972) 35 MLR 489; cf *Carlill v Carbolic Smoke Ball Co* above, n 64.

[82] E Peel, *Treitel, The Law of Contract*, 14th edn (London, Sweet & Maxwell Ltd, 2015) 2–046.

[83] But this was doubted by Kerr J in *Fairline Shipping Corpn v Adamson* [1975] QB 180 (QB) 188–89.

[84] *Tinn v Hoffman & Co* (1873) 29 LT 271, 274; *Manchester Diocesan Council for Education v Commercial & General Investments Ltd* [1970] 1 WLR 241 (Ch) 246.

(d) Time and Place of Acceptance

In the absence of express provision in the offer, the courts will apply default rules to determine such questions as when and where the acceptance takes effect—and therefore when and where the contract is concluded.

The courts have had to develop ways of dealing with delays in communication, such as where the acceptance is posted. As early as 1818 it was established that, where an offer to sell goods was sent by post, the sending of the reply by the post was the moment at which the contract was formed, even though the offeror had sold the goods before he received the acceptance.[85] This was said to be a sensible rule because if there was no contract until the acceptance arrived:

> [N]o contract could ever be completed by the post. For if the defendants were not bound by their offer when accepted by the plaintiffs till the answer was received, then the plaintiffs ought not to be bound till after they had received the notification that the defendants had received their answer and assented to it. And so it might go on ad infinitum. The defendants must be considered in law as making, during every instant of the time their letter was travelling, the same identical offer to the plaintiffs; and then the contract is completed by the acceptance of it by the latter.[86]

This is commonly referred to as the 'postal rule'. However, this is rather misleading. It might suggest that it applies automatically where the postal service is used in order to send a reply; and also that it only applies where the postal service is used. Neither is true. And in the modern development of the case-law on this topic, we can see a development in the thinking behind the rule.

In the first place, the 'postal rule' might more properly be regarded as a 'postal exception'—that is, the normal rule is that an acceptance must be actually communicated; but where the parties contemplated that the offeree might use the post, then his posting of the letter of acceptance concludes the contract.[87] Moreover, it is not limited to the sending of an acceptance by post, but includes any case, such as a telegram, where the communication is made at a distance and does not take effect more or less instantaneously. But it is limited to the case where the parties had it in contemplation that such a method of acceptance might be used—or, at least, where the offeree was entitled to think that he could properly use the post to conclude the contract, and there was nothing in the terms of the offer requiring actual communication. The language of the offer must be analysed carefully to ascertain whether it requires actual communication before the contract is formed; for example,

---

[85] *Adams v Lindsell* (1818) 1 B & Ald 681, 106 ER 250.
[86] *Ibid* 683, 251.
[87] *Holwell Securities Ltd v Hughes* [1974] 1 WLR 155 (CA) 157; *Henthorn v Fraser* [1892] 2 Ch 27 (CA) 33.

it has been held where an offer required 'notice in writing' to the vendor, the posting of a letter of acceptance did not conclude a contract of sale.[88]

Where, however, the communication of the acceptance is made by a method which, though at a distance, is instantaneous, such as telephone or telex, it has been held that it normally takes effect when and where the acceptance is received.[89] This has been explained on the basis that the party who accepts in such circumstances can know whether his message has reached the other party,[90] whereas in a case of postal acceptance there is an inherent risk that the message might be lost or delayed and it is better that the offeror should bear that risk where he has led the offeree to believe that he is entitled to use the post. But the offeror can put the risk onto the offeree if he words his offer in such a way as to require actual communication of the reply. The courts have sometimes said that these rules for the timing of acceptance are based on 'convenience'.[91] It is better, however, to view them as risk allocation mechanisms to decide who should bear the risk of the failure of the communication, and rules designed to determine the circumstances in which the offeree is entitled to rely on the contract as having been formed even before the acceptance arrives, subject always to the overriding intentions of the parties—and, in particular, of the offeror who is entitled to set in his offer the rules for the creation of the contract. And so one can say that the offeree, receiving an offer by post, is entitled to rely on his posted acceptance as concluding the contract, but only if he could reasonably interpret the offer as allowing him to do so. But if he replies by an instantaneous method, then he can know whether the acceptance has been received and, having the means to check this, he can rely on the communication as having succeeded only if he has the signs that it has been received—for example, the telephone line is still active, or there is an automated signal indicating that a fax transmission has been received. However, there may be situations where he knows that although an acceptance has been received by the machine at the other end of his communication (say, a fax machine) it has probably not in fact been received by the person to whom it was addressed—if, for example, it was sent at night to an office which is open only during the day; or if a message is left on the telephone answering machine during the day at the home of a person who the offeree knows is likely to be out at work until the evening, or away on holiday. There are few cases involving such matters, but the indications are that the courts would say that, unless the offer was clear as to what would be sufficient to constitute acceptance, the offeree could not treat his

---

[88] *Holwell Securities Ltd v Hughes* ibid.
[89] *Brinkibon Ltd v Stahag Stahl und Stahlwarenhandelsgesellschaft mbH* [1983] 2 AC 34 (HL).
[90] *Entores Ltd v Miles Far East Corporation* [1955] 2 QB 327 (CA) 333.
[91] *Brinkibon Ltd v Stahag Stahl* above, n 89, 41.

acceptance as complete until the time at which he might reasonably expect it to be received.[92]

This is linked to another issue: where a communication *should* have been made in the normal course but it was the fault of one or other party that it was not in fact made. Here the courts have taken the position that the party who was at fault cannot be heard to say that the communication did not succeed. And so an offer which is delayed through the fault of the offeror can still be accepted even if it contained a prescribed time for reply (such as 'by return of post');[93] and an acceptance which the offeror fails to read promptly will still be held to have been communicated.[94] A party who is in negotiations may therefore have a responsibility to read communications sent to him—in the sense that, if he does not read them, he may still be held to have received them.

Not all situations which might occur have been considered by the courts, and in particular questions may arise as to how to treat novel forms of communication such as e-mail or internet contracts.[95] When a new situation arises, the courts will adopt the usual common law techniques, and consider past cases which are sufficiently similar to help them to decide how to apply existing legal principles to the new factual situation; and then the new case will define for the future the approach to the new situation. When faced with a case of acceptance by telex, the courts decided that such communication should not follow the 'postal rule', but resembled more the case of acceptance by telephone since the technology involved in telex communications was almost instantaneous and in practice the sender would know whether the transmission of the message had been successful;[96] but that this would not be an invariable rule in cases where the sender knows that there may be a delay in the message being received by the offeror.[97] Similarly, a court may decide that, since an acceptance by e-mail is instantaneous in its technology, the 'postal rule' does not apply;[98] the sender can know whether the message has reached the recipient's e-mail account (it has not been rejected), and so it takes effect when it arrives at the server on which the recipient's e-mails are stored. However, since an e-mail may well not be read instantaneously,

---

[92] *Ibid* 42 (Lord Wilberforce: 'No universal rule can cover all such cases: they must be resolved by reference to the intentions of the parties, by sound business practice and in some cases by a judgment where the risks should lie'); cf *The Brimnes* [1975] QB 929 (CA) 966–67, 969–70 (exercise of right of withdrawal of charter, rather than acceptance of offer; but timing of notice by fax depends on whether there should be someone there to receive it, such as in office hours).

[93] *Adams v Lindsell* above, n 85.

[94] *The Brimnes* above, n 92.

[95] See D Nolan, 'Offer and Acceptance in the Electronic Age' in A Burrows and E Peel, *Contract Formation and Parties* (Oxford, Oxford University Press, 2010) ch 4.

[96] *Entores Ltd v Miles Far East Corporation* above, n 90.

[97] *Brinkibon Ltd v Stahag Stahl* above, n 89, 42.

[98] *Greenclose Ltd v National Westminster Bank plc* [2014] EWHC 1156 (Ch), [2014] 1 CLC 562 [138].

a likely solution would be that an e-mail acceptance (in the case where there was nothing in the language of the offer to prescribe the method or time of acceptance) would take effect when the offeror in fact reads it or, if earlier, at the time when the offeree could reasonably expect the offeror to read it.

3. Unresolved Negotiations: 'Battles of Forms'

A brief word should be said about a particular difficulty which can arise during the negotiations for a contract between commercial parties: a 'battle of forms', where each party attempts to obtain a contract on the basis of its own 'form'—its own non-negotiable standard terms of business. Some legal systems have developed special rules to deal with this situation: for example, by providing that a reply to an offer which purports to be an acceptance, but which contains additional or different terms, may still constitute an acceptance and the contract will contain the additional or different terms as long as they are not materially different from the terms of the offer and as long as the offeror has not promptly objected to the difference.[99] However, English law has no such rule.

We have already seen that this arose in *Butler Machine Tool Co Ltd v Ex-Cell-O Corporation (England) Ltd*[100] where the three members of the Court of Appeal agreed that the contract was concluded on the buyer's terms, but they were divided in their reasoning. The majority applied the traditional approach, identifying the offer and the acceptance on the facts of the case; and we have seen that this approach was later confirmed by the House of Lords as the general approach to the formation of contracts, at least where the contract is formed by correspondence.[101]

The difficulty is that the traditional method of analysis can be rather artificial in this context. Either the court must find that one or other of the parties succeeded in having their terms accepted, or it must hold that there was a failure to agree and therefore there was no contract. But disputes about the terms of the contract frequently arise at a later stage, once both parties have been acting for some time on the basis that there is a contract (although they have each been assuming that it is on their own terms), and the courts are reluctant to come to the view that there was never a contract. It seems to fly in the face of commercial reality, and so the question is not whether there was a contract, but on what terms was it concluded. But the decision as to which of the parties 'won the battle' can often seem rather unpredictable, and

---

[99] See, eg, United Nations Convention on Contracts for the International Sale of Goods (1980), art 19. However, the UK has not signed the Convention.
[100] [1979] 1 WLR 401 (CA) 404; above, p 107.
[101] *Gibson v Manchester City Council* [1979] 1 WLR 294 (HL) 297; above, p 108.

depends on the courts being able to interpret what one of the parties wrote, said or did being sufficient to constitute (objectively) an acceptance. This can be quite arbitrary, since it may well be that the acceptance is found in one party beginning to perform the contract—the last communication from the other party, which was not explicitly rejected, being then held to be the offer that was accepted. This is sometimes referred to as the 'last shot' rule—the last 'shot' is the one that wins. But it is not a rule; and all depends on how the courts interpret each of the communications between the parties, and their conduct.

Lord Denning advocated an approach which would allow the court to construct a contract from the common elements of the parties' own terms:

> There is a concluded contract but the forms vary. The terms and conditions of both parties are to be construed together. If they can be reconciled so as to give a harmonious result, all well and good. If differences are irreconcilable—so that they are mutually contradictory—then the conflicting terms may have to be scrapped and replaced by a reasonable implication.[102]

This has not, however, been adopted. It was part of Lord Denning's attempt to provide a broader objective approach to the formation of a contract than the strict 'offer and acceptance' analysis—and his approach was rejected by the House of Lords.[103] More recently, the Court of Appeal in *Tekdata Interconnections Ltd v Amphenol Ltd*[104] has reaffirmed the difficulties, but also the benefits, of insisting on finding the acceptance of an offer before a contract can be concluded following a 'battle of forms'. Although there may be cases where the parties' conduct shows that they had a different intention from that which would follow from an analysis based on offer and acceptance, such cases are the exception rather than the rule. Longmore LJ said[105] that 'it will always be difficult to displace the traditional analysis, in a battle of forms case, unless it can be said that there was a clear course of dealing between the parties'. Dyson LJ emphasised the importance of certainty in such cases:

> [T]he rules which govern the formation of contracts have been long established and they are grounded in the concepts of offer and acceptance. So long as that continues to be the case, it seems to me that the general rule should be that the traditional offer and acceptance analysis is to be applied in battle of the forms cases. That has the great merit of providing a degree of certainty which is both desirable and necessary in order to promote effective commercial relationships.[106]

---

[102] *Butler Machine Tool Co Ltd v Ex-Cell-O Corporation (England) Ltd* above, n 100, 405.
[103] *Gibson v Manchester City Council* [1979] 1 WLR 294 (HL) 297; above, p 108.
[104] [2009] EWCA Civ 1209, [2010] 1 Lloyd's Rep 357.
[105] *Ibid* [21].
[106] *Ibid* [25].

In the case of a 'battle of forms' it is therefore still necessary generally to find a contract by finding an offer which was accepted—even if this may sometimes appear rather artificial in its analysis and arbitrary in its outcome.

III. Minimum Content and Certainty

1. An Agreement (and the Offer) Must Be Complete

If the parties come to an agreement which is incomplete, it cannot form a contract. We have seen that an agreement is normally formed by offer and acceptance, and this means that an acceptance of an incomplete offer cannot form a contract. The situations where the parties have left gaps which prevent there being a valid contract are quite rare. It does not mean that the offer must contain an express statement of all the necessary terms of the contract, since gaps can be filled by implied terms. This is considered in chapter eight. For example, if the parties agree on a sale but have not agreed on the price, in general one would expect that the acceptance of an offer of sale cannot constitute a contract because the agreement on the sale does not yet contain one of the essential elements of the contract—the consideration. However, this gap can be filled, since if the agreement is silent as to the price it will be implied that the buyer must pay a reasonable price.[107] Similarly, if there is an agreement for the supply of a service which is silent as to the price to be paid, it will be implied that the recipient of the service will pay a reasonable charge.[108] But, in principle, if the parties leave gaps which cannot be filled by the implication of terms, there is not a sufficiently complete agreement for a contract to be formed.

In practice, the absence of a complete agreement most commonly becomes an issue of certainty, since the parties do not generally leave gaps, but include in their agreement matters which are not sufficiently clear and precise.

2. An Agreement (and the Offer) Must Be Certain

If the parties come to an agreement which contains elements which are not objectively certain or capable of being resolved without further negotiations between the parties, the agreement is not sufficient to form a contract.

---

[107] Sale of Goods Act 1979 s 8.
[108] Supply of Goods and Services Act 1982 s 15 (non-consumer contracts); Consumer Rights Act 2015 s 51 (consumer contracts).

For example, an agreement to sell goods at a price which 'shall be agreed upon from time to time' by the parties is void for uncertainty.[109] Silence as to the price in a contract for the sale of goods can be filled by a 'reasonable price';[110] but the insertion of a provision relating to price which is itself uncertain is fatal to the contract. This follows from the general position in English law that there cannot be an enforceable 'agreement to agree';[111] and that the parties cannot be subject to enforceable obligations to negotiate. We have seen that even an express agreement to negotiate in good faith is not accepted.[112]

If the contract provides for a mechanism for the ascertainment of a term which is not yet certain, this will be acceptable as long as the mechanism is not simply dependent on the further agreement of the parties themselves. It is sufficient, for example, if the price is to be fixed by the decision of a third party.[113]

In general the courts attempt to interpret the parties' agreement as certain, rather than uncertain, and therefore to give effect to the parties' intentions as to the validity of the transaction.[114] This is particularly so in the case of a commercial contract, where the parties have acted for a period on the basis that there is a binding contract and where there is some provision in the contract which the courts can rely upon or interpret to find a mechanism for resolving any apparent uncertainty.[115] Where the agreement provides a mechanism for the ascertainment of a term but the mechanism cannot be carried out the court will carry out the ascertainment of the term itself if the criteria for its operation are sufficiently certain (for example, that the price for the sale of land is to be a 'reasonable price') and as long as the operation of the particular mechanism was not itself an essential term of the contract.[116] And it has been held that a clause which is meaningless can be

---

[109] *May and Butcher v The King* [1934] 2 KB 17 (HL). Similarly, a contract to sell 'on hire purchase terms over a period of two years' is too uncertain: *G Scammell and Nephew Ltd v HC and JG Ouston* [1941] AC 251 (HL); as is an option to extend a lease 'at such a rental as may be agreed upon between the parties': *King's Motors (Oxford) Ltd v Lax* [1970] 1 WLR 426 (Ch).

[110] Above, n 107.

[111] *Courtney & Fairbairn Ltd v Tolaini Brothers (Hotels) Ltd* [1975] 1 WLR 297 (CA); above, p 76.

[112] *Walford v Miles* [1992] 2 AC 128 (HL); above, p 77.

[113] *Lloyds Bank Ltd v Marcan* [1973] 1 WLR 1387 (CA) (rent under lease to be fixed by person chosen by President of the Royal Institution of Chartered Surveyors).

[114] *Brown v Gould* [1972] Ch 53 (Ch) 56; *Tang v Grant Thornton International Ltd* [2012] EWHC 3198 (Ch), [2014] 2 CLC 663 [56]–[61].

[115] *Foley v Classique Coaches Ltd* [1934] 2 KB 1 (CA) 10 (sale of petrol 'at a price to be agreed by the parties in writing and from time to time' in contract which contained arbitration clause to resolve disputes over price, and had been acted on by the parties for three years, was subject to implied term that the petrol should be supplied at a reasonable price).

[116] *Sudbrook Trading Estate Ltd v Eggleton* [1983] 1 AC 444 (HL). For contracts for the sale of goods, however, Sale of Goods Act 1979 s 9 provides for the agreement to be avoided where 'the price is to be fixed by the valuation of a third party, and he cannot or does not make the valuation'.

ignored, as long as the rest of the agreement can stand as a complete contract without it.[117]

The term need not be certain from the outset, as long as it will be certain by the time that it is due to be performed. For example, the price for the sale of goods may be defined as the market price at the date of delivery, or the rent payable under a lease may rise from time to time to reflect the market value of the premises.[118] In such cases the only question is whether the 'market value' is sufficiently certain to be ascertainable when the time comes.

---

[117] *Nicolene Ltd v Simmonds* [1953] 1 QB 543 (CA): 'the usual conditions of acceptance apply'—but there were no such conditions. The parties had acted on the contract as binding. See Denning LJ at 724: 'You would find defaulters all scanning their contracts to find some meaningless clause on which to ride free'.

[118] *Brown v Gould*, above, n 114.

6

Form, Consideration and Intention

No legal system can sensibly say that every promise, or every agreement, gives rise to contractually binding obligations. There may well be moral and social obligations to keep one's promises and to give effect to agreements which one has entered into. But not all the promises and agreements that have moral or social force should necessarily have legal force. The question is how to define those promises and agreements which should be brought within the law of contract—and therefore in what circumstances persons deserve the protection of the law through some form of remedy for the fact that a promise which was made to them has not been kept, or an agreement has been broken.

This is an issue on which legal systems divide.[1] Civil systems do not have a single view about the proper approach to apply. Some will simply stress that the question is whether the promisor intended to be bound by his promise. Others will look for a 'cause' in an obligation or an agreement in order to validate it. And all systems will see some role for formalities in the creation of contracts. Common law systems also make some use of formalities, but the core doctrine here is a unique product of the common law: the doctrine of *consideration*. We shall see that this doctrine gives the notion that a contract is a bargain between its parties. We shall also see, however, that there is some unease in the common law in limiting the enforceability of promises and agreements to bargains—and that there have been some attempts to extend the doctrine, or even to give legal force to promises and agreements in the absence of consideration. This is a matter on which different common law jurisdictions take different views, and so on some points we shall look at the state of the law outside the English common law.

---

[1] For a survey of European jurisdictions, see J Gordley (ed), *The Enforceability of Promises in European Contract Law* (Cambridge, Cambridge University Press, 2001); H Kötz and A Flessner, *European Contract Law*, vol 1, T Weir (trans) (Oxford, Clarendon Press, 1997), ch 4.

I. Formality in the Formation of Contracts

1. Specific Formalities for Specific Contracts

We have already seen that English law occasionally provides for specific formality rules relating to the formation of specific contracts.[2] But these are relatively rare. The Statute of Frauds 1677 contained a range of rules requiring writing by way of *evidence* for the enforcement of particular types of contract,[3] but almost all of these have now been repealed. All that remains is the part of section 4 which requires writing signed by the guarantor or his agent before a contract of guarantee can be enforced against him, although in the modern law new formality requirements have been introduced for certain types of contract. For example, a contract of marine insurance cannot be evidenced in court without a written insurance policy;[4] and there are statutory requirements for the execution of certain consumer credit agreements, without which the agreement can be enforced against the debtor only on the order of the court.[5] Most significantly, there is also now a strengthened requirement of writing as a condition of the existence of a contract for the sale or other disposition of an interest in land (that is, a contract for the sale of land, or a contract for some other transaction which will create or transfer an interest in land). This requirement is imposed by section 2 of the Law of Property (Miscellaneous Provisions) Act 1989:

> A contract for the sale or other disposition of an interest in land can only be made in writing and only by incorporating all the terms which the parties have expressly agreed in one document or, where contracts are exchanged, in each.[6]

Each party to a contract for the sale or other disposition of an interest in land, or someone on his behalf, must sign the document (or one of identical

---

[2] Above, p 58.

[3] For further details, see above, pp 58–59. The Statute of Frauds was adopted in other common law jurisdictions, and is largely retained in the United States: EA Farnsworth, *Contracts*, 4th edn (New York, Aspen, 2006) ch 6.

[4] Marine Insurance Act 1906 s 22.

[5] Consumer Credit Act 1974, pt V.

[6] For a detailed discussion of s 2 of the 1989 Act see EH Burn and J Cartwright, *Cheshire & Burn's Modern Law of Real Property*, 18th edn (Oxford, Oxford University Press, 2011) 966–78; and for the law as it stood before that Act (under Law of Property Act 1925 s 40, which was a re-enactment of the old provision of the Statute of Frauds requiring written evidence signed by the defendant or his agent before the contract could be enforced against him), see *Cheshire & Burn* 961–66.

exchanged documents). If the requirements as to writing and signature are not complied with, there is *no contract*, although these requirements have been interpreted as including electronic communications such as e-mails, and electronic forms of signature.[7] There must of course still be an agreement between the parties which satisfies the general rules governing the formation of contracts—including offer and acceptance[8] and (as we shall see later in this chapter) consideration. But that agreement does not become a contract until the additional requirement of writing set out in section 2 is satisfied.

2. A General Formality: The Deed

By contrast with those specific requirements for specific contracts, there is also a further formality recognised by English law: the *deed*. This is a formal transaction used for various purposes, including transfers of the property rights in land, which do not concern us here. What is relevant for our context is that if a promise, or an agreement, is contained in a deed it becomes enforceable by virtue of the formality of the deed, even if the promise would not be otherwise binding because it is not supported by consideration. One could take a different perspective on the matter and say that, since the effect of the doctrine of consideration is to exclude gratuitous promises from the law of contract,[9] a deed is in effect a formality which is *required* for a legally effective promise of a gift. When looked at this way, the civil lawyer may think that there is not really a substantive difference between his system and the common law if (as is common amongst the civilian jurisdictions) his system does not exclude gratuitous promises from contracts but subjects gifts to special formality rules. However, this is not the way in which the common lawyer sees it. A contract must be supported by consideration. But, quite separately, a promise or agreement contained in a deed is enforceable by virtue of the deed—and, indeed, the law relating to deeds becomes generally applicable to the obligations set out in the deed, including rules which sometimes go beyond the normal rules of the law of contract.[10]

---

[7] Interpretation Act 1978, sch 1; cf *J Pereira Fernandes SA v Mehta* [2006] EWHC 813 (Ch), [2006] 1 WLR 1543; *Golden Ocean Group Ltd v Salgaocar Mining Industries PVT Ltd* [2012] EWCA Civ 265, [2012] 1 WLR 3674 ('writing' for Statute of Frauds 1677).

[8] *Commission for the New Towns v Cooper (Great Britain) Ltd* [1995] Ch 259 (CA) 293 (Evans LJ).

[9] Below, p 132.

[10] Eg the limitation period to enforce an obligation contained in a deed is 12 years from its breach (rather than 6 years for informal contracts): Limitation Act 1980 s 8 (as part of a general review of the law on limitation of actions, the Law Commission proposed bringing the two into line, although its proposals have not been adopted: below, p 296); and a promise can be enforceable by virtue of a deed even if it is not part of an agreement—the deed can be a unilateral act (a 'deed poll') naming the beneficiary: Lord Mackay of Clashfern (ed), *Halsbury's Laws of England* vol 32, 5th edn (London, LexisNexis Butterworths, 2012) paras 203, 261.

The reason for this difference between deeds and (informal) contracts is historical. If we look back to the thirteenth and fourteenth centuries, we find that actions of 'debt' (to enforce promises of money) could be brought only if there was a deed; and actions of 'covenant' (to enforce promises of performance), although they had earlier been enforced by virtue of the agreement, became enforceable only if the agreement was evidenced by a deed. But our modern law of (informal) contracts developed at a later stage, mainly from the fifteenth to the seventeenth centuries, from a quite different line of cases—the action of 'assumpsit', an off-shoot of the law of trespass.[11] In the modern law, we have the relics of these two separate sources of promissory obligations: deeds retain a quite separate force of their own; and promises contained in simple agreements—whether written or oral—are enforceable without a deed, but only if the promise is supported by consideration.[12]

The particular formality required for a valid deed has changed over the years. At common law,[13] a deed had to be in writing on parchment or paper; sealed by the promisor; and 'delivered' by him (that is, not a mere physical delivery, but a delivery accompanied by words or conduct signifying his intention to be bound by the provisions in the deed). Originally, a seal had to take the form of wax, impressed with a formal seal or signet ring—or even the party's fingernail. Signature was not necessary: the seal was the personal indication of the party's agreement to the deed. In practice this formality degenerated, and during the twentieth century it became common for parties simply to attach a red circle of paper to the document to serve as the seal—and the courts began to accept as a valid deed a pre-printed document which identified the place for the seal to be affixed but where the parties had not in fact attached a seal of any kind but had signed the document instead and had their signatures witnessed.[14] This was taken to the logical next step by section 1 of the Law of Property (Miscellaneous Provisions) Act 1989 which abolished the requirement of sealing for deeds by individuals, and also removed the rule that a deed must be written on paper or parchment. In their place it introduced the requirements that a deed must be clear on its face that it is intended to be a deed; and that the individual must sign the deed in the presence of a witness who attests his signature (or, if he cannot sign, the individual can direct someone to sign in his presence and in the presence of two witnesses). A company incorporated under the Companies Act 2006 may execute a deed either by affixing the common seal of the company, or by the

---

[11] JH Baker, *An Introduction to English Legal History*, 4th edn (London, Butterworths LexisNexis, 2002) chs 18–20.
[12] *Rann v Hughes* (1778) 7 TR 350n, 101 ER 1014.
[13] *Goddard's Case* (1584) 2 Co Rep 4b, 5a, 76 ER 396, 399–400.
[14] *First National Securities Ltd v Jones* [1978] Ch 109 (CA).

signature of a director and the secretary or of two directors, or by the signature of one director in the presence of a witness.[15]

It will be evident from this brief account that formalities for contracts in English law centre around writing—as in all modern legal systems; but that the written formalities can be achieved between the parties themselves. Notarisation is not used within the domestic English law of contract.[16] Registration requirements exist for certain property transactions—notably for land.[17] But the formalities for contracts are purely private.

3. The Avoidance of Formalities

In recent years the courts have considered whether the formality requirements for land contracts, guarantees and deeds are absolute. For various reasons parties may fail to comply with the formality requirements—they may not know them; may in error omit to follow them properly; or may simply find them too onerous and take the risk as to whether the other party will challenge the transaction on the ground of its failure to satisfy the formality requirement.

One particular issue has arisen: whether a party who has agreed to the contract and did not insist on the formality at the time can later be heard to say that the contract is not valid, or (in the case of guarantees) is not enforceable, where the other party has relied on his express or implied representation that the agreement is valid and binding—that is, whether a party can be 'estopped' from challenging the contract on the basis of the statutory requirements.[18]

The courts have considered this question for each separate formality by looking at the policy underlying the statutory requirement of formality. In relation to contracts for the sale of land, the Court of Appeal in *Yaxley v Gotts*[19] held that a person who was promised an interest in a building if he undertook work on the building could be granted the interest (or at least an interest which protected his expectation) under the doctrine of proprietary estoppel, in spite of the fact that the promise was not contained in a

---

[15] Companies Act 2006 s 44, expanding provisions first introduced by Companies Act 1989 s 130. For companies not incorporated under the Companies Act sealing remains an indispensable requirement.

[16] Although there has existed since the Middle Ages a profession of notary in England, it did not develop here as it did in continental Europe, and domestic English law never developed the requirement of authentication of private law documents by a notary: see, eg, W Holdsworth, *A History of English Law*, vol V, 3rd edn (London, Methuen & Co, 1945) 115. Notaries in England are generally employed in international transactions to authenticate documents as required by other legal systems: see generally *www.thenotariessociety.org.uk*.

[17] Land Registration Act 2002, replacing Land Registration Act 1925. Not all land is yet registered but the Land Registry is working to create a comprehensive land register for England and Wales. For formalities relating to land, see Burn and Cartwright, *Cheshire & Burn's Modern Law of Real Property*, above, n 6, ch 25.

[18] For 'estoppel' see below, pp 143–44.

[19] [2000] Ch 162 (CA).

contract which complied with section 2 of the Law of Property (Miscellaneous Provisions) Act 1989. Beldam LJ said:

> The general principle that a party cannot rely on an estoppel in the face of a statute depends upon the nature of the enactment, the purpose of the provision and the social policy behind it. This was not a provision aimed at prohibiting or outlawing agreements of a specific kind, though it had the effect of making agreements which did not comply with the required formalities void. This by itself is insufficient to raise such a significant public interest that an estoppel would be excluded.[20]

The court was able to hold that the statute by its own language, as well as by its context as evidenced by the background to its enactment,[21] indicated that to give effect to an informal agreement through the doctrine of proprietary estoppel would not necessarily undermine the policy requiring written contracts for the sale of land. More recently, the House of Lords in *Cobbe v Yeoman's Row Management Ltd*[22] cast doubt on whether the doctrine of proprietary estoppel should be allowed to avoid the formality requirements of section 2 of the 1989 Act. It will not apply at least in the case of experienced commercial parties who know the formality requirements for the formation of the contract and yet do not follow them, or more generally where the parties intend to make a formal contract setting out the terms of their agreement but have not yet done so.[23] However, a stronger suggestion by Lord Scott that proprietary estoppel can never avoid the statutory formality on the basis that 'Equity can surely not contradict the statute'[24] did not take account of the earlier cases such as *Yaxley v Gotts*, and has not generally been adopted.[25]

In *Shah v Shah*[26] the Court of Appeal applied dicta in *Yaxley v Gotts* to hold that the requirements of section 1 of the 1989 Act were also not absolute, in the sense that a party who had not in fact executed a document as a deed in compliance with the section could be estopped from denying it. The document in the case was expressed to be a deed, and was signed and delivered by the defendants. But the defect of formality came in its witnessing—it was attested, but by someone who signed as witness after the defendants had signed but not (as required by the Act) in their presence. The Court of Appeal held that the delivery of the document constituted an unambiguous representation of fact that it was a deed, and the claimant had acted in

---

[20] *Ibid* 191.
[21] The court relied on, inter alia, the report of the Law Commission proposing the provision, 'Formalities for Contracts for Sale etc of Land' (Law Com No 164, 1987), which at pp 18–20 discussed estoppel as a means of giving effect to an agreement which would not comply with the formality. For the general approach to interpretation of statutes and the use of background information such as Law Commission Reports see above, p 31.
[22] [2008] UKHL 55, [2008] 1 WLR 1752.
[23] *Ibid* [27] (Lord Scott), [71], [91] (Lord Walker); *Herbert v Doyle* [2010] EWCA Civ 1095, [2011] 1 EGLR 119 [57].
[24] *Ibid* [29].
[25] See eg *Whittaker v Kinnear* [2011] EWHC 1479 (QB) [27]–[30].
[26] [2001] EWCA Civ 527, [2002] QB 35.

reliance on that fact and on the deed having validly created the obligations it purported to contain. Following *Yaxley v Gotts* they considered the policy behind the Act, and the Law Commission Report which had proposed it, and concluded that estoppel could be permitted to avoid some, but not all, of the formality requirements. Pill LJ said:

> [T]here was no statutory intention to exclude the operation of an estoppel in all circumstances or in circumstances such as the present. The perceived need for formality in the case of a deed requires a signature and a document cannot be a deed in the absence of a signature. I can detect no social policy which requires the person attesting the signature to be present when the document is signed. The attestation is at one stage removed from the imperative out of which the need for formality arises. It is not fundamental to the public interest, which is in the requirement for a signature. Failure to comply with the additional formality of attestation should not in itself prevent a party into whose possession an apparently valid deed has come from alleging that the signatory should not be permitted to rely on the absence of attestation in his presence. It should not permit a person to escape the consequences of an apparently valid deed he has signed, representing that he has done so in the presence of an attesting witness, merely by claiming that in fact the attesting witness was not present at the time of signature.[27]

The question arose before the House of Lords in *Actionstrength Ltd v International Glass Engineering*[28] as to whether estoppel can be used to avoid the requirement of the Statute of Frauds that a contract of guarantee be evidenced in writing. The House held that there was no estoppel on the facts, but a majority appears to have assumed that there could in an appropriate case be such an estoppel, as long as the guarantor made a representation about its validity beyond simply making the promise of the guarantee itself, and the beneficiary of the guarantee has relied on that representation.

II. The Doctrine of Consideration

1. Consideration: The Basic Principle

The basic idea underlying the doctrine of consideration is that, where A makes a promise to B, the promise is contractually binding and enforceable by B only where B has done, or promised to do, something for A in return

---

[27] *Ibid* [30].
[28] [2003] UKHL 17, [2003] 2 AC 541.

132 FORM, CONSIDERATION AND INTENTION

for A's promise: in effect, B earns the right to enforce A's promise by doing or promising something in exchange for it. This doctrine gives English law the notion of a contract as a *bargain*. The promise by A to make a gift to B is not a contract, even if B accepts A's offer to make the gift (and therefore the parties have an agreement about the gift) because B has provided no consideration: since it is to be a gift, he has neither done nor promised to do anything in return for it. The doctrine of consideration therefore has the effect of excluding promises of gifts from the scope of the law of contract. This does not mean that a promise of a gift cannot be made to be enforceable—as we have already seen, it can be enforceable by virtue of being contained in a deed executed by the promisor.[29] Moreover, once the promise of a gift has been carried out, the gift is effective to transfer the property in the subject-matter of the gift to the donee: the law will respect a completed transfer even if it is gratuitous. English law is therefore not opposed to giving effect to a gratuitous transaction. But it excludes *promises* of gifts from the scope of informal contracts.

2. Consideration: Particular Rules

There are various particular rules within the doctrine of consideration, which can be set out in the following points (keeping throughout the example of A making a promise to B):

(a) Consideration is provided by B when he does, or promises to do, something at A's request

There are three points here.

First, the exchange of mutual promises is sufficient to make the contract binding. For example, where A and B agree today that next week A will give B his car in return for B giving A £1,000, the contract is concluded today. Such a contract, where the obligations of both parties are to be performed in the future, is called an 'executory' contract. If, on the other hand, B has performed his own promise, or done the act which was requested by A as the price of his promise, B's consideration is said to be 'executed'.

Secondly, if it is to be consideration to enforce A's promise, B's promise or act must have been given or done at A's request. B's spontaneous promise or act, even if it was foreseeable by A, is not sufficient. For example, in *Combe v Combe*[30] a man promised his wife during their divorce proceedings

---

[29] Above, p 127.
[30] [1951] 2 KB 215 (CA).

that he would make annual maintenance payments to her after the divorce. The wife later claimed that, relying on his promise, she forbore to apply to the Divorce Court for a maintenance order and that this justified her enforcing the husband's promise. However, the Court of Appeal held that the husband's promise was not binding as a contract, since the wife had not promised the husband that she would not apply to the Divorce Court for maintenance, and her failure to apply to the Court was not at the husband's request. There was a causal link between his promise and her forbearing to go to court, but that is not sufficient to make it consideration if it was not requested by the husband either expressly or impliedly. Without such a request the promise or act cannot be *in return for* the promise which is being enforced and so cannot be consideration for the promise. We shall see later, however, that in some circumstances reliance on a promise, even though the reliance was not requested by the promisor, can justify some legal effect being given to the promise through the doctrine of promissory estoppel.[31]

Thirdly, 'doing' or 'promising to do' can equally include 'not doing' or 'promising not to do'. Forbearance can be consideration as long as it satisfies the other requirements (it is at the other party's request, is of value, and so on—as we shall see below). Compromise agreements typically involve an agreement by one party not to pursue his action in return for a payment by the other of a sum in settlement of the claim.

(b) Consideration involves B doing or promising something which is to his detriment and/or to A's benefit

The justification for B having the right to enforce A's promise is that he has suffered some 'detriment' in return for the promise; or that A must fulfil his promise because A has obtained a 'benefit' from B:

> A valuable consideration, in the sense of the law, may consist either in some right, interest, profit, or benefit accruing to the one party, or some forbearance, detriment, loss, or responsibility, given, suffered, or undertaken by the other.[32]

In most cases consideration is both to the detriment of B and to the benefit of A. For example, where B pays or promises to pay £1,000 for A's car, B's payment or promise is 'detriment' to him (he incurs a payment, or undertakes a binding obligation to pay the money), and at the same time an equivalent 'benefit' to A (he obtains the benefit of the money or of the obligation to receive the money). This is the typical model of a contract where there is simply an agreed exchange between the two parties. But a contract may exist

---
[31] Below, p 143.
[32] *Currie v Misa* (1875) 10 Exch 153, 162 (Lush J).

where at first sight there is no such direct exchange: for example, if A agrees to give his car to B in return for B paying (or promising to pay) £1,000 to C. Here, B's payment (or promise to pay) to C is consideration for A's promise, because B has undertaken a 'detriment' at the request of A, in return for A's promise. The fact that the sum of £1,000 is to be paid to a third party does not prevent it in law being consideration, because it is sufficient that B suffers a detriment in return for the promise, without enquiry as to what benefit it constitutes for A.[33] However, one can rationalise it as still being a 'benefit' to A because the fact that A has requested it is enough to show that it is beneficial to him to have the payment made to C.

By contrast, there are situations where the courts have been prepared to hold that a benefit to A is sufficient even if there is no detriment to B. This was the case in *Williams v Roffey Bros & Nicholls (Contractors) Ltd*,[34] in which the Court of Appeal held that a party to a contract (B) who repeats his promise to perform his existing obligations in return for a promise from the other party (A) to increase the payments to be made under the contract provides consideration for the promise of the increased payments where, although B is not suffering any additional detriment because he is not undertaking any additional obligations, A obtains a 'practical benefit' arising out of the assurance of complete and timely performance. This case is discussed further below.[35]

We have already noted that the making of a *promise* can be sufficient detriment without it yet being performed: a promise in return for a promise creates an executory contract, in advance of either party in fact incurring the detriment by starting to perform.[36]

(c) For B's promise or act to be consideration it must have some (economic) value

There are two points here.

First, B's promise or act need not be the payment or promise of money, but it must be capable of being valued in economic terms. It is not sufficient that the promise is designed to satisfy some moral duty of the promisor. For

---

[33] *Carlill v Carbolic Smoke Ball Co* [1893] 1 QB 256 (CA) 271 (Bowen LJ: using smoke ball was detriment and therefore consideration: 'Inconvenience sustained by one party at the request of the other is enough to create a consideration;' but there was in fact also a benefit to the other party through the promotion of their product).

[34] [1991] 1 QB 1 (CA).

[35] Below, p 140.

[36] *Centrovincial Estates plc v Merchant Investors Assurance Co Ltd* [1983] Com LR 158 (CA) 159 (Slade LJ: 'provided only that the offeree has given sufficient consideration for the offeror's promise, it is nothing to the point that the offeree may not have changed his position beyond giving the promise requested of him').

example, in *Thomas v Thomas*[37] A (the executors of B's husband, who had recently died) agreed to transfer a cottage to B for her life, declaring that it was (i) in consideration of her deceased husband's desire to provide a home for B; and (ii) in return for B paying £1 a year towards the ground rent payable for the premises by A to a superior landlord. It was held that this agreement was binding—but because of the promise of the £1, and not because of deceased husband's motive, or the executors' desire to satisfy a moral obligation arising from the deceased husband's wishes:[38]

> Motive is not the same thing with consideration. Consideration means something which is of some value in the eye of the law, moving from the plaintiff: it may be some benefit to the plaintiff, or some detriment to the defendant; but at all events it must be moving from the plaintiff.[39]

Secondly, although the courts will require B to provide something which is capable of being valued in economic terms, they will not enquire into whether the bargain between the parties is fair or balanced. It is said that the courts will not investigate the 'adequacy' of the consideration. So a contract under which A promises to transfer his car (which is in fact worth £1,000 in the second-hand car market) to B in return for B's promise or payment of £1 can be a valid contract in English law. The promise or payment of £1 is good consideration. The reason usually given for this is that it is for the parties, and not for the courts, to set the balance in the agreement. There must be *an* exchange before the transaction falls within the law of contract. But the courts do not make (or adjust) the contract to provide for an objectively 'fair' exchange: the value which the parties themselves put on what they are exchanging is their own affair. This gives the English law of contract a commercial, market-centred view but not, it should be noted, one which requires the parties to accept the terms of an external market. In effect, they set their own market for the transaction.

This does not mean that the courts are insensitive to disadvantageous contracts; simply that the doctrine of consideration does not deal with this issue. If one of the parties is demonstrably in a weaker bargaining position, the courts will take into account the fact that the terms of the contract appear to be significantly disadvantageous to him as a factor which might point to

---

[37] (1842) 2 QB 851, 114 ER 330.
[38] *Ibid* 859, 333–34 (Patteson J). In argument the civilian notion of *causa* was discussed; and art 1131 of the French Civil Code was cited (through its citation in the then-current edition of *Chitty on Contracts*). The exclusion of motive as a justification of the enforceability of a promise, and the insistence on an exchange of value in return for the promise, shows that the doctrine of consideration is fundamentally different from the doctrine of *la cause* in French law and other systems which draw the principle from the French Civil Code: cf B Nicholas, *The French Law of Contract*, 2nd edn (Oxford, Clarendon Press, 1992) 123.
[39] The rule that consideration must move from the promisee is one aspect of the doctrine of privity of contract: below, p 238.

the stronger party having exercised undue influence in order to obtain the contract on favourable terms; or it might be classed as an 'unconscionable bargain'.[40]

However, these doctrines only render the contract voidable at the instance of the weaker party. If the doctrine of consideration were to be used to deal with this, it would have the consequence that the contract would not be formed if it was objectively imbalanced: not only would this be too paternalistic as a general rule but also it would prevent parties and the courts from deliberately taking advantage of the rule that consideration need not be adequate.

The parties may well use the rule in order to ensure that a promise is binding. If they agree on a transaction which is, or which might risk being analysed as, in substance gratuitous, the promise by the 'donee' to give some nominal consideration (such as a token amount of money, or a token thing such as a peppercorn) is a device to bring the gift within the law of contract. In admitting such transactions as contracts, the courts are in effect colluding with the parties to allow what is in substance a gift to be recharacterised as a contract. This is not a concern to the English lawyer, although the civil lawyer may be surprised by it. Some legal systems have rules designed to prevent the parties pretending that a gift is a contract—not because a gift cannot be a contract, but because the pretence is likely to involve an attempt to evade some other rule of law, such as tax on gifts or the rules against gratuitous alienation of property to defraud creditors or to disinherit members of the family who have inalienable succession rights. English law will sometimes have similar concerns, but it does not use the law of contract to address them.[41] On the contrary, contracts for 'nominal' consideration are not at all uncommon in England, where professional advisers draft contracts and insert a provision for nominal consideration to be paid so as to ensure that the obligations are binding. We have already seen that the parties can make an enforceable promise of a gift if the donor undertakes the promise in a deed.[42] In such a case, the donor's intention to make a gift is respected; and the use of nominal consideration can be justified on the same grounds. If a person is obviously making in substance a promise of a gift, but chooses to ask for some nominal sum or thing in return, and there are no other grounds to challenge it (such as duress

---

[40] For undue influence and unconscionable bargains see below, ch 7.

[41] There is no general tax on *inter vivos* gifts in England. Gifts made within seven years before death are brought back into account for inheritance tax on death, but the Inheritance Tax Act 1984 s 3 provides for this by determining not whether there is a 'gift', but whether the transaction has reduced the value of the person's estate. Similarly, under the Inheritance (Provision for Family and Dependants) Act 1975 s 10 the court may reverse a disposition made for less than 'full valuable consideration' less than six years before the death with the intention of defeating an application for financial provision for dependents. Fraud on creditors is dealt with under the Insolvency Act 1986 ss 238 and 423 by allowing the reversal of transactions which are made without consideration or at a consideration significantly less than the value given in exchange.

[42] Above, p 127.

or undue influence, which will be considered separately) it must be because he wishes to bring his promise within the scope of contract, and so intends his promise to be binding.

The courts, too, may sometimes take advantage of the rule which does not require consideration to be adequate, in order to give contractual effect to a promise which is not otherwise binding. That is, they may sometimes 'find' consideration even though it is not evident that the parties had it in mind that there was an exchange or a contract. An example of this is *De la Bere v Pearson*[43] where the Court of Appeal found a contract between a newspaper and a reader who (in response to a general invitation to readers to write to the newspaper) asked for investment advice and the name of a good stockbroker. The newspaper provided him with the name of an unsuitable stockbroker and he suffered losses. The newspaper published some letters but not the claimant's letter nor their reply; but the court held that there was consideration for the contract in that the prospect of publication of the claimant's letter would tend to increase the sales of their newspaper. This was very artificial, but at the time there was no ground of liability in tort given that the newspaper was not fraudulent but only negligent. When the law of tort later developed to cover economic loss caused through reliance on careless advice Lord Devlin recognised the artificiality of cases such as *De la Bere v Pearson*, and made clear that they should now be analysed within the law of tort, not contract.[44] But there are also other cases where the courts have been prepared to find consideration on very slim grounds, in order to ensure that an undertaking can be given contractual effect. Indeed, one can say that the courts are reluctant to find that there is no consideration, particularly where the agreement is between commercial parties who have assumed that their agreement is a binding contract. The courts will therefore look carefully into whether the thing done or promised by B has any value.[45] But if B promises something which has no value at all, or is entirely illusory, it cannot be consideration—such as where B agrees to accept A's promise of payment to settle a dispute when B knows that he has no valid claim to be settled.[46]

In the case of a *variation* of an existing contract, the courts have gone further, and have said that, as long as one party obtained a *practical benefit*

---

[43] [1908] 1 KB 280 (CA).
[44] *Hedley Byrne & Co Ltd v Heller & Partners Ltd* [1964] AC 465 (HL) 528. See also above, p 42.
[45] Eg *Pitt v PHH Asset Management* Ltd [1994] 1 WLR 327 (CA) (firm offer and 'lock-out' agreement for sale of property: purchaser's agreement to withdraw threat of proceedings for injunction to prevent negotiations with third party, and agreement to proceed swiftly if the contract went ahead, were consideration even though they were of doubtful value).
[46] *Wade v Simeon* (1846) 2 CB 548, 564–65; 135 ER 1061, 1067. If B mistakenly believes that he has a valid claim his agreement not to pursue it still has value and so can be consideration: *Callisher v Bischoffsheim* (1870) LR 5 QB 449, 451–52, even if A knows that the claim is not valid: *Cook v Wright* (1861) 1 B & S 559, 569, 568; 121 ER 822, 825–26.

138 FORM, CONSIDERATION AND INTENTION

as a result of the other party's promise, then that may be sufficient. This is discussed further below.[47]

(d) B's promise or act must be done at the same time as A's promise: 'past consideration' is insufficient

A bargain involves the exchange of promises or acts which are linked—the time of performance need not necessarily be linked, but the promises must themselves be linked and agreed upon contemporaneously. And so if A and B agree that A will deliver his car to B next week if B pays the price today, there is a valid contract because the promises (the car in return for the money) were exchanged by reference to each other, although the time for A's performance is deferred. On the other hand, if B rescued A from drowning in the river last week, and A promises B today that, in return for last week's rescue, A will pay £1,000, the promise is not enforceable *unless* it was made clear last week by B that he would expect to be paid in return for the rescue. This rule was stated by Lord Scarman in the Privy Council in *Pao On v Lau Yiu Long*:

> An act done before the giving of a promise to make a payment or to confer some other benefit can sometimes be consideration for the promise. The act must have been done at the promisor's request, the parties must have understood that the act was to be remunerated either by a payment or the conferment of some other benefit, and payment, or the conferment of a benefit, must have been legally enforceable had it been promised in advance.[48]

A practical example of this rule is that if the buyer of goods is to obtain an express assurance about the goods, beyond the conditions implied by law into such contracts,[49] he must do so at the time of the sale because he cannot rely on the fact that he has already bought the goods as consideration for the seller's later assurance.[50]

(e) An act done, or promise made, by B which he is already under a contractual obligation to perform in favour of a third party can be good consideration

We have already seen that there is a valid contract if A agrees to give his car to B in return for B paying (or promising to pay) £1,000 to C. The promise to pay money to a third party is sufficient consideration.[51] However,

---

[47] *Williams v Roffey Bros & Nicholls (Contractors) Ltd* [1991] 1 QB 1 (CA); below, p 140.
[48] [1980] AC 614 (PC) 629.
[49] Sale of Goods Act 1979 s 14 (non-consumer sales); Consumer Rights Act 2015 ss 9, 10 (consumer goods contracts); below, p 214.
[50] *Roscorla v Thomas* (1842) 3 QB 234, 114 ER 496.
[51] Above, p 134.

if B already owed £1,000 to C, he would in fact be undertaking no new burden—no 'detriment'.[52] But this does not prevent the promise being good consideration, because the fact that B has an existing obligation in favour of C is nothing to do with A; and although B undertakes no additional detriment by making the promise to A, A obtains the benefit of a direct right against B to have the money given to C. This was established in the middle of the nineteenth century,[53] and confirmed more recently by the Privy Council.[54]

(f) An act done, or promise made, by B which he is already under a contractual obligation to perform in favour of A, or which he has a legal obligation to perform, cannot be good consideration, unless A obtains some additional benefit

It is less easy for B to be allowed to say that he provides consideration by doing something which he is already under a duty to do under the general law, or under a contract with A.

In the case of a general legal obligation, it appears that B would be using that obligation in order to make a profit from a contract with A. If B's duty is a public duty, then there are reasons of public policy to prevent this, although not if B's promise or performance goes beyond what he had a duty to do.[55] But if the duty is not a general public duty but in the nature of a private obligation, it is not clear that the courts would take such a strict line. Certainly in *Ward v Byham*[56] Lord Denning thought that the performance of a legal obligation by B could be consideration—because in fact it provided a benefit to A, even if it was a benefit to which he was technically entitled by virtue of the pre-existing legal obligation on B to perform. In that case, the father of a child promised to pay the mother (from whom he was separated) £1 a week if the child was 'well looked after and happy'. It was held that by looking after the child the mother provided consideration for the promise of the money, even though she had a duty by statute[57] to maintain her own child. Lord Denning said:

> [T]he mother, in looking after the child, is only doing what she is legally bound to do. Even so, I think that there was sufficient consideration to support the promise.

---

[52] Above, p 133.
[53] *Scotson v Pegg* (1861) 6 H & N 295, 158 ER 121.
[54] *New Zealand Shipping Co Ltd v AM Satterthwaite & Co Ltd* [1975] AC 154 (PC) 168.
[55] *Glasbrook Bros Ltd v Glamorgan County Council* [1925] AC 70 (HL) (police provided protection beyond that which they had a public duty to offer, so contract for performance of services was valid).
[56] [1956] 1 WLR 496 (CA).
[57] National Assistance Act 1948 s 42 (the child was illegitimate; the duty under the statute was on the mother and not the father).

I have always thought that a promise to perform an existing duty, or the performance of it, should be regarded as good consideration, because it is a benefit to the person to whom it is given. Take this very case. It is as much a benefit by the mother as by a neighbour. If he gets the benefit for which he stipulated, he ought to honour his promise; and he ought not to avoid it by saying that the mother was herself under a duty to maintain the child.[58]

The thinking behind Lord Denning's judgment became very significant in a later case concerning performance of a duty owed not by law but by contract with the other party. This is the trickiest situation. If B performs or promises something for A which A was already entitled to require him to do it is not consideration—because it does not give A anything new: A receives no additional benefit, and B incurs no additional detriment. It is as if B were promising to give A something which already belongs to A. This is the analysis which the courts have traditionally made. So in *Stilk v Myrick*[59] where two sailors deserted during a voyage and the captain agreed to divide the wages of the deserters between the remaining crew if they agreed to continue to work, the crew could not enforce the promise of the additional money because their terms of engagement already included the duty to work in such emergencies and so they undertook no obligation beyond that which they already owed to the captain.

That strict approach was relaxed, however, by the Court of Appeal in *Williams v Roffey Bros & Nicholls (Contractors) Ltd*.[60] The main contractor on a building project promised to increase the payments to be made to one of his sub-contractors in circumstances where the sub-contractor was in financial difficulties and the main contractor was worried that the work would not be completed on time. Late completion would result in the contractor having to pay penalties under his own contract with the building owner. The court rejected the main contractor's argument, based on *Stilk v Myrick*, that the subcontractor gave no consideration because he had promised nothing beyond that which he already owed under the contract (to complete the work, on time). Instead, the judges focused not on what detriment was suffered by the subcontractor in repeating his promise to do the work (there was none), but on what *benefit* was received by the main contractor in return for his promise to pay the additional money. The decision in *Ward v Byham*[61] paved the way for this decision because it allowed the court to look for a 'practical benefit' received by the main contractor. And one can detect other lines of thinking in the judgments.

---

[58] [1956] 1 WLR 496, 498. Morris LJ at 498–99 emphasised that the consideration was in ensuring that the child would be happy.
[59] (1809) 2 Camp 317, 170 ER 1168. It was different in *Hartley v Ponsonby* (1857) 7 El & Bl 872, 119 ER 1471 where on the desertion of 17 out of a crew of 36 the sailors who agreed to remain in return for additional wages were doing more than they were already contractually entitled to do because it became dangerous to continue.
[60] [1991] 1 QB 1 (CA).
[61] Above, n 56.

First, that there is a risk in such re-negotiations that one party, such as a subcontractor, may put pressure on the main contractor to increase the payment because he is taking advantage of the main contractor's need to get the job completed. But if this is an underlying concern, the older cases—such as *Stilk*—were decided when the only way of dealing with such a concern was through the doctrine of consideration and so a strict line was taken. But in the modern law there is now a developed doctrine of duress, which includes a threat to break a contract within the notion of 'economic duress'.[62] The doctrine of duress is a more flexible tool, which allows the court to look at the particular circumstances in which one party agreed to increase the payment due under the existing contract, and only makes the contract voidable rather than preventing its coming into existence. Therefore:

> The modern cases tend to depend more upon the defence of duress in a commercial context rather than lack of consideration for the second agreement ... [T]he court is more ready in the presence of this defence being available in the commercial context to look for mutual advantages which would amount to sufficient consideration to support the second agreement under which the extra money is paid.[63]

Secondly, the court was influenced by the fact that this was a sensible agreement between commercial parties; and they are very reluctant to find that such an agreement fails for lack of consideration. Moreover, there is a strong emphasis on the court's desire to give effect to the intention of the parties:

> [W]hilst consideration remains a fundamental requirement before a contract not under seal can be enforced, the policy of the law in its search to do justice between the parties has developed considerably since the early 19th century when *Stilk v. Myrick* was decided by Lord Ellenborough C.J. In the late 20th century I do not believe that the rigid approach to the concept of consideration to be found in *Stilk v. Myrick* is either necessary or desirable. Consideration there must still be but, in my judgment, the courts nowadays should be more ready to find its existence so as to reflect the intention of the parties to the contract where the bargaining powers are not unequal and where the finding of consideration reflect the true intention of the parties.[64]

In *Williams v Roffey Bros* the Court held that the main contractor did obtain a 'practical benefit' in return for its promise to pay the additional money, because it would secure the timely completion of the contract and so avoid the payment of penalties under its own contract, and would also avoid the trouble and expense of finding a replacement sub-contractor, as well as obtaining the benefit of certain changes to the payment arrangements. The main contractor had not been subjected to duress in agreeing the increased price—indeed, the main contractor offered to increase the price in order to solve the sub-contractor's financial difficulties and to secure his continued performance.

---

[62] Below, pp 191–93.
[63] [1991] 1 QB 1, 21 (Purchas LJ).
[64] *Ibid* 18 (Russell LJ).

The decision in *Williams v Roffey Bros* was controversial. It has been followed at first instance, but with some hesitation about whether it can stand with the existing authorities[65] and it remains to be seen whether the relaxation of the doctrine of consideration in this area will be confirmed by the Supreme Court.

(g) Part-payment of a debt is not consideration for the release of the balance

We have seen that the decision in *Williams v Roffey Bros* relaxed the doctrine of consideration to allow the variation of an existing contract for services by B in return for payment by A, where A promised to increase the payment in return for B simply repeating his promise to perform the services, as long as the promise had the effect of giving A a 'practical benefit' in return for his promise to pay. As the case-law currently stands, this cannot be translated into a similar rule for the part-payment of a debt. If B owes a debt to A, and A agrees to relinquish part of a debt in return for B simply paying the balance but without B giving A some further advantage (such as by paying the balance earlier than is due under the contract or by giving something in place of the foregone balance of the debt) the balance remains enforceable. Part-payment of a debt is not consideration for the release of the balance of the debt. This was set out by the Court of Common Pleas in *Pinnel's Case*:

> [P]ayment of a lesser sum on the day in satisfaction of a greater, cannot be any satisfaction for the whole, because it appears to the Judges, that by no possibility a lesser sum can be a satisfaction to the plaintiff for a greater sum.[66]

This statement of principle, though in fact an obiter dictum,[67] was confirmed and applied by the House of Lords in 1884 in *Foakes v Beer*,[68] in holding that an agreement to accept payment of a debt by instalments did not have the effect of cancelling the interest that accrued during the instalment period. However, it must be noted that two members of the House, Lord Selborne[69] and Lord Blackburn, would have preferred a less rigid rule. Lord Blackburn said:

> [A]ll men of business, whether merchants or tradesmen, do every day recognise and act on the ground that prompt payment of a part of their demand may be more

---

[65] *South Caribbean Trading Ltd v Trafigura Beheer BV* [2004] EWHC 2676 (Comm), [2005] 1 Lloyd's Rep 128 [108]: 'But for the fact that *Williams v Roffey Bros* was a decision of the Court of Appeal, I would not have followed it' (Colman J); *Adam Opel GmbH v Mitras Automotive UK Ltd* [2007] EWHC 3252 (QB) at [42]: 'I am bound to apply the decision ... whatever view I might take of its logical coherence' (David Donaldson QC). See also the discussion of *Re Selectmove* [1995] 1 WLR 474 (CA), below. Courts in other common law jurisdictions have, however, been more receptive to the developments made in *Williams v Roffey Bros*.
[66] (1602) 5 Co Rep 117a, 77 ER 237.
[67] The payment was made earlier than the due date, therefore giving the creditor a benefit.
[68] (1884) 9 App Cas 605 (HL).
[69] *Ibid* 613.

beneficial to them than it would be to insist on their rights and enforce payment of the whole. Even where the debtor is perfectly solvent, and sure to pay at last, this often is so. Where the credit of the debtor is doubtful it must be more so.[70]

However, the House regarded the well-established rule in *Pinnel's Case* as one which they should follow, even though of course it was not binding on them. This is a good illustration of the reluctance of the courts to overturn long-standing principles of the common law.[71]

Looking at the question afresh, one might think that Lord Blackburn's argument points towards an application of the principle in *Williams v Roffey Bros*; in effect, he argued that the debtor who agrees to accept less than the full payment of the debt will do so because he recognises a benefit in doing so: the receipt of some money now, for certain, rather than risking the uncertainty of whether any of the debt will in practice be enforceable. This argument—that the strictness of the rule in *Pinnel's Case* has been superseded by the decision in *Williams v Roffey Bros*—was put to the Court of Appeal in *Re Selectmove*.[72] But the Court refused to accept it, not because they could not see merit in the extension of *Williams v Roffey Bros* to this situation, but because they regarded themselves as bound by the decision of the House of Lords in *Foakes v Beer* in relation to the part payment of a debt.[73] This step—and the full implications of the relaxation of the doctrine of consideration as already effected by the Court of Appeal in *Williams v Roffey Bros*—therefore awaits a decision of the Supreme Court.

III. Promissory Estoppel

1. The Core Principle of Estoppel: Reliance on a Representation

There are various forms of 'estoppel' in English law.[74] The core meaning of this rather unusual word is quite simple, as explained by Lord Denning:

> The word 'estoppel' only means stopped. You will find it explained by Coke in his *Commentaries on Littleton* (19th ed, 1832), vol. II, s. 667, 352a. It was brought over

---

[70] *Ibid* 622.
[71] Above, p 21.
[72] Above n 65, 479–81.
[73] The same approach was taken in *Collier v P & MJ Wright (Holdings) Ltd* [2007] EWCA Civ 1329, [2008] 1 WLR 643 [6].
[74] J Cartwright, 'Protecting Legitimate Expectations and Estoppel in English Law' *Electronic Journal of Comparative Law* (vol 10.3, Dec 2006: *www.ejcl.org/103/art103-6.pdf*).

by the Normans. They used the old French 'estoupail.' That meant a bung or cork by which you stopped something from coming out. It was in common use in our courts when they carried on all their proceedings in Norman-French.[75]

In essence, a party who is 'estopped' is stopped, or prevented, from denying something. Under 'estoppel by convention', for example, where the parties to a transaction act on an assumed state of facts or law, communicated by each party to the other, then each party is estopped from denying the assumed facts or law if it would be unjust to allow him to go back on the assumption.[76] In any litigation between the parties neither is allowed to argue that the facts or the law are not as they had both assumed. And similarly under 'estoppel by representation' a person who has made a representation to another may be estopped from denying the content of his representation.

2. The Modern Development of Promissory Estoppel in English Law

'Estoppel by representation' is well established in English law, but it was restricted to representations of *existing fact*, and not to statements of intention, or promises.[77] A party who had made a representation of fact would not be permitted to lead evidence to contradict that fact in an action by or against the party to whom he had made the representation and who had relied on it—had changed his position in some way to his detriment on the faith of the representation. The doctrine of promissory estoppel is a development of this to cover representations as to future conduct: promises. Two separate lines of development are relevant here: proprietary estoppel and promissory estoppel.

In the first place, *proprietary estoppel* is now a well-established doctrine within land law, developed in a line of cases dating from the mid-nineteenth century.[78] Where one party (A) makes a representation or promise to another party (B) to the effect that B has or shall have an interest in, or right over, A's property, or acquiesces in B's mistaken belief that he has or shall have such an interest or right, then if A intends B to act in reliance on the representation, promise or mistaken belief, and B does so act in reliance, equity may intervene to prevent (*estop*) A from asserting his own strict legal rights to his property. It is a method by which B can acquire an interest in land, and can

---

[75] *McIlkenny v Chief Constable of the West Midlands* [1980] QB 283 (CA) 316–17.
[76] *Republic of India v Indian Steamship Co Ltd (No 2)* [1998] AC 878 (HL) 913.
[77] *Jorden v Money* (1854) 5 HL Cas 185, 214–15, 226–27; 10 ER 868, 881–82, 886.
[78] Especially *Ramsden v Dyson and Thornton* (1866) LR 1 HL 129, 170; *Wilmott v Barber* (1880) 15 ChD 96, 105–106. This doctrine might also apply outside land law, but still within the law of property: *Western Fish Products Ltd v Penwith DC* [1981] 2 All ER 204 (CA) 218. See generally Burn and Cartwright, *Cheshire and Burn's Modern Law of Real Property*, above, n 6, 906–22, 936–42.

have positive rights to enforce that interest, although the remedy is discretionary and will not necessarily be to enforce the particular interest which B expected to receive: it might be only the reimbursement of the expenditure he incurred in reliance on the representation.[79] We shall see later that, although proprietary estoppel is limited to property, its link to promissory estoppel is significant for possible future developments in the law of contract.[80]

The doctrine of *promissory estoppel* was developed in English law only later. It is generally attributed to the decision of Denning J in *Central London Property Trust v High Trees House*[81] who, however, drew on earlier cases to justify the principle which he stated:

> With regard to estoppel, the representation made in relation to reducing the rent, was not a representation of an existing fact. It was a representation, in effect, as to the future, namely, that payment of the rent would not be enforced at the full rate but only at the reduced rate. Such a representation would not give rise to an estoppel, because, as was said in *Jorden v. Money*,[82] a representation as to the future must be embodied as a contract or be nothing.
>
> But what is the position in view of developments in the law in recent years? The law has not been standing still since *Jorden v. Money*. There has been a series of decisions over the last fifty years which, although they are said to be cases of estoppel are not really such. They are cases in which a promise was made which was intended to create legal relations and which, to the knowledge of the person making the promise, was going to be acted on by the person to whom it was made and which was in fact so acted on. In such cases the courts have said that the promise must be honoured… In each case the court held the promise to be binding on the party making it, even though under the old common law it might be difficult to find any consideration for it. The courts have not gone so far as to give a cause of action in damages for the breach of such a promise, but they have refused to allow the party making it to act inconsistently with it. It is in that sense, and that sense only, that such a promise gives rise to an estoppel.[83]

This may seem to be a radical decision of a judge at first instance. But, at least on the surface, the judgment is a normal application of common law technique. Denning J looked back to earlier cases which had not themselves acknowledged a new principle but which, when taken together, he could say showed that there was a general principle at play—that a person who made a representation about his intentions could be estopped from acting

---

[79] In recent cases the English courts have tended to take the expectation as the starting-point, at least where the representation is precise about the interest or right in question, but to award less if the value of the expectation is disproportionate to the value of the detriment incurred: *Jennings v Rice* [2002] EWCA Civ 159, [2003] 1 P & CR 8.
[80] Below, pp 154–55.
[81] [1947] KB 130 (KB). The facts are set out below.
[82] (1854) 5 HL Cas 185 (above, n 77).
[83] [1947] KB 130 (KB) 134.

inconsistently with his intentions by the party to whom the representation was made, and who had been intended to, and had in fact, acted upon it. It was an extension and development of the old doctrine of estoppel by representation; and although the decision of the House of Lords in *Jorden v Money* appeared to be an obstacle to such a development, Denning J was able to include amongst the cases on which he drew as authority another decision of the House of Lords, later than *Jorden v Money: Hughes v Metropolitan Railway Co*.[84]

In *Hughes* a landlord agreed to a suspension of the tenant's obligation to complete repairs to the leased property which, under the terms of the lease, had to be completed within a fixed period. The suspension was given during a period when the parties were negotiating for a possible surrender of the lease by the tenant, but when the negotiations broke down the landlord sought to terminate the lease on the ground that the repairs had not been completed within the period required by the lease. The landlord was not allowed to evict the tenant, but had to give further time to effect the repairs. The language of 'estoppel' was not used in the case, but in *High Trees* Denning J interpreted this as a case of estoppel, the landlord being prevented in equity from going back on his promise to suspend the tenant's obligation.

High Trees is itself an interesting case for an understanding of how the common law develops, not only to see how Denning J deduced a new general principle from the earlier cases, but also to see how influential a decision at first instance can be in the later development of the law. As a decision of the High Court, *High Trees* was not binding on the High Court or on the courts above.[85]

In fact, much of what was said by Denning J in the case was *obiter dictum*. The case involved the long lease of a block of flats at an annual rent of £2,500. During the war, when the tenant was unable to secure sub-tenants to take all the flats, the landlord agreed to reduce the annual rent to £1,250. After the war a claim was brought by the landlord's receiver to test the level of rent payable, although the claim was brought only for the rent due in the last two quarters of 1945, and by that period the flats were again all fully let. The receiver succeeded, on the basis that the landlord's promise had been only to reduce the rent for the period when the block of flats was not fully let, or not substantially fully let, because of the war. This is hardly a radical decision: the landlord had not (on a proper interpretation of his promise) in fact agreed to a lower rent for the period for which it was being claimed. Much more interesting is what Denning J had to say about the general doctrine of estoppel, and what its effect *could* have been. He made clear that, if the claim

---

[84] (1877) 2 App Cas 439 (HL).
[85] Above, pp 24–25.

had not been just for the period at the end of the war, but had been to recover the balance of the rent which had not been claimed during the period when the flats were not fully let, the receiver would have failed. That is, the balance of the rent due during the war had been extinguished by the operation of the estoppel—the landlord, having represented that he would not require it to be paid, and the tenant having acted on that representation, the landlord would be estopped from going back on it. As Denning J said, this doctrine has the potential to undermine the rule of the common law that the balance of a debt cannot be released without consideration:

> The logical consequence, no doubt is that a promise to accept a smaller sum in discharge of a larger sum, if acted upon, is binding notwithstanding the absence of consideration: and if the fusion of law and equity leads to this result, so much the better. That aspect was not considered in *Foakes v. Beer*.[86] At this time of day however, when law and equity have been joined together for over seventy years, principles must be reconsidered in the light of their combined effect.[87]

The full implications of this have not yet been settled, but it is at least arguable that the doctrine of promissory estoppel can be used to provide a defence to a debtor who has been led to pay part of a debt which the creditor has voluntarily accepted in full satisfaction of the whole, where the creditor then seeks to claim the balance of the debt.[88]

3. The Elements of Promissory Estoppel in English Law

Although the decision in *High Trees* is seen as the origin of the doctrine of promissory estoppel in the modern law, it has been subject to further discussion and refinement in the later cases, and in particular by the higher courts. We shall here outline the elements of the doctrine. A useful starting-point is a general statement of the doctrine by Lord Hodson in the Privy Council in *Ajayi v RT Briscoe (Nigeria) Ltd*:

> The principle, which has been described as quasi estoppel and perhaps more aptly as promissory estoppel, is that when one party to a contract in the absence of fresh consideration agrees not to enforce his rights an equity will be raised in favour of the other party. This equity is, however, subject to the qualifications (1) that the other party has altered his position, (2) that the promisor can resile from his promise on giving reasonable notice, which need not be a formal notice, giving the promisee a

---

[86] (1884) 9 App Cas 605 (above, pp 142–43).
[87] [1947] KB 130, 135.
[88] *Collier v P & MJ Wright (Holdings) Ltd* above, n 73, [42] (Arden LJ, referring to the 'brilliant obiter dictum of Denning J in the *High Trees* case'), [48] (Longmore LJ). See also below, p 151.

reasonable opportunity of resuming his position, (3) the promise only becomes final and irrevocable if the promisee cannot resume his position.[89]

The account in this section is only of the doctrine of promissory estoppel in English law which, as we shall see, is of very limited scope. It has been extended much more broadly in American and (more recently) Australian law; this will be mentioned in the following section.[90]

(a) The Doctrine is Limited to the Variation of an Existing Contract, in the Absence of Fresh Consideration

Lord Hodson's statement refers to a party to a contract agreeing not to enforce his rights in the absence of fresh consideration. We shall consider this in further detail below[91] but it is important from the outset to realise that the context in which the doctrine of promissory estoppel is used in English law is in the variation of existing contracts;[92] and only where there is no contractual variation. If the parties agree to the variation of a contract with fresh consideration for the variation, estoppel is irrelevant. For example, if A contracts to deliver 100 bags of sugar to B in return for £100, but before performance there is an agreement to vary this to 75 bags for £75, each party is providing consideration for the variation: B has given up the right to 25 bags, in return for A giving up the right to £25.[93] Depending on how the parties arrange the variation, there is now either a contractual variation of the old contract, or a discharge of the old contract replaced by a new contract. But, in either case, B now has a right to (only) 75 bags of sugar, and A has the right to receive (only) £75.

Promissory estoppel becomes relevant only where there is a variation of the contract without consideration: in effect, where there is a variation only of one party's obligations. And on the case-law as it stands, it is only where that variation is by one party agreeing to *reduce* his entitlement to the other party's performance: where one party agrees not to enforce his contractual rights fully against the other party.[94]

---

[89] [1964] 1 WLR 1326 (PC) 1330.
[90] Below, p 153.
[91] Below, p 152 ('sword' or 'shield').
[92] In fact, it can be used outside the law of contract where one party has a right against another which he agrees not to enforce: *Durham Fancy Goods Ltd v Michael Jackson (Fancy Goods) Ltd* [1968] 2 QB 839 (QB) (obligation arose not by contract but by statute: director's personal liability for signing bill of exchange without company's proper name).
[93] The variation need not be at £1 per bag: it is for the parties to decide what price to put on those particular bags of sugar (the court will not inquire into its adequacy: above, p 135), so there will be consideration as long as, in return for giving up the right to the 25 bags of sugar, A has given up something of value.
[94] In *Williams v Roffey Bros & Nicholls (Contractors) Ltd* [1991] 1 QB 1 (CA) above, p 140, Glidewell and Russell LJJ declined to consider whether promissory estoppel could be developed to enforce the promise to *increase* the payment due under the contract: at 13, 17–18.

(b) The Representation

The doctrine of promissory estoppel is designed to prevent a party from going back on his promise: there must therefore be a promise, or representation, by one contracting party to the other. We have already seen that the representation is of the party's intention not to insist on his strict legal rights against the other party under the contract—a promise not (or not fully) to enforce the contract. The representation need not be express, but can be implied;[95] but it must be 'clear and unequivocal'[96]—and this will be tested (like a contractual promise) by the way in which the recipient could reasonably have understood it.[97] But, as with a communication alleged to have formed a contractual agreement,[98] it will normally be insufficient for the 'representation' to be made by silence alone: 'it is difficult to imagine how silence and inaction can be anything but equivocal'.[99]

(c) The Representee Must Have Relied on the Representation—Altered His Position

The core element of promissory estoppel—as any form of estoppel by representation—is the representee's reliance on the representation. It is the fact that he has done something which he would (or, at least, might)[100] not otherwise have done as a result of receiving the other party's promise not to enforce his strict legal rights, that allows the representee to be heard to say that he should not be bound to perform the contract. The representee's reliance makes it *inequitable* for the representor to go back on his representation. There has been some debate in the cases as to whether this means that the representee must just have 'acted' on the representation; or whether he must in some sense have acted 'to his detriment'. But the real question is whether, when the representor seeks to go back on his promise and to claim the right to enforce the contract fully in accordance with its terms, the position in which the representee now

---

[95] In *Hughes v Metropolitan Railway Co*, above, n 84, the landlord's representation not to hold the tenant to his obligation to repair the premises during their negotiations was implied, rather than express.
[96] *Woodhouse AC Israel Cocoa Ltd SA v Nigerian Produce Marketing Co Ltd* [1972] AC 741 (HL).
[97] *Bremer Handelsgesellschaft mbH v Vanden Avenne-Izegem PVBA* [1978] 2 Lloyd's Rep 109 (HL) 126.
[98] Above, p 115.
[99] *Allied Marine Transport Ltd v Vale do Rio Doce Navagacao SA (The Leonidas D)* [1985] 1 WLR 925 (CA) 937 (Robert Goff LJ).
[100] Following the same approach taken to other situations in which the question is whether a representee relied on a representation, the courts can infer reliance from the fact that the representation was likely to be relied upon in the circumstances: *Brikom Investments Ltd v Carr* [1979] QB 467 (CA) 482–83 (Lord Denning MR); cf below, p 178.

finds himself as a result of his actions in reliance on the representation is such that it would be inequitable to require him to perform.[101]

(d) The Representor Can Revoke His Promise: Estoppel is Normally Only Temporary

It is clear from Lord Hodson's statement of the doctrine of promissory estoppel that it is normally only temporary: the promisor can revoke his promise on giving reasonable notice. In a case where the representation promised a release from the contract for only a limited period, then no notice will be necessary at the end of the period.[102] But if there is no limit on the release, the representor can require the contract to be performed again if he gives *reasonable notice*—but what constitutes reasonable notice will depend on the facts. The underlying principle, as made clear by Lord Hodson, is that notice is to be given to allow the representee to put himself back into the position of being able to perform. It was his acting in reliance on the representation which made it 'inequitable' for the representor to insist on strict performance of the contract. So to 'undo the inequity' the representor has to allow the representee to 'undo his reliance'—or at least to give him the opportunity to do what the court judges necessary to put himself once more in the position to perform. For example, if A contracts to sell 100 bags of sugar to B, and B tells A that he need deliver only 75 bags, then B may be estopped from insisting on the remaining 25 bags at the time required by the contract for delivery, if A has acted in reliance on not having to perform—for example, he has sold the rest of his supply to a third party. But B still has a contractual entitlement to the 25 bags, and can give notice that he will require them; and then the question becomes how long it will reasonably take for A to obtain a further supply of 25 bags.

(e) The Representation May Be Irrevocable

In exceptional cases, however, the representor may no longer be able to revoke his representation: in such cases the effect of the estoppel is to vary the contract permanently. It will arise only where it is permanently 'inequitable' to require the representee to perform the contract fully according to its terms— and this means not only that he has relied on the representation, but also

---

[101] *Societe Italo-Belge Pour le Commerce et L'Industrie SA (Antwerp) v Palm and Vegetable Oils (Malaysia) Sdn Bhd (The Post Chaser)* [1982] 1 All ER 19 (QB) 25–27.

[102] *High Trees*, above, n 81 (the reduction of rent was only for such period as the flats could not be fully let during the war).

that he cannot now reasonably be required to get back into a position where he can perform. For example, A contracts to sell an antique table and eight chairs to B, and B tells A that he will require only six chairs (whilst still paying the full price). As long as A still has the remaining two chairs B can change his mind. But once A has sold them, and can therefore no longer obtain the goods necessary to fulfil his contract, he can no longer be required to perform. In the *High Trees*[103] case Denning J said that this principle can have the effect of allowing the part payment of a debt to cancel the whole debt, since the creditor can be estopped from claiming back the balance of the debt where the debtor has acted in reliance on the representation that the balance will not be enforced. This will circumvent the rule in *Pinnel's Case*, as applied by the House of Lords in *Foakes v Beer*,[104] but the full implications remain to be settled. One might expect promissory estoppel to be applied cautiously in this context, both because it will have the effect of undermining the rule set out in *Foakes v Beer*, and for the practical reason that, if it is accepted that promissory estoppel generally gives rise to a permanent variation in the contract only where it is no longer equitable to expect the representee ever to perform the original contract, this will not normally arise in the case of a remission of part of a debt because it is difficult to show that the payment of money (the balance of the debt) is permanently impossible. However, the Court of Appeal has accepted that the doctrine of promissory estoppel may be used to provide a defence to a debtor who has been led to pay part of a debt. In *Collier v P & MJ Wright (Holdings) Ltd*[105] Arden LJ said:

> [I]f (1) a debtor offers to pay part only of the amount he owes; (2) the creditor voluntarily accepts that offer, and (3) in reliance on the creditor's acceptance the debtor pays that part of the amount he owes in full, the creditor will, by virtue of the doctrine of promissory estoppel, be bound to accept that sum in full and final satisfaction of the whole debt. For him to resile will of itself be inequitable.[106]

Longmore LJ was more cautious. He emphasised the need for the debtor to show that he has relied on the representation that the balance of the debt would be forgone, and warned against too easily construing agreements between debtor and creditor as intended to forgo permanently the creditor's rights.[107] However, the Court of Appeal in this case did not have to determine the circumstances in which the doctrine of promissory estoppel may have the effect of circumventing the decision in *Foakes v Beer*, because the only question before the court was to decide whether there was an arguable case

---

[103] Above, n 87.
[104] Above, n 86.
[105] Above, n 73.
[106] *Ibid* [42].
[107] *Ibid* [48].

152 FORM, CONSIDERATION AND INTENTION

which should be allowed to proceed to trial—and the Court was unanimous that there was an arguable case.

(f) Promissory Estoppel Does Not Create New Rights— It is a 'Shield' Not a 'Sword'

As the law currently stands in England, promissory estoppel has the very limited operation which has been described above. It involves the (normally temporary) release of existing contractual obligations. It does not involve the enforcement of promises to increase obligations under an existing contract; and it certainly does not allow a new obligation to be created. This was made clear as early as 1951 in *Combe v Combe*.[108] We have already seen that, in that case, a wife failed in her claim that her forbearance to apply to the Divorce Court for a maintenance order constituted consideration to justify her enforcing her husband's promise of maintenance. She sought in the alternative to claim that the husband was estopped from denying his obligation to pay the maintenance on the basis of the *High Trees* doctrine. But this was also rejected by the Court of Appeal. Denning LJ said:

> Much as I am inclined to favour the principle stated in the *High Trees* case,[109] it is important that it should not be stretched too far, lest it should be endangered. That principle does not create new causes of action where none existed before. It only prevents a party from insisting upon his strict legal rights, when it would be unjust to allow him to enforce them, having regard to the dealings which have taken place between the parties
>
> … Seeing that the principle never stands alone as giving a cause of action in itself, it can never do away with the necessity of consideration when that is an essential part of the cause of action. The doctrine of consideration is too firmly fixed to be overthrown by a side-wind. Its ill-effects have been largely mitigated of late, but it still remains a cardinal necessity of the formation of a contract, though not of its modification or discharge.[110]

It is sometimes said that promissory estoppel can be used only as a 'shield', not a 'sword'[111]—that is, it can be raised as a defence to a claim by the other party to enforce the contract, but it cannot be used by the representee to claim to enforce new rights which would exist only by virtue of the representation. The representation is not a cause of action; the reliance on a representation is not, within the doctrine of promissory estoppel, a source of new obligations.

---

[108] [1951] 2 KB 215 (CA); above, pp 132–33.
[109] [1947] KB 130.
[110] *Ibid* 219–20.
[111] *Combe v Combe* above, n 108, 224 (Birkett LJ).

This limited view of the role of promissory estoppel in English law has been confirmed more recently by the Court of Appeal—an illustration of the application of the rules of precedent, since the Court of Appeal is bound by its own decision in *Combe v Combe*, and it will take a decision of the Supreme Court, or statute, to change it.[112]

4. The Relationship between Consideration and Estoppel: Differences within the Common Law, and Possible Developments in England

In English law, as we have seen, promissory estoppel is not a source of obligations. This is not, however, a unified view amongst the common law jurisdictions.

In American law it has been accepted since early in the twentieth century that the doctrine of promissory estoppel can work, alongside the doctrine of consideration, to make promises enforceable. Paragraph 90(1) of the American Law Institute's Restatement (2d) Contracts says:

> A promise which the promisor should reasonably expect to induce action or forbearance on the part of the promisee or a third person and which does induce such action or forbearance is binding if injustice can be avoided only by enforcement of the promise. The remedy granted for breach may be limited as justice requires.[113]

This allows a promise to be enforceable if *either* the promisee has given consideration for it *or* the promisee has relied on it: a much wider doctrine than in English law. In consequence, there is less need for the American courts to 'find' consideration in order to make a promise enforceable, although the remedy for promissory estoppel is not necessarily the protection of the claimant's expectation but is more commonly damages to reflect his reliance on the promise.[114]

In Australian law, too, there has been some development in this area. We have already seen that in *Waltons Stores (Interstate) Ltd v Maher*[115] a party who was negotiating to take a lease of property was estopped from denying

---

[112] Above, p 25; *Baird Textiles Holdings Ltd v Marks and Spencer plc* [2001] EWCA Civ 274, [2002] 1 All ER (Comm) 737 [55]: 'there is no real prospect of the claim succeeding unless and until the law is developed, or corrected, by the House of Lords' (Judge LJ).

[113] *Restatement of the Law (2d), Contracts* (St Paul, Minnesota, American Law Institute, 1981), para 90. The 'Restatements' are not statutory texts, but are highly influential statements of the rules of law, generally deduced from the case-law but sometimes containing new ideas and new rules which then themselves influence the developing case-law: EA Farnsworth, *Contracts*, 4th edn (New York, Aspen, 2004) para 1.8.

[114] Farnsworth, *Contracts*, above, n 113, para 2.19. A good example is *Hoffman v Red Owl Stores Inc* 133 NW 2d 267 (Wisconsin, 1965), above, p 83.

[115] (1988) 164 CLR 387 (HCA); above, p 82. Followed in *Commonwealth v Verwayen* (1990) 95 ALR 321 (HCA).

that he was bound to complete the lease where he had encouraged the landowner to continue to build the property when he had already decided not to take the lease. The High Court of Australia held that it would be unconscionable for the prospective tenant to retreat from his implied promise to complete the contract. The remedy was not enforcement of the contract, but damages in place of specific performance,[116] but in substance promissory estoppel was here used as a 'sword'—to allow the representee to enforce the representation on the basis that he had relied on it, and it would be inequitable (or 'unconscionable') for the representor not to give effect to it.

The court took this step to extend the scope of the doctrine of promissory estoppel:

> [T]he respondents ask us to drive promissory estoppel one step further by enforcing directly in the absence of a pre-existing relationship of any kind a non-contractual promise on which the representee has relied to his detriment.[117]

The High Court of Australia regarded promissory estoppel as part of a wider general doctrine of estoppel which includes proprietary estoppel[118]—under which it is well established that the representee may sue the representor on his promise that he has or will have a property right:

> One may ... discern in the cases a common thread which links them together, namely, the principle that equity will come to the relief of a plaintiff who has acted to his detriment on the basis of a basic assumption in relation to which the other party to the transaction has 'played such a part in the adoption of the assumption that it would be unfair or unjust if he were left free to ignore it.[119] Equity comes to the relief of such a plaintiff on the footing that it would be unconscionable conduct on the part of the other party to ignore the assumption.[120]

It has also been emphasised in the Australian cases that the remedy is not simply the enforcement of the representation but the starting-point is to avoid the detriment suffered by the representee in reliance on the representation; and, in any event, there must be a proportionality between the remedy and the detriment which is its purpose to avoid.[121]

It remains to be seen whether the Supreme Court will be willing to take a similar step and to view the hitherto limited doctrine of promissory estoppel

---

[116] Below, p 281.
[117] (1988) 164 CLR 387 [22] (Mason CJ and Wilson J).
[118] Above, p 144.
[119] Per Dixon J in *Grundt v Great Boulder Pty Gold Mines Ltd* (1937) 59 CLR 641, at p 675; see also *Thompson v Palmer* (1933) 49 CLR 507, at 547.
[120] (1988) 164 CLR 387, [30] (Mason CJ and Wilson J). This development has not, however, been made without criticism in some of the Australian state courts: see eg *Saleh v Romanous* [2010] NSWCA 274, (2010) 79 NSWLR 453 [74] (Handley JA).
[121] *Commonwealth v Verwayen* above, n 115. In the English cases on proprietary estoppel, by contrast, the approach has generally been to protect the representee's expectation (subject to the proportionality test): *Jennings v Rice*, above, n 79, at [30], [54].

as part of a wider general doctrine, by reference in particular to the well-established and wider doctrine of proprietary estoppel. But until such a step is taken, the decision of the Court of Appeal in *Combe v Combe*[122] remains the authority against the use of promissory estoppel as a means of creating new obligations. At present, therefore, the only general ways in which a promise becomes enforceable in English law are if the promisee has given consideration for it, or if the promise is contained in a deed.

IV. Contractual Intention

1. The Role of the Parties' 'Intentions' in the Formation of a Contract

Some legal systems give an overriding significance to the intentions of the parties in the formation of the contract—in the sense that the distinction between a legally (contractually) binding promise and a promise which is only morally or socially binding is that in a contract the party intends to be legally bound. In such a case, the test of the parties' intention is a key test to determine the existence of a contract.

English law, as we have seen, uses two other fundamental tests to determine whether a promise or agreement is legally enforceable: the doctrine of *consideration*, which defines the scope of enforceable promises within the law of contract; and the use of a *deed*, which by its formality renders a promise enforceable even if it is not supported by consideration. So a promise in English law is binding if either the promisee has given consideration for it, or the promisor has included it in a deed which he has properly executed. 'Intention to be legally bound' is not a third possibility. A party who intends to be bound, but who does not make his promise either in a deed or in return for consideration, is not legally bound.

However, we can see that the rules of English law do tend to hold promises enforceable where there was an intention to be bound. Certainly this is so in the case of a deed: the use of a deed is a conscious use of a formality which will inevitably be associated with an intention that the deed should create legally enforceable rights against the party executing the deed. This is one of the purposes generally attributed to formalities—to ensure that the party entering into a transaction realises its significance.[123] But it might also

---

[122] Above, n 108; *Baird Textiles Holdings Ltd v Marks and Spencer plc*, above, n 112.
[123] A 'cautionary' function: LL Fuller, 'Consideration and Form' (1941) 41 *Colum L Rev* 799, 800.

be argued that the doctrine of consideration will tend to limit informal contracts to those where the parties intend to be bound. The use of nominal consideration is a deliberate attempt to bring within the law of contract (and therefore enforceability) a promise which is in substance gratuitous.[124] And even in other informal contracts which embody a more usual bargain, the fact that there is an exchange might suggest that each of the parties has thought about the value of the transaction. It should also be added that the courts are reluctant not to find consideration where they perceive that there was in fact an intention on the part of the parties to be bound.[125] But it must not be forgotten that the test is *not* the parties' intention, but whether there is consideration for the promise, or a deed.

2. 'Intention to Create Legal Relations'

The English courts do, however, sometimes refer to a doctrine of 'intention to create legal relations'. One might say that the elements required for the formation of a contract are an agreement formed by offer and acceptance; consideration; and an intention to create legal relations. But it must be understood that the role of intention is subsidiary. In the case of a contract between commercial parties, and even between a consumer and a business or professional party, the courts will generally presume from the fact of the agreement and the existence of consideration that the parties intended to be bound. This is not surprising, since the question of whether the parties intended to be legally bound will be tested objectively.[126] A deal between commercial parties can normally be expected to have legal consequences, and a consumer dealing with a commercial party similarly normally expects to enter into a binding transaction. In such cases, therefore, the question of the parties' intentions becomes relevant only if there is a claim by one of the parties that they did *not* intend to be bound. Of course, this may be shown expressly, in the language of the offer or the acceptance: the reason for using a 'subject to contract' label[127] is to ensure that one does not yet become legally bound simply because the agreement has been reached in principle; and the agreement may itself be declared to be one which is not to be legally binding.[128] Whether

---

[124] Above, pp 136–37.
[125] See eg *Williams v Roffey Bros and Nicholls* (Contractors) Ltd [1991] 1 QB 1 (CA); above, p 141. For the emphasis on the significance of giving effect to the intentions of the parties in relation to the enforcement of third-party rights, see *Darlington BC v Wiltshier Northern Ltd* [1995] 1 WLR 68 (CA) 76; below, p 239.
[126] *RTS Flexible Systems Ltd v Molkerei Alois Muller GMBH* [2010] UKSC 14, [2010] 1 WLR 753, [45]. For the general test of objectivity in contract formation see ch 5.
[127] Above, p 79.
[128] *Rose and Frank Co v JR Crompton & Bros Ltd* [1925] AC 445 (HL) ('honourable pledge' clause); *Kleinwort Benson Ltd v Malaysia Mining Corporation Bhd* [1989] 1 WLR 379 (CA) (language of 'comfort letter' made clear it was not binding).

there can be a successful challenge to the contract on the basis that a party did not intend it to have legally binding consequences therefore depends on a proper construction of the agreement, but in a purely commercial case the burden is on the party seeking to prove that there is no binding contract:

> In the present case, the subject-matter of the agreement is business relations, not social or domestic matters. There was a meeting of minds—an intention to agree. There was, admittedly, consideration for the company's promise. I accept the propositions of counsel for the plaintiff that in a case of this nature the onus is on the party who asserts that no legal effect was intended, and the onus is a heavy one.[129]

However, it is in the case of a purely domestic agreement—such as between husband and wife,[130] or between other family members[131] or friends[132]—that the courts will normally look specifically to see whether there is evidence of an intention to be bound. The domestic or social context raises the presumption that there is no intention to create legal relations. Day-to-day agreements between domestic parties—such as agreements for housekeeping or personal allowances—may not constitute contracts, but:

> There is nothing to stop a husband and wife from making legally binding arrangements, whether by contract or settlement, to regulate their property and affairs while they are still together.... These days, the commonest example of this is an agreement to share the ownership or tenancy of the matrimonial home, bank accounts, savings or other assets.[133]

---

[129] *Edwards v Skyways* [1964] 1 QB 349 (QB) 355 (Megaw J).
[130] *Balfour v Balfour* [1919] 2 KB 571 (CA).
[131] *Jones v Padavatton* [1969] 1 WLR 328 (CA) (mother's agreement to provide maintenance to adult daughter).
[132] *Coward v Motor Insurers' Bureau* [1963] 1 QB 259 (CA) (agreement to give fellow workman a lift to work).
[133] *Granatino v Radmacher* [2010] UKSC 42, [2011] 1 AC 534, [142] (Baroness Hale). The case involved the award of (financial) ancillary relief where a marriage had broken down, but the parties had entered into an ante-nuptial agreement. In such a case, although the court will give weight to the parties' agreement, it cannot be decisive because the parties cannot oust the court's jurisdiction. Baroness Hale dissented in the result in the case.

7

Vitiating Factors: Void, Voidable and Unenforceable Contracts

If the formation of a contract requires the consent of the parties to the agreement, it also follows that the law must devise rules to determine the impact on the validity of the agreement of things such as mistakes made by one or both parties at the time of entering into the agreement, and pressure to which one of the parties was subjected in giving consent. Indeed, legal systems which define a contract by reference to the agreement formed through the exchange of the parties' consents generally have a unified theory of the factors which render the consent—and therefore the agreement—defective. This is not how English law traditionally sees this area of the law. There are doctrines of mistake, misrepresentation, duress and undue influence, which we shall discuss in this chapter. But it is not common for all these topics to be brought together into a single chapter—or, sometimes, even adjacent chapters—in the English textbooks. The reason is that English law does not focus on the consent of the parties but, as we have seen in chapters five and six, views a contract as an (objectively ascertained) agreement where each party has provided consideration for the other's promises in the agreement. The contract is a bargain between the parties giving effect to their agreement. The *contract* can be vitiated ('void' or 'voidable', as we shall see below), but the courts do not generally use the language of the 'consent' being vitiated. So rather than grouping all the so-called vitiating factors into a single overarching theory based on a general principle linked to the vitiation of a party's consent, English law follows its typical pattern of having separate specific rules for separate specific defects in the formation of the contract. And we shall see that even in the modern law there are some relics of the historical distinction between the common law and equity, which developed different rules as to the circumstances in which a contract can be vitiated. However, even though there are these traditional separations between the vitiating factors, it is in fact beneficial to consider them together, because we shall see that they have certain common themes.

In addition to the vitiating factors, we shall also mention in this chapter the (in)capacity of parties, and the intervention of the courts in a contract on the basis of illegality and public policy, which are related to the vitiating factors in that they affect the validity or enforceability of contracts. We have already considered the rather different case in which a contract may be unenforceable for lack of formality.[1]

I. The Vitiating Factors in English Law; Void and Voidable Contracts

1. An Overview of the Vitiating Factors

A contract may be vitiated by mistake, misrepresentation, non-disclosure, duress, undue influence or by being an 'unconscionable bargain'. There are links between these different categories.

Mistake and misrepresentation are closely linked in that a misrepresentation only vitiates the contract when it causes a mistake. However, English law does not traditionally make this link. The textbooks tend to treat them separately—and we shall see below that a 'mistake' (that is, a pure mistake) rarely renders a contract void: the courts are very reluctant to allow a party to avoid a contract by simply proving that he was mistaken. The operation of mistake will depend on the category of mistake in question—that is, what the party made the mistake *about*—but the limited scope of remedies for mistake is clear. The range of remedies for misrepresentation, however, is wide—perhaps too wide, giving rise to a real complexity in the law of misrepresentation. One can make sense of the fundamental difference of attitude in relation to mistake and misrepresentation by seeing that in the case of a misrepresentation the defendant has caused the claimant's mistake. The claimant is not simply trying to avoid a contract because of his own (subjective) mistake but can attribute the mistake to the defendant's words or actions. On the other hand, the courts are also reluctant to give remedies for simple non-disclosure. Again, a party who seeks a remedy because the other party should have disclosed information has to justify why that other party had such a duty at all. It is an omission, rather than (as in the case of misrepresentation) a positive action.

---

[1] Above, p 126.

Duress, undue influence and 'unconscionable bargains' are also closely linked. Duress involves the use of illegitimate pressure to obtain the contract; undue influence includes less overt forms of pressure, but can also extend to the exercise of more subtle influences or the abuse of a position of trust or confidence which result in a 'stronger' party obtaining a contract at (in some sense) the expense of the 'weaker' party. Both of these doctrines are well established, although there has been some re-definition of each by the courts in recent years. The doctrine of 'unconscionable bargains' is much more limited in English law—the law of undue influence tends to cover most of the relevant ground. But all three doctrines are linked by a general approach that requires a party (who may appear to be, or claim to be, 'weaker' than the other) to justify why he should obtain release from a contract—and the mere fact of relative weakness or a disadvantageous contract (even a grossly disadvantageous contract) is not sufficient justification. Again, rather like in the contrast between mistake and misrepresentation, we see that the claimant's own position is not here normally sufficient to enable him to obtain a remedy—English law looks as much to the question 'why should the defendant lose the contract?' as to the question 'why should the claimant be allowed to be released from the contract?' These are, of course, two sides of a single question when considering remedies for the vitiating factors. But the focus on requiring justification for depriving the defendant of the contract emphasises the concern in English law to protect the contracting party's security of contract. That security should be undermined only where there is a good reason to do so—and typically that is limited to cases where the defendant bears some responsibility (in the most general sense) for what has happened.

There are situations where English law will focus more on the claimant than on the defendant, and hold that protection of the claimant is the overriding policy—such as where the claimant has a lack of capacity to contract. This will be considered briefly towards the end of the chapter, but we shall see that even in this situation there is sometimes a surprising reluctance to allow a simple incapacity to vitiate the contract where the other party had no knowledge of it or any reason to know it. There are also situations where the courts will hold that a contract is void or unenforceable because of its content or its purpose—where the contract is illegal or immoral or otherwise contrary to public policy. Again, this will be considered just briefly at the end of the chapter.

2. 'Void' and 'Voidable' Contracts

The range of remedies available for each of the vitiating factors will be outlined below. First, it is important to understand the difference between a void contract and a voidable contract.

A *void* contract is one which, although there has been (apparently) a contract formed by offer, acceptance and consideration, does not create any rights or obligations at all. It is void *ab initio* (from the beginning) and so it was not effective at any time. For example, if a contract for the sale of goods was void, then the purchaser did not acquire any property rights in the goods even if they were physically delivered to him by the seller. It is an automatic remedy, in the sense that the court and the parties do not have to do anything to make the contract void: if there is a dispute, the court simply makes a decision that the contract was always void, from the very beginning. The only 'vitiating factor' which has the effect of making the apparent contract void is mistake, although contracts may also sometimes be said to be void on the ground of illegality.

A *voidable* contract is one which was validly formed by offer, acceptance and consideration, but has a defect in it from the moment of formation. The contract is valid to create rights and obligations, but is liable to be made void; but if it is not made void, then it remains in full force. Usually the defect which makes a contract voidable is the responsibility of one of the contracting parties, and so it is only the other ('innocent') party who can have the contract made void. One should notice the terminology here: the contract is 'avoided', or is 'rescinded' the remedy by which a voidable contract is avoided is 'rescission'. Sometimes rescission is a remedy awarded by a court; but sometimes (as for misrepresentation)[2] rescission can be effected by the innocent party without a court order. If the voidable contract is rescinded, it is then retrospectively (*ab initio*) reversed: the rights and duties which were created by it are treated as if they had never been created. This means that if, for example, the property rights in goods were transferred under a contract of sale which is later rescinded, then the rights re-vest in the seller, and the parties must each make restitution of what they have received from the other under the contract. But the courts have developed various rules which prevent a contract from being rescinded, even though it was voidable because of some defect in its formation—such as where the factual reversal of performance is not in substance possible (that is, restitution is not possible); or where an innocent third party would be prejudiced by rescission of the contract (such as where the goods under a contract of sale have already been sold on to an innocent third party). A contract may be voidable for misrepresentation, or duress, or undue influence, or if it is an unconscionable bargain.

From the examples given above, it will be clear that there is sometimes a good reason for a party to seek to show that the contract is void, rather than merely voidable. If rescission would no longer be available, a party who transferred property under the contract will no longer be able to rescind the contract and recover the property. But if he can show that the contract was void, then he can show that the property rights are still his—even if the goods have been sold on to a third party. English law normally applies the rule *nemo dat quod non habet*: one cannot transfer what one does not have. If the

---

[2] Below, p 179.

apparent purchaser of goods contracted to sell them to a third party, then if the first contract, by which he 'purchased' them, was void the purchaser acquired no property rights and therefore had nothing to transfer to the third party. So the original owner can bring a claim against the third party to assert his rights.[3] Only after the limitation period has passed for the original owner to bring a claim for his property which has passed out of his possession will he lose his right to claim for it.[4] This issue has commonly arisen in relation to alleged mistakes of identity, and is discussed further below.[5]

3. The Range of Remedies for the Vitiating Factors

The party who makes a claim based on one of the vitiating factors may seek various remedies. We have already seen that he may wish to establish that there is no contract—that the contract is void. Or he may wish to obtain the rescission of the contract (through a court order or, as we shall see below, by his own act). These claims are both designed to enable him to escape the contract and be put in the position as if the contract had never existed through restitution by each party of benefits received from the other under the contract.

On the other hand, the party may seek a monetary remedy—normally damages to compensate his loss; and the claim is typically focused on the loss suffered by entering into the contract which has turned out to be unprofitable. However, a cause of action must be found for a claim for damages, which involves the claimant establishing that the defendant has committed a wrong—a breach of contract, or a tort. Mistake does not give rise to damages, because a claim of mistake does not involve an assertion that the defendant has done anything wrong, but that the contract is void because of the claimant's own mistake. Misrepresentations often give rise to claims for damages. If the defendant did not simply make a false statement during the negotiations but went further and expressly or impliedly affirmed his false statement in the terms of the contract itself, the fact that the statement is false means that there is a breach of contract. Or the making of a false statement, either dishonestly or carelessly, can give rise to an action in tort for damages

---

[3] In English law this is a claim in tort—typically the tort of conversion, for damages for the value of the goods against a party who deals with them inconsistently with the rights of the owner. The common law awarded only damages, and did not develop a general remedy of specific recovery of personal property, although the courts were given the power to order delivery of a chattel by the Common Law Procedure Act 1854 s 68. This power still exists under the Torts (Interference with Goods) Act 1977 s 3, although the more usual remedy is damages, whereupon the original owner's title to the goods is extinguished: s 5.

[4] Limitation Act 1980 s 3(2) (owner's title extinguished where no action brought for 6 years after the first conversion during which the owner has not recovered possession; in the case of a theft, or obtaining by blackmail or fraud, the time starts to run not from the theft but from the sale to the purchaser in good faith: *ibid* s 4).

[5] See *Shogun Finance Ltd v Hudson* [2003] UKHL 62, [2004] 1 AC 919, below, p 169.

to compensate the losses suffered by reliance on the statement.[6] Duress is not itself a tort, but the overt act involved in putting illegitimate pressure on the other party to procure his assent to the agreement will often constitute a tort. But there will be fewer instances when a claim based on non-disclosure or undue influence or unconscionable bargains will be covered by the law of tort. On the other hand, in some situations in which undue influence is proved there will also be a duty to account for profits made from a position of influence—a fiduciary duty between the parties.

Moreover, the conduct of a trader in making a misrepresentation to a consumer, or which constitutes duress or undue influence by a trader against a consumer, may also constitute an 'unfair commercial practice' (a 'misleading action' or an 'aggressive commercial practice') which gives the consumer other remedies: the right to 'unwind' the contract, or to a discount or to damages.[7]

Sometimes in the case of mistake, where the contract is entered into in the form of a written document agreed to by both parties, one party may seek a different remedy altogether: rectification of the written contract. This is not to escape the contract, nor to claim damages, but to have the court give effect to the version of the agreement as the claimant understood it to be rather than as it is in fact written.

More than one remedy may sometimes be available on the facts—and a claimant may sometimes be able to obtain more than one remedy, but sometimes he may have to choose between the available remedies. The context in which this most commonly arises is misrepresentation, so we shall consider this issue under that heading.

II. Mistake[8]

1. Different Ways of Categorising Mistakes

One could categorise mistakes in different ways. The primary categorisation used in this chapter is by reference to *what the mistake is about*: the terms

---

[6] For the difference between the measure of damages in contract and in tort see below, pp 180, 183.
[7] Consumer Protection from Unfair Trading Regulations 2008 SI 2008/1277, as amended by SI 2014/870; below, pp 183, 193, 196.
[8] J Cartwright, *Misrepresentation, Mistake and Non-Disclosure*, 3rd edn (London, Sweet & Maxwell, 2012) Pt II discusses this in more detail. For an overview of the approach of European legal systems, see R Sefton-Green, *Mistake, Fraud and Duties to Inform in European Contract Law* (Cambridge, Cambridge University Press, 2005).

of the contract; the identity of the other party; or the subject-matter of the contract. However, we shall also consider (but as a secondary element of the categorisation) whether the mistake was *unilateral* (made by one party alone) or was *shared* (or *common*: both parties made the same mistake). These are distinctions which have legal significance and can point towards or against a remedy for the party who made a mistake. Although this arrangement and terminology will be used in this book, it must be noted that the courts and textbook writers do not agree on the arrangement of this topic,[9] nor even on the terminology to be used.[10]

2. Mistakes About the Terms of the Contract

(a) Mistake in the Formation of a Contract

We have considered this area already in detail in chapter five. Making a mistake about the terms of the contract is not really a case of 'mistake' at all, but of the absence of agreement in the formation of the contract. If A thinks that the contract is on one set of terms, and B thinks that it is on a different set of terms, there is no agreement between them—and so no contract—unless there is some basis on which one party's 'mistake' can be overridden. This then becomes a matter of the application of the objective test for the formation of a contract. If the lack of subjective agreement can be resolved by the court holding that B's understanding of the terms is to prevail on the basis that it was reasonable for B to believe (and he did in fact believe) that A was agreeing to a contract on those terms,[11] then the court holds that A is bound on those terms in spite of his contrary intentions, and he can now be said to have been under a 'mistake' as to the terms. But it is better simply to say that there is no agreement unless B (and not A) can establish that his understanding of the terms was what he could reasonably conclude from his observation of the other party's words and conduct.

---

[9] E Peel, *Treitel: The Law of Contract*, 14th edn (London, Sweet & Maxwell, 2015) ch 8 and M Furmston, *Cheshire, Fifoot and Furmston's Law of Contract*, 16th edn (Oxford, Oxford University Press, 2012) ch 8 use as the primary division whether the mistake was shared or unilateral; until its 11th edn (2003) Treitel followed Lord Atkin in *Bell v Lever Bros Ltd* [1932] AC 161, 217 in distinguishing the effect of the mistake—whether it 'negatives consent' or 'nullifies consent'. J Beatson, A Burrows and J Cartwright, *Anson's Law of Contract*, 30th edn (Oxford, Oxford University Press, 2016) ch 8 uses the same primary division as in this book: mistakes about the terms of the contract, about the other party's identity, and about the subject-matter of the contract.

[10] Sometimes a shared mistake is described as 'mutual' (*Bell v Lever Bros Ltd* [1932] AC 161 (HL)), sometimes it is 'common' (Treitel ch 8; Anson ch 8; Cheshire, Fifoot and Furmston ch 8; *Solle v Butcher* [1950] 1 KB 671 (CA) 686, 693). But some books use the word 'mutual' to describe the very different situation where the parties are at cross-purposes, holding different beliefs or understandings, rather than the same (Cheshire, Fifoot and Furmston ch 8).

[11] Above, pp 100–02.

(b) Written Contracts: Rectification for Mistake

One situation where the language of 'mistake' is more appropriate is where the parties' agreement is put in the form of a single written contract, and one or both parties misunderstand the document so that it fails accurately to record the terms which he or they agreed. The courts will normally interpret a written contract objectively, taking into account the context of the contract (for example, its particular commercial context) but not the parties' own subjective intentions or understandings about the meaning of the document.[12] In that sense, the written document *is* the contract. The parties are then properly said to be mistaken about the written document in so far as it fails to set out their intended terms. A party to the written contract who made a mistake about its terms will sometimes be able to seek *rectification* of the document— a court order that the contract be given effect for all purposes, from the very beginning, in the terms ordered by the court rather than in the terms of the original document. Such a mistake about a written contract can be either common or unilateral.

If it is a common mistake, the purpose of the order is to correct the inaccurate recording of the parties' agreement.[13] The court must therefore be satisfied that the document fails to record the agreement, which means showing what the agreement was—the parties' common intentions—and that it continued up to the time when the contract was formed by the creation of the document. Because the document is evidence that the parties did not agree in the terms into which the claimant seeks to have the document rectified, the party seeking the remedy has a significant burden of producing evidence to substantiate his claim although here, as always in civil cases, the burden is only that he must prove his case on the 'balance of probability' (that is, more likely than not to be true).[14] It has recently been said in an obiter dictum in the House of Lords that the parties' prior 'common intention' is to be tested objectively.[15] This has not, however, met with unanimous approval,[16] and even if rectification is to be available to bring the written document into line with the parties' objectively evidenced agreement, it seems unlikely that the courts would wish to refuse rectification where the document fails to reflect the proved common subjective intentions (regardless of what the objective interpretation may be). We have seen already that in the formation

---

[12] Below, p 207.
[13] See generally *Swainland Builders Ltd v Freehold Properties Ltd* [2002] EWCA Civ 560, [2002] 2 EGLR 71 [33].
[14] *Thomas Bates and Son Ltd v Wyndham's (Lingerie) Ltd* [1981] 1 WLR 505 (CA) 521.
[15] *Chartbrook Ltd v Persimmon Homes Ltd* [2009] UKHL 38, [2009] 1 AC 1101 [60] (Lord Hoffmann).
[16] Eg *Crossco No 4 Unlimited v Jolan Ltd* [2011] EWHC 803 (Ch), [2011] All ER (D) 13 (Apr) [253].

of a contract, although the courts apply an objective test, they do not do so to override the parties' actual, subjective agreement.[17]

It is important to remember that rectification is available only if the document fails to record the terms as the parties intended them. If it accurately records the agreement, but it appears that the parties made a common mistake in their underlying agreement, or about its legal effect, that is not a matter that can be remedied by rectification. For example, in *Frederick E Rose (London) Ltd v William H Pim Jnr & Co Ltd*[18] the parties contracted in writing for sale of 'horsebeans', having agreed on the use of that (generic) term which covers a range of beans, although they both thought that it referred to a particular kind of bean, feveroles, which they knew the purchaser required in order to fulfil another contract. Rectification was refused because the mistake was in the underlying agreement: the document was an accurate expression of what the parties had in fact agreed.

Rectification for unilateral mistake is more difficult to obtain. A party who seeks the remedy claims only that the document does not reflect his *own* intentions at the time when the contract was formed, and he seeks to deprive the other party of the terms which the latter did intend. Given that the document was written so as to accord with the non-mistaken party's intentions, it will be rectified only if the claimant can show not only his mistake, but also that the other party either knew of the mistake or at least wilfully failed to take proper steps to understand what the mistaken party intended.[19] In cases in which rectification has been ordered for unilateral mistake about the terms, the judges have often phrased their reasoning in terms that the defendant obtained the contract by 'sharp practice', or 'unconscionable conduct'.

The remedy of rectification was devised by the old courts of equity, and retains the discretionary character that typified the equitable remedies although here, as elsewhere, the courts no longer exercise a broad and general discretion.[20] But it will not be ordered if the claimant has delayed bringing his claim so long that it is unjust to order rectification (the equitable doctrine of *laches*);[21] and where the order would prejudice an innocent third party.[22]

---

[17] Above, pp 100–01.
[18] [1953] 2 QB 450 (CA).
[19] *Commission for the New Towns v Cooper* [1995] Ch 259 (CA) 280–81, 292. Cf, however, D McLaughlin, 'The "Drastic" Remedy of Rectification for Unilateral Mistake' (2008) 124 LQR 608, 640 (rectification brings the written document into line with the parties' agreement as determined by the ordinary test for contract formation).
[20] Above, p 5.
[21] *Lindsay Petroleum Company v Hurd* (1873) 5 PC 221, 239.
[22] The same limitation is placed on the remedy of rescission: below, p 179.

(c) Written Contracts: Non Est Factum

Sometimes a party who has signed a document will wish to say that he is simply not bound by the document at all because of his mistake. We shall see that the courts are reluctant to allow a party to avoid the full consequences of a contract which he has signed even when the contract contains unexpected and onerous clauses.[23] But to go further and to say that the document is not binding at all because of a mistake even where the party has signed it is a very difficult claim to establish. This is the plea of *non est factum* ('it is not my deed')—which in the modern law can be raised to justify a claim that the contract is void because although the signature appears to show assent, it was assent based on mistake. But in order to raise the plea successfully it is necessary for the person who in fact signed the document to show that, at the time of the signature, he was unable to understand the document as a result of some disability (whether permanent or temporary), that the document was fundamentally different from the document which he believed that he was signing, and that he was not careless.[24]

3. Mistakes About the Identity of the Other Party

(a) Identity is Not Normally of Determining Significance

In most contracts the identity of the other party is not significant. In a contract for the sale of goods, for example, the buyer is interested in receiving good title to the goods, and the seller is interested in receiving the price. The buyer is not normally concerned to buy the goods from a particular person (rather than another), nor is the seller concerned to sell only to a particular person.

However, there are situations in which one party can legitimately say that the identity of the other contracting party was fundamental; it was with this person and *only* this person that he was prepared to enter into the contract. 'Identity' here is not just the name which a person uses: the name may be simply a label. I refer to 'John Smith' because that is the name he gave me, but if it turns out that his name is not John Smith it does not mean that I was intending to deal with a different person. It was this person, who happened to be using the name John Smith. It should be noted that in English law it easy to change one's name, even without formality, so that the use of a name may have less formal legal significance than in some other jurisdictions.

---

[23] Below, pp 206–07.
[24] *Saunders v Anglia Building Society* [1971] AC 1004 (HL).

And since there is no system of compulsory identity cards in the United Kingdom,[25] it can be difficult to verify a person's name, so names can often have simply a factual significance (to refer to a person) without necessarily defining the person. Nor is a mistake about a person's 'identity' simply a mistake about his qualities and characteristics (such as his educational qualifications to take up a contract of employment; or his creditworthiness to take goods on credit rather than paying for them on the spot in a contract of sale). The 'identity' is his very person, the things which distinguish him from other individuals for the purposes of the party's decision to enter into the contract with him.

(b) A Mistake of Identity Prevents the Formation of the Contract

At the root of a successful claim based on mistake of identity is the proposition that the parties never in fact agreed: there was no exchange of consents to form the contract, because the party who was under a mistake did not intend to deal with the other person who in fact communicated with him. One could put it in the language of the failure of offer and acceptance: A addressed his offer to B; but the person who in fact received it and purported to accept the offer was not B but C, who was pretending to be B. There was therefore no consensus between the parties. But when it is put this way it is evident that the circumstances in which such a claim will be successful are limited.

We have already seen that before there can be any prospect of succeeding in a claim based on mistake of identity, the claimant must show that it was with B *rather than* with C that A intended to contract. But if A makes the contract face-to-face with C, then it will not be easy for him to say this: he will normally choose to enter into the contract with the person who is present. This is indeed what the courts have held as a general rule: there is a presumption in face-to-face cases that each party was intending to deal with the person who was physically present.[26]

---

[25] The Identity Cards Act 2006 established a National Identity Register and provided for the introduction of identity cards, but that Act was repealed by the Identity Documents Act 2010, under which identity cards were cancelled and all information recorded in the National Identity Register was destroyed.

[26] *Ingram v Little* [1961] 1 QB 31 (CA), where it was held by a majority that the presumption was rebutted on the facts and so the contract (to sell a car to a fraudster who answered a newspaper advertisement using the name of a real person) was void. The decision on the facts has been criticised in later cases. The presumption was also applied but not rebutted in *Lewis v Averay* [1972] 1 QB 198 (CA), again a contract of sale of a car to a fraudster pretending to be another person. But Devlin LJ in *Ingram* and Lord Denning MR in *Lewis* appeared to think that the presumption was of law not fact; and may not normally be rebuttable. The most recent review is by HL in *Shogun Finance Ltd v Hudson*, below, n 29.

Where the parties did not meet, but formed their agreement through long-distance communications, it can be easier to show that the contract was void for mistake of identity, because the name used by a party during the negotiations acquires a higher significance: A receives a letter which appears to come from B (whom A knows, either personally or by reputation) and sends a reply addressed to B (and not to C).[27] But it is still necessary, as in all claims based on mistake of identity, to show that B's identity was fundamental that A was prepared to enter into this particular contract with B but not with C. The construction of A's communications here becomes crucial—to determine the person to whom they were addressed. And if there was not a separate person, B, with whom A intended to deal, but 'B' is simply a name used as an alias by C to hide his own identity and to make him sound more respectable, then there is no mistake of identity because there are not two separate identities (B and C) between which A makes a mistake.[28]

These issues, and the distinction between contracts face-to-face and other contracts, were reviewed and, by a majority, broadly confirmed by the House of Lords in *Shogun Finance Ltd v Hudson*[29] which is now the leading authority. The case involved a contract between a finance company and the hirer/purchaser under a contract for the hire-purchase of a car. The purchaser was a fraudster, who used the name (and, as evidence, the stolen driving licence of) a Mr Patel. The contract was in writing between 'Mr Patel' and Shogun, the finance company. By the time that Shogun discovered the fraud, the car had been sold to Mr Hudson, who claimed that the hire-purchase contract was only voidable not void, and that he had bought it from the person who was the hirer under the hire-purchase contract, in good faith and without notice of the defect in the earlier contract, and he had therefore acquired title to it.[30] But the majority in the House of Lords held that the hire-purchase contract was void, and so Shogun retained title. The decision was based on the fact that it was a written contract, expressed to be between Shogun and 'Mr Patel'. The parties to the contract could therefore only be those two named persons. And since the real Mr Patel was clearly not a party (he had not signed it or otherwise given his assent to the contract, of which he knew nothing), and the person signing the contract as debtor was *not* 'Mr Patel', there could be no contract.

However, even though the actual decision was taken on the narrow ground of the interpretation of the written contract, the House of Lords took the opportunity to review the identity mistake cases more generally, and were divided. The majority maintained the distinction between face-to-face

---

[27] *Cundy v Lindsay* (1878) 3 App Cas 459 (HL).
[28] *King's Norton Metal Co Ltd v Edridge, Merrett and Co Ltd* (1897) 14 TLR 98 (CA).
[29] [2003] UKHL 62, [2004] 1 AC 919.
[30] Hire Purchase Act 1964 s 27(1), (2).

contracts, in which there is a strong presumption that there is no mistake of identity, and other contracts, where the crucial issue will be the construction of the communications between the parties, viewed objectively from the position of the recipient of the communications[31] in order to determine to whom they were addressed. However, the minority would have rejected the distinction between face-to-face contracts and other contracts, and would have extended the presumption to all cases: the contract is between the parties (present or not) who actually deal with each other, and, it seems, it would normally not be possible to rebut this presumption. And so in a case like *Shogun* itself, the contract would be with the fraudster who signed the contract (even though he used the name of Mr Patel). One real concern which underpinned the reasoning of the minority (and which followed a line of argument put by Devlin LJ[32] and Lord Denning[33] in earlier cases) was the unsatisfactory position of third parties. If a contract is void (as held by the majority in *Shogun*) a third party who acquires the property in good faith and without notice of the earlier defect is unprotected. And so the minority preferred a rule which would normally hold the contract to be voidable, under which purchasers in good faith would be protected since rescission cannot be obtained if it would prejudice innocent third parties.[34] Lord Millett[35] drew attention to the difference here between English law and other systems where a purchaser in good faith from a non-owner in possession can obtain title—a rule of the law of property, rather than the law of contract. In English law, however, where a contract of sale is void, the purported transfer of the title to the goods under the contract is also void; and the application of the rule *nemo dat quod non habet*[36] means that a purchaser of a void title, even in good faith without notice of the defect in the seller's title, does not generally obtain title. The result of the majority decision in *Shogun*, therefore, in holding that a mistake of identity renders the contract void, is that in such cases English law favours the property rights of the original owner over the rights of a third-party purchaser. This remains controversial, but the Law Commission, having suggested in 2005 in the aftermath of *Shogun* that the area should be reviewed,[37] has not pursued it.[38]

---

[31] That is, in line with the general rule for the interpretation of communications between the parties negotiating for a contract: above, p 101; *Shogun Finance Ltd v Hudson* above, n 29, [123], [170].

[32] *Ingram v Little* above, n 26, 73–74.

[33] *Lewis v Averay* above, n 26, 207.

[34] Above, p 161.

[35] *Shogun Finance Ltd v Hudson* above, n 29, [84]–[85]. He used the specific example of German law. Lord Hobhouse rejected this firmly at [55].

[36] Above, p 56.

[37] Law Commission, 'Ninth Programme of Law Reform' (Law Com No 293, 2005) paras 1.16, 3.51–3.57.

[38] Law Commission, 'Tenth Programme of Law Reform' (Law Com No 311, 2008) paras 4.2–4.4; 'Eleventh Programme of Law Reform' (Law Com No 330, 2011) paras 3.4–3.6.

4. Mistakes About the Subject-Matter

(a) The 'Subject-Matter'

A mistake about the 'subject-matter' of the contract is a mistake of fact or of law which bears on the subject-matter of the obligations of one of the parties. For example, it might be a mistake about the existence of the goods under a contract of sale, or some factual characteristic or quality of the goods, or the seller's title to them. It is important to understand that this kind of mistake is different from mistakes about the terms of the contract. The terms of the contract are the parties' obligations under the contract, and without an agreement on the terms there can be no contract. But the parties can contract on an agreed set of terms (say, a contract under which the parties agree on the sale of specific goods at a particular price) whilst still making a mistake about the subject-matter of the contract (the existence or qualities of the goods). This is illustrated by *Smith v Hughes*[39] where there was a contract for the sale of oats: the buyer (a racehorse trainer) believed that they were old oats, suitable for feeding to his horses; the seller (a farmer) knew that they were new oats. The Court of Queen's Bench, hearing the case on appeal from the County Court, sent the case back for a re-trial because in instructing the jury[40] the judge had failed properly to draw the distinction between a mistake about the *terms* of the contract—the buyer believed that the seller was promising that the oats were old, whereas the seller intended no such promise; and a mistake about the *quality* of the subject-matter—the parties were agreed on their respective promises (a quantity of oats identified by a sample, in return for a price) but the buyer simply misunderstood the age of the oats.

If a contract is void for a mistake about the subject-matter, it is therefore on a different basis from a mistake about the terms, or a mistake about the other party's identity. In these latter cases, there is no contract because there was no properly-formed agreement between the parties. But if the mistake is only about the subject-matter, there *is* an agreement, but it is based on a misunderstanding by one or both parties.

(b) Unilateral Mistake

A unilateral mistake about the subject-matter does not affect the validity of the contract.[41] If the mistake was created by the other party's misrepresentation

---

[39] (1871) LR 6 QB 597.

[40] In the 19th century juries were still commonly used to determine the facts in civil trials. In the modern law jury trials are still possible, but are almost obsolete. Except in tort cases involving claims of fraud, malicious prosecution or false imprisonment there is now a presumption against a jury trial: Senior Courts Act 1981 (formerly known as Supreme Court Act 1981: above, p 7 n 11) s 69. Juries are never used in practice in claims for breach of contract.

[41] *Smith v Hughes* above, n 39, 603, 606–07; *Statoil ASA v Louis Dreyfus Energy Services LP (The Harriette N)* [2008] EWHC 2257 (Comm), [2008] 2 Lloyd's Rep 685 [88].

there may well be remedies for misrepresentation, as was shall see below. But one party's mistake, however fundamental to his decision to enter into the contract, does not make the contract void. This is the basis of the common law's approach of *caveat emptor* ('let the buyer beware') in contracts of sale. But it is not simply a question of allocating the risk to buyers under sale contracts. In all contracts each party bears the risk as to whether the subject-matter of the contract is as he believes it to be; and if he wishes to have remedies in the event that he is mistaken, he should either ask the other party for a contractual undertaking about it (that is, make the matter a term of the contract)[42] or at least ask questions so that, if he is given inaccurate answers, he will have remedies for the misrepresentation. This is so, even if the other party *knows* about the mistake since the latter has no duty to tell the mistaken party about his mistake:

> I agree that on the sale of a specific article, unless there be a warranty making it part of the bargain that it possesses some particular quality, the purchaser must take the article he has bought though it does not possess that quality. And I agree that even if the vendor was aware that the purchaser thought that the article possessed that quality, and would not have entered into the contract unless he had so thought, still the purchaser is bound, unless the vendor was guilty of some fraud or deceit upon him, and that a mere abstinence from disabusing the purchaser of that impression is not fraud or deceit; for, whatever may be the case in a court of morals, there is no legal obligation on the vendor to inform the purchaser that he is under a mistake, not induced by the act of the vendor.[43]

(c) Common (Shared) Mistake

A common mistake may, however, make a contract void, but only in very limited circumstances. In the most recent review of this area, in *The Great Peace*,[44] the Court of Appeal have said that a mistake will be sufficient only if it makes the contract 'impossible' to perform, although this does not mean only physical impossibility.

The court first asks whether the parties have provided in the contract (expressly or impliedly) for the issue about which it is said that they have made a mistake—that is, whether the *risk* of the mistake is part of the risk allocation in the contract itself. If one or other party has undertaken the risk

---

[42] In practice such matters will be often covered by implied terms in the contract, even if there is no express term. Eg in non-consumer contracts of sale by a business seller the Sale of Goods Act 1979 s 14 implies conditions as to satisfactory quality of the goods and their fitness for purpose; and if the seller knows the purpose to which the buyer intends to put them he guarantees that they can be used for that purpose. A consumer goods contract is treated as including similar terms: Consumer Rights Act 2015 ss 9, 10. See below, p 214.

[43] *Smith v Hughes* above, n 39, 606–07 (Blackburn J).

[44] *Great Peace Shipping Ltd v Tsavliris Salvage (International) Ltd (The Great Peace)* [2002] EWCA Civ 1407, [2003] QB 679.

of the 'mistake' in the contract then it is not a case of mistake at all, but simply a matter of giving effect to the contract. A good example of this is *McRae v Commonwealth Disposals Commission*[45] where the High Court of Australia held that, on the facts, the seller of a wrecked oil tanker which did not in fact exist had guaranteed its existence in the contract. The seller could not therefore claim that the contract was void for mistake, but had to pay damages under the contract to the buyer for the failure to provide the non-existent tanker—the damages being necessary to compensate the buyer for the wasted costs of the salvage expedition to look for the tanker. This case will alert the civil lawyer to the fact that there is no obstacle in English law to a contract to do the impossible. Although it might be unlikely that a party has in fact undertaken to do something which is physically impossible, this is only a matter of the construction of his undertakings—and if he has promised to do something which he cannot do, or to transfer something which does not in fact exist, then he is still bound, although he will not, of course, be bound to perform the impossible, but to pay damages to the other party. But since English law sees damages as the primary remedy, and sees the promise in economic terms rather than as having in principle to be performed,[46] this is not as strange to the English lawyer as it might be to one trained in a system which gives priority to the binding force of the performance obligation and may have a rule that the promise to do the impossible is an inherent contradiction.

If there is no express or implied allocation in the contract of the risk of the mistake, then a common mistake may be argued. The question is then whether it is possible for the parties to perform the contract according to its terms, not only in the literal sense but in the broader sense of whether the 'contractual adventure' or 'purpose' can be fulfilled. The approach was first set out in Lord Atkin's speech in *Bell v Lever Brothers Ltd* in very narrow terms: a contract can be void where both parties make a mistake as to the existence of the subject-matter, but:

> Mistake as to quality of the thing ... will not affect assent unless it is the mistake of both parties, and is as to the existence of some quality which makes the thing without the quality essentially different from the thing as it was believed to be.[47]

Lord Atkin made clear that this was to be applied narrowly:

> [I]t is of paramount importance that contracts should be observed, and that if parties honestly comply with the essentials of the formation of contracts—i.e., agree in the same terms on the same subject-matter—they are bound, and must rely on

---

[45] (1951) 84 CLR 377 (HCA), adopted as equally applicable in English law by Steyn J in *Associated Japanese Bank (International) Ltd v Crédit du Nord SA* [1989] 1 WLR 255 (QB), and by CA in *The Great Peace*.
[46] Below, p 301.
[47] [1932] AC 161 (HL) 217–18.

the stipulations of the contract for protection from the effect of facts unknown to them.[48]

The policy is against allowing mistakes to undermine contracts; and so it is only in extreme cases that the contract can be void for mistake. This can be illustrated by examples given by Lord Atkin of situations in which a mistake would not be sufficient to satisfy the test—including cases of mistake which in many civil law jurisdictions would satisfy their test and, indeed, may even constitute typical cases to illustrate the operation of mistake in the formation of a contract:

> A. buys B.'s horse; he thinks the horse is sound and he pays the price of a sound horse; he would certainly not have bought the horse if he had known as the fact is that the horse is unsound. If B. has made no representation as to soundness and has not contracted that the horse is sound, A. is bound and cannot recover back the price. A. buys a picture from B.; both A. and B. believe it to be the work of an old master, and a high price is paid. It turns out to be a modern copy.[49] A. has no remedy in the absence of representation or warranty. A. agrees to take on lease or to buy from B. an unfurnished dwelling-house. The house is in fact uninhabitable. A. would never have entered into the bargain if he had known the fact. A. has no remedy, and the position is the same whether B. knew the facts or not, so long as he made no representation or gave no warranty. A. buys a roadside garage business from B. abutting on a public thoroughfare: unknown to A., but known to B., it has already been decided to construct a byepass road which will divert substantially the whole of the traffic from passing A.'s garage. Again A. has no remedy.[50]

The test for the circumstances in which a contract will be void for common mistake was restated in *The Great Peace* as follows:

> [T]he following elements must be present if common mistake is to avoid a contract: (i) there must be a common assumption as to the existence of a state of affairs; (ii) there must be no warranty by either party that that state of affairs exists; (iii) the non-existence of the state of affairs must not be attributable to the fault of either party; (iv) the nonexistence of the state of affairs must render performance of the contract impossible; (v) the state of affairs may be the existence, or a vital attribute, of the consideration to be provided or circumstances which must subsist if performance of the contractual adventure is to be possible.[51]

Two further points must be noted about recent developments in the law relating to common mistake.

First, until recently the cases spoke of the contract being void only for a mistake of fact, and not of law. This parallels a similar traditional distinction

---

[48] *Ibid* 224.

[49] By contrast, the authenticity of a work of art is a typical case of a sufficient mistake of fact in other jurisdictions, such as France: B Nicholas, *The French Law of Contract*, 2nd edn (Oxford, Clarendon Press, 1992) 86–88.

[50] *Ibid* 224.

[51] Above, n 44 [76]. This parallels the test for frustration of the contract: below, ch 11.

between misrepresentations of law and of fact.[52] However, in both areas the distinction between law and fact has now been rejected, and a common mistake of law can now render a contract void if it satisfies the other requirements of a common mistake set out above.[53]

Secondly, after the decision of the Court of Appeal in *Solle v Butcher* in 1949[54] it appeared to become established that the court had an equitable jurisdiction to set aside a contract on the basis of a common mistake which was 'fundamental'—but this was interpreted as meaning *less* 'fundamental' than the narrow common law test for a contract to be void for common mistake. That is, even if the common mistake was insufficient to render the contract void at common law, the court could still avoid it (the contract was voidable, rather than void); and could do so in its discretion and could impose terms on the grant of the order of rescission. This principle was attributed to Denning LJ although he claimed to be drawing on some older cases from the courts of equity to justify it (hence the reference to it being an 'equitable' jurisdiction). It appears from his judgment in *Solle v Butcher* that in making this development in the law he was motivated by a reluctance to allow contracts to be void for mistake, preferring that they should be voidable (and therefore that innocent third parties would be protected if, for example, they later purchased the goods transferred under the contract);[55] but it also had the effect of giving the courts a discretionary control of the remedy, and of allowing the courts to take a more generous approach to the avoidance of contracts than the strict approach taken by the courts applying the rules of common mistake recognised by the common law. This development of the law was firmly rejected by the Court of Appeal in *The Great Peace*, not only on the basis that it had been without authority and contrary to the established caselaw including the binding decision of the House of Lords in *Bell v Lever Brothers Ltd*;[56] but also because it was wrong in principle to introduce a test which was inherently uncertain, and so gave a wide discretion to the court, and which in allowing a contract to be rescinded which would not be void at common law undermined the policy of the common law approach which is set firmly against allowing a common mistake to avoid a contract except in the most extreme cases. The extension of the law made in *Solle v Butcher*

---

[52] Below, p 177.
[53] *Brennan v Bolt Burdon* [2004] EWCA Civ 1017, [2005] QB 303 (contract of compromise, but not sufficient mistake on facts: parties had contracted on basis of risk of correctness of their assumptions about the law).
[54] [1950] 1 KB 671 (CA).
[55] Above, p 161.
[56] Above, pp 173–74. This raises an interesting issue of precedent, since the Court of Appeal must normally follow its own previous decisions, unless there is a later decision of the House of Lords (here there was not) or the earlier decision was decided per incuriam (but this normally means that it failed to take it into account; but in *Solle v Butcher* Denning LJ did discuss *Bell v Lever Bros Ltd* and sought to distinguish it): above, p 25; SB Midwinter, '*The Great Peace* and Precedent' (2003) 119 LQR 180.

can no longer be relied upon; *The Great Peace* is now the leading authority in England[57] (together with *Bell v Lever Brothers Ltd* of which it provides an interpretation). The narrowness of the operation of the doctrine of common mistake has been reinstated.

III. Misrepresentation and Non-disclosure[58]

1. Misrepresentation Contrasted with Mistake

We have already noted that misrepresentation and mistake are closely linked: to give rise to any remedy the defendant's misrepresentation must have been believed by the claimant. In the context of a misrepresentation made during the negotiations for a contract, it must have been an *inducement* to the claimant to enter into the contract. So it caused him to believe something which is not true—to make a mistake, and the mistaken belief was at least one of his reasons for entering into the contract. We have just seen that English law is very reluctant to admit that a contract is void for mistake, particularly in the case where the mistake is about the subject-matter of the contract—the facts or the state of the law which bear on the subject-matter of the contract and therefore constitute the backdrop for his decision to enter into the contract. This is largely because the English courts take a strict view of each party's responsibility for his own understanding of the facts and the law surrounding the contract: neither party can complain that he simply made a mistake about the subject-matter; and even if both parties made a mistake it only affects the validity of the contract if the mistake is so fundamental that is renders the subject-matter essentially different, or makes the planned performance in some sense impossible.

Where, however, the claimant makes a mistake by virtue of a misrepresentation made by the other party (or, sometimes, even a third party) the picture changes.

Instead of being reluctant to find a remedy at all, the courts produce a wider range of possible remedial responses. The claimant is no longer simply

---

[57] Judges in some other common law jurisdictions have been less welcoming of the decision in *The Great Peace*, criticising it for the removal of the flexibility which the had been given by *Solle v Butcher*; see eg, in Canada, *Miller Paving Ltd v B Gottardo Construction Ltd* (2007) 285 DLR (4th) 568 [26].

[58] Cartwright, *Misrepresentation, Mistake and Non-Disclosure* above, n 8, Pts I and III discuss this in more detail.

saying that he made a mistake (his fault?—at least, his risk). He is now saying that the defendant caused the mistake. Even if, as we shall see, the misrepresentation was wholly innocent (not even negligent) the claimant can rely on it to rescind the contract. In such a case, it may not be easy to say that the defendant is now the one 'at fault', but at least we can say that he is responsible for having caused the undesirable state of affairs in which the claimant finds himself. So whereas in the case of a mistake the courts were reluctant to allow a claimant to escape the contract because that would deprive the defendant of the contract—would disturb the security of contract to which he is entitled—in the case of a misrepresentation they have no such reluctance. In a sense, the defendant has deprived himself of the right to rely on the security of the contract by having caused the claimant's mistake. This link (and contrast) between mistake and misrepresentation does not often appear in the reasoning of the courts; but it explains the fundamental difference of attitude to the two areas of the law.

2. The Range of Remedies for Misrepresentation

If one party to a contract can establish a misrepresentation made by the other party, or his agent (or, sometimes, a third party), then a range of remedies is available.

We should first be clear what is meant by a 'misrepresentation'. In essence, it is the communication of false information—which may be by words (a false statement) or by conduct; but silence is not usually sufficient. There must at least be some positive action by the person making the statement (the 'representor')—such as a landlord's covering up patches of dry rot in a building so as to mislead a prospective tenant about the state of the premises.[59] But merely failing to disclose a known defect in the building is not a misrepresentation—and normally there will not even be a duty of disclosure in such circumstances.[60] A statement which is true can still be a misrepresentation if, in context, it carries an implication which is false—such as the truthful statement by the seller of land that it has been occupied until recently by a tenant at a particular level of rent which may give the false impression that this is still its rentable value.[61] Until recently the courts required that a misrepresentation must be a false statement of *fact*, and held that a statement of *law* is not a 'misrepresentation', but the law/fact distinction has been abandoned and so a misrepresentation of law can now be actionable.[62] Statements of

---

[59] *Gordon v Selico Co Ltd* [1985] 2 EGLR 79 (Ch).
[60] See below, p 186.
[61] *Dimmock v Hallett* (1866) 2 Ch App 21.
[62] *Pankhania v Hackney LBC* [2002] EWHC 2441 (Ch), [2002] All ER (D) 22 (Aug), approved in *Brennan v Bolt Burdon* [2004] EWCA Civ 1017, [2005] QB 303 (where the mistake of law rule was similarly abandoned: above, p 175).

opinion cannot generally give rise to remedies, unless either they are fraudulent (so the person making the statement is then misrepresenting his actual state of mind)[63] or the statement, though literally one of opinion, carries also an implication of fact which is false. Similarly, statements of *intention* or of *future fact* are not misrepresentations: if the person receiving such a statement (the 'representee') wishes to obtain a remedy from the representor who does not fulfil his stated intention, he should obtain a promise from him—that is, a contractually binding undertaking. Although the courts do not put it in quite this way, what they are really doing is identifying statements which the representee should be entitled to take seriously (so 'sales talk' is excluded) and on which he should be entitled to rely in entering into the contract.

To have a remedy the representee must have relied on the misrepresentation. In the context we are considering, this means that it must have induced the representee to enter into the contract. Even if the representee cannot show that he relied on the misrepresentation (and this is a difficult thing to show—generally contracting parties are motivated by a range of things in agreeing to a contract), as long as the representation is one which a reasonable person in the claimant's position would be likely to have relied on in the circumstances, a court is entitled to infer that the representee did in fact rely on it. So, in effect, the representor has to produce evidence that the representee *did not* rely on the representation. In this respect the law of misrepresentation is very favourable to the representee—and this emphasises the contrast between a pure mistake (where there is rarely a remedy) and misrepresentation (where the courts seem very favourably disposed to the party whose mistake was induced by the other).

Once it is shown that the other party made a misrepresentation, and that it induced the contract, the representee may have various possible remedies: rescission of the contract, damages in tort if the misrepresentation was made either fraudulently or negligently in breach of a duty to take care; damages (calculated on the same basis as if for fraud) under the Misrepresentation Act 1967, section 2(1), except where the misrepresentation is made by a trader to a consumer and constitutes an 'unfair commercial practice' (a 'misleading action') which then gives the consumer other remedies: the right to 'unwind' the contract, or to a discount or to damages; and damages for breach of contract if the representor not only made the misrepresentation but undertook contractual responsibility for it in the terms of the contract itself. A little needs to be said about this range of different remedies, as well as about the extent to which the claimant has the right to choose between them.

---

[63] *Edgington v Fitzmaurice* (1885) 29 ChD 459 (CA) 483 (Bowen LJ: 'the state of a man's mind is as much a fact as the state of his digestion').

3. Rescission of the Contract

Regardless of whether the representation was made fraudulently (dishonestly), or negligently (without reasonable grounds for believing it to be true) or wholly innocently, the representee is entitled to rescind the contract: the contract is voidable for misrepresentation. This is an area where the old courts of common law and of equity differed: the common law only allowed rescission in cases of fraud; but the courts of equity allowed rescission for all misrepresentations which induced the contract, and not only those made fraudulently. As usual, this is resolved in the modern law by giving priority to the equitable rule.[64]

Rescission does not require a court order; the right to rescind the contract is the right of the representee, and he can achieve it simply by an act which gives notice to the representor that he elects to rescind the contract. This may be by giving notice directly to the representee, or by doing an act (such as taking back the goods delivered under a contract of sale) which clearly shows the intention to rescind. It has even been held that attempting to find a fraudulent representor who has absconded is sufficient.[65] This is controversial because it allows a representee to avoid the contract and recover title to the goods without retaking them—and therefore might prejudice later purchasers in good faith who acquire no title.[66] But it is an example[67] of the willingness of the common law to allow self-help remedies: the innocent contracting party is able to obtain the remedy himself without the time and trouble of going to court to obtain a release from the contract. This then facilitates his being able to enter into a substitute contract more speedily. Of course the operation of any self-help remedy carries risks; and there is always the risk that the representor will challenge the validity of the rescission. But even if the court is called upon to adjudicate, the court does not itself effect the rescission but either confirms or denies that the earlier act by the representee was effective to rescind the contract.

If the contract is rescinded it is retrospectively avoided (*ab initio*), and the parties must make restitution by returning the benefits they have received from each other under the contract. But the remedy ceases to be available if (i) rescission would prejudice an innocent third party, such as a purchaser in good faith of property transferred pursuant to the contract; or (ii) the representee 'affirms' the contract—that is, he discovers that he has the right

---

[64] Above, p 7; *Redgrave v Hurd* (1881) 20 ChD 1 (CA).
[65] *Car and Universal Finance Co Ltd v Caldwell* [1965] 1 QB 525 (CA).
[66] Law Reform Committee 12th Report, Transfer of Title to Chattels (Cmnd 2958, 1966) para 16; Law Commission, Ninth Programme of Law Reform (Law Com No 293, 2005) paras 3.51–3.57. The Law Commission has not, however, pursued this: above, n 38.
[67] See also the right of an innocent party to terminate a contract for fundamental breach or breach of condition by giving notice to the party in breach: below, p 283.

to rescind but makes clear that he does not want to do so; or (iii) the representee has taken more than a 'reasonable time' to seek the remedy—which in the case of a non-fraudulent misrepresentation means a reasonable time from the contract, although time runs only from discovery of a fraud; or (iv) restitution is impossible. On this last point, it should be noted that the English courts require reversal of the actual performance for restitution to take place—and therefore if property has been sold to a third party restitution will no longer be possible. There is no principle of allowing restitution 'by equivalent' (such as by requiring the representor to hand over the purchaser money he received in exchange for the property if he has already sold it). In addition to these 'bars' to rescission which were developed by the courts, section 2(2) of the Misrepresentation Act 1967 gives the court a discretion to deny rescission, and to require the representee to take damages instead of rescission, if the misrepresentation was not fraudulent and if, in the circumstances, the court decides that allowing rescission would on balance be too harsh on the representor, given the loss that the representation has caused to the representee.[68]

The contract is voidable only if the misrepresentation was made by the other party to the contract, or his agent, or a third party of whose misrepresentation the other party had knowledge.[69] If it is made by an independent third party, the validity of the contract is not affected by the misrepresentation: as against the other contracting party the representee can claim only mistake, and not misrepresentation.

4. Damages in Tort

Sometimes a person by making a misrepresentation during the negotiations for a contract will commit a tort[70]—and the loss suffered by the representee in entering into the contract is then recoverable as damages in tort.

If the misrepresentation is fraudulent—that is, the representor did not honestly believe it to be true[71]—then he may be liable in the tort of *deceit* for all the losses suffered by the representee in reliance on the misrepresentation.

---

[68] Under s 2(4) of the 1967 Act, however, s 2 does not apply, and the court therefore has no discretion to refuse rescission, in the case of a misrepresentation made by a trader to a consumer which constitute a 'misleading action' giving the consumer a right to redress under Part 4A of the Consumer Protection from Unfair Trading Regulations 2008: below, p 183.
[69] *Royal Bank of Scotland plc v Etridge (No 2)* [2001] UKHL 44, [2002] 2 AC 773 [40].
[70] English law has a series of separate torts, each with their own separate rules: above, p 38.
[71] *Derry v Peek* (1889) 14 App Cas 337 (HL) 374 (Lord Herschell, making clear that fraud includes making a false statement '(1) knowingly, or (2) without belief in its truth, or (3) recklessly, careless whether it be true or false': but this does not include honest carelessness). See also above, p 84.

Where the fraudulent misrepresentation induced the representee to enter into a contract, this will normally be the loss suffered in consequence of entering into the contract. The burden lies on the representee to establish the defendant's fraud, and although the standard of proof is the usual civil standard of the balance of probability the courts require strong evidence before they are satisfied that it is more likely than not that the defendant was dishonest. Fraud is not easy to establish.

If the misrepresentation was made negligently—that is, where the representor did not fulfil a duty to take care in making the statement—then he may be liable in the tort of *negligence* for the losses suffered by the representee in consequence of the breach of duty. The claim in negligence is easier for the claimant than a claim in deceit since he need not establish fraud on the part of the defendant. But in other respects the claim in negligence is less potent. First, the representee must show that the representor owed him a duty to take care in making the statement. This is normally the case only where the representor had special skill or knowledge in relation to the subject-matter of the statement, and knew or ought to have known the purpose to which the representee would put the information without independently verifying it,[72] but this can certainly include information given by one party to another during the negotiations for a contract.[73] Secondly, the representee must show that the defendant breached his duty—that he failed to exercise reasonable care in making the false statement. Just because he owed a duty of care and in fact made a false statement does not show that he was in breach: even a careful representor might give inaccurate information. Thirdly, the range of loss covered by the tort of negligence can be less than the loss covered by the tort of deceit. A fraudulent defendant cannot be heard to say that he should not be liable for all the damage which he has caused by his fraud;[74] but a negligent defendant is only careless and can only be held liable for the foreseeable consequences of his actions.[75]

A claim in tort can be brought against anyone who commits the tort; and the torts of deceit and negligence can be committed not only by parties to the contract by making misrepresentations during the negotiations, but also by third parties, including the agents of the parties who can then incur personal liability.

Damages in tort are calculated to compensate the loss suffered by the person against whom the tort is committed; and 'loss' in this context means the amount by which his wealth is diminished by the tort. In the context of a

---

[72] *Caparo Industries Plc v Dickman* [1990] 2 AC 605 (HL) 638 (Lord Oliver, setting out a test drawn from *Hedley Byrne & Co Ltd v Heller & Partners Ltd* [1964] AC 465 (HL) and later cases).
[73] *Esso Petroleum Co Ltd v Mardon* [1976] QB 801 (CA). See also above, p 85.
[74] *Smith New Court Securities Ltd v Scrimgeour Vickers (Asset Management) Ltd* [1997] AC 254 (HL).
[75] *The Wagon Mound* [1961] AC 388 (PC).

precontractual misrepresentation actionable in deceit or in negligence, this generally means that the core measure of loss is the amount by which he is worse off (in economic terms) as a result of relying on the misrepresentation and entering into the contract. It is important to note that the profits which the representee hoped to make from the contract are not recoverable in tort—that would be a claim for 'expectation' measure damages and is available only for breach of contract.[76]

5. Damages under Section 2(1) of the Misrepresentation Act 1967

A general claim to damages for precontractual misrepresentation was established by section 2(1) of the Misrepresentation Act 1967:

> 2.—(1) Where a person has entered into a contract after a misrepresentation has been made to him by another party thereto and as a result thereof he has suffered loss, then, if the person making the misrepresentation would be liable to damages in respect thereof had the misrepresentation been made fraudulently, that person shall be so liable notwithstanding that the misrepresentation was not made fraudulently, unless he proves that he had reasonable ground to believe and did believe up to the time the contract was made that the facts represented were true.

Under this provision a party to a contract who made a misrepresentation to the other party before the contract was concluded is liable to pay damages for the loss caused, unless he can prove that he honestly believed the representation, and had reasonable grounds for so believing. Although the subsection does not mention 'negligence' this is in substance what it aims to cover, because it holds a representor liable only if he did not have reasonable grounds to believe in the truth of his statement. However, the claim is significantly better for the representee than a claim in the tort of negligence, since he does not have to prove that the defendant owed a duty of care (simply that he made a precontractual misrepresentation), nor even that he was negligent (it is for the defendant to prove that he honestly and on reasonable grounds believed his statement—that is, he must prove that he was *not* negligent). Moreover, it has been held that the reference to fraud in the subsection results in the damages being calculated on the same basis as in the tort of deceit, rather than the tort of negligence—including, therefore, unforeseeable losses.[77] Following an amendment made in 2014, however, section 2 of the 1967 Act does not apply in the case of a misrepresentation made by a trader to a consumer which constitutes a 'misleading action' giving the consumer a right to redress under Part 4A of the Consumer Protection from Unfair Trading Regulations 2008 (see below).

---

[76] Below, p 184.
[77] *Royscot Trust Ltd v Rogerson* [1991] 2 QB 297 (CA).

6. Right to Redress under the Consumer Protection from Unfair Trading Regulations 2008

The Consumer Protection from Unfair Trading Regulations 2008[78] prohibited unfair commercial practices by traders against consumers, but the Regulations as originally introduced did not give private law remedies to consumers.[79] The Regulations were amended in 2014, however, to provide 'rights to redress' for consumers against traders where an unfair commercial practice is either a 'misleading action' or an 'aggressive commercial practice', which is a significant factor in the consumer's decision to enter into the contract. These rights to redress are the right to 'unwind' the contract (the contract comes to an end, payments made are refunded and goods transferred are returned); the right to a discount in respect of the payments made or due under the contract; and damages for consequential financial loss, alarm, distress or physical inconvenience or discomfort.[80]

Where the conduct which constitutes a 'misleading action' takes the form of a misrepresentation, the Regulations provide the consumer with new remedies in addition to the other remedies that may be available for the misrepresentation, except for claims to damages under section 2 of the Misrepresentation Act 1967, which are excluded in cases where the 2008 Regulations apply.[81]

7. Remedies for Breach of Contract

Statements made during the negotiations do not necessarily become part of the contract itself. If, however, the representor promised in the contract, either expressly or impliedly, that a statement was true, then he is in breach of contract if the statement is not true, and the representee can pursue remedies for breach of contract: typically damages for the loss caused by the breach, but also sometimes termination of the contract for breach.[82] It is common for express provision to be made in negotiated commercial contracts to incorporate particular representations into the contract: for example, certain representations which were made during the negotiations for a sale of shares on a company take-over may be listed and repeated in the contract itself, and given contractual force (commonly referred to as 'representations and warranties').

---

[78] SI 2008/1277, implementing Directive 2005/29/EC.

[79] Regulation 29 provided that an agreement should not be void or unenforceable by reason only of a breach of the Regulations.

[80] Part 4A of the 2008 Regulations, as amended by SI 2014/870.

[81] Misrepresentation Act 1967 s 2(4), added by the 2014 amendment to the 2008 Regulations. The 'rights to redress' for aggressive commercial practices will in practice overlap with the remedies for duress and undue influence: below, pp 193, 196.

[82] For termination see below, p 281.

It is also very common for a clause to be inserted into a written contract denying contractual force to any statement which is not expressly repeated in the contract (a so-called 'entire agreement' or 'integration' clause). These clauses are designed to give certainty to the contracting parties about the existence and scope of the contract terms, and in particular in relation to pre-contractual representations. In the absence of such clauses, a court might hold that a representation made during the negotiations impliedly became a term of the contract, particularly where it was a representation by a party who was in a better position than the other to know the detail of the information which he was providing.[83]

In the case of consumer contracts for the supply of goods, digital content or services, however, most statements made by the trader to the consumer during the negotiations will become terms of the contract, since traders are now required to provide certain information to consumers about the goods, digital content and services,[84] and the Consumer Rights Act 2015 provides that the contract is to be treated as including such information as a term, as well as any description of the goods or digital content given by the trader to the consumer, and anything said or written by the trader to the consumer about the trader or the service under a services contract.[85] This will therefore provide the consumer with remedies for breach of contract in addition to the other remedies that may be available for the misrepresentation.[86]

Damages for breach of contract are calculated to put the innocent party into the financial position in which he would have been had the contract not been broken.[87] So if there is a contractual guarantee that a statement is true, the damages payable for breach of contract if the statement is not true are designed to put the representee into the position as if it *had been* true: it protects (in financial terms) his 'expectations' arising from the representation.

8. Choosing between the Remedies

The remedies outlined above are not all mutually exclusive. A claimant may obtain rescission of the contract, and at the same time recover damages on the tort measure (in deceit or negligence or under section 2(1) of the Misrepresentation Act 1967) because there is no logical inconsistency between

---

[83] For incorporation of precontractual representations into the contract see below, pp 203–05.

[84] Consumer Contracts (Information, Cancellation and Additional Charges) Regulations 2013 (SI 2013/3134); below, p 187.

[85] Consumer Rights Act 2015 ss 11–12 (goods contracts), ss 36–37 (digital content contracts) and s 50 (services contracts).

[86] For additional remedies available to the consumer where the breach of contract consists in a breach of the terms treated as included by the Consumer Rights Act 2015, see below, p 297.

[87] Below, p 288.

them: rescission, with its attendant restitution, is designed to put the parties back into the position as if the contract had never been formed, and tort damages are to compensate loss similarly in order to put the claimant in the financial position as if he had not entered into the contract. If the claimant rescinds, he will reduce much of his tort loss—but if (after rescission) he still has out-of-pocket losses he may wish to claim them as damages in tort. On the other hand, the claimant cannot both rescind and claim damages for breach of contract, because the contract has to continue in existence for the breach of contract claim, but is avoided *ab initio* in rescission: they are logically inconsistent.

The law of remedies for misrepresentation is complex but gives a wide range of choice to claimants who have been misled by the other contracting party in entering into the contract. Which remedy the claimant will prefer depends on his circumstances and the relative merits of each on the facts.

9. Exclusion of Remedies for Misrepresentation

It is common, particularly in commercial contracts, for the parties to include express provision relating to misrepresentation. We have already seen that the contract may regulate the contractual remedies flowing from precontractual representations by expressly repeating representations in the contract, and providing by an 'entire agreement' clause that such representations will alone have contractual force.[88] However, given the fact that parties often make statements during the negotiations for a contract, which could (if found later not to be accurate) give rise not only to claims for breach of contract but also to a range of other remedies described earlier in this chapter, the parties may seek to manage the risk of later litigation by excluding or limiting the remedies that would otherwise be available for misrepresentation. Such clauses may take the form not only of exclusion and limitation of liability clauses, but also of clauses which purport to prevent the liability arising, such as by providing that neither party has made any representation, or that neither party has relied on any representation that has been made ('no representation' and 'non-reliance' clauses). Even if misrepresentations were in fact made and relied on, the party who has agreed in the contract to such a clause will be unable to plead the other party's misrepresentation to obtain a remedy,[89] although where the effect of the clause is to exclude or restrict a liability or remedy which would otherwise have been been available for a precontractual

---

[88] Above, p 184.
[89] It is a 'contractual estoppel': each party is estopped by the terms of the contract from pleading the misrepresentation: *Peekay Intermark Ltd v Australia and New Zealand Banking Group Ltd* [2006] EWCA Civ 386, [2006] 2 Lloyd's Rep 511, [57]; *Springwell Navigation Corp v JP Morgan Chase Bank* [2010] EWCA Civ 1221, [2010] 2 CLC 705.

misrepresentation, the statutory control on clauses excluding or restricting liability for misrepresentation will still apply.[90]

10. Non-disclosure

At the start of this chapter we saw that English law is reluctant to allow a party to escape from a contract by simply proving that he made a mistake. We have now seen that, where the mistake was induced by the other party's misrepresentation, the picture is quite different: a range of remedies is available, including rescission of the contract even where the misrepresentation was innocent (not even negligent). The fact that the defendant was responsible for causing the claimant's mistake changes the picture completely. A claim for a remedy based on the defendant's non-disclosure lies between mistake and misrepresentation. The claimant is not simply asserting his own mistake. But nor is he saying that the defendant did anything which actively caused it—rather, that the defendant could and should have given him information which would have affected his decision to contract.

English law is very reluctant to impose duties of disclosure. A successful claim of non-disclosure is a claim based on the defendant's *omission* to provide information. It is much easier to find a (negative) duty not to provide false information (misrepresentation) than to find a (positive) duty to provide information (non-disclosure). The starting-point in the common law is that there is no such positive duty:

> [W]hatever may be the case in a court of morals, there is no legal obligation on the vendor to inform the purchaser that he is under a mistake, not induced by the act of the vendor.[91]

This is consistent with the general approach in English law to the arm's-length relationship between the parties during negotiations.[92] However, there are certain situations in which a party will be required to disclose information during the negotiations for a contract.

There are certain types of contract in which the law attributes to the parties the obligation to disclose information during its formation and where the remedy for breach of the duty of disclosure is rescission of the contract (that is, the same remedy as where a contract is induced by the other party's

---

[90] Misrepresentation Act 1967 s 3 (non-consumer contracts), below, p 229; *Springwell Navigation Corp v JP Morgan Chase Bank* above, n 89, [181]; *Axa Sun Life Services plc v Campbell Martin Ltd* [2011] EWCA Civ 133, [2011] 1 CLC 312, [51]. An 'entire agreement' clause does not exclude liability for misrepresentation and so s 3 does not apply: *Inntrepreneur Pub Co (GL) v East Crown Ltd* [2000] 2 Lloyd's Rep 611 (Ch) 614. For consumer contracts, the general controls on unfair terms in Part 2 of the Consumer Rights Act 2015 apply: see below, p 230.

[91] *Smith v Hughes* (1871) LR 6 QB 597, 607 (Blackburn J).

[92] Above, p 78.

misrepresentation). Such contracts have sometimes been given by the courts the label '*uberrimae fidei*' ('utmost good faith') but this is a curious expression, given that English law does not have a more general category of (normal) 'good faith' contracts. The most common example used to be the contract of insurance, in which each party had at common law a duty of disclosure towards the other of material facts within his knowledge (including, in certain cases, facts which he ought to know) which are material to the risk to be covered by the contract.[93] However, the consumer's duty of disclosure has now been removed and replaced by a duty to take reasonable care not to make a misrepresentation to the insurer,[94] and the non-consumer's common law duty of disclosure has been replaced by a new statutory duty to make to the insurer a 'fair presentation of the risk'.[95] It has also been held that there are mutual duties of disclosure of material facts amongst parties who are negotiating to create a contract of partnership,[96] and between members of a family who settle a dispute amongst themselves (such as the division of property).[97] There are more limited duties of disclosure on creditors in favour of sureties,[98] and some more particular obligations on creditors where the contract of surety consists of a bank guarantee in favour of a debtor with whom the surety has a non-commercial relationship, such as a wife's guarantee of her husband's business debts in which she has no commercial interest.[99] In addition, there are certain types of contract where statute imposes duties of disclosure, attaching various different remedies. Particularly significant are duties imposed on traders in favour of consumers in the case of many 'off-premises' (or 'doorstep') contracts and 'distance' contracts for goods or services,[100]

---

[93] *Carter v Boehm* (1766) 3 Burr 1905, 97 ER 1162; *Banque Financière de la Cité SA v Westgate Insurance Co Ltd* [1991] 2 AC 249 (HL).
[94] Consumer Insurance (Disclosure and Representations) Act 2012.
[95] Insurance Act 2015 (in force from 12 August 2016).
[96] *Conlon v Simms* [2006] EWHC 401 (Ch), [2006] 2 All ER 1024; [2006] EWCA Civ 1749, [2008] 1 WLR 484.
[97] *Greenwood v Greenwood* (1863) 2 De GJ & S 28, 46 ER 285.
[98] *Hamilton v Watson* (1845) 12 Cl & Fin 109, 8 ER 1339 (HL Sc, but applied also in England): the duty is only to disclose any unusual feature of the contract with the debtor which is being guaranteed by the surety.
[99] *Royal Bank of Scotland Plc v Etridge (No 2)*, above, n 69 (the duty is not necessarily one of personal disclosure but to take steps to ensure that the surety has understood the implications of the transaction, in order to minimise the risk of misrepresentation or undue influence by the debtor against the surety).
[100] Consumer Contracts (Information, Cancellation and Additional Charges) Regulations 2013 SI 2013/3134, implementing Directive 2011/83/EU (exclusions from the application of the Regulations are set out at reg 6). Failure to provide the required information does not make the contract voidable, but extends the consumer's statutory right to cancel the contract, and under reg 18, the contract is treated as including a term that the trader has complied with his duty to provide information. Where information is in fact provided under the 2013 Regulations, it is treated as being included as a term of the contract under the Consumer Rights Act 2015: above, p 184.

or 'distance' contracts for financial services;[101] and duties imposed on persons responsible for the issue of company prospectuses and listing particulars.[102]

Taken together, the provisions governing consumer contracts appear to come close to imposing a general duty of disclosure on traders in dealing with consumers. But the English courts regard all these particular duties as exceptions to the general rule that there is no duty of disclosure. For the common lawyer, the fact that there are specific duties—and even specific statutory duties of disclosure—does not lead by a process of inductive reasoning to a general duty of disclosure. It would be open to a court to take such a step as a matter of the development of the common law on disclosure, but given the fundamental difference between misrepresentation and non-disclosure, and the general approach of the courts to the (arm's length) relationship between the parties during the negotiations for a contract, the courts are likely to be very cautious indeed in making any extension to the duties of disclosure.

Moreover, there is generally no liability in tort for failing to disclose relevant information to the other party during negotiations. The tort of deceit requires a misrepresentation: even a deliberate withholding of information does not give rise to liability.[103] There have been some recent suggestions in the case-law that if the defendant owes a duty of disclosure by virtue of the nature of the contract which the parties are negotiating, the fraudulent failure to disclose might give rise to damages in deceit.[104] But there are contrary authorities[105] so this cannot yet be regarded as settled. And although the duty of care in negligence can impose a duty to provide information—for example, a professional adviser can undertake a continuing duty to offer advice when it should be relevant to his client's circumstances—the courts will not use this tort to impose general duties of disclosure because it would undermine the nature of the relationship between the negotiating parties.[106]

Sometimes, however, the courts will require a party to disclose information to the other as part of his duty to act in the latter's interests—not because of the type of contract in question, but because of the type of relationship

---

[101] Financial Services (Distance Marketing) Regulations 2004 SI 2004/2095, implementing Directive 2002/65/EC: failure to provide the required information does not make the contract voidable or give rise to damages, but extends the consumer's statutory right to cancel the contract.

[102] Financial Services and Markets Act 2000 ss 80, 81: the remedy under s 90 is damages payable to anyone who has acquired securities to which the prospectus or listing particulars relate and has suffered loss as a result of the omission.

[103] *Peek v Gurney* (1873) LR 6 HL 377, 391, 403.

[104] *HIH Casualty and General Insurance Ltd v Chase Manhattan Bank* [2001] EWCA Civ 1250, [2001] 2 Lloyd's Rep 483 [48], [164], [168]; *Conlon v Simms* [2006] EWHC 401 (Ch), [2006] 2 All ER 1024, [202]; [2006] EWCA Civ 1749, [2008] 1 WLR 484 [130].

[105] *HIH Casualty and General Insurance Ltd v Chase Manhattan Bank* [2003] UKHL 6, [2003] 2 Lloyd's Rep 61 [75].

[106] Above, pp 81–82.

which already exists between the parties at the time when the contract is negotiated. If, for example, the parties who negotiate a contract are already partners, they already independently owe each other the duty of good faith in their mutual dealings; or if one party is a trustee of the other, or owes him fiduciary duties, he has inherent duties in favour of the other party under the trust or fiduciary relationship. This is a point at which the law of contract (the nature of the duty owed during the negotiations) intersects with the legal rules for the protection of particular individuals by virtue of their position. In this respect there is a similar close link also in the law of undue influence, discussed below.

Moreover, parties will sometimes disclose information because it is in their interest to do so—the rules of the law of contract provide some incentives to disclose. For example, once the seller of goods is on notice about purposes to which the purchaser proposes to put the goods, he may be held impliedly to have promised that the goods will be suitable for those purposes[107] and so will be liable for breach of contract if he does not inform the buyer about any relevant limits to the purposes which the goods might fulfil. Rather than imposing duties of disclosure, the law uses the doctrine of implied terms—and so the risk allocation in the contract itself—to remedy the failure to provide certain relevant pieces of information. But this is still quite limited in scope, and is a long way from being in substance a general duty of disclosure.

IV. Duress, Undue Influence and Unconscionable Bargains

1. Pressure and Abuse of Position

Duress, undue influence and the doctrine of 'unconscionable bargains' are related because they involve one party to the contract either having applied some form of pressure on the other, or having abused his position vis-à-vis the other in order to obtain the contract. The party who gave his assent to the contract under such pressure or in response to such an abuse of his position by the other party is entitled to revoke his assent: the contract is voidable.

---

[107] Sale of Goods Act 1979 s 14(3) (non-consumer contracts); Consumer Rights Act 2015 s 10 (consumer contracts); below, p 214.

These areas are similar to misrepresentation in providing protection to a party whose freedom to form an independent judgment about the merits of the contract has been impaired because of what the other party has said or done (more or less overtly). In misrepresentation, the informational basis of the party's judgment is impaired because he is misled by the other party's false statement; and—as in the case of a pure mistake—he unwittingly enters into the contract in circumstances where, had he known the truth, he might not have done. In duress, however, and in some cases of undue influence, the party knows what he is doing, but has no real choice in the matter. On the other hand there are also cases of undue influence where the party exercising the influence does so in more subtle ways and the victim may not realise that he is the victim of an abuse of the other party's position.

It is clear, however, that these are all separate doctrines in English law with their own separate rules. In *Lloyds Bank Ltd v Bundy* Lord Denning tried to bring them together into a single general doctrine of 'inequality of bargaining power':

> By virtue of it, the English law gives relief to one who, without independent advice, enters into a contract upon terms which are very unfair or transfers property for a consideration which is grossly inadequate, when his bargaining power is grievously impaired by reason of his own needs or desires, or by his own ignorance or infirmity, coupled with undue influences or pressures brought to bear on him by or for the benefit of the other. When I use the word 'undue' I do not mean to suggest that the principle depends on proof of any wrongdoing. The one who stipulates for an unfair advantage may be moved solely by his own self-interest, unconscious of the distress he is bringing to the other. I have also avoided any reference to the will of the one being 'dominated' or 'overcome' by the other. One who is in extreme need may knowingly consent to a most improvident bargain, solely to relieve the straits in which he finds himself. Again, I do not mean to suggest that every transaction is saved by independent advice. But the absence of it may be fatal.[108]

Before it could be further developed in the later cases this generalisation was rejected on the basis that the individual doctrines are sufficiently clearly defined by their own separate rules; Lord Denning's principle did not in fact accurately cover the existing law in the separate doctrines; and it was not appropriate for the courts to create a 'general principle of relief against inequality of bargaining power—this task is appropriate to the legislator, not the courts'.[109] On this last point, it is important to be clear what is involved in all the doctrines covered in this section: a contracting party is able to avoid a contract where he entered into it under pressure from the other party

---

[108] [1975] QB 326 (CA) 339.
[109] *National Westminster Bank Ltd v Morgan* [1985] AC 686 (HL) 707–08 (Lord Scarman).

(or of which the other party had notice), or where the other party has in some sense abused his position vis-à-vis the claimant. None of these doctrines is designed to give a remedy to a party simply because of the 'unfairness' of the terms of the contract; nor to give a remedy to a 'weaker' party simply because of his weakness in relation to the other contracting party, although we shall see that in some circumstances it can be very relevant to consider the terms of the contract (one party gets significantly the better side of the bargain) or the balance of the relationship between the parties (one party is significantly 'stronger' than the other).

2. Duress

A contract is voidable on the ground of duress where the other party induced the claimant to contract by applying 'illegitimate' pressure which gave him no practical choice but to submit. Until the 1970s the courts had not developed duress beyond the cases of threats to harm the claimant's person or his property—and it was not even certain that threats to harm property were sufficient. But in the last forty years they have extended it to cover threats to the claimant's economic interests, commonly referred to as 'economic duress'.

The older cases, dealing with threats to the person, were relatively straightforward. It is not difficult to see that a contract entered into under such threats should not be enforceable by the party who made the threats. One question which the courts had to address was the necessary link between the threats and the contract: the test of causation. They held that, as long as the threat was *a* reason for the claimant having decided to enter into the contract, that was sufficient to entitle him to avoid the contract, even if he had other reasons which might still have led him to enter into the same contract if there had been no threat.[110] This matches the test in misrepresentation—the false statement need only be a reason (an inducement) for the contract.

Once duress is extended to cover not only threats to the person and to property but also to purely economic interests, however—such as the threat to break a contract and thereby to cause loss—it is less obvious that the pressurised party should be able to escape the contract entered into under such a threat. The wrongfulness of the threat is less immediately obvious; and it is less clear that the claimant should have given in to the threat by agreeing to enter into the contract, rather than being expected to take some other course of action. A context in which this issue may arise is in the pressurised variation of an existing contract: one party threatens not to continue unless he is paid more money, and the other party agrees to increase the payments. The resulting agreement can be a new contract or a contractual variation

---

[110] *Barton v Armstrong* [1976] AC 104 (PC).

of the original contract as long as there is consideration for the new agreement;[111] but is the new or varied contract voidable for duress? Even if the threat to break a contract is capable of being 'economic duress', should the payor simply give in and agree to the new price rather than using other remedies (such as by enforcing the original contract itself)? In the earliest cases which accepted the extension of duress to include threats of economic consequences, the courts began to draw the distinction between 'illegitimate pressure' which is capable of being duress, and 'commercial pressure' which is not.[112] This admits that sometimes one is expected by the law to put up with threats and pressure directed against one's economic interests, but that sometimes the threat or pressure may go beyond that and become unacceptable. It is inevitably a difficult line to draw.

The House of Lords reviewed the developing doctrine of economic duress in *The Universe Sentinel*,[113] and made clear that where a party raises duress either as a claim (to have the contract rescinded) or as a defence to the enforcement of the contract against him, he must show that the pressure was 'illegitimate', and that he had no practical choice but to submit. Pressure is illegitimate if the thing threatened was unlawful (a crime, a tort or a breach of contract) or if the way in which a (lawful) thing was threatened made the use of the threat itself illegitimate: that is, the nature of the demand can make the threat of something lawful into 'illegitimate' pressure, as in the crime of blackmail.[114] But the legitimate threat of something that one is entitled to do is not duress—such as the threat not to enter into future contracts unless the other party agrees to a particular contract now.[115] Steyn LJ has emphasised that it would destabilise commercial contracts if the threat of lawful action could constitute duress:

> We are being asked to extend the categories of duress of which the law will take cognisance. That is not necessarily objectionable, but it seems to me that an extension capable of covering the present case, involving 'lawful act duress' in a commercial

---

[111] *Williams v Roffey Bros & Nicholls (Contractors) Ltd* [1991] 1 QB 1 (CA), which relaxed the doctrine of consideration in this context because of the developments in economic duress: above, pp 140–42; *Atlas Express Ltd v Kafco (Importers and Distributors Ltd)* [1989] 1 QB 833 (QB) (variation vitiated by duress).

[112] *Occidental Worldwide Investment Corp v Skibs A/S Avanti (The Siboen and the Sibotre)* [1976] 1 Lloyd's Rep 293 (QB) 336; *Pao On v Lau Yiu Long* [1980] AC 614 (PC) at 635.

[113] *Universe Tankships Inc of Monrovia v International Transport Workers Federation (The Universe Sentinel)* [1983] 1 AC 366 (HL). See Lord Diplock at 383–84 and Lord Scarman at 400–01. *The Universe Sentinel* involved a claim for restitution of money paid under duress rather than a contract entered into under duress, but it was applied to a case of contract in *Dimskal Shipping Co SA v International Transport Workers Federation* [1992] 2 AC 152 (HL).

[114] Theft Act 1968 s 21(1): 'A person is guilty of blackmail if, with a view to gain for himself or another or with intent to cause loss to another, he makes any unwarranted demand with menaces; and for this purpose a demand with menaces is unwarranted unless the person making it does so in the belief (a) that he has reasonable grounds for making the demand; and (b) that the use of the menaces is a proper means of reinforcing the demand.'

[115] *CTN Cash and Carry Ltd v Gallaher Ltd* [1994] 4 All ER 714 (CA).

context in pursuit of a bona fide claim, would be a radical one with far-reaching implications. It would introduce a substantial and undesirable element of uncertainty in the commercial bargaining process. Moreover, it will often enable bona fide settled accounts to be reopened when parties to commercial dealings fall out. The aim of our commercial law ought to be to encourage fair dealing between parties. But it is a mistake for the law to set its sights too highly when the critical inquiry is not whether the conduct is lawful but whether it is morally or socially unacceptable... Outside the field of protected relationships, and in a purely commercial context, it might be a relatively rare case in which 'lawful act duress' can be established.[116]

The illegitimate pressure will constitute duress if the victim had no practical choice but to submit: there was no alternative course of action which he could reasonably have been expected to take. But it has been suggested that the test of causation in economic duress is different from that in duress to the person. In the latter case, it is sufficient that the illegitimate pressure was 'a' cause. But where the pressure is only economic, the link between the pressure and the contract takes on a higher significance: it must be 'decisive' or 'clinching'.[117]

If the contract is voidable for duress, rescission will be barred for some of the same reasons as rescission can be barred for misrepresentation: if rescission would prejudice an innocent third party; if restitution is impossible;[118] or if the claimant has affirmed the contract.[119] But the contract will be taken to be affirmed only if the party subjected to the duress expressly or impliedly accepts it (for example, he acts on the contract without making any objection based on the duress) *after* the pressure has ceased.

The remedy for duress is rescission of the contract. But the tort of 'intimidation' may often be committed by a person who applies duress, which will allow the victim of duress (whether he affirms or rescinds the contract), or a third party, to claim his loss from the party who applied the threats.[120] In the case of a contract between a trader and a consumer, the conduct of a trader in subjecting the consumer to duress may also constitute an 'aggressive commercial practice' which gives the consumer the right to 'unwind' the contract, or to a discount or to damages.[121]

---

[116] *Ibid* 719.
[117] *Huyton SA v Peter Cremer GmbH & Co* [1999] 1 Lloyd's Rep 620 (QB) 636.
[118] *Halpern v Halpern* [2007] EWCA Civ 291, [2008] 1 QB 195.
[119] *North Ocean Shipping Co Ltd v Hyundai Construction Co Ltd* [1979] QB 705 (QB).
[120] *Rookes v Barnard* [1964] AC 1129 (HL).
[121] Consumer Protection from Unfair Trading Regulations 2008 SI 2008/1277, as amended by SI 2014/870; above, p 183.

3. Undue Influence

We have seen that before the 1970s duress was very limited in its scope: it only applied to open, direct threats; and only to threats to harm a person (or, possibly, his property). The principles of duress were originally developed by the common law courts. The courts of equity developed a parallel principle undue influence which allowed them to hold voidable a contract which had been induced by one party's pressure on the other, or some other abuse of the relationship between the parties, but which did not constitute duress at common law either because it was less openly threatening (for example, implicit pressure, not a threat but giving the other party no real choice but to comply—such as a wife being given no choice but to comply with her husband's wishes in signing documents to allow him to have rights over her property)[122] or not even threatening at all but constituted the abuse of a relationship of trust (for example, the willing submission of a sister to the rules of her sisterhood and the instructions of her spiritual advisor in transferring property to the sisterhood);[123] or because it was threatening something less than harm to the other party's person or his property (such as threats to report a member of the other party's family to the police unless the party agrees to enter into a contract).[124]

The courts also developed a distinction between 'actual' undue influence, where there was evidence on the facts that one party had in fact applied unfair pressure or influence over the other; and 'presumed' undue influence, where there was no such evidence but the court inferred it from a combination of (a) the 'influencing' party being in a dominant position in which he could take advantage of the other by exerting pressure; and (b) the terms of the resulting contract being such that the 'influencing' party obtained a very significant advantage; and (c) there being no evidence that the 'influenced' party had in fact exercised independent will in entering into the contract (such as by taking independent legal advice). However, in *Royal Bank of Scotland plc v Etridge (No 2)*[125] the House of Lords reviewed this distinction, and emphasised that there is just a single doctrine of undue influence, although there are different ways of *proving* that undue influence has been applied: either undue influence can be shown on the evidence, or it is open to the court as a matter of fact to infer that the stronger party has obtained the contract by applying undue influence because the transaction cannot otherwise be explained.

---

[122] *Turnbull & Co v Duval* [1902] AC 429 (PC). In the modern law see *Barclays Bank plc v O'Brien* [1994] 1 AC 180 (HL) and *Royal Bank of Scotland plc v Etridge (No 2)*, above, n 69.
[123] *Allcard v Skinner* (1887) 36 ChD 145 (CA).
[124] *Williams v Bayley* (1866) LR 1 HL 200.
[125] Above, n 69.

The so-called 'presumed' undue influence is based only on a rebuttable evidential presumption:

> Proof that the complainant placed trust and confidence in the other party in relation to the management of the complainant's financial affairs, coupled with a transaction which calls for explanation, will normally be sufficient, failing satisfactory evidence to the contrary, to discharge the burden of proof.[126]

The courts have identified certain relationships as requiring one party to exercise his rights with due regard for the other—to prefer the other's interests over his own—such as the relationship of trust and confidence between a doctor and his patient, or a solicitor and his client.[127] In such cases the court will be satisfied from proof of the relationship that one party was in a position in which he *could* have take advantage of the other. But in other cases—including the relationship of husband and wife, and between a bank and its customer—it is a question of fact as to whether one party was placing trust and confidence in the other party in relation to the transaction which he now challenges. But in all cases it is not sufficient to prove the fact that one party placed trust and confidence in the other; in addition, for the court to be entitled to infer that the stronger party exercised undue influence in order to obtain the contract, it is necessary to show that the contract cannot be explained except on the assumption that the trust and confidence has been abused: there must be a 'transaction which cannot be explained by reference to the ordinary motives by which people are accustomed to act'.[128] In considering this question all the circumstances in which the contract was entered into will be relevant, including whether the party claiming to have been influenced took independent advice and therefore had the opportunity to understand the significance of the transaction.[129] Such an issue will not arise where the parties are both commercial parties. One commercial party may be held to have exercised undue influence over a non-commercial party; but the courts are most unlikely to infer undue influence between two parties who are bargaining at arm's length, regardless of the balance of the bargain contained in the contract.

The terms of the contract—the fact that one party obtains a transaction significantly in his favour—is part of the evidence from which the court may infer that the stronger party exercised undue influence in order to obtain the contract. But it is important to remember that the imbalance in the bargain is not sufficient to imply undue influence: it is the nature of the bargain, taken in

---

[126] *Ibid* [14] (Lord Nicholls of Birkenhead); see also [219] (Lord Scott of Foscote).
[127] *Bank of Credit and Commerce International SA v Aboody* [1990] QB 923 (CA) 954; *Royal Bank of Scotland plc v Etridge (No 2)* above, n 69, [157], [161].
[128] *Royal Bank of Scotland plc v Etridge (No 2)* above, n 69, [220] (Lord Scott of Foscote, applying *Allcard v Skinner* above, n 123, 185).
[129] *Inche Noriah v Shaik Allie Bin Omar* [1929] AC 127 (PC); however, the fact of independent advice is not conclusive against there being undue influence: *Royal Bank of Scotland plc v Etridge (No 2)* above, n 69, [20].

the context of the particular relationship between the parties (the relationship of trust and confidence), that leads the court to infer that the relationship has been abused. If there is in fact evidence of the exercise of undue influence then the court need go no further to consider the terms of the bargain, since undue influence is a form of wrongdoing:[130] the party who has exercised undue influence is not allowed to argue that the party who was subjected to the influence cannot have the contract rescinded because the contract was in fact to his advantage.[131]

As in the case of misrepresentation and duress, the contract will be voidable not only if the undue influence is exercised by the other party to the contract (or his agent), but also if it is exercised by a third party and the contracting party knows about it at the time of entering into the contract.[132] In the case of non-commercial bank guarantees, such as a wife's guarantee of her husband's business debts in which she has no commercial interest, the bank can also be affected by *constructive* notice of the risk of undue influence or misrepresentation by the husband against the wife, which will render the guarantee voidable by the wife against the bank if the bank did not take steps to ensure that the wife understood the implications of the transaction.[133]

Furthermore, the right to have the contract rescinded for undue influence will be barred if the influenced party has expressly or impliedly affirmed it after he is freed from the effect of the influence; or if rescission would prejudice innocent third parties; or if mutual restitution by the parties of benefits received from each other under the contract is now impossible. The defendant's conduct in exercising undue influence is not necessarily a tort and so there may not be a claim by the victim for damages, although in many circumstances where undue influence is established the relationship between the parties will be categorised as 'fiduciary', which will carry an equitable obligation to account to the victim for profits made from the abuse of the relationship.[134] In the case of a contract between a trader and a consumer, the conduct of a trader in exercising undue influence may also constitute an 'aggressive commercial practice' which gives the consumer the right to 'unwind' the contract, or to a discount or to damages.[135]

---

[130] *Attorney-General v R* [2003] UKPC 22, [2003] EMLR 24 [21] (Lord Hoffmann): 'Like duress at common law, undue influence is based upon the principle that a transaction to which consent has been obtained by unacceptable means should not be allowed to stand. Undue influence has concentrated in particular upon the unfair exploitation by one party of a relationship which gives him ascendancy or influence over the other'.

[131] *CIBC Mortgages plc v Pitt* [1994] 1 AC 200 (HL) 209, drawing the analogy with misrepresentation, where the terms of the contract are irrelevant: once the misrepresentation is proved to have induced the contract, the representee is entitled to rescind.

[132] *Royal Bank of Scotland plc v Etridge (No 2)* above, n 69, [40].

[133] *Ibid* [43], [87].

[134] J Glister and J Lee, *Hanbury & Martin, Modern Equity*, 20th edn (London, Sweet & Maxwell, 2015) 22-017.

[135] Consumer Protection from Unfair Trading Regulations 2008 SI 2008/1277, as amended by SI 2014/870; above, p 183.

The co-existence of the rules of duress (originally from the common law) and undue influence (originally from equity) in the modern law is an illustration of how the abolition of the separate jurisdictions in the Judicature Acts 1873–5 was only a matter of procedure, and did not change the basic rules of law, which are now applied by all courts, and continue to be developed by them.[136]

4. Unconscionable Bargains

There is a line of cases in which the courts of equity held that a bargain could be set aside if it was 'unconscionable'. This originates in some old cases in which expectant heirs were protected—that is, those who were presently in financial difficulty but relied on the fact (or hope) of their future inheritance to take credit on onerous terms[137]—but was generalised into a broader principle in *Fry v Lane*:

> [W]here a purchase is made from a poor and ignorant man at a considerable undervalue, the vendor having no independent advice, a Court of Equity will set aside the transaction.[138]

If these elements are established, the onus shifts to the purchaser to show that the transaction was fair, just and reasonable.

The elements of this test were further developed in *Cresswell v Potter* in 1968 in a way which appeared to open it up as a more generally useful ground of avoidance of a contract:

> Eighty years ago, when *Fry v. Lane* was decided, social conditions were very different from those which exist today. I do not, however, think that the principle has changed, even though the euphemisms of the 20th century may require the word 'poor' to be replaced by 'a member of the lower income group' or the like, and the word 'ignorant' by 'less highly educated.'[139]

But although there are some cases in which this principle has been applied, they are relatively rare in England. It has however been developed into a more general principle in some other common law countries.[140] In practice, in England parties have more commonly brought their claims under the heading of undue influence, and it may be rather unusual for a case to fail on the plea of undue influence and yet succeed as an 'unconscionable bargain'. Like

---

[136] Above, pp 7–8.
[137] Eg *Earl of Aylesford v Morris* (1873) 8 Ch App 484.
[138] (1888) 40 ChD 312 (Ch) 322 (Kay J).
[139] [1978] 1 WLR 255 (Ch) 257 (Megarry J).
[140] Notably Australia: JW Carter, *Contract Law in Australia*, 6th edn (Chatswood, LexisNexis, 2013) ch 24; and the United States: Uniform Commercial Code s 2-302 and EA Farnsworth, *Contracts*, 4th edn (New York, Aspen, 2004), para 4.28.

undue influence, the basis for the rescission of the contract is not the unfairness of the terms of the contract, but the fact that the claimant has (or, in the circumstances, it can be inferred that he has) obtained the contract by improper means.[141]

V. Capacity

A party to a contract who is an individual (that is, a natural person rather than a corporation with legal personality) may claim not to be bound by a contract where he can demonstrate a lack of capacity to enter into the contract.

We shall not consider this topic in detail, but in outline it should be noted that contracts entered into by a minor are (depending on the type of contract in question) either voidable by him on attaining his majority (the age of 18), or not binding on him unless he ratifies them after his majority, except contracts for 'necessaries', which are immediately binding. 'Necessaries' are things required for his immediate use (such as food, clothing, lodging, and contracts of apprenticeship and employment). These rules are all designed to protect the minor, and do not depend on the other party's knowledge of his age.

Claims based on a lack of mental capacity, however, are different in that although (again, apart from contracts for necessaries) a contract may be voidable for a proven lack of capacity, this is only where the mental condition is such that the party could not understand the transaction, and the other party knew of the incapacity.[142] This has been identified by the Privy Council as similar to the general doctrine of unconscionable bargains: it is not the incapacity in itself, nor the terms of the contract, which are remedied, but the fact that the other party has taken advantage of the party who lacks capacity.[143] Similarly, claims based on incapacity arising from drunkenness depend not on the lack of capacity to understand the transaction, but on whether the other party knew about the incapacity and so took advantage of him.[144]

---

[141] *Multiservice Bookbinding Ltd v Marden* [1979] Ch 84 (Ch) 106; *Hart v O'Connor* [1985] AC 1000 (PC) 1017–18.

[142] *Hart v O'Connor* above, n 141, 1019. Cf *Dunhill v Burgin (Nos 1 and 2)* [2014] UKSC 18, [2014] 1 WLR 933, [25] (Baroness Hale: it is 'generally accepted' that it is sufficient if the other party 'ought to have known' of the incapacity).

[143] *Ibid* 1024, 1027. A disability can however render a *written* contract void under the doctrine of *non est factum*: above, p 167.

[144] *Gore v Gibson* (1845) 13 M & W 623, 626; 153 ER 260, 262.

The capacity of statutory corporations depends on the powers with which they are endowed by virtue of their constituent documents—the memorandum of a company incorporated under the Companies Acts defines its powers, and any contract entered into outside those powers is in principle void on the ground of *ultra vires*. However, since this could prejudice third parties dealing with a company, the *ultra vires* doctrine was reversed in relation to third parties by the Companies Act 1989.[145]

VI. Illegality and Public Policy

In certain circumstances the courts will find that a contract is from the beginning[146] illegal or contrary to public policy. We shall not discuss this complex topic in detail, beyond noting that the ground of illegality can be either a statute which the contract by its terms contravenes, or a principle of the common law. For example, the courts have held that certain contracts contravene public policy if their objects are immoral (such as to further prostitution)[147] or if they interfere with the course of justice or if, in certain circumstances, they purport to oust the jurisdiction of the courts.[148] One important rule in the commercial context is that a term which places a restriction on a party's freedom to pursue a trade or profession (a covenant 'in restraint of trade'), is unenforceable unless the particular restriction can be shown to be reasonable not only in relation to the parties' own interests, but also in relation to the public interest.[149]

The effects of illegality and public policy on the validity of the contract vary, and the law is in a state of some uncertainty as a result of clear disagreement amongst the judges at the highest level about the underlying principles of the doctrine of illegality, and in particular about whether there are clear rules about the operation of doctrine, or whether the court should take a

---

[145] Companies Act 1989 s 108; see now Companies Act 2006 s 39 ('The validity of an act done by a company shall not be called into question on the ground of lack of capacity by reason of anything in the company's constitution').

[146] Supervening illegality is dealt with under the doctrine of frustration: below, p 265.

[147] *Pearce v Brooks* (1866) LR 1 Exch 213.

[148] This is a further ground on which the agreement in *Combe v Combe* [1951] 2 KB 215 (CA), above, p 132, would not have been enforceable even if there had been consideration for it: see Denning LJ at 221.

[149] *Nordenfelt v Maxim Nordenfelt Guns and Ammunition Co Ltd* [1894] AC 535 (HL).

less rigid approach and balance the relevant factors on the facts of the case in hand.[150] If the illegality is a result of a particular statutory rule, then the statute might itself prescribe the consequence. In other cases, the courts sometimes describe the contract as 'void' and sometimes as 'unenforceable'; but this is not the same as a contract void for mistake[151] because it is possible for property to pass under an illegal contract, and therefore for the property rights of the transferee to be given legal effect provided that he does not need to rely on the illegal contract for any purpose other than providing the basis of his claim to a property right.[152] In the case of a covenant in restraint of trade, just the particular offending covenant may be unenforceable; and in other contracts if there is a severable term which is affected by illegality the rest of the contract may be able to stand without it. In order to avoid the risk of a whole contract being void or unenforceable on the basis of a particular provision, it is common for negotiated commercial contracts to contain an express provision to the effect that if any term of the contract is found to be illegal, invalid or unenforceable, in whole or in part, it shall be severed and deemed not to form part of the contract.

---

[150] The cases have arisen in various areas: in contract, see *ParkingEye Ltd v Somerfield Stores Ltd* [2012] EWCA Civ 1338, [2013] QB 840; however, for cases in the Supreme Court in other areas of the law, see *Les Laboratoires Servier v Apotex Inc* [2014] UKSC 55, [2015] AC 430; *Hounga v Allen* [2014] UKSC 47, [2014] 1 WLR 2889; *Bilta (UK) Ltd v Nazir (No 2)* [2015] UKSC 23, [2015] 2 WLR 1168. In the *Bilta* case at [15] Lord Neuberger PSC suggested that the proper approach to the defence of illegality should be addressed by the Supreme Court 'as soon as appropriately possible'.
[151] Above, pp 160–61.
[152] *Tinsley v Milligan* [1994] 1 AC 340 (HL) 370 (still applied as the law, but criticised by judges who prefer a more flexible approach balancing the factors on the facts of the case: above).

8

Finding the Terms of the Contract

Given that a contract gives legal effect to an agreement between the parties, the search for the terms of the contract is the search for what the parties have agreed as the scope of their legally binding obligations and the mechanisms for the regulation of their relationship. Indeed, at least in theory, the terms of the contract are defined in English law by the intention of the parties—their agreement. We have already seen[1] that English law attributes less significance to 'special contracts'—the classification of contracts by type—than modern systems which draw on the Roman law tradition of contractual classification, difference between the approach of the common law and the civil law to finding the terms of the contract is a notable consequence of this. The common lawyer does not expect the law to fill out the details of the contract in the way that many civil codes do; he expects to be able to find the terms from a proper interpretation of the parties' actual agreement, combined with an application of various rules designed to fill the gaps in the parties' express agreement by 'implying' terms—but the implication of terms is also notionally attributable to the intentions of the parties. We shall see that, although the general theory for finding the terms of the contract is based on the parties' agreement, the contrast with the approach in the civil law is not quite as stark as this may suggest, although it does have a significant impact on the different way in which contracts are drafted by common lawyers.

I. The 'Terms' of a Contract

The 'terms' of a contract can take various forms. Central to the contract are the promises which each party has made to the other. These may be

[1] Above p 58.

obligations of performance (to perform a service, to pay money, to deliver property under a contract of sale, and so on) or other particular promises which one party may have undertaken in favour of the other (such as a promise about the quality of goods, or a promise that certain statements made during the negotiations are true). All such obligations and promises were termed by Lord Diplock the 'primary obligations' of the contract: the obligations which, if not performed, will give rise to remedies for breach of contract.[2] It cannot be assumed that the parties will make every primary obligation clear in their express negotiations, or even in the written document if they commit their contract to writing: they will often leave gaps in their negotiations for a contract, and the law must find ways of filling the gaps. The *express* terms will often be supplemented by *implied* terms.

Apart from the classification into express and implied terms, the primary obligations can be classified in other ways for—example, as being 'conditions', 'warranties' or 'intermediate terms', a classification which has consequences for the remedies which are available to the innocent party for breach of contract. We shall consider such matters in chapter 12 (remedies).

In addition to the obligations of performance and the other promises referred to above, a contract will commonly contain other terms, such as a clause designed to exclude or limit one party's liability under the contract;[3] or a clause which provides for disputes to be resolved in a particular way (such as by arbitration); or a clause which identifies the governing law of the contract.

II. Finding and Interpreting the Express Terms

Finding the express terms of the contract will depend on the way in which the contract was formed. But the search for the express terms also involves an exercise in the interpretation of those terms. The purpose of the analysis of the express provisions of the contract is not simply to identify their existence, but also to determine their meaning—the content of the obligations to which each party is subject under the contract.

---

[2] *Photo Production Ltd v Securicor Ltd* [1980] AC (HL) 848–49. This terminology could be misleading if Lord Diplock's use of it is not understood: he does not use 'primary' to mean the 'most important' obligations of the contract. Rather, all performance obligations are 'primary obligations', and he contrasts such obligations with the 'secondary' obligation to pay damages for breach of primary obligations: below, p 274.

[3] Below, ch 9.

1. Contracts Not Reduced to Writing

(a) Finding the Terms

We have seen that, apart from cases in which the parties enter into a written contract, the courts will generally look for an offer and an unequivocal acceptance of the offer in order to find sufficient agreement to form a contract; and that this is certainly required where the contract is alleged to have been formed between two parties negotiating by correspondence.[4] The search for the express terms of the contract will then depend upon identifying the relevant communications—typically, therefore, the final offer and its acceptance.

However, it can sometimes be quite difficult to piece together the terms of the contract as the parties agreed them through their offer and acceptance, particularly where the agreement follows upon a period of negotiations where each of the parties has made various suggestions for the terms of their intended agreement, and it is not entirely clear from the final exchange (identified as the final offer and acceptance) whether the offer constitutes a complete proposal, or whether the agreement on the matters which were being discussed at the last stage also carries forward into the contract other things which were said at an earlier stage. This is a question of fact for the court. One context in which this can arise is where one party claims that a representation made by the other during the negotiations became part of the final bargain so as to give rise to remedies for breach of contract if the representation was false (a *mis*representation).[5] The test developed by the courts to answer this is deceptively simple: whether the parties intended the statement to be incorporated into the contract; whether, therefore, the defendant intended to make a contractually binding promise about the accuracy of his statement.[6] The application of this test, however, is less straightforward. In determining the parties' intentions the courts take into account the significance of the statement (it is more likely to be incorporated if the representee made clear that is was important to him);[7] the timing of the statement (if it was made or repeated at the time of the contract,[8] and in particular if it was made in order to clinch the deal,[9] it will be more likely to be incorporated); and the reliance that the representee is likely to have placed on the representor in relation to the statement (a party who is in a position to know about what he says is more likely to be held to give a contractual assurance if the other party was not in such a position of skill or knowledge). This last point is illustrated well

---

[4] Above, p 109.
[5] Above, pp 183–84.
[6] *Heilbut, Symons & Co v Buckleton* [1913] AC 30 (HL).
[7] *Couchman v Hill* [1947] KB 554 (CA).
[8] *Ibid* 43, 49.
[9] *Andrews v Hopkinson* [1957] 1 QB 229 (QB).

by two contrasting cases. In *Dick Bentley Productions Ltd v Harold Smith (Motors) Ltd*[10] a motor dealer who made statements about the condition of a car he was selling was held to have given a contractual assurance about the condition to the purchaser of a car. By contrast, however, in *Oscar Chess Ltd v Williams*[11] the private seller who made statements about the age of a car on selling it to a dealer was held not to have guaranteed the truth of his statements in the contract. In the latter case it was the buyer, rather than the seller, who had the expertise and the means of verifying the information; the seller was able to rely on only the registration document (which had been fraudulently altered by a previous owner) and so it was obvious to both sides that the seller was not in a position to guarantee the statement which he made.[12]

In the case of consumer contracts for the supply of goods, digital content or services, however, statements by the trader to the consumer at or before the formation of the contract will now very often become terms of the contract under the Consumer Rights Act 2015,[13] removing the need to determine the parties' 'intention' under the common law test.

A further issue is whether written terms which one party did not in fact see were incorporated into the contract—for example, where there is an offer and acceptance between a bus driver and a customer, with the delivery of a ticket which contains a term, or refers to some other document containing a term, or there is a notice on the bus or on the timetable at the bus stop referring to the bus company's standard terms. This has most commonly arisen in the context of exclusion clauses and other adverse terms, where one party is seeking to show that the other is bound by a term even though it was not an explicit part of the offer which was accepted. Because of that context, the courts have been particularly careful before interpreting the facts of the cases so as to hold that such terms are incorporated into the contract.[14] But a party will have succeeded in including such terms in the contract if he took such steps as were reasonably necessary to attempt to bring the terms to the other party's attention[15]—a test which has been said to be consistent with the general objective test for the formation of a contract, in that a party who takes a ticket in circumstances where he could and should reasonably have realised that there were terms incorporated into the contract is indicating to the party offering the ticket that he was agreeing to those terms. In other words, his conduct is such as to lead the other party reasonably to believe that he is agreeing to the terms being incorporated by reference—and so the

---

[10] [1965] 1 WLR 623 (CA).
[11] [1957] 1 WLR 370 (CA).
[12] *Ibid* 376.
[13] Above, p 184.
[14] There was a particular reluctance before the Unfair Contract Terms Act 1977 gave the courts another means of tackling unfair exclusion (etc) clauses: below, p 223.
[15] *Parker v South Eastern Railway* (1877) 2 CPD 416.

terms will be incorporated unless the other party knows that he is not in fact assenting to them.[16] But the more onerous the terms which are sought to be incorporated by this means, the less likely it is that the party who has not seen the terms can be taken by the other party to have been indicating his assent:

> [T]he more unreasonable a clause is, the greater the notice which must be given of it. Some clauses which I have seen would need to be printed in red ink on the face of the document with a red hand pointing to it before the notice could be held to be sufficient.[17]

Moreover, one party will not have taken reasonable steps to bring the terms to the other party's attention unless it was made sufficiently clear, at or before the time of the contract,[18] that there were terms to be incorporated. If the incorporation is sought to be made by a ticket, but the ticket is issued in circumstances where the customer is reasonably entitled to think that it is simply a voucher or receipt rather than a contractual document, the terms are not incorporated.[19]

(b) Interpreting the Terms

We have already seen that in the interpretation of the communications (whether oral or written) which passed between the parties the courts will apply an 'objective' test, viewed from the perspective of the parties themselves: each party is taken in law to have agreed to what by his words and conduct he led the other party in fact—and reasonably—to understand.[20]

2. Written Contracts

(a) Finding the Terms

Where the parties have concluded the contract in a single written document, the written document will normally contain the express terms, either all set out in the document, or some in the document itself and others being incorporated into the contract by express reference within the document. In the case of a contract for the sale or other disposition of an interest in land,

---

[16] *Harris v Great Western Railway Co* (1876) 1 QBD 515, 530–32 (Blackburn J). For the 'objective test', based on Blackburn J's judgment in *Smith v Hughes* (1871) LR 6 QB 597, 607, see above, ch 5.

[17] *Spurling v Bradshaw* [1956] 1 WLR 461 (CA) 466 (Denning LJ). See also *Thornton v Shoe Lane Parking Ltd* [1971] 2 QB 163 (CA) 170 (automatic ticket machine at entry to car park).

[18] *Olley v Marlborough Court Ltd* [1949] 1 KB 532 (CA) (notice in hotel bedroom; but contract was already formed at check-in).

[19] *Chapelton v Barry UDC* [1940] 1 KB 532 (CA).

[20] Above, pp 100–02.

the contract must be in writing, signed by both parties or their agents, and the written document (or identical documents which are exchanged) must contain all the terms which the parties have expressly agreed.[21] In other cases, however, the parties may agree that their contract shall be reduced to written form, and in such cases there will be no concluded contract until the writing is created. But there will be an inference that any statements or promises made by either party to the other during the negotiations, which are not repeated in the written document, were not intended to be contractually binding. This is not conclusive: it is possible for a separate contract, either oral or separately constituted by correspondence or in writing but in either case *collateral* to the principal written document, to have come into existence as a result of the statements or promises being made and not recorded in the written document, but having been intended to have contractual effect.[22] It will normally have to be a separate collateral contract because the general rule is that oral evidence is not to be used to add to, vary or contradict the written terms (the 'parol evidence rule'), although there are exceptions to this rule, including where one or both parties can show that the written document fails to reflect their agreement, and so should be rectified.[23]

If, however, the parties have included in their written contract an 'entire agreement' clause, such as one which provides that[24] 'this Agreement constitutes the entire agreement between the parties', there cannot be any claim based on a collateral contract. Such a clause constitutes an agreement between the parties that the full contractual terms[25] to which the parties agree to bind themselves are to be found in the written contract itself and nowhere else.

A party to a written contract cannot normally deny that he is bound by whatever terms are contained in the document or are incorporated by an express reference in the document. This is particularly so where the party has signed the document: a signature is conclusive unless the other party has misled him about the terms of the document, in which case he is entitled to say that he is bound only by the terms as they were told to him. In the context of written contracts, the courts are therefore less disposed to allow a party to avoid being bound by a contract by saying that sufficient steps were not taken to bring them to his notice:

> In cases in which the contract is contained in a railway ticket or other unsigned document, it is necessary to prove that an alleged party was aware, or ought to

---

[21] Law of Property (Miscellaneous Provisions) Act 1989 s 2(1); above, p 126.
[22] *Record v Bell* [1991] 1 WLR 853 (Ch).
[23] Above, p 165.
[24] *Inntrepreneur Pub Co (GL) v East Crown Ltd* [2000] 2 Lloyd's Rep 611 (Ch).
[25] At least the express terms. Whether the clause excludes implied terms will depend on its construction. In *Exxonmobil Sales and Supply Corporation v Texaco Ltd* [2003] EWHC 1964 (Comm), [2003] 2 Lloyd's Rep 686, [25]–[27] an entire agreement clause was held to exclude terms which might otherwise have been implied by usage and course of dealing, but it might not exclude implication based on business efficacy. For these different bases of implication of terms, see below, pp 211–12.

have been aware, of its terms and conditions. These cases have no application when the document has been signed. When a document containing contractual terms is signed, then, in the absence of fraud, or, I will add, misrepresentation, the party signing it is bound, and it is wholly immaterial whether he has read the document or not.[26]

By his agreement to the document a party represents that he agrees to be bound by the contents of the document.[27] One might expect that it would be different if the other party in fact knows that he has not read them and that he would not have agreed to the terms—because normally a party can only insist on his own understanding of the terms if the other has led him reasonably *and in fact* to believe that he was agreeing to them.[28] In Canada a court has followed this reasoning, even in the case of a signed document, and held that a car hire company could not hold a customer to an unusual and unexpected clause in a signed document where the company's clerk knew that the customer was in a hurry and did not read the document before signing it—and, indeed, the company advertised itself as offering a quick service.[29] But the English courts have not taken this approach,[30] and it has been said that the rule that a signature is binding 'is an important principle of English law which underpins the whole of commercial life; any erosion of it would have serious repercussions far beyond the business community.'[31] A signature on a document is treated as a sign that the party who signs accepts what the document contains—or is prepared to bear the risk of not reading it—unless the other party has actively caused him to misunderstand the document by a fraudulent or innocent misrepresentation about its contents.[32]

(b) Interpreting the Terms

Traditionally the courts have favoured an approach to interpretation of written contracts and other legal documents which relies on the objective, ordinary meaning of the words used in the document; and here the 'objective' test of interpretation takes an external perspective, rather than the perspective

---

[26] *L'Estrange v Graucob* [1934] 2 KB 394 (CA) 403 (Scrutton LJ).
[27] *Harris v Great Western Railway Co* (1876) 1 QBD 515, 530.
[28] Above, p 101.
[29] *Tilden Rent-a-Car Co v Clendenning* (1978) 83 DLR (3d) 400 (CA Ontario).
[30] An exception is one of the judges (Sir Edward Eveleigh) in *Lloyds Bank plc v Waterhouse* [1993] 2 FLR 97 (CA). See also JR Spencer, 'Signature, Consent, and the Rule in *L'Estrange v Graucob*' [1973] CLJ 104.
[31] *Peekay Intermark Ltd v Australia and New Zealand Banking Group Ltd* [2006] EWCA Civ 386, [2006] 2 Lloyd's Rep 511 [43] (Moore-Bick LJ).
[32] *Curtis v Chemical Cleaning and Dyeing Co* [1951] 1 KB 805 (CA) (innocent misrepresentation about the meaning of words on a 'receipt' which customer signed when leaving dress for dry-cleaning). The doctrine of *non est factum* (above, p 167) is an exception to the signature rule—but a very narrow exception, and one with drastic consequences (the contract is void, not simply in force but with the clause as it was represented to be).

of the party who received a communication.[33] The process by which the parties came to their agreement, through the communications between themselves which have to be interpreted in order to discover the content of the agreement, is superseded by the document itself. The parties have agreed that the document reflects the agreement, so the focus of the interpretation is on the document itself.

In *Prenn v Simmonds*[34] Lord Wilberforce made clear that a contract must not be interpreted in isolation from 'the matrix of facts' in which it was set: it is necessary to 'inquire beyond the language and see what the circumstances were with reference to which the words were used, and the object, appearing from those circumstances, which the person using them had in view.' And in a series of cases[35] the House of Lords has re-assessed the general approach to the interpretation of documents, and has emphasised that whilst the test is objective, ignoring the parties' own subjective intentions and the parties' own interpretation of the document, the interpretation of a written contract or other document should take into account its *context*. Lord Hoffmann's statement in *Investors Compensation Scheme Ltd v West Bromwich Building Society* is very frequently quoted now as a summary of the modern approach to interpretation:

(1) Interpretation is the ascertainment of the meaning which the document would convey to a reasonable person having all the background knowledge which would reasonably have been available to the parties in the situation in which they were at the time of the contract.

(2) The background was famously referred to by Lord Wilberforce[36] as the 'matrix of fact,' but this phrase is, if anything, an understated description of what the background may include. Subject to the requirement that it should have been reasonably available to the parties and to the exception to be mentioned next, it includes absolutely anything which would have affected the way in which the language of the document would have been understood by a reasonable man.

(3) The law excludes from the admissible background the previous negotiations of the parties and their declarations of subjective intent. They are admissible only in an action for rectification. The law makes this distinction for reasons of practical policy and, in this respect only, legal interpretation differs from the way we would interpret utterances in ordinary life. The boundaries of this exception are in some respects unclear. But this is not the occasion on which to explore them.[37]

---

[33] Above, p 98.
[34] [1971] 1 WLR 1381 (HL) 1384.
[35] *Mannai Investment Co Ltd v Eagle Star Life Assurance Co Ltd* [1997] AC 749 (HL); *Investors Compensation Scheme Ltd v West Bromwich Building Society* [1998] 1 WLR 896 (HL); *Bank of Credit and Commerce International SA v Ali* [2001] UKHL 8, [2002] 1 AC 251.
[36] *Prenn v Simmons*, above, n 34.
[37] In *Chartbrook Ltd v Persimmon Homes Ltd* [2009] UKHL 38, [2009] 1 AC 1101, HL re-examined the rule that precontractual negotiations are to be excluded from the interpretation of a written contract, but was not persuaded to depart from its earlier decision in *Prenn v Simmons*, above, n 34.

(4) The meaning which a document (or any other utterance) would convey to a reasonable man is not the same thing as the meaning of its words. The meaning of words is a matter of dictionaries and grammars; the meaning of the document is what the parties using those words against the relevant background would reasonably have been understood to mean. The background may not merely enable the reasonable man to choose between the possible meanings of words which are ambiguous but even (as occasionally happens in ordinary life) to conclude that the parties must, for whatever reason, have used the wrong words or syntax: see *Mannai Investments Co. Ltd. v. Eagle Star Life Assurance Co. Ltd*.[38]

(5) The 'rule' that words should be given their 'natural and ordinary meaning' reflects the common sense proposition that we do not easily accept that people have made linguistic mistakes, particularly in formal documents. On the other hand, if one would nevertheless conclude from the background that something must have gone wrong with the language, the law does not require judges to attribute to the parties an intention which they plainly could not have had. Lord Diplock made this point more vigorously when he said in *Antaios Compania Naviera S.A. v. Salen Rederierna A.B.*:[39]

> 'if detailed semantic and syntactical analysis of words in a commercial contract is going to lead to a conclusion that flouts business commonsense, it must be made to yield to business commonsense.'[40]

In another case Lord Steyn emphasised that the rules for interpretation of written contracts and other documents, in a commercial context, must reflect commercial expectations:

> In determining the meaning of the language of a commercial contract, and unilateral contractual notices, the law therefore generally favours a commercially sensible construction. The reason for this approach is that a commercial construction is more likely to give effect to the intention of the parties. Words are therefore interpreted in the way in which a reasonable commercial person would construe them. And the standard of the reasonable commercial person is hostile to technical interpretations and undue emphasis on niceties of language.[41]

The Supreme Court has also made clear that, if there are two possible interpretations of a commercial contract, the court is entitled to prefer the interpretation which is consistent with business common sense.[42]

The courts have traditionally been particularly careful in the interpretation of clauses which exclude or limit the liability of one of the parties, or

---

[38] Above, n 35.
[39] [1985] AC 191, 201.
[40] *Investors Compensation Scheme Ltd v West Bromwich Building Society* [1998] 1 WLR 896, 912–13.
[41] *Mannai Investment Co Ltd v Eagle Star Life Assurance Co Ltd* above, n 35, 771. The case involved the interpretation of a tenant's notice to terminate a lease rather than a contract, but HL emphasised that the approach is the same.
[42] *Rainy Sky SA v Kookmin Bank* [2011] UKSC 50, [2011] 1 WLR 2900; *Arnold v Britton* [2015] UKSC 36, [2015] AC 1619.

which are otherwise onerous to one party and inserted for the benefit of the other. As a general rule, where a clause is uncertain or ambiguous it will be construed *contra proferentem*—against the person putting it forward. But this has been developed most particularly in the context of exclusion and limitation clauses, so that a party seeking to rely on such a clause must show that the clause clearly covers the case he wishes to make. We shall see this in more detail in chapter nine.

III. Implied Terms

In very many cases the parties will not make express provision in their agreement for all the obligations necessary to make a full set of contractual terms. In the case of a negotiated commercial contract the parties may attempt to include all the terms in their written contract and to avoid gaps; and business parties may also seek to provide a full set of terms in their 'standard forms' which they insist on incorporating into their contracts with other businesses and consumers.[43] But in other contracts—including many day-to-day contracts such as contracts for the sale of goods and the supply of services entered into either orally or following an exchange of correspondence—there will be no attempt to make express provision for a full set of terms. If the parties leave gaps which cannot otherwise be filled, and where the gap is such that it prevents the contract being complete, or makes it uncertain, then the contract fails.[44] But very often the gaps can be filled using *implied terms*: that is, the parties have not expressly included a particular term, but the courts are able to determine that the term should be implied into the contract, to complete it.

A number of tests have been developed in the cases to assist the court to determine whether the parties can be held impliedly to have agreed to terms which do not appear in the express agreement, whether the agreement takes the form of a single written document, or has to be constructed from the communications (written or oral) between the parties during the formation of the contract. In 2009, in *Attorney-General of Belize v Belize Telecom Ltd*,[45] the Privy Council said that, at least where the question is whether terms can be

---

[43] For the problem of unfair terms in standard forms see below, ch 9; and for 'battles of the forms' between commercial parties see above, p 120.

[44] Above, pp 122–24.

[45] [2009] UKPC 10, [2009] 1 WLR 1988 [21] (Lord Hoffmann).

implied into a written document, such tests are only part of a single broader question: what the instrument, read as a whole against the relevant background, would reasonably be understood to mean, thereby assimilating the test for implication of terms to the test for interpretation of a written contract.[46] However, this test has not in practice replaced the traditional tests for implication of terms, which the courts have continued to apply. The Supreme Court[47] has recently reaffirmed the traditional tests, which are therefore set out in the following sections of this chapter.

1. Obvious Terms; Regular and Customary Terms

The court may decide that, on the facts, the parties must have intended a particular term to have been included because it was obvious, although not expressly stated. The test for this is sometimes referred to as the 'officious bystander' test, after a statement of MacKinnon LJ:

> Prima facie that which in any contract is left to be implied and need not be expressed is something so obvious that it goes without saying; so that, if, while the parties were making their bargain, an officious bystander were to suggest some express provision for it in their agreement, they would testily suppress him with a common 'Oh, of course!'[48]

This is simply filling out the (unexpressed) agreement of the parties. Similarly, the court may be able to say that it can infer from a regular and consistent course of past dealings between the same parties on the same set of terms that they must have intended to incorporate those same terms into their present contract: there is nothing in the actual agreement to negative it, and it can be interpreted as just an oversight or as a tacit intention to use the usual set of contract terms. However, this is not an easy test to satisfy.[49]

Another context in which terms can sometimes be implied is where the parties are both in the same trade and of equal bargaining strength, and there are standard terms used in the trade. For example, in *British Crane Hire Corporation Ltd v Ipswich Plant Hire Ltd* the contract of hire of a crane formed orally at short notice and without completing a formal contract was held to incorporate a term of the standard conditions of hire used by the party hiring out the crane (even though they were not sent to the other party until later) where both parties were plant hire companies and the party hiring

---

[46] *Investors Compensation Scheme Ltd v West Bromwich Building Society*, above, n 40.
[47] *Marks and Spencer plc v BNP Paribas Services Trust Company (Jersey) Ltd* [2015] UKSC 72, [2015] 3 WLR 1843, [22]–[31], [77].
[48] *Shirlaw v Southern Foundries Ltd* [1939] 2 KB 206 (CA) 227.
[49] *McCutcheon v David Macbrayne Ltd* [1964] 1 WLR 125 (HL Sc) (no incorporation); *Hollier v Rambler Motors (AMC) Ltd* [1972] 2 QB 71 (CA) (three or four occasions in five years not sufficient).

out the crane was entitled to assume that the other was accepting the contract on its terms because such a term was standard in the trade.[50]

2. Terms Necessary to Give the Contract 'Business Efficacy'

The court may decide that, on the facts, the parties must have intended the term because it is *necessary* to make the contract work, and is consistent with all the other terms of the contract. It is said that such a term, implied to give 'business efficacy' to the contract, is based on the intentions of the parties but this is moving away from the real intentions of the parties and starting to allocate the risks between them as the court decides that they should have done. In *The Moorcock*[51] the claimants contracted to use the defendants' jetty for unloading their ship. The defendants did not own the adjacent river bed, but had not checked whether it was suitable for the ship to dock and unload. The ship sustained damage, and the claimants were able to recover from the defendants on the basis of the breach of an implied term to the effect that the defendants had warranted (that is, promised) that they had taken care to check the safety of the jetty for the ship. Bowen LJ said:

> an implied warranty, or, as it is called, a covenant in law, as distinguished from an express contract or express warranty, really is in all cases founded on the presumed intention of the parties, and upon reason. The implication which the law draws from what must obviously have been the intention of the parties, the law draws with the object of giving efficacy to the transaction and preventing such a failure of consideration as cannot have been within the contemplation of either side ... In business transactions such as this, what the law desires to effect by the implication is to give such business efficacy to the transaction as must have been intended at all events by both parties who are business men; not to impose on one side all the perils of the transaction, or to emancipate one side from all the chances of failure, but to make each party promise in law as much, at all events, as it must have been in the contemplation of both parties that he should be responsible for in respect of those perils or chances.[52]

But it is clear that the courts do not go further and imply terms simply to rebalance the risks of the contract as the courts think that the parties should reasonably have agreed between themselves. Lord Denning sought to extend the implication of terms to cover terms which it would have been 'reasonable' for the parties to include; but this was firmly rejected by the House of Lords.[53] Even where the courts have followed the new *Belize*[54] test for the implication

---

[50] [1975] QB 303 (CA) 311 (Lord Denning MR: 'It is just as if the plaintiffs had said: "We will supply it on our usual conditions," and the defendants said "Of course, that is quite understood"').
[51] (1889) 14 PD 64 (CA).
[52] *Ibid* 68.
[53] *Liverpool CC v Irwin* [1977] AC 239 (HL) 253–54, 258, 262, 266.
[54] Above, n 45.

of terms, it has been emphasised that the test is still narrow, and based on what is necessary to enable the parties' express agreement to be given effect.[55]

3. Particular Terms in Particular Types of Contract

Although English law looks to the intention of the parties (express or implied) in order to find the terms of the contract, the law will also imply particular terms in particular types of contract. This was made clear by Diplock LJ:

> The task of ascertaining what the parties to a contract of any kind have agreed shall be their legal rights and liabilities to one another as a result of the contract is a familiar one in all systems of law. It is accomplished not by determining what each party actually thought those rights and liabilities would be, but by what each party by his words and conduct reasonably led the other party to believe were the acts which he was undertaking a legal obligation to perform. There are some rights and liabilities which arise by implication of law from the nature of the contract itself such as a contract of sale of goods or land, a contract of carriage or bailment, a contract of service or a contract of insurance. In offering to enter into a contract of a particular kind a party leads the other party reasonably to believe that he undertakes a legal obligation to perform all those acts which a person entering into a contract of that kind usually performs, unless his words or conduct are such as would make it reasonably clear to the other party that this is not so and also makes it clear which of those acts he does not intend to undertake to perform and which of them he intends to undertake to perform only in some other and specified manner.[56]

This can look rather like a system of 'special contracts', familiar to the civil lawyer whose code lays down the incidents of a wide range of types of contract. However, Diplock LJ still attributed these implied terms to the intention of the parties, objectively indicated to each other. Such terms may be implied at common law (by the courts' own characterisation of particular types of contract carrying particular implied terms) or by statute.

(a) Terms Implied at Common Law

The courts have held that there are certain typical situations where the parties will normally be held to have intended to include a particular term, whether or not they stated it expressly. For example, it has been held that the landlord of a block of flats will normally (in the absence of contrary terms in

---

[55] *Marks and Spencer plc v BNP Paribas Securities Services Trust Co (Jersey) Ltd* [2014] EWCA Civ 603, [2014] L & TR 26 [23]–[28], aff'd [2015] UKSC 72, [2015] 3 WLR 1843, above, n 47.
[56] *Hardwick Game Farm v Suffolk Agricultural Poultry Producers Association* [1966] 1 WLR 287 (CA) 339.

the particular contract of letting) be held to have intended to undertake the obligation to keep the means of access and the common areas reasonably fit for use, and therefore such an undertaking will be implied into a contract of letting between the landlord and a tenant of a flat in the block.[57] In relation to leases in general it is well established that (if there is no express provision) the landlord impliedly promises that a tenant shall have quiet enjoyment of the premises;[58] and in the case of a letting of a furnished house, that the premises shall be reasonably fit for habitation at the beginning of the tenancy.[59] And in employment contracts there are implied duties on both parties: for example, the employee has the duty to serve the employer with fidelity and in good faith[60] and in return the employer owes the duty to conduct himself in a manner likely to preserve the relationship of confidence and trust between employer and employee.[61]

(b) Terms Implied by Statute

Various standard terms are implied by statute into particular types of contract. For example:

(i) In a contract for the sale of goods, there are implied terms on the part of the seller that he has a right to sell the goods, that the goods are and will remain free from undisclosed charges or incumbrances and that the seller will enjoy quiet possession;[62] where the contract is by description or sample, that the goods will correspond with the description or the sample;[63] and where the seller sells the goods in the course of a business, that the goods are of satisfactory quality and that they are reasonably fit for any purpose of the buyer which the buyer expressly or by implication makes known to the seller.[64] There are similar terms implied into contracts for the transfer of goods (otherwise than under a sale contract) or hire of goods.[65]

---

[57] *Liverpool CC v Irwin*, above, n 53.
[58] *Markham v Paget* [1908] 1 Ch 697 (Ch).
[59] *Collins v Hopkins* [1923] 2 KB 617 (KB).
[60] *Robb v Green* [1895] 2 QB 315 (CA).
[61] *Malik v Bank of Credit and Commerce International SA* [1998] AC 20 (HL).
[62] Sale of Goods Act 1979 s 12 (non-consumer contracts); Consumer Rights Act 2015 s 17 (consumer goods contracts). The 2015 Act does not use the language of 'implied terms', but of terms which the contract 'is to be treated as including', yet there is no apparent difference of principle or effect in this formulation.
[63] Sale of Goods Act 1979 ss 13, 15 (non-consumer contracts); Consumer Rights Act 2015 ss 11, 13 (consumer goods contracts).
[64] Sale of Goods Act 1979 s 14 (non-consumer contracts); Consumer Rights Act 2015 ss 9, 10 (consumer goods contracts).
[65] Supply of Goods and Services Act 1982 ss 2–4, 7–9 (non-consumer contracts); in the Consumer Rights Act 2015, a consumer goods contract (above, nn 62, 63, 64) includes sales, hire, hire-purchase and contracts for the transfer of goods: s 3.

(ii) In a contract for the supply of a service, where the supplier is acting in the course of a business there is an implied term that the supplier will carry out the service with reasonable care and skill.[66]

(iii) Various terms are implied into particular kinds of tenancy: for example, the landlord under a lease of a dwelling-house for a term of less than seven years has the implied obligation to keep in repair the structure and exterior of the property, as well as certain installations in the premises (water, gas, electricity, sanitation and heating).[67]

Some of these implied terms are statutory formulations of terms which the courts had already decided that parties to such contracts impliedly owed at common law; for example, the Sale of Goods Act (which was first passed in 1893) largely put the common law on the subject into a statutory text. But others are specific provisions created by statute in order to protect a contracting party—to allocate certain risks in typical contracts to one or other of the parties. In the modern law, the use of the automatic implication of terms in particular contracts can be simply an efficient way of presuming the content of the contract, in the absence of contrary provision in the express terms of the contract. But sometimes it is a mandatory allocation of risk under the contract to one of the parties—and in such cases the freedom for parties to vary the statutory implications by the terms of the contract is limited or excluded altogether.[68]

4. The Exclusion of Implied Terms: Drafting Styles in the Common Law

The general theory about how to identify the terms of the contract in English law is based on the intentions of the parties. Throughout the rules for the formation of a contract, the test is objective, rather than purely subjective; but within the constraints of an objective test the 'intentions' of the parties about the terms may be more or less real. Express terms are the articulation of the parties' intentions; terms implied because they are obvious are still close to

---

[66] Supply of Goods and Services Act 1982 s 13 (non-consumer contracts); Consumer Rights Act 2015 s 49.

[67] Landlord and Tenant Act 1985 s 11.

[68] Parties cannot exclude or limit of the terms implied by Landlord and Tenant Act 1985 s 11 unless authorised by the County Court: s 12. The Sale of Goods Act 1893 s 55 allowed the parties freely to negative or vary the implied terms, but in the case of non-consumer contracts this is now limited by the Unfair Contract Terms Act 1977 s 6: below, p 228. Similarly (but subject to the 1977 Act) terms implied into non-consumer contracts of transfer or hire of goods, or for the supply of a service, may be negative or varied by express agreement, or by course of dealing between the parties, or by usage: Supply of Goods and Services Act 1982 ss 11, 16. The terms which are treated as included in a consumer contract by virtue of the Consumer Rights Act 2015 (above, nn 62–66) cannot be excluded or restricted by the trader: ss 31 (goods contracts), 57 (services contracts).

being based on the real intentions. But as the courts move to terms imposed through necessity and then by reference to the particular type of contract, they may seem to be moving further away from the parties' intentions. But even here the courts hold to the general theory that the role of implied terms is only to fill out—to complete—the parties' agreement by reference to what they can be taken to have intended by entering into such a contract. This is emphasised by the fact that—except where there is a mandatory rule to the contrary, imposed by statute—the courts will not imply a term which conflicts with an express term. In the case of the typical contracts into which particular terms are normally implied at common law, it has been said that the courts will require an express contrary provision in the contract to negative the normal implied term.[69] But even so the express term will normally in principle override the implied term—because the implied term cannot fill out the intentions of the parties when they clearly stated in the contract that their intention was not to include a provision on the lines of the implied term.

Implied terms are generally seen by the English lawyer as a gap-filler: to be used to fill out the terms of the contract when the parties have not made express provision. As such, implied terms are vital in many contracts: for example, in day-to-day contracts to purchase goods, the terms routinely implied by the Sale of Goods Act 1979 or the Consumer Rights Act 2015 provide the basis of the remedies most commonly sought by buyers—to reject the goods, or claim damages or other remedies for defects in the goods. Making provision by law not only to imply terms (since these are not matters usually stated expressly by a seller) but to imply particular terms, set out in detail in a statutory text, provides certainty for the buyer. But if the parties have the opportunity to make express provision, rather than relying on the implied terms—even the clearest implied terms, those provided by statute—they will do so. This usually occurs in the context of commercial contracts, given that it is commercial parties that are in a position to negotiate and draft their contracts in detail, and that terms implied by statute into consumer contracts can often not be excluded or restricted.[70] But, in the case of negotiated commercial contracts, it is not usual for a party (or, rather, his legal adviser) to leave gaps in the drafting of the contract to be filled by implied terms, even the statutory implied terms. It is always risky to leave gaps, since it leaves to the court's discretion the interpretation of the nature and scope of the 'gap' which has been left between the express terms, and therefore the nature and scope of any term which the court might decide is 'obvious' or 'necessary' to fill the gap. Certainty for the parties is enhanced by removing

---

[69] *Liverpool CC v Irwin* above, n 53, 257 (Lord Cross of Chelsea: 'When it implies a term in a contract the court is sometimes laying down a general rule that in all contracts of a certain type—sale of goods, master and servant, landlord and tenant and so on—some provision is to be implied unless the parties have expressly excluded it').

[70] Above, n 68.

such discretion from the courts, and by making express provision in a written contract for all the terms which the parties are to include in their contract—including, typically, an 'entire agreement' clause[71] to avoid any precontractual representations becoming terms of the contract if they are not expressly included. This helps to explain the familiar style of drafting of commercial contracts by English practitioners. The civil lawyer may draft a much shorter contract, saying that he need not include in the document all the details of the terms which the code will necessarily import into a contract of this kind. But the English lawyer sees implied terms (even statutory implied terms) as a last resort, to be avoided if at all possible.

---

[71] Above, p 206.

9

Controlling the Content of the Contract: 'Unfair' Contracts

All legal systems show some concern for the 'fairness' of a contract, and develop various techniques for control over the substantive content of contracts—the 'fairness' (or, rather, the *un*fairness) of contractual terms. Most systems will not inquire into the simple economic balance of the transaction, starting instead from the proposition that the balance between what the parties bring to a contract is for the parties themselves to decide. To take the most extreme case: a promise of a gift is capable of being a valid contract in most civil law systems. And although a promise of a gift is not, as such, a contract in English law because of the doctrine of consideration which requires a contract to embody an exchange of values between the parties,[1] this does not in practice prevent the parties from making enforceable promises of gifts, either through the use of nominal consideration[2] or through the use of the formality of a deed.[3] However, although there is no general control over the balance of the bargain, there are particular situations, or particular types of contract, where legal systems intervene either to re-balance the contract or to invalidate the contract on the basis of its imbalance. Such intervention may be direct or indirect. There are direct controls where the courts will strike down or vary terms for the reason that the terms are in themselves unfair. There are also, however, indirect controls over the fairness of contracts where the courts will take the substantive terms into account as part of the operation of other rules relating to the validity of contracts. Different legal systems will use such controls in different ways, and will define in different ways the types of contract, or the types of term, or the standards of 'unfairness', on the basis of which intervention is permitted. There is an economic and political judgement inherent in this issue: whether, for example, only consumers should be able to challenge the validity of contract terms on the basis of their 'unfairness', or whether

---

[1] Above, ch 6.
[2] Above, pp 136–37.
[3] Above, p 127.

such protection (and, if so, how much protection) should also be offered to businesses. In this chapter we shall consider the approach which has been adopted by the courts, and by the legislator, in England towards both indirect and direct controls over the substantive terms of the contract.

I. Indirect Controls over the 'Fairness' of the Contract

1. Procedural and Substantive Unfairness

The courts have frequently said that they will not intervene simply on the basis of an unfairness in the balance of the bargain ('*substantive* unfairness'). We saw in chapter seven that a contract will be voidable in favour of a party who has been induced to enter into it by the misrepresentation, duress or undue influence of the other party. But in these doctrines the courts' intervention is based on what the other party has done in order to obtain the contract ('*procedural* unfairness'). Even if the defendant loses the contract because of conduct which does not appear to be morally culpable such as a wholly innocent misrepresentation, the rationale is still that he cannot be allowed to insist on the contract because he caused the claimant's mistake. It is not based on an assessment of the terms of the contract, which are generally irrelevant where the question is whether the contract was voidable for misrepresentation. This firm distinction between procedural and substantive unfairness was drawn by Lord Brightman in *Hart v O'Connor*:

> If a contract is stigmatised as 'unfair', it may be unfair in one of two ways. It may be unfair by reason of the unfair manner in which it was brought into existence; a contract induced by undue influence is unfair in this sense. It will be convenient to call this 'procedural unfairness.' It may also, in some contexts, be described (accurately or inaccurately) as 'unfair' by reason of the fact that the terms of the contract are more favourable to one party than to the other. In order to distinguish this 'unfairness' from procedural unfairness, it will be convenient to call it 'contractual imbalance.' The two concepts may overlap. Contractual imbalance may be so extreme as to raise a presumption of procedural unfairness, such as undue influence or some other form of victimisation. Equity will relieve a party from a contract which he has been induced to make as a result of victimisation. Equity will not relieve a party from a contract on the ground only that there is contractual imbalance not amounting to unconscionable dealing.[4]

---

[4] [1985] AC 1000 (PC) 1017–18.

This makes clear that there is no general power to intervene to strike down a contract on the basis of substantive unfairness—not even a power in 'equity', the line of cases which come from the old equitable jurisdiction. 'Unconscionable bargains'[5] in English law are also based on procedural unfairness—or, at least, must include procedural unfairness. But Lord Brightman also said that the substantive unfairness of the bargain can be relevant as *evidence* of procedural unfairness: for example, evidence from which the court may infer that the stronger party exercised undue influence in order to obtain the contract: the transaction 'calls for explanation'.[6] This is not making the contract voidable because of the unfairness of the terms of the contract to one party, but because of the unfairness of the stronger party's conduct in applying pressure or in abusing his position of trust and confidence in procuring the contract in his favour. But it does show that the courts can investigate the substantive imbalance of the contract with a view to checking whether it is a symptom of an underlying defect in the formation of the contract.

2. Judicial Controls over Unfair Terms: Incorporation and Construction

Where one party claims that he has included in the contract a term which operates in his favour, and against the interests of the other party—typically, but not exclusively,[7] a term which excludes or limits his liability for breach of the contract—the courts will view the term with some suspicion. They do not claim the jurisdiction to strike the term down, however unreasonable it might be: if the parties have in fact agreed it, and it properly covers the situation in which one party now seeks to rely on it, then that is simply the exercise by the parties of their freedom of contract[8] and any challenge to the validity of the term must be sought elsewhere, such as in the statutory controls over unfair contract terms.[9] But the courts can (indirectly) prevent an unreasonable or onerous term from having effect by controlling its incorporation into the contract, and its interpretation. In other words, before the court is prepared to enforce an onerous term it must be satisfied that the term was properly incorporated into the contract, and that on its proper construction it is applicable in the circumstances.

---

[5] Above, p 197.
[6] *Royal Bank of Scotland plc v Etridge (No 2)* [2001] UKHL 44, [2002] 2 AC 773 [14] (Lord Nicholls of Birkenhead); above, pp 194–96.
[7] *Interfoto Picture Library Ltd v Stiletto Visual Programmes Ltd* [1989] QB 433 (CA) (clause imposing exorbitant fee for failure to comply with obligation to return photographic transparencies in accordance with terms of loan agreement).
[8] *Photo Production Ltd v Securicor Transport Ltd* [1980] AC 827 (HL) 848, 851.
[9] Below, pp 226–34.

(a) Incorporation of the Term

We have already seen that, in identifying the terms of the contract, the courts will take into account the fact that an alleged term was unusual or onerous in order to determine whether the party against whom it is to operate can be taken to have given his assent to it.[10] This issue most commonly arises where the party against whom the term is to be used has not put his signature to any document containing or referring to the term,[11] nor is the agreement (including or referring to the term) contained in a single written document, but the term was on a notice or a ticket or some other similar document, and the party did not in fact see it. In such circumstances the courts will say that the party who asserts that the term is part of the contract must show that, at the time when the contract was concluded, he had taken such steps as were reasonably necessary to attempt to bring the term to the other party's attention; and that the more onerous the term, the more onerous is his duty to bring it to the other party's attention.[12]

At first sight this is simply part of the court's normal analysis of the content of the contract. But it goes beyond this; and the courts have treated it as a tool which can be used specifically to target terms which they perceive to be unfair. In *Interfoto Picture Library Ltd v Stiletto Visual Programmes Ltd* Bingham LJ noted that, although there is no general principle requiring the parties to make and carry out contracts in good faith, various doctrines of the English law of contract fulfil a similar function, including the rules for the incorporation of onerous terms:

> The well known cases on sufficiency of notice are in my view properly to be read in this context. At one level they are concerned with a question of pure contractual analysis, whether one party has done enough to give the other notice of the incorporation of a term in the contract. At another level they are concerned with a somewhat different question, whether it would in all the circumstances be fair (or reasonable) to hold a party bound by any conditions or by a particular condition of an unusual and stringent nature.[13]

(b) Interpretation of the Term: Construction Contra Proferentem

In chapter eight we saw some of the rules relating to the interpretation of contracts, and in particular the interpretation of written contracts. However, the

---

[10] Above, pp 204–05.
[11] The signature is normally conclusive if there was no misrepresentation about the contents of the document which was signed: above, pp 206–07.
[12] Above, pp 204–05.
[13] Above, n 7, 439.

courts have traditionally been particularly careful in the interpretation of terms which exclude or limit the liability of one of the parties, or which are otherwise onerous to one party and inserted for the benefit of the other.

Where there is doubt about the meaning of a term, it will be construed *contra proferentem*—which means, in this context, against the party who is seeking to rely on it to his own advantage. It is for that party to show that the clause clearly and unambiguously confers on him the benefit which he claims. This most typically arises in the context of exclusion or limitation clauses; and in practice it means that the party seeking to rely on such a clause as a defence to a claim made against him must show that the clause clearly and unambiguously covers the particular liability which is otherwise established by the claim. If the clause might have been intended to cover a different liability, it will not be held to cover the particular liability in question, and so cannot be used as a defence. In the context of a clause purporting to exclude liability for misrepresentation Jacob J said:

> [I]f a clause is to have the effect of excluding or reducing remedies for damaging or untrue statements then the party seeking that protection cannot be mealy-mouthed in his clause. He must bring it home that he is limiting his liability for falsehoods he may have told.[14]

This is very strictly applied: even if the clause might cover the particular liability *and liabilities arising in other circumstances*, then it may be held not to apply in the present case. For example, the courts have held that clauses which by their language are wide enough to cover breaches of duty which are committed either negligently or non-negligently do not in fact exclude liability for the breach of duty committed negligently—it is to be presumed that the clause was only meant to cover non-negligent breach of duty. This follows from the courts' assumption that:

> [I]t is inherently improbable that one party to the contract should intend to absolve the other party from the consequences of the latter's own negligence. The intention to do so must therefore be made perfectly clear, for otherwise the court will conclude that the exempted party was only intended to be free from liability in respect of damage occasioned by causes other than negligence for which he is answerable.[15]

The courts have also—as with their approach to incorporation, discussed above—developed an approach to construction which differentiates between more and less onerous clauses. On the one hand, a clause which seeks to exclude liability for a fundamental breach of contract will have to be particularly clear and unambiguous before a court is satisfied that the innocent party was really intending to exclude liability for such a serious breach.[16] On the

---

[14] *Thomas Witter Ltd v TBP Industries Ltd* [1996] 2 All ER 573 (Ch) 595–96.
[15] *Gillespie Bros & Co Ltd v Roy Bowles Transport Ltd* [1973] QB 400 (CA) 419 (Buckley LJ).
[16] *Photo Production Ltd v Securicor Transport Ltd*, above, n 8, 850.

other hand, a clause which only limits the defendant's liability to a particular sum of money[17] or limits the range of recoverable losses[18] rather than excluding the liability altogether, or which limits only his rights of set-off arising from a breach of contract rather than excluding the liability,[19] will still be construed *contra proferentem* and so must be clearly expressed, but it will not be treated as strictly as an exclusion clause. This reflects the courts' view that such clauses are more likely to be part of the risk allocation in the contract:

> Whether a clause limiting liability is effective or not is a question of construction of that clause in the context of the contract as a whole. If it is to exclude liability for negligence, it must be most clearly and unambiguously expressed, and in such a contract as this, must be construed contra proferentem. I do not think that there is any doubt so far. But I venture to add one further qualification, or at least clarification: one must not strive to create ambiguities by strained construction, as I think that the appellants have striven to do. The relevant words must be given, if possible, their natural, plain meaning. Clauses of limitation are not regarded by the courts with the same hostility as clauses of exclusion: this is because they must be related to other contractual terms, in particular to the risks to which the defending party may be exposed, the remuneration which he receives, and possibly also the opportunity of the other party to insure.[20]

Lord Wilberforce here rejected the argument which would 'strive to create ambiguities by strained construction' in the case of limitation clauses. This hints at an approach which the courts have sometimes applied in relation to onerous clauses, such as exclusion clauses: where the only way in which a court could prevent an unreasonable exclusion clause from having its literal effect was by interpreting it as not covering the breach, there was a tendency to adopt a rather strained interpretation. However, whilst the courts have now openly admitted that this is what they have in the past sometimes done, they have also made clear[21] that such strained constructions are not now generally appropriate since, in addition to the courts' own controls through the rules of incorporation and construction of terms, there are now statutory controls which can strike down unfair terms, as we shall see in the next section.

The courts will interpret the clause first, before considering the impact of the statutory controls over it. And so the construction *contra proferentem* involves a narrow construction, which may prevent the clause from applying to the particular claim by virtue of its lack of clear and unambiguous drafting. In such a case there is no need to go further to subject the clause to

---

[17] *Ailsa Craig Fishing Co Ltd v Malvern Fishing Co Ltd* [1983] 1 WLR 964 (HL Sc).
[18] *EE Caledonia Ltd v Orbit Valve Co Europe* [1994] 1 WLR 1515 (CA) 1521 (clause limiting both parties' liability for consequential losses).
[19] *Continental Illinois National Bank & Trust Co of Chicago v Papanicolaou (The Fedora)* [1986] 2 Lloyd's Rep 441 (CA) 443–44.
[20] *Ailsa Craig Fishing Co Ltd v Malvern Fishing Co Ltd*, above, n 17, 966 (Lord Wilberforce).
[21] *Photo Production Ltd v Securicor Transport Ltd*, above, n 8, 851.

the statutory controls at all. In some other legal systems, the *contra proferentem* rule of interpretation would operate in exactly the opposite direction: to interpret the clause as widely as possible, so that it can then more easily be struck down by the statutory controls. But this has not been adopted in the English cases, no doubt because the rules of interpretation were in place and already well established as a means of narrowing the operation of exclusion clauses before the statutory controls were first introduced.

II. Direct Controls over the 'Fairness' of the Contract

1. Control by the Common Law

We have already noted that the courts do not have a general power to strike down or vary clauses which they perceive to be 'unreasonable'. However, there are certain very particular rules which the courts have developed to deal with terms of particular substantive content.

In the context of exclusion clauses, the courts have held that as a matter of policy it is not possible in law for a party to exclude liability for his own personal fraud. This was confirmed in 2003 by the House of Lords, although the House did not firmly decide whether it is possible for a party to exclude his secondary liability for the fraud of his agent.[22]

Penalty clauses are also struck out. Until recently, a penalty clause has been defined as a clause which provides for the payment of a sum of money on breach of contract, where the clause is 'stipulated as in terrorem of the offending party',[23] or has as its 'predominant contractual function' to deter the other party from breach rather than to compensate the claimant.[24] The penalty clause is contrasted with a 'liquidated damages' clause, which is a 'genuine pre-estimate of damage'—that is, an attempt at the time of the contract to agree in advance what the likely damage will be if there is a breach.[25]

---

[22] *HIH Casualty and General Insurance Ltd v Chase Manhattan Bank* [2003] UKHL 6, [2003] 2 Lloyd's Rep 61, confirming dicta in *S Pearson & Son Ltd v Dublin Corporation* [1907] AC 351 (HL) 353–54, 362.
[23] *Dunlop Pneumatic Tyre Co Ltd v New Garage and Motor Co Ltd* [1915] AC 79 (HL) 86–88 (Lord Dunedin).
[24] *Lordsvale Finance plc v Bank of Zambia* [1966] QB 752 (QB) 762 (Colman J).
[25] *Dunlop Pneumatic Tyre Co Ltd v New Garage and Motor Co Ltd* above, n 23, 86–88.

A liquidated damages clause is enforceable—indeed, it is a good thing, because instead of claiming for damages and having an assessment of the loss in fact caused by the breach, it allows a pre-agreed sum to be claimed against the party in breach simply as a debt. The Supreme Court has now reviewed the rule against penalty clauses in response to arguments that it was unclear in its operation and contrary to the general principle of freedom of contract, given that even an agreed penalty cannot be enforced. However, the Court has retained the rule against penalties, whilst clarifying it and redefining some of its underlying principles.[26] The judgments emphasise that the penalty rule does not regulate the fairness of the parties' primary obligations under the contract, but only clauses defining secondary obligations—the remedies available for breach of a party's primary obligations under the contract,[27] and that it should not be limited to clauses providing for the payment of money, but that a clause withholding the payment of money or imposing an obligation to transfer assets in the event of breach of contract could also be a penalty.[28] However, the test to be applied to determine whether a clause is a penalty is one of proportionality in protecting a legitimate interest under the contract:

> [W]hether the impugned provision is a secondary obligation which imposes a detriment on the contract-breaker out of all proportion to any legitimate interest of the innocent party in the enforcement of the primary obligation. The innocent party can have no proper interest in simply punishing the defaulter. His interest is in performance or in some appropriate alternative to performance.[29]

In many civil law systems there is judicial control of penalty clauses: the courts are given the power to reduce manifestly excessive, or disproportionate, penalties. This is not, however, the approach adopted in English law.[30] Proportionality is now included within the test to determine whether the clause is a penalty, but if the stipulated sum is excessive, or disproportionate, and is held to be a penalty, it is not reduced (to, for example, a 'reasonable penalty'), but is simply struck out and the claimant is left to prove his actual loss by way of damages.

There are also certain particular types of contract where the courts will intervene to strike out clauses which undermine the rights of one of the parties. We have seen that English law does not have such a firm theory of 'special contracts' as many civil law systems,[31] but there are contractual relationships

---

[26] *Cavendish Square Holdings BV v El Makdessi* and *ParkingEye Ltd v Beavis* [2015] UKSC 67, [2015] 3 WLR 1373.
[27] For the distinction between 'primary' and 'secondary' obligations, see also *Photo Production Ltd v Securicor Ltd* [1980] AC 827 (HL) 848–89, below, p 274.
[28] *Cavendish Square Holdings BV v El Makdessi*, above, n 26, [13], [16], [170], [226], [230].
[29] *Ibid* [32] (Lord Neuberger and Lord Sumption); see also [152], [255].
[30] Cf *ibid* [37], [164], [165], [265] (comparing civil law approaches).
[31] Above, p 58.

which the courts have identified as deserving of special control and protection. For example, the courts of equity devised rules to protect the mortgagor of land against oppressive terms in the mortgage. In the modern law, much of this is now covered by the general law of contract under which an apparently harsh term will be enforceable if it has been genuinely agreed and if there is no evidence of misconduct on the part of the mortgagor in procuring the mortgagee's agreement to it.[32] However, the courts have retained the principle that there are certain terms which will undermine fundamentally the mortgagor's rights under a contract of mortgage, and which will therefore be struck out—such as an option for the mortgagee (the lender) to purchase the mortgaged property: the borrower must have the right to recover the mortgaged property on payment of the sums due under the mortgage.[33] There are also circumstances where the courts have devised controls over the *exercise* of contractual rights, rather than over the terms of the contract—such as relief against forfeiture of proprietary rights. Such controls are very limited, but are discussed in chapter 12.[34]

2. Control by Statute

In a range of legislative texts the courts have been given the power to control certain types of contract term. Before 1 October 2015, there were two general statutory provisions: the Unfair Contract Terms Act 1977 (which regulated exclusion and limitation clauses in both consumer and non-consumer contracts) and the Unfair Terms in Consumer Contracts Regulations 1999 (which regulated a wide range of terms, but only in consumer contracts). There were also some other more specific statutory controls over contract terms, including section 3 of the Misrepresentation Act 1967, which regulated terms in both consumer and non-consumer contracts that exclude or restrict a party's liability for misrepresentation. Since 1 October 2015, however, most of the provisions relating to exclusion and limitation clauses in consumer contracts are found in the Consumer Rights Act 2015, and the Unfair Contract Terms Act 1977 and section 3 of the Misrepresentation Act 1967 are now limited to non-consumer contracts. The Unfair Terms in Consumer Contracts Regulations 1999 have also been replaced by new provisions in Part 2 of the Consumer Rights Act.

---

[32] Such as the doctrines of undue influence or 'unconscionable bargains': *Multservice Bookbinding Ltd v Marden* [1979] Ch 84 (Ch); above, pp 197–98. There are also statutory controls over the terms of loan agreements: below, p 234.

[33] *Samuel v Jarrah Timber and Wood Paving Corpn Ltd* [1904] AC 323 (HL). See generally EH Burn and J Cartwright, *Cheshire & Burn's Modern Law of Real Property*, 18th edn (Oxford, Oxford University Press, 2011) 814–25.

[34] Below, p 286.

(a) Exclusion and Limitation Clauses in Non-consumer Contracts: The Unfair Contract Terms Act 1977

This title of this statute is misleading. It does not regulate unfair contract terms in general, but only clauses which have the effect of excluding or restricting liability, and it is not limited to the control of contract terms, but also regulates the exclusion or restriction of non-contractual liability by non-contractual notices as well as by contract terms.[35] Its scope has also now been restricted to non-consumer contracts (and non-consumer notices) by the Consumer Rights Act 2015, and in relation to exclusions or restrictions of liability by contract terms, the present scheme of the Act is broadly as follows:

(i) For almost all of the relevant situations which are covered by the Act, it regulates the exclusion or restriction of only 'business liability':[36] liability for breach of obligations or duties arising—
  (a) from things done or to be done by a person in the course of a business (whether his own business or another's); or
  (b) from the occupation of premises used for business purposes of the occupier.

  That is, this Act does not generally prevent a non-business contracting party from excluding or restricting his liability.[37]

(ii) In the case of clauses in non-consumer contracts which attempt to exclude or restrict liability, the nature of the control imposed by the Act depends on the type of liability to which the clause refers:
  (a) if it is liability for negligence (such as a breach of a contractual duty to take care)[38] section 2 prohibits any exclusion or restriction of the defendant's liability for death or personal injury; and it allows an exclusion or limitation of liability for other loss or damage only if the clause satisfies the requirement of 'reasonableness';
  (b) if it is liability for breach of contract, and the contract is on the defendant's 'written standard terms of business', then under section 3 the clause is effective only if it satisfies the requirement of 'reasonableness';

---

[35] Eg notices at the entry to premises purporting to exclude liability in tort to visitors who do not enter under the terms of a contract. Contractual liability can be modified or excluded only by contractual terms.

[36] Section 1(3).

[37] The exception is s 6, which also applies to non-business contracts. It regulates the exclusion or limitation of the conditions as to the title of the seller under a contract for the sale of goods or of the hirer under a hire-purchase contract, or compliance of the goods with the description by reference to which they were sold or hired under such contracts, even where the contract is between individuals neither of whom acts in the course of business.

[38] This also covers the tort of negligence, and the 'common duty of care' owed by occupiers of premises to their lawful visitors under the Occupiers' Liability Act 1957: Unfair Contract Terms Act 1977 s 1(1).

(c) if it is liability for breach of terms (as to title, conformity with description and sample, and quality of goods and their fitness into a contract for the sale of goods) under the Sale of Goods Act 1979,[39] or a contract of hire-purchase under the Supply of Goods (Implied Terms) Act 1973, then under section 6 the clause is effective only if it satisfies the requirement of 'reasonableness'.

(iii) Parties may try to avoid the operation of the Act by drafting their clauses in such a way that they do not 'exclude or restrict' liability—for example, by modifying the duty so as to prevent the liability arising at all. The courts have two separate techniques to deal with such situations. First, they interpret clauses on the basis of their 'substance rather than form'—that is, if the clause has the effect of excluding or restricting a liability which (in the absence of the clause) would have arisen they will treat it as a clause to which the Act applies.[40] Secondly, the draftsman of the Act anticipated this problem, and made specific provision for clauses which purport to allow a party to offer substantially different contractual performance, or no performance at all, in place of the contracted performance,[41] and more generally for clauses which exclude or modify the duty rather than excluding or restricting the liability, or which impose restrictive conditions or exclude or restrict remedies in respect of a liability.[42]

(iv) Some of the controls exercised by the Act depend on whether the clause satisfies the requirement of 'reasonableness'. The Act provides a definition of 'reasonableness' in section 11:

> the term shall have been a fair and reasonable one to be included having regard to the circumstances which were, or ought reasonably to have been, known to or in the contemplation of the parties when the contract was made.

Where the clause restricts liability to a specified sum of money, the court is to take into account the party's resources and how far it was open to him to cover himself by insurance. There are also guidelines for the operation of the 'reasonableness test' in Schedule 2 which show that in assessing the reasonableness of an exclusion or limitation clause the Act is concerned with procedural fairness as well as substantive fairness: it includes such things as the strength of the relative bargaining positions of the parties; whether the customer received an inducement to agree to the term, or had an opportunity of entering into a similar contract with others but without having to accept

---

[39] Above, p 214. Section 7 contains similar provisions for similar terms implied into non-consumer contracts under which possession or ownership of goods pass other than contracts of sale or hire purchase (eg contracts for the hire of goods).
[40] *Phillips Products Ltd v Hyland* [1987] 1 WLR 659 (CA).
[41] Section 3(2)(b).
[42] Section 13(1).

a similar term; and whether the customer knew or ought reasonably to have known of the existence and extent of the term. Schedule 2 strictly applies only in the case of clauses which exclude or restrict the implied terms in contracts for sale or supply of goods (sections 6 and 7), but it has been treated by the courts as containing generally applicable guidelines.

Where a clause is subject to the reasonableness test it is for the defendant, who seeks to rely on it, to show that it satisfies the test.[43] And it is the whole clause, or a separate and severable part of it, which must be shown to be reasonable. If a clause is not reasonable the whole clause fails: the court cannot rewrite the clause so that it constitutes only a reasonable exclusion or limitation clause.[44]

(b) Exclusion and Restriction of Liability for Misrepresentation by Clauses in Non-consumer Contracts: Section 3 of the Misrepresentation Act 1967

The Misrepresentation Act 1967 contains in section 3 a separate control over contract terms in non-consumer contracts which would exclude or restrict any liability or any remedy arising from a pre-contractual misrepresentation. Such clauses are of no effect unless the party relying on the term can show that it satisfies the requirement of reasonableness set out in the Unfair Contract Terms Act 1977.

This provision applies to clauses which are aimed at excluding the liabilities and remedies that arise from the misrepresentation—such as rescission of the contract[45] or damages under section 2(1) of the Misrepresentation Act 1967.[46] It applies to clauses which have the effect of excluding the liability or remedies for misrepresentation, even if they do so by taking the form not of an exclusion or limitation of liability clause, but of a denial of some element of the claim for misrepresentation.[47]

The separate existence of this special control over clauses which relate to misrepresentation can be explained by the fact that it was introduced in the partial reform of the law of misrepresentation in 1967 by the Misrepresentation Act, at a time when there was not yet any general statutory control of exclusion and limitation clauses. It later became a model for the more general provisions of the Unfair Contract Terms Act 1977, although it was not integrated into the 1977 Act, but was simply amended[48] to refer to the (new) definition of the 'requirement of reasonableness' in the 1977 Act.

---

[43] Section 11(5).
[44] *Stewart Gill Ltd v Horatio Myer & Co Ltd* [1992] QB 600 (CA).
[45] Above, p 179.
[46] Above, p 182.
[47] 'No representation' and 'non-reliance' clauses: above, p 185.
[48] Unfair Contract Terms Act 1977 s 8.

(c) Exclusion and Limitation Clauses in Consumer Contracts: The Consumer Rights Act 2015

We saw (above) the controls in relation to exclusions or restrictions of liability set out in the Unfair Contract Terms Act 1977, which is now limited to *non-consumer* contract terms and notices. The Consumer Rights Act 2015 contains some similar provisions in relation to *consumer* contracts and notices; that is, contracts between a trader and a consumer, and notices relating to rights or obligations as between a trader and a consumer or purporting to exclude or restrict a trader's liability to a consumer.[49] As in the case of clauses in non-consumer contracts under the 1977 Act, the nature of the control imposed by the Consumer Rights Act depends on the type of liability to which the clause refers, but it does not subject clauses to a requirement of 'reasonableness' but provides simply that terms that would exclude or restrict the trader's liability are not binding on the consumer in the following cases:

(a) if it is liability for negligence (such as a breach of a contractual duty to take care),[50] section 65 prohibits any exclusion or restriction of the defendant's liability for death or personal injury;

(b) if it is liability for breach of a term treated by Part 1 of the Consumer Rights Act as being included in the contract for goods, digital content or services,[51] then the clause is not binding.[52]

This list is shorter than that contained in the Unfair Contract Terms Act 1977,[53] because in the case of consumer contracts there is also a general provision regulating unfair contract terms, contained in Part 2 of the Consumer Rights Act 2015, to which we now turn.

(d) Unfair Terms in Consumer Contracts: Part 2 of the Consumer Rights Act 2015

The Consumer Rights Act 2015 implements in the UK the EC Directive on Unfair Terms in Consumer Contracts.[54] This is the third implementation of the Directive: Regulations were first made in 1994,[55] replaced by 1999

---

[49] Consumer Rights Act 2015 s 1 (pt 1), s 61 (pt 2). 'Trader' and 'consumer' are defined in s 2.

[50] This also covers the tort of negligence and the 'common duty of care' owed by occupiers of premises to their lawful visitors under the Occupiers' Liability Act 1957: Consumer Rights Act 2015 s 65(4).

[51] Eg terms as to quality, fitness for purpose, matching description, pre-contract information and sample, and title: Consumer Rights Act 2015 ss 9–13, 17, 34–36, 41 (goods and digital content); reasonable care and skill, price and time of performance: ss 49–52 (services).

[52] Consumer Rights Act 2015 ss 31 (goods), 47 (digital content), 57 (services).

[53] Above, pp 227–28.

[54] Council Directive 93/13.

[55] SI 1994/3159.

Regulations in order to reflect more closely the wording of the Directive as well as to provide improved enforcement mechanisms.[56] The new implementation in the 2015 Act extends the provisions to consumer notices, as well as consumer contract terms, and makes certain changes to the regime governing contract terms in light of a review by the Law Commission.[57]

The basic provisions relating to contract terms are contained in section 62:

> (1) An unfair term of a consumer contract is not binding on the consumer.
>
> ...
>
> (3) This does not prevent the consumer from relying on the term or notice if the consumer chooses to do so.
>
> (4) A term is unfair if, contrary to the requirement of good faith, it causes a significant imbalance in the parties' rights and obligations under the contract to the detriment of the consumer.
>
> (5) Whether a term is fair is to be determined—
>
> (a) taking into account the nature of the subject matter of the contract, and
> (b) by reference to all the circumstances existing when the term was agreed and to all of the other terms of the contract or of any other contract on which it depends.

and section 67:

> Where a term of a consumer contract is not binding on the consumer as a result of this Part, the contract continues, so far as practicable, to have effect in every other respect.

There is general obligation on the trader to ensure that any written term of a consumer contract is transparent (that is, expressed in plain and intelligible language and legible),[58] and if a term could have different meanings, the meaning that is the most favourable to the consumer is to prevail (a version of the *contra proferentem* rule).[59] But, provided that it is not only transparent but

---

[56] SI 1999/2083. The 1999 Regulations extended the enforcement powers beyond the Director General of Fair Trading to include other bodies. The Consumer Rights Act 2015 s 70 confers investigatory and enforcement powers on the Competition and Markets Authority and other regulators. The regulatory mechanisms (such as the power of regulators to obtain injunctions to prevent the continued use of unfair standard terms by businesses) are in practice much more significant than the purely private control of individual contracts with which we are concerned here. Unfair contract terms guidance from the Competition and Markets Authority can be found on the Government website: *www.gov.uk/government/organisations/competition-and-markets-authority*.

[57] Law Commission, 'Unfair Terms in Consumer Contracts: Advice to the Department for Business, Innovation and Skills' (March 2013), available on the Law Commission website, *www.lawcom.gov.uk*.

[58] Section 68.

[59] Section 69(1). For the *contra proferentem* rule, see above, p 221.

also prominent (that is, brought to the consumer's attention in such a way that an average consumer would be aware of it) a term cannot be assessed for fairness if it specifies the main subject-matter of the contract, or the assessment is of the appropriateness of the price payable under the contract by comparison with the goods, digital content or services supplied under it.[60]

In Part 1 of Schedule 2 there is an 'indicative and non-exhaustive' list of types of term which *may* be regarded as unfair: a 'grey list', rather than a 'black list' which would determine conclusively the invalidity of terms which it included. The list contains a range of familiar types of clause, some of which are exclusion or limitation clauses but others which are unduly onerous in other ways to the consumer or unduly beneficial to the business.

The challenge to a contract term on the basis that it is unfair is not left only to the consumer: the court must consider whether the term is fair even if none of the parties to the proceedings has raised that issue or indicated that it intends to raise it, but only if the court considers that it has before it sufficient legal and factual material to enable it to consider the fairness of the term.[61]

The language of the Regulations tracks that in the Directive; and this includes a definition of 'unfairness' which looks rather strange to the English lawyer: '*contrary to the requirement of good faith*, it causes a significant imbalance in the parties' rights and obligations ...'. We have seen that English law does not generally use the language of 'good faith' to define the standards expected of the parties in the formation of a contract.[62] However, the Preamble to the Directive includes an indication of what is intended here:

> Whereas, in making an assessment of good faith, particular regard shall be had to the strength of the bargaining positions of the parties, whether the consumer had an inducement to agree to the term and whether the goods or services were sold or supplied to the special order of the consumer; whereas the requirement of good faith may be satisfied by the seller or supplier where he deals fairly and equitably with the other party whose legitimate interests he has to take into account.

The first part of this extract bears a striking similarity to some of the guidelines for the application of the 'reasonableness test' under Schedule 2 of the Unfair Contract Terms Act 1977;[63] and the second part makes clear that there

---

[60] Section 64. The requirement that the term relating to the price or subject-matter be exempt from review only if it is transparent and prominent implements a proposal of the Law Commission in its Advice in March 2013 (above, n 57) pts 2–4, made in light of the decision of the Supreme Court in *Office of Fair Trading v Abbey National plc* [2009] UKSC 6, [2010] 1 AC 696 (charges for unauthorised bank overdrafts were within the 'price or remuneration' so could not be challenged).

[61] Section 71, implementing the decision in of the ECJ in Case C-243/08 *Pannon GSM Zrt v Sustikné Györfi* (4 June 2009), [2010] 1 All ER (Comm) 640.

[62] Above, p 64.

[63] Above, p 228.

is an element of procedural fairness in the notion of good faith. Discussing the requirement of 'good faith' under the Directive Lord Bingham said:

> The requirement of good faith in this context is one of fair and open dealing. Openness requires that the terms should be expressed fully, clearly and legibly, containing no concealed pitfalls or traps. Appropriate prominence should be given to terms which might operate disadvantageously to the customer. Fair dealing requires that a supplier should not, whether deliberately or unconsciously, take advantage of the consumer's necessity, indigence, lack of experience, unfamiliarity with the subject matter of the contract, weak bargaining position or any other factor listed in or analogous to those listed in Schedule 2 to the Regulations. Good faith in this context is not an artificial or technical concept; nor, since Lord Mansfield was its champion, is it a concept wholly unfamiliar to British lawyers. It looks to good standards of commercial morality and practice.[64]

The Court of Justice of the European Union has said that, in deciding whether an imbalance arises 'contrary to the requirement of good faith', 'the national court must assess ... whether the seller or supplier, dealing fairly and equitably with the consumer, could reasonably assume that the consumer would have agreed to such a term in individual contract negotiations'.[65]

(e) Other Statutory Controls over Particular Types of Term

Other statutes have provided particular controls over the parties' freedom to vary the terms of the contract, generally where a particular relationship attracts the protection of the law for reasons of policy.

For example, there is extensive statutory protection for an employee under the Employment Rights Act 1996, and the general rule is that any provision in an agreement is void in so far as it purports to exclude or limit the operation of any provision of the Act or to preclude a person from bringing any proceedings before an employment tribunal.[66] Tenants of various types of property are also given extensive protection through a range of statutes: for example, the parties to a lease of a dwelling-house for a term of less than seven years cannot without the authorisation of the County Court exclude or limit the landlord's obligations to repair which are implied by the Landlord and Tenant Act 1985.[67] Over the years there have been statutory controls

---

[64] *Director General of Fair Trading v First National Bank Plc* [2001] UKHL 52, [2002] 1 AC 481, [17]. This was a decision on the language of the 1994 Regulations, which included in its text the criteria for assessing 'good faith' set out in the preamble to the Directive.

[65] Case C-415/11 *Aziz v Caixa d'Estalvis de Catalunya, Tarragona i Manresa* (14 March 2013), [2013] 3 CMLR 5 [69]. In *ParkingEye Ltd v Beavis* [2015] UKSC 67 the UK Supreme Court applied *Aziz* as the leading case.

[66] Employment Rights Act 1996 s 203.

[67] Above, p 215; Landlord and Tenant Act 1985 s 12.

over the terms of various types of tenancy, limiting the landlord's power to exercise his contractual right to terminate and to regain possession, as well as in some cases limiting the level of rent which can be charged. Such provisions are based on the policy from time to time in favour of tenants against landlords.[68]

There have long been statutory controls over the terms of loan agreements, to give relief to borrowers against unfair contracts. Under the Money-lenders Act 1900[69] a court could re-open a transaction with a money-lender where the interest or other charges were excessive and the transaction was 'harsh and unconscionable'. The current provision is found in the Consumer Credit Act 1974,[70] under which the court has wide powers to make orders where the relationship between the creditor and the debtor is unfair to the debtor because of any of the terms of their agreement, the way in which the creditor has exercised or enforced any of his rights under the agreement, or any other thing done (or not done) by or on behalf of the creditor. The orders available include requiring the creditor to repay any sum paid by the debtor; to reduce or discharge any sum payable by the debtor under the agreement; or to alter the terms of the agreement.

---

[68] The control over the terms of leases still exists, but is now significantly less than it was during the middle part of the twentieth century. For an overview, see Burn and Cartwright, above, n 33, ch 11.

[69] Section 1.

[70] Sections 140A–C, inserted by Consumer Credit Act 2006 ss 19–21 and replacing narrower provisions in ss 137–40 which gave the court the power to re-open an 'extortionate' credit agreement—where the payments to be made under it were 'grossly exorbitant' or if it 'otherwise grossly contravenes ordinary principles of fair dealing'.

10

Who has the Benefit of the Contract? Who is Bound by the Contract?

A fundamental question in any legal system is the extent of the legal reach of the contract. If one starts from the proposition that a contract is created from the agreement between its parties, it will be natural to say that the contracting parties are within the reach of the contract: they can enforce it and be bound by it. Under a bilateral contract—the typical case—a set of obligations is owed by each party to the other. In relation to each contractual obligation one party has the benefit of it—has the right arising under it; and the other party has its burden—has the duty. In this context we often speak about who may 'enforce' the contract, but this does not presuppose that any particular remedy is available—'enforcing' the contract here means simply having the benefit of the obligation and thereby having the legal remedies which are available to protect the rights arising from that benefit, whether is it through the literal enforcement of the contract (specific performance), or damages, or any other remedy. We shall consider remedies in chapter 12.

Such a discussion already makes some assumptions about how we identify the 'parties' to a contract, and this must be considered first. But the real enquiry is to discover how far the contract reaches beyond the parties: in what circumstances can a person who is, so to speak, 'outside' the contract acquire the right to the fulfilment of an obligation, or be bound himself to fulfil it or in some way to respect its existence.

Legal systems have generally started from the position that a contract is personal to the parties because of its very nature, and therefore not only can the contracting parties not confer a burden on a person outside their contract (a 'third party'), nor can they even confer enforceable rights on the third party. However, such a limited view of the reach of the contract has generally been rejected, or at least undermined, so as to allow third parties to have directly enforceable rights to benefits created by a contract, although the pace of such reform has varied from one legal system to another, English law being particularly slow to create a general doctrine of enforceable third-party rights.[1] Until very recently, English law took the position that a person who was not a party to a contract could not acquire directly enforceable rights under it: this is known as the doctrine of 'privity of contract'—that is, only those who are 'privy' to the contract (parties to it) acquire rights under it. The law in this area was reformed very significantly by the Contracts (Rights of Third Parties) Act 1999. But long before this Act parties had found ways of avoiding the strict rule of privity by structuring their transactions so as to create rights for third parties; and the courts were sometimes able to find remedies which in effect gave protection to third parties. Moreover, there are well-established circumstances in which a person may acquire rights to existing contractual obligations through assignment; and (although only in narrowly defined circumstances) a third party may become liable in tort for interference with a contractual obligation.

I. Who is a 'Party' to the Contract? The Doctrine of Privity of Contract

1. A Party to the Agreement or to the Bargain?

We saw in chapter five that a contract in English law is based on an agreement between the parties, normally formed through the acceptance by one party of an offer by the other. The language which we commonly use in that context shows that we identify the parties to the contract as being the *parties to the agreement*: those persons, whether individuals or legal persons (such as companies) who communicated to each other their assent to a set of terms in such form as is sufficient to create a contract.

---

[1] European jurisdictions generally developed doctrines of third-party rights in the later stages of the nineteenth century, in response to such developments as life insurance contracts: see, eg, B Nicholas, *The French Law of Contract*, 2nd edn (Oxford, Clarendon Press, 1992) 184–85. The English response in this case was to give the beneficiaries of such insurance contracts rights by statute, rather than to generalise an exception to the rule denying third-party rights: Married Women's Property Act 1882 s 11 (below, p 247). The development of a more general provision admitting enforceable third-party rights in English law was slowed down by the link to the doctrine of consideration (below, pp 237–39) and the restrictions on judicial reform set by the doctrine of precedent (below, pp 240–41). Some other common law systems have still not introduced general third-party rights: eg, not all States and Territories in Australia have modified the privity rule: JW Carter, *Contract Law in Australia*, 6th edn (Chatswood, LexisNexis, 2013) paras 16-16, 16-18–16-23.

However, in chapter six we saw that an agreement is not in itself sufficient to create a contract: except where the undertaking is contained in a deed, the contract also requires consideration. Here we analyse the contract in terms of the promises between the parties: and what makes one party's promise enforceable is that the other party gave consideration for it. The promisee earned the legal right to the promise—the right to the obligation—by doing or promising something in return at the express or implied request of the promisor. We may describe the contract as a bargain between the parties. And so another way of identifying the parties to the contract is as the *parties to the bargain*—the one who undertook the obligation, and the one who gave consideration for it.

In most bilateral contracts these are two sides of the same coin. The parties' agreement consists in their mutual undertakings, and the undertakings of one party provide consideration for the undertakings of the other. So whether one looks at the agreement or the bargain the identity of the parties is the same. But the choice between these two approaches is critical for understanding the nature of the doctrine of privity as it was developed by the common law—and in turn to understand the nature of a contract and of contractual obligation. It also explains why the English courts found it so difficult to break down the doctrine of privity of contract, even when they thought that it was not satisfactory and should be reformed.

2. The Link between Privity and Consideration: *Tweddle v Atkinson*

The origin of the doctrine of privity in the modern law is generally identified as *Tweddle v Atkinson*.[2] The claimant, William Tweddle, was the son of John Tweddle. He married the daughter of William Guy. Before the marriage the two fathers agreed that they would each give a sum of money to the claimant, and they recorded the agreement in a written memorandum which said:

> Memorandum of an agreement made this day between William Guy, of &c. of the one part, and John Tweddle, of &c. of the other part. Whereas it is mutually agreed that the said William Guy shall and will pay the sum of £200 to William Tweddle, his son-in-law; and the said John Tweddle, father to the aforesaid William Tweddle, shall and will pay the sum of £100 to the said William Tweddle, each and severally the said sums on or before the 21st day of August, 1855. And it is hereby further agreed by the aforesaid William Guy and the said John Tweddle that the said William Tweddle has full power to sue the said parties in any Court of law or equity for the aforesaid sums hereby promised and specified.

The claimant said that he had ratified and assented to the agreement. William Guy died without making the payment, and the question was

---

[2] (1861) 1 B & S 393, 121 ER 762.

whether the claimant could require Guy's executors to pay. There was no suggestion that Guy would not have made the payment had he lived—that is, no evidence that he had changed his mind. But executors can properly pay money from the deceased's estate only if it is to discharge a liability of the estate, otherwise they may become personally liable for improperly paying away the estate's property.[3] This no doubt explains their reluctance to pay in this case.

The Court of Queen's Bench held that the claim failed. This is a very strong decision. It can be seen from the parties' written memorandum that the terms of the agreement were clear, the intention to benefit the claimant (identified by name) was clear, and it was even made explicit that he should have the right to sue to enforce it. But the court thought it self-evident that he had no right to sue. They put it in terms of the doctrine of consideration: the claimant had not provided consideration for William Guy's promise, and so could not enforce it. '[N]o stranger to the consideration can take advantage of a contract, although made for his benefit.'[4] And:

> The modern cases ... shew that the consideration must move from the party entitled to sue upon the contract. It would be a monstrous proposition to say that a person was a party to the contract for the purpose of suing upon it for his own advantage, and not a party to it for the purpose of being sued.[5]

In effect, this decision identifies the 'party to the contract'—in the sense of the one who obtains legally enforceable rights under it—as the party to the consideration. One becomes a party not simply by giving one's assent to an agreement (the claimant had done that, by ratifying the agreement and agreeing to receive the benefits under it), but by undertaking an obligation or doing some other thing requested by the promisor[6] as the price of acquiring the right to the obligation.

The doctrine of privity was applied in 1915 by the House of Lords in *Dunlop Pneumatic Tyre Co Ltd v Selfridge & Co Ltd*.[7] Although *Tweddle v Atkinson* was not discussed, the reason for the decision of the House of Lords was the same: a company named as a third party to the agreement was not entitled to enforce the agreement because it had not provided any consideration. The House here did not speak in the language of 'privity of contract'; the enforceability of the contract was seen as necessarily a part of the doctrine of consideration. However, in emphasising the fundamental nature

---

[3] *Ministry of Health v Simpson* [1951] 1 AC 251 (HL).
[4] (1861) 1 B & S 393, 398; 121 ER 762, 764 (Wightman J).
[5] *Ibid* (Crompton J).
[6] Crompton J's reference to a party acquiring contractual rights only if he is also a party 'for the purpose of being sued' is misleading, since a party may not be liable to be sued under, eg, a unilateral contract: *Carlill v Carbolic Smoke Ball Co* [1893] 1 QB 256 (CA). But there the claimant had still earned the right to enforce the promise by providing consideration by using the smoke ball: above, p 134 n 33.
[7] [1915] AC 847 (HL).

of this principle, Viscount Haldane noted that there were in fact two separate principles:

> My Lords, in the law of England certain principles are fundamental. One is that only a person who is a party to a contract can sue on it. Our law knows nothing of a jus quaesitum tertio arising by way of contract. Such a right may be conferred by way of property, as, for example, under a trust, but it cannot be conferred on a stranger to a contract as a right to enforce the contract in personam. A second principle is that if a person with whom a contract not under seal has been made is to be able to enforce it consideration must have been given by him to the promisor or to some other person at the promisor's request. These two principles are not recognized in the same fashion by the jurisprudence of certain Continental countries or of Scotland, but here they are well established.[8]

Later it became more usual to separate out the doctrine of privity from the doctrine of consideration, and to suggest that reform of the doctrine of privity might be possible.

3. Development of Judicial Attitudes to the Doctrine of Privity During the Twentieth Century

During the twentieth century there was a remarkable change in the attitude to the doctrine of privity. We have seen that the Queen's Bench in 1861 and the House of Lords in 1915 saw it as obvious that a third party could not sue to enforce a contract, even when he was named as an intended beneficiary of it. By 1994, however, Steyn LJ could say:

> The case for recognising a contract for the benefit of a third party is simple and straightforward. The autonomy of the will of the parties should be respected. The law of contract should give effect to the reasonable expectations of contracting parties. Principle certainly requires that a burden should not be imposed on a third party without his consent. But there is no doctrinal, logical or policy reason why the law should deny effectiveness to a contract for the benefit of a third party where that is the expressed intention of the parties. Moreover, often the parties, and particularly third parties, organise their affairs on the faith of the contract. They rely on the contract. It is therefore unjust to deny effectiveness to such a contract.[9]

This rather overstates the argument: if one thinks that the right to enforce a contractual obligation arises from the fact that one has 'bought' it by doing or promising something in return—the doctrine of consideration—then there is indeed a doctrinal reason to deny that a third party should have a direct right of action. That was the starting-point for the doctrine of privity of contract in the earlier cases. However, Steyn LJ's statement shows a shift in judicial attitude not only to third-party rights, but also to the underlying basis of

---

[8] *Ibid* 853.
[9] *Darlington BC v Wiltshier Northern Ltd* [1995] 1 WLR 68 (CA) 76.

the law of contract: the emphasis is on the intentions of the parties, rather than the bargain. Again, this is a particularly strong statement. English contract law has not become based on the 'autonomy of the will of the parties': that would suggest that the doctrine of consideration should also be overturned, but the courts have not taken that step—although we have seen that there has also been a tendency in the later twentieth century to emphasise the application of the doctrine of consideration in such a way as to give effect to the intentions of the parties.[10] However, the traditional English approach to the doctrine of privity of contract was seen as not only liable to frustrate the intentions of the parties, but also out of step with other legal systems:

> [W]e do well to remember that the civil law legal systems of other members of the European Union recognise such contracts. That our legal system lacks such flexibility is a disadvantage in the single market. Indeed it is a historical curiosity that the legal system of a mercantile country such as England, which in other areas of the law of contract (such as, for example, the objective theory of the interpretation of contracts) takes great account of the interests of third parties, has not been able to rid itself of this unjust rule deriving from a technical conception of a contract as a purely bilateral vinculum juris.[11]

The attack on the doctrine of privity of contract was not new. During the course of the twentieth century the courts had become uncomfortable with the strict application of the doctrine because it could prevent third parties from obtaining the benefit of contracts which the contracting parties had intended should be conferred. As early as 1937 the Law Revision Committee[12] considered the matter and recommended that a third party should be able to enforce a contract which by its express terms purported to confer a benefit directly on him. This reform was never taken forward because of the outbreak of war in 1939, but later the courts began openly to criticise the doctrine and even to suggest that they might themselves reverse it. The delay in taking this step, however, can be explained at least in part by the doctrine of precedent in English law. The decision of the House of Lords in *Dunlop v Selfridge*,[13] accepting the doctrine of privity, was binding on all courts, including the House of Lords itself until the Practice Statement of 1966 when the House announced its changed view of the binding force of its own previous decisions.[14] In 1961, we still find Lord Reid saying:

> Although I may regret it, I find it impossible to deny the existence of the general rule [of privity of contract][15]

---

[10] *Williams v Roffey Bros & Nicholls (Contractors) Ltd* [1991] 1 QB 1 (CA) above, pp 140–41.
[11] *Darlington BC v Wiltshier Northern Ltd* above, n 9, 77 (Steyn LJ).
[12] Sixth Interim Report, 'Statute of Frauds and the Doctrine of Consideration' (Cmd 5449, 1937) para 48.
[13] Above, n 7.
[14] Above, p 26.
[15] *Scruttons Ltd v Midland Silicones Ltd* [1962] AC 446 (HL) 473.

although in 1967 he was able not only to criticise the doctrine but also to suggest that the courts might themselves find the means of changing it.[16] The criticism of the doctrine gathered some momentum during the last quarter of the century; for example, Lord Scarman said:

> I respectfully agree with Lord Reid that the denial by English law of a 'jus quaesitum tertio' calls for reconsideration. In *Beswick v. Beswick*[17] Lord Reid, after referring to the Law Revision Committee's recommendation in 1937[18] that the third party should be able to enforce a contractual promise taken by another for his benefit, observed:
>
> 'And, if one had to contemplate a further long period of Parliamentary procrastination, this House might find it necessary to deal with this matter.'
>
> The committee reported in 1937: *Beswick v. Beswick* was decided in 1967. It is now 1979: but nothing has been done. If the opportunity arises, I hope the House will reconsider *Tweddle v. Atkinson*[19] and the other cases which stand guard over this unjust rule.[20]

The 'Parliamentary procrastination' finally ended with the Contracts (Rights of Third Parties) Act 1999.[21] But before the passing of the Act contracting parties (or, rather, their legal advisers who knew the limitations on third party rights through the doctrine of privity of contract) and the courts found various ways in which the doctrine could in practice be avoided.

II. Avoiding the Doctrine of Privity

There were some techniques available to parties negotiating an agreement to enable them to ensure that a third party could have an enforceable right under the agreement. And sometimes the courts, to avoid the agreement being of no effect, developed rules of law, or further developed existing rules of law, so as to protect third parties by giving them direct rights of action or by giving the

---

[16] *Beswick v Beswick* [1968] AC 58 (HL) 72.
[17] Above, n 16.
[18] (Cmnd 5449) p 31.
[19] Above, n 2.
[20] *Woodar Investment Development Ltd v Wimpey Construction UK Ltd* [1980] 1 WLR 277 (HL) 300. See also *Swain v Law Society* [1983] 1 AC 598 (HL) 611 (Lord Diplock: 'an anachronistic shortcoming that has for many years been regarded as a reproach to English private law').
[21] Below, p 250.

contracting parties themselves better remedies in order to protect the third parties for whom they had contracted.

1. Creating Rights for the Third Party

(a) Make the Third Party a Party

Perhaps the most obvious way to ensure that an intended beneficiary could have the right to enforce a contract was to bring him within the regular scope of the contract—that is, make him a party. However, simply naming him as a party and securing his agreement to the terms of the contract is not sufficient because the doctrine of privity is based on the principle that a party is one who has the right to an obligation by having provided consideration. It would therefore be necessary for the third party at least to undertake an obligation in return for the promise which he is to enforce. In the alternative, it was quite common for practitioners to ensure that a contract which sought to confer a benefit on a third party was executed as a deed, which avoids the need for the beneficiary of the deed to provide consideration.[22]

Making the third party into a contracting party could also be achieved using a separate (collateral) contract. For example, builders and professionals involved in a building project were commonly required to enter into direct contracts (generally referred to as 'collateral warranties') in favour of all those who may need to have rights of action against them for their defective work, such as tenants and future owners of the property.

(b) Trusts

A right could be given under a trust, rather than just as a contractual right. Under a trust one person (the 'beneficiary') has a right in equity to property which is vested in another (the 'trustee'). As far as the common law is concerned, the trustee is the owner, and can transfer the property or deal with it as his own. But equity regards the beneficiary as the true, underlying owner and allows his rights to be enforced not only against the trustee (who has taken on the duty to hold the property for the benefit of the beneficiary) but also against anyone else into whose hands the property comes except a person who acquired rights in the property for value (a purchaser) without notice of the existence of the trust.[23] The beneficiary has directly enforceable rights and can require the trustee to take action for him, or can bring an action himself

---

[22] Above, p 127.
[23] For an introduction to the trust, see S Gardner, *An Introduction to the Law of Trusts*, 3rd edn (Oxford, Oxford University Press, 2011).

in the name of the trustee.[24] A trust can be set up with property (land or personal property) as its subject-matter, but also with another right, such as a debt or the benefit of a contractual obligation, as its subject-matter—a 'trust of a promise'. So it is possible to construct a transaction under which, say, A, who has a contract with B, agrees to hold his right to B's obligations under that contract on trust for C. The contract is between A and B; but C's right to B's obligations is legally enforceable. Parties could set up such a transaction deliberately so as to ensure that C has enforceable rights even though he was not a party to the contract. But a trust requires proof of an intention to create a trust and the courts were reluctant to imply a trust because (amongst other reasons) a trust is irrevocable.[25] To hold that A and B must (impliedly) have intended to set up a trust involves holding that they have irrevocably created enforceable rights, and so cannot without C's consent vary the terms of the trust (nor, therefore, the terms of the contract of which the benefit is now the subject-matter of the trust). In the case of contracts, however, the parties are normally able to agree to vary the contract.

(c) Assignment

Once a contractual right has been created, it can often be assigned to a third party. So although before 1999 it was not possible for A and B to confer a directly enforceable contractual right on C, it was possible for something similar to be done in two stages: A and B enter into a contract, under which B makes a particular promise to A; and then A assigns to C the right to that promise. In the end, C receives (by assignment from A) a benefit that he can then enforce in his own right. This shows that there ought to be no objection in principle to a third party having an enforceable contractual right for which he did not personally give consideration. Assignment is discussed further below.[26]

(d) Agency

Agency is not an exception to the doctrine of privity of contract, because where one person (the 'principal') expressly or impliedly authorises another (the 'agent') to enter into a contract on his behalf it is the principal, and not the agent, who is party to the contract. It may look as though the contract is between the agent and the other contracting party, and that the principal acquires rights under it as a third party, but in fact the agent is not a party to

---

[24] *Vandepitte v Preferred Accident Insurance Corp of New York* [1933] AC 70 (PC) 79.
[25] *Re Schebsman* [1944] Ch 83 (CA).
[26] Below, p 256.

the contract at all; and this is normally clear to the other contracting party, who knows that he is dealing with an agent. However, there is one situation in which the principles of agency look very like an exception to the doctrine of privity: where the agent does not disclose that he is acting as agent. The other party deals with him on the basis that he is the other party. But in fact the agent is acting within his authority as agent, although in his own name. English law here accepts that the undisclosed principal can intervene and take the benefit of the contract which his agent has intended to enter into on his behalf, as long as there is nothing in the terms of the contract to contradict this. The other contracting party therefore finds that he is in a contract with a person with whom he had no intention to contract. However, he is able to raise against the principal any defences that he could have raised against the agent; and he can require the principal to take the burden of the obligations under the contract, as well as the benefits.

Sometimes the courts have used agency analysis rather creatively to solve problems arising through the application of the doctrine of privity. For example, in contracts concerning carriage of goods by sea, it is common for the owner of goods to agree that he limits his claims against the carrier (with whom he contracts) and also against other persons such as stevedores engaged by the carrier to load or unload the goods. If the goods are damaged in unloading, and the owner brings a claim (in tort) against the stevedore, the stevedore needs to be able to use the exclusion clause in the contract between the owner and carrier—but he is not a party to it. The courts could solve this if they were able to find that the carrier was contracting not only in his own right for the carriage of goods, but also as agent for the stevedore for the purposes of a second, direct contract between the owner and stevedore, which contained the clause limiting the stevedore's liability.[27] This became accepted as the normal analysis for that particular situation, as a way of giving effect to the clear intentions of the parties.[28]

(e) Tort

The law of tort can be used indirectly to give effect to both the benefits which a contract was intended to confer on a third party, and its burdens.

Sometimes a person who claims that he has suffered a loss as a result of the failed performance, or defective performance, of a contract to which he

---

[27] *New Zealand Shipping Co Ltd v AM Satterthwaite & Co Ltd* [1975] AC 154 (PC) 167–68 (Lord Wilberforce: 'the bill of lading brought into existence a bargain initially unilateral but capable of becoming mutual, between the shipper and the appellant, made through the carrier as agent. This became a full contract when the appellant performed services by discharging the goods').

[28] *Ibid* 169; *Port Jackson Stevedoring Pty Ltd v Salmond & Spraggon (Australia) Pty Ltd* [1981] 1 WLR 138 (PC) 144 (Lord Wilberforce: 'their Lordships would not encourage a search for fine distinctions which would diminish the general applicability, in the light of established commercial practice, of the principle').

is not party can find a claim in tort which allows him to recover that loss against the defaulting party to the contract. This is not a general solution to the doctrine of privity of contract: a breach of contract which causes loss to a third party does not automatically constitute a tort; and even where a tort claim does arise, the law of tort normally protects a claimant only against out-of-pocket losses and does not award compensation designed to fulfil his disappointed expectations.[29] But sometimes a court can allow a claim in tort which in substance covers losses of expectation—such as the case of *White v Jones*[30] in which the House of Lords held that a solicitor who failed to exercise due care in favour of his client by failing to draw up a will for the client to sign before the client died, owed a duty to those members of the client's family who would have benefited under the will had it been properly drawn up and executed.

A person can sometimes be burdened by a contract to which he is not a party but of which he knows, if without reasonable justification or excuse he intentionally induces one of the parties to break the contract.[31] He is liable to pay damages to the person who suffers loss by the tort.

(f) Property Law

We have already seen that a third party can enforce a contractual right if he is the beneficiary of a trust, where the contractual right has been made the subject-matter of the trust. This is an example of the use of the law of property to give effect to third-party rights, since in equity the beneficiary is treated as having a property right in the subject-matter of the trust. There are other contexts in which the law of property can be used to give effect to third-party rights.

Under the principles of English land law both the benefit and the burden of a covenant—a contractual obligation entered into by deed—can in certain circumstances be annexed to the land, or to an estate in the land, so that it passes automatically with the land when it is transferred. This allows whoever is the owner of the land for the time being to enforce the covenant because it was created for the benefit of the landowner, rather than simply for the benefit of the person who was the original beneficiary of the covenant; and it allows the covenant to be enforced against whoever has the land which was originally owned by the person who gave the covenant. This principle applies

---

[29] Above, pp 181, 184 (liability in tort for misrepresentation, contrasted with liability in contract).
[30] [1995] 2 AC 207 (HL).
[31] *Lumley v Gye* (1852) 2 El & Bl 216, 118 ER 749; *OBG Ltd v Allan* [2007] UKHL 21, [2008] 1 AC 1.

to covenants between landlord and tenant in a lease,[32] which run with the land (so as to benefit and bind an assignee of the tenant) and with the reversion (so as to benefit and bind an assignee of the landlord). As long as the parties to any claim hold the same estate as the original landlord and tenant (or, as it is often said, there is 'privity of estate' between the claimant and defendant), then the covenants remain mutually enforceable. The scope of the principle is narrower in relation to freehold land, although here it is still possible for the benefit of a covenant to be annexed to the land which was intended to be benefited by it. But the burden is only enforceable against successors to the original covenantor if the covenant is 'restrictive'—imposing negative obligations—and if it is to be enforceable against a purchaser it must have been registered so that he has the opportunity of discovering it.[33]

This idea that the benefit and burden of contractual obligations can be attached to property so as to become enforceable by and against later owners of the property is not generally extended outside the context of land in English law, although in one case involving a ship which was subject to a charterparty the Privy Council appeared to accept it as a wider principle.[34] It is certainly not applicable in the normal case of the transfer of goods: and so, for example, a warranty given in respect of goods does not attach to the goods so as to be enforceable by a sub-acquirer.[35] However, where A gives possession of goods to B under a contract of bailment—a contract, such as a contract of deposit or hire, under which B agrees to hold the goods or to use them for a particular purpose before returning them to A—and B enters into a further contract of bailment of the goods in favour of C (a 'sub-bailment') with the consent of A, C's acquisition of the goods allows him to take advantage of any relevant clauses in the contract between A and B, such as exclusion clauses if A sues C in tort for damage to the goods. A is also subject to an exclusion clause in the contract between B and C in any claim he makes

---

[32] A lease is not simply a contract, but is also an estate in land in English law: see generally EH Burn and J Cartwright, *Cheshire & Burn's Modern Law of Real Property*, 18th edn (Oxford, Oxford University Press, 2011) chs 8 (general characteristics of leases) and 9 (covenants, including the effect of assignment).

[33] *Tulk v Moxhay* (1848) 2 Ph 774, 41 ER 1143 used the principle of notice: 'the question is ... whether a party shall be permitted to use the land in a manner inconsistent with the contract entered into by his vendor, and with notice of which he purchased' (Lord Cottenham LC at 777–8, 1144); this has been superseded in the modern law by the entry of a notice of the burden of the covenant in a publicly-searchable register: Land Registration Act 2002 s 29 (where the title to the burdened land is registered); Land Charges Act 1972 s 2(5)(ii), 4(6) (unregistered land).

[34] *Lord Strathcona Steamship Co Ltd v Dominion Coal Co Ltd* [1926] AC 108 (PC) (purchaser of a ship who had notice of the terms of a charterparty entered into for its use was constructive trustee and could can be prevented from using the ship inconsistently with the charterparty); but this was disapproved in *Port Line Ltd v Ben Line Steamers Ltd* [1958] 2 QB 14 (QB). It might be better analysed on the basis of the grant of an injunction to restrain the purchaser from committing the tort of interfering with the earlier contract of which he had actual notice: *Swiss Bank Corporation v Lloyds Bank Ltd* [1979] Ch 548 (Ch) 569–75.

[35] This means that there is no equivalent to the French doctrine of 'accessory rights' except in the case of covenants affecting land: B Nicholas, *The French Law of Contract*, above, n 1, 172–73.

against C even though he is thereby bound by a term in a contract to which he is not a party. Giving consent to B sub-bailing the goods is sufficient to allow the terms of that authorised sub-bailment to be raised against him.[36]

(g) Third-Party Rights by Statute

Statutory exceptions to the doctrine of privity of contract have been created from time to time. The most general of these is now the Contracts (Rights of Third Parties) Act 1999 which is discussed later in this chapter. But before that Act there were various particular statutory interventions in order to give third parties the right to enforce a contract—for example, various statutes dealing with insurance contracts, to cover the situation of persons who are intended to acquire rights under an insurance policy which was taken out by another.[37]

2. Enforcement of the Contract by the Promisee for the Benefit of a Third Party

(a) The Problem: The Loss is Suffered by the Third Party

Sometimes the problem of privity could be solved not by finding remedies for the third party directly, but by giving the contracting party a claim to enforce the third party's right. At first sight, this is an uncontroversial application of the normal principles of contract law. The contract is between A and B, for the benefit of C. And so to allow B to sue A in order to enforce A's promise to confer a benefit on C is just giving an action for the beneficiary of the promise (the promisee—B, the contracting party) against the promisor. But there is a technical difficulty here: as we shall see in chapter 12, the normal position in English law is that a contracting party can bring a claim for damages—but only for the claimant's *own* loss. And here it is the third party who suffers the loss. However, the courts have devised some particular solutions for this situation.

(b) Specific Performance

We shall see the remedy of specific performance later.[38] For the moment it is important to realise that it is an exceptional remedy in English law: damages

---

[36] *The Pioneer Container* [1994] 2 AC 324 (PC). For bailment, see also above, p 54.
[37] Eg Married Women's Property Act 1882 s 11 (life insurance in favour of husband or wife, or children); Road Traffic Act 1988 s 148(7) (third-party beneficiaries of motor insurance policy).
[38] Below, pp 245 ff.

are the normal remedy for breach of contract. The traditional approach of the courts has been to say that the claimant can obtain specific performance—a court order that the promisor fulfil his promise under the contract—only if it can be shown that damages would be an inadequate remedy on the facts. That is, the first question is how damages would be calculated to compensate the claimant's loss. If an award of damages would not adequately compensate the loss which he has suffered, then the court might make an order for specific performance, although there are also other limitations on the availability of the remedy—such as that performance must now be possible, and that the court will not normally order a party to perform a purely personal service obligation. But if a promisee can obtain an order for specific performance of a promise in favour of a third party, it appears to be a good solution to the problem of privity of contract: the claim is brought by the party who has the right to the obligation, and the court makes an order which has the consequence that the third party receives the promised benefit directly from the promisor.

It is not obvious that specific performance should be available to protect a third party. If the promisee suffers no loss by virtue of the promisor's failure to confer the benefit on the third party, the promisee will obtain an award of only nominal[39] damages because he has no substantial loss to compensate. And nominal damages are perfectly adequate to compensate his loss. They are not, of course, adequate to compensate the third party's loss. But the third party has no right to the obligation. However, the House of Lords developed the rules of specific performance to fill this gap in *Beswick v Beswick*.[40] Peter Beswick transferred his coal delivery business to his nephew, John Beswick, and John undertook to make weekly payments to Peter for the rest of his life, and then £5 a week to Ruth Beswick, Peter's wife, after Peter's death. The payments were made to Peter in accordance with the contract, but after Peter died John made only one payment to Ruth. Ruth sued, making claims in two separate legal capacities: first, as the administratrix of her deceased husband's estate (his personal representative, enforcing his claim as contracting party) and secondly as herself, the third-party beneficiary of the contract between Peter and John. She failed in her second claim, on the basis that she was prevented by the doctrine of privity from having a direct claim as third party. However, she succeeded in the first claim, and obtained an order of specific performance (that is, in her capacity as representing the promisee she obtained an order which resulted in her receiving the benefit in her

---

[39] An award of nominal damages (eg a token £5) will be awarded even if there is no substantial loss: below, p 289.
[40] [1968] AC 58 (HL).

private capacity). The House of Lords rejected the argument that an award of nominal damages for the promisee would be an adequate remedy, and said that they could take a broader view of whether damages were a 'just' or 'adequate' remedy.

(c) Damages Calculated to Cover the Third Party's Losses

There are some particular situations where the courts have allowed a contracting party to sue for damages which are calculated to cover not the promisee's loss but the third party's loss.

For example, when a representative member of a group enters into a contract, even though he is not technically acting as the agent of each member, it has been suggested that he might be able to sue for loss suffered by the whole group. There are some cases of family holiday contracts which adopt this approach, where it has been suggested that the parent who entered into the contract can sue for the distress and disappointment suffered by all the members of the family in consequence of the holiday company providing a very poor holiday in breach of contract.[41]

In a line of cases concerned with defective buildings the courts have held that where a builder contracts to build or do work on a building which he knows is, or will be, owned or occupied by a third party, the person who originally contracted for the work to be done can sue the builder for any losses suffered by the third-party owners or occupiers.[42] But this has been treated as an exception to the normal rules for the assessment of damages, confined to building cases: it has not been generalised to a right for every contracting party to sue for losses suffered by third parties.

It has even been suggested that one might find a general solution to the problem of the doctrine of privity by holding that the promisee suffers a loss by virtue of the fact that he does not receive what he bargained for— that is, that the promisor's failure to confer the promised benefit on the third party is in itself a loss to the promisee.[43] But this fiction has not been developed.

---

[41] *Jackson v Horizon Holidays Ltd* [1975] 1 WLR 1468 (CA), as explained in *Woodar Investment Development Ltd v Wimpey Construction UK Ltd* [1980] 1 WLR 277 (HL) 283.

[42] *Linden Gardens Trust Ltd v Lenesta Sludge Disposals Ltd* [1994] 1 AC 85 (HL); *Darlington BC v Wiltshier Northern Ltd* [1995] 1 WLR 68 (CA); *Alfred McAlpine Construction Ltd v Panatown Ltd* [2001] 1 AC 518 (HL).

[43] *Woodar Investment Development Ltd v Wimpey Construction UK Ltd* above, n 41, 300–01; *Alfred McAlpine Construction Ltd v Panatown Ltd* above, n 42, 547, 585–92. The reasoning is based on the notion that the promisee will need to pay for the benefit to be conferred by another means.

III. Reform by the Contracts (Rights of Third Parties) Act 1999

1. The Law Commission's Proposals for Reform

We have seen that in 1937 the Law Revision Committee[44] had recommended a reform of the doctrine of privity of contract, together with reform of the doctrine of consideration, although these reforms were not taken forward because of the outbreak of war in 1939. The question of the reform of the doctrine of privity of contract had been considered by the Law Commission in the 1960s when it was considering a general codification of the law of contract. This project was abandoned, but the Law Commission took up the particular issue of the privity doctrine in the early 1990s, and in 1994 it recommended reform by legislation.[45] On this occasion no recommendation was made for the reform of consideration, although it was noted that 'the doctrine of consideration may be a suitable topic for a future separate review by the Law Commission'.[46] Nor were any recommendations made for the reform of the remedies available to the promisee.[47] The Law Commission's recommendations centred around reforming the law so as to allow the contracting parties to confer a benefit on a third party which the third party could enforce directly.

2. The Contracts (Rights of Third Parties) Act 1999

In 1999 Parliament legislated to create a new rule of English law under which contracting parties can confer rights on third parties which are enforceable directly by the third parties themselves. The Contracts (Rights of Third Parties) Act 1999 is reproduced in the Appendix.

---

[44] Sixth Interim Report, 'Statute of Frauds and the Doctrine of Consideration' (Cmd 5449, 1937); above, p 240.

[45] Law Commission, 'Privity of Contract: Contracts for the Benefit of Third Parties' (Law Com No 242 Cm 3329, 1996) paras 1.3, 1.4. The Law Commission Report included a draft Bill, which formed the basis of the Act although some of its details were amended before and during the passage through Parliament.

[46] *Ibid* para 6.17.

[47] *Ibid* para 5.17; above, p 247.

REFORM BY THE CONTRACTS ACT 1999

The basic scheme of the Act is to allow third parties in defined circumstances to enforce contractual terms directly—that is, to reform the doctrine of privity of contract. Key issues to notice are as follows:

(a) Which Contracts are Covered?

The Act covers most types of contract. There are some specific exceptions in section 6, but the aim of the Act is to constitute a general exception to the doctrine of privity.

(b) In what Circumstances Does a Third Party Acquire the Right to Enforce a Term?

A third party can enforce a term of the contract if he can show two things.

First, he must show *either* that the contract expressly provides that he may enforce the term; *or* that the contract by its language confers a benefit on him (it 'purports to confer a benefit on him') and on a proper construction of the contract it does not appear that the parties did not intend him to have the right to enforce it.[48] In other words, even if the contract does not expressly provide for the third party to be entitled to enforce a term, there is a presumption that he may do so from the fact that the contract by its language confers a benefit on him. The presumption is rebuttable on evidence that, properly construed, the contract shows that the parties did not intend it. But unless the contract expressly excludes the third party's right, there is a risk that it will be implied that he has a right of enforcement.

Secondly, the third party must show that he is expressly identified in the contract by name, or as a member of a class, or as answering a particular description. But he need not be in existence at the time of the contract.[49] This means that a third party could be (for example) 'the owner for the time being' of property—which will then allow any owner, present or future, to enforce the term in question. But the third party must be *expressly* identified. A person who cannot point to the language of the contract and show that he is referred to in it does not acquire a right to enforce it. And so a person cannot incidentally take advantage of a contract simply by showing that the contract in fact benefits him.

It will be evident that *Tweddle v Atkinson*[50] would now be covered by the Act, since the claimant was expressly identified in the contracting parties'

---

[48] Section 1(1), (2).
[49] Section 1(3).
[50] Above, p 237.

written memorandum, which also expressly provided that he should have the right to enforce it.

(c) Parties can Always Contract out of the Act Expressly

In the early days after the Act was first passed it became quite common for commercial parties to contract expressly out of the operation of the Act, in order to avoid any risk of third parties having unexpected (implied) rights of enforcement. For example, many of the standard forms of contract used in the construction industry were re-issued when the Act came into force with a clause designed to avoid the operation of the Act: parties preferred to continue to use their tried and tested ways of ensuring that third parties could have rights to sue—such as requiring builders and professionals involved in a building project to enter into collateral warranties in favour of tenants and future owners of the property.[51] However, there is a growing perception that the Act can be used to achieve this in a simpler form and some construction industry standard form contracts are now drafted so as to give the parties the option of creating direct rights in favour of defined third parties using the 1999 Act, thus removing the need for collateral warranties.

(d) What Rights Does the Third Party Acquire?

The third party has a right to 'enforce' the relevant term or terms of the contract, within the context of the contract as a whole. 'Enforcement' does not refer narrowly to the remedy of specific performance, but means that the third party is to be treated as if he were a party to the contract for the purposes of claiming remedies.[52] This means that he is able to obtain damages to compensate his own loss, and to obtain specific performance in the same situations in which a contracting party may do so.

However, the third party's right of enforcement is subject to (i) the promisor's right to raise defences or set-offs against him as if the claim had been brought by the other contracting party, or the third party had been a party to the contract;[53] and (ii) being reduced by such amount as the court thinks appropriate where the promisee has already recovered from the other contracting party a sum in respect of the losses claimed by the third party or the promisee's expenses in making good the promisor's default.[54]

---

[51] Above, p 242.
[52] Section 1(5).
[53] Section 3: see below.
[54] Section 5: see below.

REFORM BY THE CONTRACTS ACT 1999   253

(e) The Act also Applies to Exemption Clauses

'Term of the contract' includes an exemption clause as well as promissory terms.[55] This means that in a case where an exemption clause in a contract purports to extend to someone outside the contract it will be easier to give effect to the clause and allow the third party to rely on it, without having to rely on doctrines such as agency.[56]

(f) Can the Third Party's Right to Enforce be Taken Away by the Contracting Parties?

The parties can always negative or limit the third party's right in the first place, in the terms of the contract.[57] But can they change the contract to vary or remove the right, once the contract has been concluded? Under section 2 they are free to do so only until the third party has 'communicated his assent to the term' to promisor;[58] or has relied on the term and the promisor knows of, or ought reasonably to have foreseen, such reliance.[59]

This introduces into English law the concept that a person acquires vested rights under a contract not by providing consideration, but by simple communication of acceptance of the right, or by his reliance on the term in question. The third party's right is created by the contract itself (regardless of whether the third party yet knows about it). But it becomes indefeasible when the third party has accepted it or relied on it. It should be noted that neither acceptance nor reliance is sufficient to create an obligation directly between the parties to an agreement—consideration is required. But in this context the third party, who by definition has not provided consideration for the promise which he is being allowed to enforce, can acquire an indefeasible right to the obligation by his acceptance or reliance—although of course the term which he has the right to enforce is a promise in the contract for which consideration was given (but it was given by the promisee).

(g) The Position of the Promisor

The promisor is meant to have the same rights against the third party that he would have had if the claim had been brought by the other contracting party, or if the third party had been made a contracting party—and so he is not

---

[55] Section 1(6).
[56] Above, pp 243–44.
[57] Section 1(2).
[58] Section 2(1)(a).
[59] Section 2(1)(b), (c).

in a worse position by virtue of the claimant being a third party rather than a contracting party. He can therefore use defences or set-offs which would have been available against a contracting party,[60] although the parties can always contract to vary this by either extending or reducing his defences and set-offs.[61]

Furthermore, the promisor is protected against double liability: if the promisee has claimed and recovered a sum in respect of the third party's loss, then the third party's claim is reduced accordingly—although it is not, strictly, an automatic and equivalent reduction, but a reduction by such amount as the court thinks appropriate.[62]

(h) The Position of the Promisee

The promisee's general right at common law to bring claims in his own name under the contract is unaffected by the Act; and this includes his right to bring any available claims which cover the losses in fact suffered by the third party,[63] or for remedies which in fact protect the third party's position, such as specific performance.[64] If the promisee obtains such a remedy, the promisor is protected against double liability in any later claim by the third party.[65] And if the third party has already recovered before the promisee's action, then that will be relevant to the loss which the promisee himself can claim, under the normal rules for contract remedies.

(i) Interaction of the Act with Other Remedies for Third-Party Losses

The Act only adds a new right of action for the third party; it does not change any existing rules or remedies which are available to either the third party or the contracting parties.[66] And so, for example, the use of tort claims, or claims using property law rules (including trusts) to enforce third party rights will be unaffected—although courts may find that there is less need to 'develop' rules in these areas to give protection to third parties now that there is a direct action available under the Act to protect the third party's rights.

---

[60] Section 3(2), (4).
[61] Section 3(3), (5).
[62] Section 5.
[63] Such as under the principle applicable to building contracts discussed above, p 249.
[64] *Beswick v Beswick* [1968] AC 58 (HL); above, p 248.
[65] Section 5.
[66] Section 7.

3. Interaction of the Doctrines of Privity of Contract and Consideration after the 1999 Act

The Contracts (Rights of Third Parties) Act 1999 does not make any change to the doctrine of consideration. However, given that the common law doctrine of privity of contract was grounded in the doctrine of consideration, it is natural to wonder whether a reform of consideration might follow. The Law Commission argued that consideration and privity are independent doctrines in the developed law:

> [T]he third party rule determines who can enforce a contract; while the rule that consideration must move from the promisee determines the types of promises that can be enforced.[67]

But they also accepted that the reform of privity has an impact on the policy underlying the doctrine of consideration, since the 1999 Act allows a party to acquire rights for which he has not provided anything in return:

> [W]e see no objection to accepting that, while formally, our reform does not affect the requirement of consideration, at a deeper policy level, and within the area of third party rights, it may represent a relaxation of the importance attached to consideration.[68]

The third party's rights arise under the Act by virtue of the *intention* of the contracting parties; and the rights become indefeasible by the third party's *acceptance* or *reliance* on the term. These are not the tests for the creation of contractual obligations: a party acquires the right to an obligation by doing or promising something in return for the right—he provides consideration for it.[69] In order to provide a mechanism for third-party rights, and to place limits on their creation and enforceability, it was necessary to devise tests based on criteria such as intention, acceptance and reliance which are different from those used in the case of the formation of the contract itself, since the absence of consideration is the very bar to the third party's rights at common law. But the use of such tests opens the door to the argument that if a third party can be recognised as acquiring legally enforceable rights in order to give effect to the intention of the parties, and if his acceptance of the promise or his reliance on it can also be relevant criteria which justify protecting his 'right', should not those same ideas be translated across to the rules for the formation of the contract as between the two parties themselves? If the third party's rights should be given effect because the 'autonomy of the will of the parties should be respected'[70] can that not equally apply to the intention of

---

[67] Law Commission Report (above, n 45) para 6.1.
[68] *Ibid* para 6.17.
[69] Above, pp 236–37.
[70] *Darlington BC v Wiltshier Northern Ltd* [1995] 1 WLR 68 (CA) 76 (Lord Steyn, quoted more fully above, p 239).

one party to be bound by his promise to the other party to the agreement even if the agreement is not supported by consideration provided by the promisee? Or if reliance is accepted as a trigger for the enforceability of a third party's right under the 1999 Act, can that not equally apply as justification for the enforceability of a promise by the direct promisee who provides no consideration but relies on the promise? Such steps would be a radical change to the existing law of contract in England. We saw in chapter six that the intention of the parties, however serious, is not a substitute for consideration provided by the promisee,[71] and that reliance is not sufficient to create new obligations under the doctrine of promissory estoppel—although estoppel has the potential to develop in this way in England as it has done already in America and Australia, if the Supreme Court chooses to permit it.[72]

IV. Assignment and Novation of Contractual Rights and Duties

The obligations contained within a contract are initially owed by one party to the other. But it is possible for there to be a change of parties using either assignment or novation. Assignment can transfer only the benefit of an obligation—the right to it. Novation allows a change in both the burden and the benefit of an obligation—the duty, as well as the right. Both assignment and novation are very commonly used in commercial contexts to effect a change in contractual arrangements for commercial purposes—for example, debt factoring involves assignment of the right to enforce a debt; and novation may be used in the context of a building contract when there is a change of building contractor, or where an architect, originally employed by the client in the planning of the project, is transferred into the employment of the contractor once the contractor has been appointed.

1. Assignment

(a) Assignment is of Only the Benefit, Not the Burden

Assignment is the transfer of the benefit of rights. It does not involve the creation of a new right, but only transfers an existing right (a debt or 'chose

---

[71] Above, pp 155–56.
[72] Above, pp 153–55.

in action',[73] such as right under a contract). In principle, there is no change to the content of the obligation, nor any change to the identity of the debtor—the person by whom the obligation is owed. There is only a change in the identity of the creditor—the person to whom it is owed. There can be no assignment of the burden of a debt or other obligation:

> Although it is true that the phrase 'assign this contract' is not strictly accurate, lawyers frequently use those words inaccurately to describe an assignment of the benefit of a contract since every lawyer knows that the burden of a contract cannot be assigned.[74]

(b) Legal and Equitable Assignments

An assignment may be *legal* or *equitable*. The old common law courts accepted that the benefit of a right could be assigned but only in limited circumstances—and this (still referred to in the modern law as a 'legal' assignment) is now found in section 136 of the Law of Property Act 1925: the assignment must be *absolute* (unconditional), not purporting to be by way of charge only, of the *whole* of the debt or other legal chose in action, *in writing* and *notice* must be given to the debtor. If the assignment fulfils these requirements the assignment transfers to the assignee the legal right to enforce the debt or chose in action in his own name: the assignor falls out of the picture completely.

The old courts of equity allowed an assignment to take effect even though it did not fulfil the requirements of a legal assignment—either because the right was not capable of legal assignment (it was an equitable right, rather than a legal right); or because of the nature of the assignment or the way in which it was effected (for example, it was an assignment of only part of the debt not the whole debt; or it was the assignment of a legal right but done orally and not in writing). In such cases the assignee was treated as acquiring the benefit of the right, but he could not enforce it in his own name: he had to join the assignor in any enforcement action. Equitable assignments are still used (and still referred to by that name) in the modern law.

(c) Rights Which are Capable of Assignment

Not all rights arising under contracts are assignable. For example, the right to performance of an obligation which is personal as between the original

---

[73] A 'chose in action' is a thing which is recoverable by action, contrasted with a 'chose in possession' which is a thing which can be physically possessed.
[74] *Linden Gardens Trust Ltd v Lenesta Sludge Disposals Ltd* [1994] 1 AC 85 (HL) 103 (Lord Browne-Wilkinson).

contracting parties is not assignable. The underlying principle is that a right should be assignable if it makes no difference to the party whose obligation is in issue whether he performs for the original contracting party, or for another person over whose identity he has no control (since an assignment is effective without his consent). But if the nature of the obligation is such that it might make a difference to whom it is owed, the right to the performance of the obligation will be impliedly non-assignable. The right to the damages payable for non-performance of the (personal) obligation is however assignable, because once the issue becomes simply payment of money rather than performance of the obligation, it ceases to be regarded as of consequence for the party in breach to whom he has to pay the money.

Whether the benefit of a particular obligation is by its character assignable or non-assignable, this may be overridden by the contract between the parties.[75] Even if the right is in principle assignable, the parties may expressly place limits (or a total prohibition) on its assignment. An express contractual prohibition on assignment is effective, and prevents an assignee from receiving the rights which were purportedly assigned.[76] This is a matter of contract, and so the scope of the prohibition is subject to the normal rules on interpretation of contracts.[77] It is therefore possible to prohibit the assignment of the right to performance of the contract, whilst leaving intact the right to assign the claim for damages for breach once it has occurred; or to allow assignment only subject to certain conditions, such as requiring the debtor's consent for any particular future assignment which the creditor wishes to make; or to limit the type of person to whom the right may be assigned, such as allowing assignment only to a bank or a financial institution fulfilling certain characteristics; or to limit the number of times that the right may be assigned. Commercial contracts commonly contain detailed provisions for the circumstances (if any) in which assignment is to be permitted.

(d) The Effect of a Valid Assignment

Assignment does not change the nature of the right: the assignee is entitled to the same remedies as the assignor would have had, if he had not assigned—and therefore the assignee of a debt can recover the debt, and the assignee of a right to performance of a contract can require performance of the contract or damages calculated to remedy his losses arising from breach, as long as they are the same kind of losses as would have been suffered by the original assignor.[78]

---

[75] *Don King Productions Inc v Warren* [2000] Ch 291 (Ch) 318–19.
[76] *Linden Gardens Trust Ltd v Lenesta Sludge Disposals Ltd*, above, n 74.
[77] Above, pp 202–10.
[78] *Dawson v Great Northern and City Railway Co* [1905] 1 KB 260 (CA).

However, an assignment (legal or equitable) is always 'subject to equities'—that is, the assignee's rights of enforcement are subject to any limitations, defences and set-offs to which an enforcement claim by the assignor would have been subject had he not assigned. The assignee can be in no better position than his assignor, since this would prejudice the other party to the contract.

2. Novation

Novation is the creation of a new right, usually in place of and by extinction of an old right. It is generally a new contract under which one party takes the place of one of the existing parties, and the old party is released—in effect, a variation of the existing contract, by the substitution of one of the parties—although it can also be a variation of the existing contract between the same two parties, either by the replacement of the old contract with an entirely new contract, or by the replacement of just one or more individual terms. The name is derived from Roman law, and has been commented on in English cases:

> '[N]ovation,' which as I understand it means this—the term being derived from the Civil Law—that there being a contract in existence, some new contract is substituted for it, either between the same parties (for that might be) or between different parties; the consideration mutually being the discharge of the old contract.[79]

A novation imposes contractual burdens on the new party, and can introduce new terms, whereas an assignment involves only a transfer of the existing contractual rights. Consequently, a novation requires the consent of both parties because it involves the creation of new obligations, whereas assignment can be effected without the consent of the debtor because his obligation is not changed.

Because a novation involves the substitution of a new contract for an old contract, the usual rules for the formation of a contractual obligation apply; and so either there must be consideration both for the release of the old obligations and for the creation of the new obligations, or the novation must be contained in a deed executed by all the parties releasing or undertaking obligations.

---

[79] *Scarf v Jardine* (1882) 7 App Cas 345 (HL) 351 (Lord Selborne LC).

11

Change of Circumstances

A contract is a legally enforceable agreement—a bargain between the parties—to which each party has given his assent on the basis of the circumstances as he believed them to be at the time of the contract. The contract binds each party to fulfil obligations which necessarily contain a balance to which the parties have agreed and therefore an allocation of risks between the parties. In a contract of sale of goods, for example, the seller undertakes the risk of being able to deliver the goods on the agreed date; and he is bound to accept the price set out in the contract—a price which he will have agreed on the basis of the circumstances as he believed them to be, such as the market in the goods in question. If, unknown to one or both parties, things had already changed before the contract, there is a question about the validity of the contract itself—we are then in the realm of the doctrine of mistake.[1] If things change after the performance of the contract, it is normally irrelevant because the contract has by then fulfilled its purpose. But if there is a change of circumstances after the formation of the contract, but before it has been fully performed, one of the parties may seek to argue that the changed circumstances affect the contractual balance and that he is therefore entitled to some remedy—such as release from the contract, or an adjustment of the terms of the contract to take into account the new circumstances.

Many day-to-day contracts are performed immediately. There is no (or no significant) delay between the formation of the contract and its performance, and so there is little scope for changes of circumstances which might affect the bargain which the parties have entered into. However, where there is a delay between the formation of the contract and its performance, or where there is a contract for performance to be made over an extended period, there is a much greater chance of changes of circumstances having an impact on the balance of the bargain. The question is therefore how this can and should be addressed.

Legal systems differ significantly in their approach to how changes of circumstances may impact upon the contract: differences not only about how significant the change of circumstances must be in order to give rise to any

[1] Above, ch 7.

remedy (must performance of the contract become 'impossible', or will something less suffice?), but also in the remedy which is appropriate (discharge of the contract, either automatically or by order of the court—or even the power for the court to adjust the terms of the contract to accord with the changed circumstances?).[2] We shall see in this chapter that the rules of English law governing changes of circumstances during the lifetime of the contract are in some respects more limited than those in many civil law systems. In consequence, parties are generally advised to make specific provisions in their contracts for possible future events which might affect the balance of the bargain—often under the name of *'force majeure'* or 'hardship' clauses—and negotiated commercial contracts do very commonly contain such provisions in order to avoid the operation of the general legal rules. However, there can be some difficulties with the operation of such clauses.

I. The Doctrine of Frustration

1. Development of the Doctrine of Frustration

Originally English law took the strict view that if a party promised in a contract to do something, then he could not use any excuse for not keeping his promise even if performance was impossible by reason of some external event beyond his control. This was illustrated by a case in the seventeenth century in which it was held that a tenant who had undertaken to pay rent under a lease of property was still bound to pay where he had been evicted from the premises by the King's enemies:

> [W]hen the party by his own contract creates a duty or charge upon himself, he is bound to make it good, if he may, notwithstanding any accident by inevitable necessity, because he might have provided against it by his contract.[3]

But from the second half of the nineteenth century the courts developed the doctrine of *frustration*. At first it was put in the language of an 'implied term' in the contract: the parties must have intended that the contract would no

---

[2] For an overview of the approach of European legal systems, see E Hondius and HC Grigoleit, *Unexpected Circumstances in European Contract Law* (Cambridge, Cambridge University Press, 2011). American law distinguishes 'impossibility' or 'impracticability' of performance, and 'frustration of purpose': EA Farnsworth, *Contracts*, 4th edn (New York, Aspen, 2006) paras 9.5–9.7.

[3] *Paradine v Jane* (1647) Aleyn 26, 27; 82 ER 897, 897.

longer bind them if it became impossible to perform. This was the approach taken by Blackburn J in *Taylor v Caldwell*,[4] a case in which there was a contract for the use of a music hall which was destroyed by fire before the time for performance. Both parties were excused from performance of their obligations under the contract, and so the party who had contracted to use the music hall did not have to pay but could not hold the owner of the hall liable for breach of contract in not providing it. Blackburn J developed this principle through the usual common law technique:[5] by a process of inductive reasoning he held that certain particular cases in which the courts had released parties from their contract because of supervening impossibility (such as where the contract was for personal performance but the contracting party died) demonstrated a general underlying principle:

> [I]n contracts in which the performance depends on the continued existence of a given person or thing, a condition is implied that the impossibility of performance arising from the perishing of the person or thing shall excuse the performance.[6]

This was said to be based on an implied term in the contract. But it was not based on the assumption that the parties had in fact thought about the possibility of the music hall being destroyed. It was a term implied as a general rule of law, rather than simply to fill out the unexpressed intentions of the parties:

> The parties when framing their agreement evidently had not present to their minds the possibility of such a disaster, and have made no express stipulation with reference to it, so that the answer to the question must depend upon the general rules of law applicable to such a contract.[7]

The first question is construction of the contract. If it is a 'positive contract to do a thing' the party continues to have the obligation to perform even if 'in consequence of unforeseen accidents, the performance of his contract has become unexpectedly burthensome or even impossible'. But:

> [T]his rule is only applicable when the contract is positive and absolute, and not subject to any condition either express or implied: and there are authorities which, as we think, establish the principle that where, from the nature of the contract, it appears that the parties must from the beginning have known that it could not

---

[4] (1863) 3 B & S 826, 122 ER 309.

[5] Above, p 41.

[6] Above, n 4, 839, 314. He also considered Roman law and the French writer Pothier, and concluded that English law on this matter was consistent with certain rules of the civil law. Four years later Blackburn J introduced into the English law of contract a general principle of mistake, again basing his discussion on Roman law and Pothier: *Kennedy v The Panama, New Zealand and Australian Royal Mail Co Ltd* (1867) LR 2 QB 580, 587–88. Blackburn J's particular use of the rules of the civil law may be open to criticism, but it is evidence of some influence of civilian ideas on the English law of contract in its formative stages: J Cartwright, 'The Rise and Fall of Mistake' in R Sefton-Green (ed), *Mistake, Fraud and Duties to Inform in European Contract Law* (Cambridge, Cambridge University Press, 2005) 67–71.

[7] *Ibid* 833, 312. On implied terms see above, pp 210–17.

be fulfilled unless when the time for the fulfilment of the contract arrived some particular specified thing continued to exist, so that, when entering into the contract, they must have contemplated such continuing existence as the foundation of what was to be done; there, in the absence of any express or implied warranty that the thing shall exist, the contract is not to be construed as a positive contract, but as subject to an implied condition that the parties shall be excused in case, before breach, performance becomes impossible from the perishing of the thing without default of the contractor.[8]

This was not yet described as the doctrine of 'frustration'—and that term was not used by Blackburn J in his judgment, although it soon came to be used in relation to the 'purpose' or 'object' of the contract being frustrated by supervening circumstances.[9] But it was later recognised that it was really fictitious to say that the doctrine was based on the parties' intentions. The 'implied term' theory was rejected, and the modern test set out, in the speech of Lord Radcliffe in *Davis Contractors Ltd v Fareham UDC*:

> [T]here is something of a logical difficulty in seeing how the parties could even impliedly have provided for something which ex hypothesi they neither expected nor foresaw; and the ascription of frustration to an implied term of the contract has been criticized as obscuring the true action of the court which consists in applying an objective rule of the law of contract to the contractual obligations that the parties have imposed upon themselves ... The legal effect of frustration 'does not depend on their intention or their opinions, or even knowledge, as to the event.'[10] On the contrary, it seems that when the event occurs 'the meaning of the contract must be taken to be, not what the parties did intend (for they had neither thought nor intention regarding it), but that which the parties, as fair and reasonable men, would presumably have agreed upon if, having such possibility in view, they had made express provision as to their several rights and liabilities in the event of its occurrence' (*Dahl v. Nelson*,[11] per Lord Watson).
>
> By this time it might seem that the parties themselves have become so far disembodied spirits that their actual persons should be allowed to rest in peace. In their place there rises the figure of the fair and reasonable man. And the spokesman of the fair and reasonable man, who represents after all no more than the anthropomorphic conception of justice, is and must be the court itself. So perhaps it would be simpler to say at the outset that frustration occurs whenever the law recognizes that without default of either party a contractual obligation has become incapable of being performed because the circumstances in which performance is called for would render it a thing radically different from that which was undertaken by the contract. Non haec in foedera veni. It was not this that I promised to do.[12]

---

[8] *Ibid* 833–34, 312.
[9] *Jackson v Union Marine Insurance Co Ltd* (1874) LR 10 CP 125.
[10] *Hirji Mulji v Cheong Yue Steamship Co Ltd* [1926] AC 497 (PC) 509.
[11] (1881) 6 App Cas 38.
[12] [1956] AC 696 (HL) 728–29. This is accepted as the test in the modern law: *Pioneer Shipping Ltd v BTP Tioxide Ltd* [1982] AC 724 (HL) 744, 751–52.

264 CHANGE OF CIRCUMSTANCES

In order to understand the operation of the doctrine of frustration two separate issues must be considered: first, what constitutes frustration; and secondly, the consequences once frustration has occurred.

2. Application of the Test for Frustration

The test for frustration is set out above in the extract from Lord Radcliffe's speech: in essence, it is that without the fault of either party something has happened which means that performance according to the terms of the contract would be 'radically different' from that which the parties intended at the time of the contract. This requires a little explanation and refinement in the light of its application in the cases.

Most important is that if the contract by its terms makes provision for the supervening event it is not a case of frustration. The doctrine of frustration is designed to cover the case where the parties have not made provision for a change in circumstances, and the new circumstances have the effect of radically changing the nature of the contractual obligations. If the contract contains a provision dealing with the situation, the change in circumstances cannot involve a radical change to the nature of the contract which the parties intended, and so it is simply a matter of giving effect to the provision of the contract. It is very common for parties negotiating commercial contracts to include *'force majeure'* or 'hardship' clauses, which lay down what is to happen to the contract and the performance due under it if certain specified events occur. Such clauses are discussed further below. Although the doctrine of frustration is not now based on the 'implied term' theory, there are still situations in which the courts may decide that the contract impliedly allocates the risk of the alleged frustrating event. For example, where there is a contract for the provision of goods or services for an indefinite period at a fixed price, the court may well decide that the parties cannot sensibly have intended the contract to be given effect literally in accordance with its terms, but must have intended that either party would have the right to terminate on giving reasonable notice.[13] The right to terminate in such circumstances arises under the contract rather than by the operation of the doctrine of frustration.

A related issue is whether the change in circumstances must have been unforeseeable by the parties at the time of the contract if it is to constitute a frustrating event, or whether it is sufficient that they failed to make provision

---

[13] *Staffordshire Area Health Authority v South Staffordshire Waterworks Co* [1978] 1 WLR 1387 (CA) (contract in 1929 to supply water 'at all times hereafter' at a fixed price held terminable on reasonable notice, either on the basis of interpretation of the words of the contract or (Lord Denning MR) because the right to terminate on reasonable notice should normally be implied into a contract to supply goods or services over an unlimited period in return for a fixed payment).

for it in the contract. This is not entirely settled. Lord Denning suggested that it is possible for a contract to be frustrated by an event which the parties in fact foresaw.[14] But the failure by the parties to deal with a known risk should normally indicate the parties' willingness to bear the consequences of that risk materialising—that is, if the contract were to be frustrated in such circumstances it would reverse the risks as the contract in fact allocated them.

It is clear, however, that the change in circumstances must be outside the parties' control: it must have occurred 'without default of either party'. If the alleged frustrating event was caused by one of the parties, or the impossibility of performance arises because of a choice made by one of the parties, it is not a case of frustration, but will usually constitute a breach of contract by that party. This has been applied quite narrowly, to reject a claim of frustration in a case where the defendants had contracted to transport equipment for the claimants on one of two named ships, and where the ship which the defendants had intended to use sank after the contract had been formed but before performance. The transportation contract was not frustrated because the defendants could still have used the other named ship in order to perform the contract—and the fact that they did not do so because they already had another contract under which that second ship was to be used was irrelevant: it was still their election not to use it to fulfil the claimant's contract.[15]

Although it is commonly said that the frustrating event must make the contract impossible to perform—'incapable of being performed' in Lord Radcliffe's language—this is in fact too narrow. It is not only a question of whether the contractual obligations can be physically performed, but also whether they can legally be performed: a supervening event which renders the contractual performance illegal can frustrate the contract.[16] And it is not even necessary that a change in the factual circumstances renders the performance literally impossible. The question is whether continued performance would be *radically different* from that which was intended by the parties when the contract was formed. There are a number of cases where the English courts have admitted that a contract was frustrated when it was not physically impossible to perform the obligations, but the *purpose* of the contract was no longer possible. In *Krell v Henry*,[17] for example, the claimant agreed to hire out a flat in Pall Mall, London, to the defendant for two days, 26 and 27 June 1902, when it had been announced that processions to mark the coronation of King Edward VII would pass along Pall Mall. After the contract was entered into, the King became ill and the coronation was postponed. It was held that the contract of hire of the flat was frustrated. Although the terms of the contract

---

[14] *Ocean Tramp Tankers Corp v V/O Sovfracht (The Eugenia)* [1964] 2 QB 226 (CA) 239.
[15] *J Lauritzen AS v Wijsmuller BV (The Super Servant Two)* [1990] 1 Lloyd's Rep 1 (CA).
[16] *Denny Mott & Dickson Ltd v James B Fraser & Co Ltd* [1944] AC 265 (HL Sc) (wartime regulation prohibiting trading of the particular kind covered by the contract).
[17] [1903] 2 KB 740 (CA).

could literally be performed (the payment of the hire charge in return for the use of the flat), the coronation procession was the 'foundation of the contract' in the minds of both parties when the contract was entered into. Where the 'foundation of the contract' or the 'contractual adventure'[18] as it was intended by both parties fails as a result of a change in circumstances, the contract can be frustrated.

However, the courts have made clear that it is not sufficient that the cost of performance is significantly increased for one of the parties. English law does not admit 'economic' frustration. In *Davis Contractors Ltd v Fareham UDC*[19] Davis entered into a contract to build 78 houses for the Council, for a fixed price, within a fixed period of eight months. Davis claimed that the contract had been entered into on the basis that adequate supplies of labour and materials would be available to complete the work within the contracted period, but that, without fault of either party, there was a shortage of labour with the result that work took 22 months, and that this delay amounted to frustration of the contract. The House of Lords unanimously rejected the claim based on frustration:

> [I]t is not hardship or inconvenience or material loss itself which calls the principle of frustration into play. There must be as well such a change in the significance of the obligation that the thing undertaken would, if performed, be a different thing from that contracted for.[20]

Frustration is exceptional, and cannot be invoked lightly. If frustration extended to cover the case where the fixed price becomes 'so unfair to the contractor that he ought not to be held to his original price', then 'there would be an untold range of contractual obligations rendered uncertain and, possibly, unenforceable'.[21]

3. Consequences of Frustration

If there is a change of circumstances which satisfies the test for frustration, then the contract is *terminated*. This remedy, and the way in which it is effected, is significantly different from the remedies which most civil law systems will recognise in such a context.

In the first place, the remedy of 'termination' is not retroactive. When a contract is terminated, the primary obligations of both parties—that is, the obligations which each party undertook in favour of the other in the

---

[18] *Jackson v Union Marine Insurance Co Ltd* above, n 9.
[19] Above, n 12.
[20] *Ibid* 729 (Lord Radcliffe).
[21] *Ibid* 730–31 (Lord Radcliffe).

contract[22]—are discharged in so far as they have not yet accrued due to be performed. But those obligations which have already accrued due are left undisturbed. And so, in effect, both parties are released from performance of the contract for the future, but there is no automatic reversal of the performance which has been rendered under the contract. This is the same remedy as we shall see can sometimes be available for a breach of contract;[23] and there again the effect of the contract being 'terminated' for breach is to discharge the future primary obligations, but not to disturb the past performance.

Where there is a breach of contract which justifies termination, the innocent party is able also to sue for damages for the loss which flows from the breach. In the case of frustration, however, there is no claim for damages, because—by definition—neither party is at fault in having brought about the circumstances which have frustrated the contract. This can mean that the (non-retroactive) termination of the contract, without restoring the parties to the original positions in which they were placed before they entered into the contract, can leave one party at a significant disadvantage. If the contract was one where each party has already performed his obligations to an equal degree—for example, it is a contract for the performance of services over a period of time, the services to be paid for as they are rendered—then termination does not create difficulties in this respect. If, however, the contract did not call for the parties' obligations to be performed more or less simultaneously, it is possible for one party to have done much more than the other by the time of frustration—and therefore he is relieved of much less of his total contractual obligation than the other party. It was recognised that this caused difficulties in some cases. Sometimes the law of restitution could assist, because if one party has received nothing of what is due to him under a contract, but has already paid money, he can have restitution of the money: it is said in such a case the there is a 'total failure of consideration'— 'consideration' here meaning the performance of the other party's contractual obligations. For example, in *Fibrosa Spolka Akcyjna v Fairbairn Lawson Combe Barbour Ltd*[24] there was a contract for the delivery of machinery for a particular price. Before the time came for delivery of the machinery, but after a deposit had been paid by the buyer, the contract was frustrated. It was held that the deposit was recoverable because there was a total failure of consideration. However, this would not have been possible if there had already been partial performance of the contract by the seller.

In order to provide at least a partial solution to this problem Parliament passed the Law Reform (Frustrated Contracts) Act 1943 to give the court certain powers to adjust the financial positions of the parties after frustration

---

[22] Above, p 202.
[23] Below, p 281.
[24] [1943] AC 32 (HL).

has taken effect. The Act does not define frustration, nor does it change the basic remedy (termination). However, it makes specific provision for two situations. First,[25] if money has been paid (or has become payable) by either party to the other before the moment of frustration, it must be repaid (or ceases to be payable)—but if the party to whom the sums have been paid or are payable has incurred expenses in performance of the contract before the time of frustration, the court may allow him to retain a sum up to the total of his expenses. The decision on the sum to be awarded is within the court's broad discretion 'to do justice in a situation which the parties had neither contemplated nor provided for, and to mitigate the possible harshness of allowing all loss to lie where it has fallen'.[26] But it is limited to allowing the party who has incurred expenses to retain them out of the pre-payment which the contract required. If there was no sum already paid or payable by the time of the frustration, there is nothing out of which the court can allow him to retain his expenses. Secondly,[27] if before the time of frustration one party has conferred a benefit on the other which has not yet been paid for under the contract, the court may require the party who received the benefit to pay for it. Again, the sum payable is within the court's discretion, although the court is required by the Act to take into consideration the expenses incurred by the party who has received the benefit, and the effect on the value of the benefit of the circumstances which frustrated the contract. There are very few reported cases in which these provisions have been applied.

The remedy of termination for frustration takes effect not by election of either party, nor by the order of a court, but automatically on the occurrence of the frustrating event even if neither party yet knows that it has occurred. If the issue of frustration is raised in court—typically where one party sues for breach of contract and the other raises a defence that he was not in breach because his obligations had already been discharged by a frustrating event—the court is simply deciding whether the alleged event was sufficient in law to frustrate the contract. If it was, then the termination took effect at the moment of the frustrating event.

It should also be noted that the only remedy for frustration at common law is termination of the contract; and termination is permanent—English law does not recognise partial frustration (termination of only part of the contract) nor temporary frustration (suspension, rather than permanent termination). So either the event constitutes frustration, and the contract is permanently terminated; or it does not, and it remains fully enforceable. The court has no power to adjust the terms of the contract to reflect the changed circumstances; and, unless it is possible to resolve the difficulties which arise

---

[25] Law Reform (Frustrated Contracts) Act 1943 s 1(2).
[26] *Gamerco SA v ICM/Fair Warning Ltd* [1995] 1 WLR 1226 (QB) 1237 (Garland J).
[27] *Ibid* s 1(3). See *BP Exploration Co (Libya) Ltd v Hunt (No 2)* [1979] 1 WLR 783 (QB).

following the changed circumstances by interpretation of the contract or by the implication of a term on the facts,[28] the court can give no relief where there is a change of circumstances which falls short of frustration.[29] Some civil law jurisdictions have developed broader powers for the courts to adjust the terms of the contract in cases involving changes of circumstances which undermine fundamentally the basis on which the parties had entered into the contract; and the development of such judicial powers in relation to the contract is commonly based on the inherent duty of contracting parties to act in good faith in the performance of the contract. We have seen that there is no such general duty of good faith in the English law of contract;[30] and even though there are circumstances where a duty to perform in good faith may be implied,[31] it would be much too serious an inroad on the parties' contract for the English courts to base on such an implied duty the development of a power to intervene to adjust the contract.[32] The contract is for the parties, rather than for the court.

II. Using Contract Terms to Anticipate Changes of Circumstances

The doctrine of frustration, set out above, contains various rules which are hardly satisfactory, and commercial parties will often include clauses in their contracts to make express provision for the effects of supervening circumstances which may arise during the lifetime of the contract. If there is an express clause dealing with the matter, the doctrine of frustration cannot apply.

---

[28] Cf *Staffordshire Area Health Authority v South Staffordshire Waterworks Co*, above, n 13.
[29] Cf *Lloyds TSB Foundation for Scotland v Lloyds Banking Group plc* [2013] UKSC 3, [2013] 1 WLR 366 [47], where HL (Sc) contemplated the possibility of equitable adjustment by interpretation of the contract where the contract has become impossible of performance, but not where it is 'nearly frustrated but not quite': 'To hold otherwise would be to undermine the principle enshrined in the maxim pacta sunt servanda which lies at the root of the whole of the law of contract' (Lord Hope of Craighead DPSC).
[30] Above, pp 64, 77.
[31] *Yam Seng Pte Ltd v International Trade Corp Ltd* [2013] EWHC 111 (QB), [2013] 1 Lloyd's Rep 526; above, p 67.
[32] American law recognises an implied duty of good faith in performance of contracts (Farnsworth, above, n 2, para 7.17; Uniform Commercial Code para 1-304), but the development of equitable adjustment, whilst recognised in the Restatement (2d) Contracts para 272, and sometimes applied, has received a limited general acceptance in the courts: Farnsworth, above, n 2, para 9.9.

Parties will generally wish to define more precisely the sort of circumstances which will have an effect on the continuing obligations under the contract, and the consequences of those circumstances. It is common for negotiated commercial contracts and industry-standard contracts (such as building contracts) to contain a clause listing the events which will trigger a remedy. Such a list gives greater certainty than the general test for frustration ('radical change in the obligation'); and it allows the parties to make either a narrower or a wider provision for such events than the common law test might allow. A clause of this kind is often headed '*force majeure*', and sometimes parties are even tempted to include '*force majeure*' in the list of events which trigger the remedy—but this is unfortunate. The term '*force majeure*' is well known in French law and other systems which have drawn their codes from France, because it appears as a term in the French Civil Code, and has been interpreted by the French courts and so has a clearly defined (and very narrow)[33] meaning. But it is not a term of art in English law and the courts have struggled to give it meaning when they have been faced with a reference to it in a contract:

> The precise meaning of [*force majeure*], if it has one, has eluded the lawyers for years. Commercial men have no doubt as to its meaning. Unfortunately no two commercial men can be found to agree upon the same meaning, so perhaps in this, as in so many other matters, there is very little difference between the commercial and legal fraternity.[34]

Parties will also choose to include detailed clauses in their contracts in order to define the consequences of supervening circumstances. They may, for example, wish to allow for a suspension of the contract in the case of an event which may be temporary; or for financial adjustments to be made to the contract in the case of certain events. Neither of these would be covered by the general common law of frustration. But one solution to the problem of supervening circumstances which one might expect the parties sometimes to favour is problematic in English law: there are difficulties in drafting a contract so as to impose on the parties the obligation to renegotiate.

This is a significant limitation on the parties' ability to anticipate supervening circumstances—and one which contrasts with the solution adopted in some civil law jurisdictions. We have seen that the solution of the common law in the case of significant changes of circumstances is for the contract to be automatically terminated for frustration. If the circumstances are not sufficient to frustrate the contract, then it remains in force. The court does not have any general jurisdiction to intervene—and so, for example, English law knows no principle by which a court could revise the terms of the contract

---

[33] B Nicholas, *The French Law of Contract*, 2nd edn (Oxford, Clarendon Press, 1992) 202–05.
[34] *Thomas Borthwick (Glasgow) Ltd v Faure Fairclough Ltd* [1968] 1 Lloyd's Rep 16 (QB) 28 (Donaldson J).

so as to maintain the contractual relationship but to re-balance the contract in the light of the changed circumstances.[35] In practice, where the contract is frustrated, no doubt it will often be in the interests of both parties to renegotiate the terms to avoid losing the whole transaction. But this is a commercial matter between the parties. The court cannot require them to renegotiate, nor can the court itself impose a new contract. In those civil systems which accept a power for the courts to intervene in this way, the judicial intervention is often justified by reference to the parties' duty to perform their contracts in good faith, which can extend to the duty to renegotiate in good faith in cases where the basis of the contract is fundamentally changed. In English law, however, not only is there no general, inherent duty of good faith between parties during the negotiations,[36] but the House of Lords has rejected even an express duty to negotiate in good faith.[37] As the law currently stands, this also prevents the parties from successfully imposing on themselves the duty to renegotiate in good faith. It may change: one judge has said in the Court of Appeal that it is not acceptable for the courts to refuse to give effect to an express term requiring the parties to renegotiate the contract in defined circumstances, because such a refusal would frustrate the intentions of the parties: 'it would be a strong thing to declare unenforceable a clause into which the parties have deliberately and expressly entered'.[38] It will take a decision of the Supreme Court to reverse the general rule which holds that an express duty to (re)negotiate is unenforceable. But that rule is based as least in part[39] on the claim that the duty to negotiate 'in good faith' is inherently uncertain, and so if the parties draft an express renegotiation clause which the court can say is sufficiently certain, perhaps by providing for a mechanism to settle the dispute if the parties fail to resolve the matter by their renegotiations, the clause can be given effect—and this is clearly what the courts seek to do in the case of a negotiated commercial contract.[40]

---

[35] Above, p 269.
[36] Above, pp 64, 77.
[37] *Walford v Miles* [1992] 2 AC 128 (HL); above, p 77.
[38] *Petromec Inc v Petroleo Brasileiro SA* [2005] EWCA Civ 891, [2006] 1 Lloyd's Rep 121 [121].
[39] Above, pp 75–79.
[40] *Cable & Wireless plc v IBM United Kingdom Ltd* [2002] EWHC 2059 (Comm), [2002] 2 All ER (Comm) 1041 (clause to resolve disputes by negotiation in good faith was saved by additional clause which referred unresolved disputes to an alternative dispute resolution procedure: 'This may seem a somewhat slender basis for distinguishing this type of reference from a mere promise to negotiate. However, the English courts should nowadays not be astute to accentuate uncertainty (and therefore unenforceability) in the field of dispute resolution references': Colman J at [25]). Cf also *Yam Seng Pte Ltd v International Trade Corp Ltd*, above, n 31, [144], [152], where Leggatt J rejected the argument that a duty to perform a contract in good faith is too uncertain.

12

Remedies for Breach of Contract

The remedies provided by a legal system for breach of contract tell us much about the system's notion of contract. In this chapter we shall outline some of the rules of English law concerning the remedies for breach, and discover some key ideas about the way in which English law views a contract and the nature of the parties' rights. In considering this topic we need to consider not just the range of available remedies, and the particular rules of each remedy, but also such questions as the hierarchy of remedies (which remedy is normally awarded in preference to the others, and why?); the role of the court in awarding remedies (not only whether the court has some discretion, overt or covert, over the remedy to be awarded but also whether the court necessarily has any role at all—the place of 'self-help' remedies, activated by one of the contracting parties without recourse to the courts); and the extent to which the parties are permitted to dictate the remedies in the contract itself. Furthermore, a fundamental question—which will also highlight the approach of the common law to the contract, the parties' rights and their remedies—is in what sense the legal system sees an event of non-performance as a 'wrong': how 'wrong' is it to break a contract? In each of these areas the answers given by English law are in some respects significantly different from those given by many civil law systems.

I. 'Breach of Contract'

1. What is a Breach of Contract? The Significance of the Obligation to Perform

The language of the common law here gives an indication of an underlying approach. We speak of remedies for 'breach of contract', rather than the consequences of 'non-performance' or 'defective performance'. As we shall see, a breach of contract does involve the failure by one party to fulfil an obligation under the contract through non-performance or defective performance. But there is less focus on the infringement of the claimant's right to performance.

Some common lawyers have gone so far as to suggest that there is not really any right to receive performance at all. The strongest statements were made by the American lawyer and judge Oliver Wendell Holmes in two separate writings:

> The remedy [of specific performance] is an exceptional one. The only universal consequence of a legally binding promise is, that the law makes the promisor pay damages if the promised event does not come to pass. In every case it leaves him free from interference until the time for fulfilment has gone by, and therefore free to break his contract if he chooses.[1]

and:

> Nowhere is the confusion between legal and moral ideas more manifest than in the law of contract. Among other things, here again the so called primary rights and duties are invested with a mystic significance beyond what can be assigned and explained. The duty to keep a contract at common law means a prediction that you must pay damages if you do not keep it,—and nothing else. If you commit a tort, you are liable to pay a compensatory sum. If you commit a contract, you are liable to pay a compensatory sum unless the promised event comes to pass, and that is all the difference. But such a mode of looking at the matter stinks in the nostrils of those who think it advantageous to get as much ethics into the law as they can ...
>
> I have spoken only of the common law, because there are some cases in which a logical justification can be found for speaking of civil liabilities as imposing duties in an intelligible sense. These are the relatively few in which equity will grant an injunction ... But I hardly think it advisable to shape general theory from the exception.[2]

The English lawyer would not generally make such a strong statement.[3] The primary obligation is seen as the obligation to perform and, as we shall see, the obligation of performance is normally to be kept alive even in the event of non-performance. Breach of contract does not of itself discharge the performance obligations of the party in breach. However, the way in which the remedies for breach of contract operate does in practice translate non-performance or defective performance into money—damages. The courts are reluctant to order a party to perform, and therefore the party in breach can in most cases pay damages rather than performing his obligations if he so

---

[1] OW Holmes, *The Common Law* (Boston, Little, Brown & Co, 1881) 301.
[2] OW Holmes [Mr Justice Holmes], *The Path of the Law* (1896) 10 Harv L Rev 457, 462.
[3] Nor would the modern American lawyer: eg EA Farnsworth, *Contracts*, 4th edn (New York, Aspen, 2006) paras 12.2–12.3.

chooses. English law certainly does not see a party's duty to perform, and the other party's correlative right to receive that performance, as having the same overriding significance—either theoretical or practical—as civil law systems commonly do. There is no doubt a moral duty generally to keep one's promises; but that is not the legal notion of contractual obligation.

The approach in English law to breach of contract was conveniently summarised by Lord Diplock in *Photo Production Ltd v Securicor Ltd*:

> Leaving aside those comparatively rare cases in which the court is able to enforce a primary obligation by decreeing specific performance of it, breaches of primary obligations give rise to substituted or secondary obligations on the part of the party in default, and, in some cases, may entitle the other party to be relieved from further performance of his own primary obligations ...
>
> Every failure to perform a primary obligation is a breach of contract. The secondary obligation on the part of the contract breaker to which it gives rise by implication of the common law is to pay monetary compensation to the other party for the loss sustained by him in consequence of the breach; but, with two exceptions,[4] the primary obligations of both parties so far as they have not yet been fully performed remain unchanged.[5]

The obligations (typically, to perform) which the parties undertake in the contract, either expressly or impliedly, are 'primary obligations' and a breach of contract is the failure to perform a primary obligation. This does not distinguish between non-performance, defective performance or delay in performance; all are simply breaches of contract. The breach gives rise automatically to a 'substituted or secondary obligation'—the obligation to pay damages for the loss caused by the breach. But in most cases the primary obligations remain unchanged: a breach of contract creates the new obligation to pay damages; but does not terminate the contract, nor does the court normally intervene to order specific performance.

2. The Range of Remedies

As the statement by Lord Diplock makes clear, damages are the normal and automatic remedy for breach of contract in English law. Specific performance is an exception. And termination of the contract is also an exception—although we shall see that it is much more common than specific performance, and is often a very useful remedy for the innocent party. There are also other remedies which need to be considered. Injunctions are closely related to specific performance and these two remedies will be discussed together.

---

[4] For the two 'exceptional' cases in which the innocent party is entitled to terminate the contract, see below, p 282.

[5] [1980] AC 827 (HL) 848–9; see also above, p 202.

An action to enforce a specific sum of money such as a debt, or the price payable under a contract of sale, or a sum agreed by the parties in the contract as payable in the event of breach, can sometimes look rather like either specific performance or damages, but is distinct and must be considered separately. And there are remedies (or 'rights') peculiar to consumer contracts for the supply of goods, digital content or services: rights to the repair or replacement of the goods, or a reduction in the price, under a consumer goods contract, together with statutory rights to reject the goods which take effect in place of the common law remedy of termination; rights to the replacement or reduction in price under a consumer contract for digital content; and rights to repeat performance or reduction in price under a consumer services contract. These remedies will be considered in the following sections.

II. Specific Performance and Injunction

1. Specific Performance and Injunction as Equitable Remedies

Orders for specific performance and injunctions were not awarded by the old common law courts: the remedy for breach of contract at common law was damages. But the courts of equity developed orders, directed at the individual who had failed to fulfill his contractual obligations or was threatening not to fulfil them, requiring him personally to perform (specific performance) or to do or refrain from doing a particular act (injunction). This is an illustration of the courts of equity developing remedies to supplement the common law. Before the fusion of the old jurisdictions of common law and equity by the Judicature Acts 1873 and 1875, therefore, a claimant who sought only damages would take his case to a common law court; but if he sought specific performance of a contract he would go to a court of equity.

We have seen that the effect of the Judicature Acts was to join the separate courts of common law and equity into one single 'Supreme Court of Judicature'; but not to fuse the substantive rules of common law and equity.[6] So the old 'equitable' remedies still coexist with the common law remedies, and they continue to be developed by the courts today. In the case of conflict between

---

[6] Above, pp 7–8. The 'Supreme Court of Judicature' created by the Judicature Acts was what is now known as the 'Senior Courts' (the High Court and the Court of Appeal) and should not be confused with the present 'Supreme Court': see above, p 7, n 11.

a rule of common law and a rule of equity, it is the equitable rule which prevails:[7] and so the remedy of specific performance or injunction will still be awarded, in preference to an award of damages, if the principles for its award which were developed by 1875, and as they have been further developed since then, so determine.

In the modern law it is still normal to refer to specific performance and injunctions as 'equitable' remedies. They are also commonly described as 'discretionary' remedies—that is, the court has an overt discretion in deciding whether to order them. But it is important to realise that this is not simply a question of whether the court thinks that it is in a broad sense 'fair' or 'equitable' to make an order. The 'discretion' involved is a principled discretion: although it is for the court to decide whether on the facts they should order specific performance or an injunction, there are well-established rules which the courts will apply to determine whether it is appropriate to make an order.

2. The Content of the Order and the Remedy for Non-compliance

'Specific performance' in English law means just that: an order of the court that the defaulting party perform the contract personally and literally in accordance with its terms. Similarly, an injunction is an order that the defaulting party personally do a positive act to remedy a breach of contract (a 'mandatory' injunction: such as to destroy a building which he has built in contravention of a contractual obligation) or not do a particular act in order to avoid being or becoming in breach of contract (a 'prohibitory' injunction: such as not to enter into or perform another contract which would be a breach of the present contract). Unlike many civil law systems, English law has not developed a remedy under which the court can order performance by a third party, paid for by the debtor, except in the very limited situation where the defendant has already failed to comply with an order of (personal) specific performance or injunction.[8] The equitable jurisdiction is exercised only against the particular individual—it is said that equity acts '*in personam*'— and so specific performance or an injunction will be ordered only where it is possible and appropriate for the defaulting party personally to be required to perform and (as we shall see below) where a remedy in damages cannot equally well serve the case for the claimant.

The sanction applied by the courts of equity to a defendant who had failed to comply with the court's order to perform was drastic: his non-compliance put him in contempt of court. This meant that the court acted against him

---

[7] Senior Courts Act 1981 (formerly known as Supreme Court Act 1981) s 49(1), replacing Supreme Court of Judicature Act 1873 s 25(11).
[8] CPR r 70.2A.

personally in the most direct sense: fining him and if necessary imprisoning him. This extreme sanction remains in the modern law—and, indeed, Lord Hoffmann gave it as a factor to be taken into account by the courts in exercising their discretion as to whether to make an order for specific performance.[9]

3. Specific Performance in the Modern Law

There are certain general criteria which the courts have devised over the years to determine the circumstances in which an order of specific performance is appropriate.

A clear limitation on the remedy is that it will not be awarded to enforce an obligation of personal service. There is a statutory prohibition against the courts ordering employees to work;[10] but other cases are covered by the general equitable rule designed to avoid turning service contracts into 'contracts of slavery'.[11] But many contracts to perform services are not personal and so will not normally fall within this principle—such as a contract to build a house. On the other hand, specific performance of such a contract will not normally be awarded, but for a different reason: damages will be an adequate remedy, since they will allow the claimant to obtain equivalent services from a third party.

There are other limitations which the courts have adopted against an award of specific performance. For example, a gratuitous undertaking will not be enforced because it is said that 'equity will not assist a volunteer'—that is, a court exercising the equitable jurisdiction will not lend its assistance to a party to enforce an obligation which was entered into in his favour where he has given nothing in return for it. This does not, of course, constitute an obstacle to specific performance of most contracts, since the requirement of consideration means that a party enforcing a contract is not normally a 'volunteer', although if a promise is gratuitous and is binding only because it is contained in a deed[12] it will not be specifically enforceable. Moreover, the courts have held that they will not normally make an order for specific performance of an obligation where the court would have to undertake constant supervision to check on compliance with its order; nor where enforceability of the contract lacks 'mutuality'—that is, the claimant will not be awarded specific performance of the defendant's obligations where the defendant would not be able to obtain an equivalent order for performance of the claimant's own

---

[9] *Co-operative Insurance Society Ltd v Argyll Stores (Holdings) Ltd* [1998] AC 1 (HL) 13.
[10] Trade Union and Labour Relations (Consolidation) Act 1992 s 236.
[11] *De Francesco v Barnum* (1890) 45 ChD (CA) 438 (Fry LJ).
[12] Above, p 127.

obligations (for example, a minor cannot obtain specific performance because he could not himself be subject to a similar order); nor where (given that this is an equitable remedy) the defendant does not come to the court 'with clean hands'—his behaviour in relation to the contract which he is seeking to enforce has been such that the court is not prepared to assist him.[13]

The most significant general rule, however, is that the court will not order specific performance unless damages would be an inadequate remedy. This derives from the original basis of the equitable jurisdiction—the remedy was awarded by the courts of equity to address a defect in the common law; and so if the common law could give an adequate remedy for the claimant's particular circumstances it was not appropriate for equity to intervene. This general approach was carried into the modern law after the fusion of the jurisdictions by the Judicature Acts.

There have been some suggestions in recent years that the courts might be more disposed to exercise their discretion to order performance of contractual obligations, and that the old rule to the effect that specific performance will be awarded only if damages are 'inadequate' is moving to a broader rule: that specific performance will be awarded if it would be the more 'appropriate' remedy. For example, we have seen that in *Beswick v Beswick*[14] the House of Lords used specific performance to solve a problem of the doctrine of privity of contract, by allowing the promisee to obtain an order that the promisor perform his obligations in favour of the third party: they rejected the argument that an award of nominal damages for the promisee would be an adequate remedy, and said that they could take a broader view of whether damages were a 'just' or 'adequate' remedy. Lord Upjohn said[15] that 'Equity will grant specific performance when damages are inadequate to meet the justice of the case'.

However, there have not been significant signs of a general development in favour of granting specific performance more readily; and in *Co-operative Insurance Society Ltd v Argyll Stores (Holdings) Ltd*[16] the House of Lords discussed at some length the general approach to the remedy and largely reaffirmed the traditional approach. In that case the Court of Appeal had granted specific performance of a tenant's undertaking to keep its supermarket open for trade during the usual hours of business in the landlord's

---

[13] *Coatsworth v Johnson* (1886) 54 LT 520 (CA) (specific performance of contract to grant a lease refused where claimant had already broken covenants contained in the contract for lease).

[14] [1968] AC 58 (HL); above, p 248.

[15] *Ibid* 102.

[16] [1998] AC 1 (HL). Scots law does not follow the English approach: enforcement of the contract ('specific implement') is one of the ordinary remedies to which a claimant is entitled unless there is a reason for denying it; and a contract such as that in *Co-operative Insurance Society Ltd v Argyll Stores (Holdings) Ltd* is capable of specific enforcement in Scotland: *Co-operative Insurance Society Ltd v Halfords Ltd (No 2)* 1999 SLT 685 (Outer House of the Court of Session).

shopping centre during the whole period of the lease.[17] This was reversed by the House of Lords, which made clear that specific performance is an exceptional remedy which will only be granted within the court's discretion where damages would be an inadequate remedy; in any event the court will normally not order a defendant to continue to run a business because the covenant, and so the court's order, cannot be sufficiently precise to avoid the risk of costly litigation to enforce it: there may therefore be uncertainty over whether it has been complied with, which risks the defendant becoming in contempt of court for non-compliance; and ordering the tenant to keep open the business when it was not an economic venture would involve a loss to him and a consequent benefit to the landlord greater than the loss to the landlord by allowing closure. On this last point, Lord Hoffmann said:

> It is true that the defendant has, by his own breach of contract, put himself in such an unfortunate position. But the purpose of the law of contract is not to punish wrongdoing but to satisfy the expectations of the party entitled to performance. A remedy which enables him to secure, in money terms, more than the performance due to him is unjust. From a wider perspective, it cannot be in the public interest for the courts to require someone to carry on business at a loss if there is any plausible alternative by which the other party can be given compensation. It is not only a waste of resources but yokes the parties together in a continuing hostile relationship. The order for specific performance prolongs the battle. If the defendant is ordered to run a business, its conduct becomes the subject of a flow of complaints, solicitors' letters and affidavits. This is wasteful for both parties and the legal system. An award of damages, on the other hand, brings the litigation to an end. The defendant pays damages, the forensic link between them is severed, they go their separate ways and the wounds of conflict can heal.[18]

Lord Hoffmann here took into account the economic consequences of an order: a reason for not ordering the defendant to perform is that it would be a waste of resources, and would in effect punish him whereas the aim of remedies in the law of contract is not to punish defendants but to compensate claimants.

In the light of this clear reluctance to order specific performance, one might well ask: in what circumstances will the courts generally make an order? In practice, the context in which an order is most likely to be made is where the contract is for the delivery of a specific thing for which there is no available market. A contract for personal services will not be specifically enforced; and a contract for non-personal services will normally be adequately compensated by an award of damages to enable the claimant to

---

[17] The lease was for a term of 35 years, of which almost 20 years still remained when the tenant, a national chain of supermarkets, closed the particular supermarket on the basis that was loss-making.
[18] [1998] AC 1, 15–16.

obtain substitute performance from a third party. A contract for the sale of non-specific goods will not normally be enforced, because the claimant can go into the market to obtain them—although in rare cases (such as where the defendant has the only supply of such goods) a court might be persuaded to order specific performance precisely because there is no alternative market.[19] But specific performance may be awarded in the case of specific goods for which there is no market, such as antiques;[20] or a contract for the sale of land, since the courts have long accepted that an award of damages in inadequate to protect the disappointed purchaser of a particular plot of land, with or without a building on it. The most common type of contract of which specific performance will be ordered is therefore a contract for the sale of a house.[21]

4. Injunction

In claims for actual or threatened breach of contract the courts adopt a general approach to the award of injunctions similar to their approach to specific performance. The injunction is a discretionary remedy, although there are well-established criteria for the exercise of the discretion; breach is contempt of court; a court will not order an injunction in circumstances where specific performance would not be ordered—for example, there can be no injunction to prevent a person from taking up an alternative service contract if its indirect effect would be inevitably to require him to continue in the contract of service of which he is in breach.[22] And the courts will not normally order a party who has constructed a building in breach of contract to pull down the building where 'to grant it would subject the defendant to a loss out of all proportion to that which would be suffered by the plaintiff if it were refused'[23] or where it would be 'an unpardonable waste of much needed houses to direct that they now be pulled down'.[24]

---

[19] *Sky Petroleum Ltd v VIP Petroleum Ltd* [1974] 1 WLR 576 (Ch).
[20] *Falcke v Gray* (1859) 4 Drew 651, 62 ER 250.
[21] The fact that a contract for the sale of land or an interest in land is normally capable of specific performance is fundamental to the doctrine of *Walsh v Lonsdale* (1882) 21 ChD 9 (CA) under which equitable interests in land are created: above, p 56 n 22. Cf *Southcott Estates Inc v Toronto Catholic District School Board* 2012 SCC 51, (2012) 351 DLR (4th) 476 (Supreme Court of Canada, refusing specific performance for land contract which was merely an investment where claimant could find other property).
[22] *Warner Bros Pictures Inc v Nelson* [1937] 1 KB 209 (limited injunction awarded which would not have such effect).
[23] *Jaggard v Sawyer* [1995] 1 WLR 269 (CA) 288 (Millett LJ).
[24] *Wrotham Park Estate Co Ltd v Parkside Homes Ltd* [1974] 1 WLR 798 (Ch) 811 (Brightman J).

5. Damages in Place of Specific Performance or Injunction

By statute the courts of equity were given the power to order damages in substitution for, or as well as, an award of specific performance or injunction.[25] However, it has been held that the measure of such damages is not in principle different from the measure of damages at common law,[26] and in practice in the modern law, where the remedy for breach is determined by the single court which applies both the old common law rules and the old equity rules, the claimant who is successful in a claim for breach of contract will normally simply be awarded common law damages for breach if specific performance is refused.

III. Termination for Breach

1. The Nature of Termination

We have already seen the remedy of termination in the context of the doctrine of frustration.[27] As Lord Diplock explained,[28] where a contract is terminated for breach the primary obligations of both parties are discharged in so far as they have not yet accrued due to be performed. But those obligations which have already accrued due are left undisturbed. We have seen that this is an exceptional remedy—in the sense that a breach of contract does not normally give rise to termination but the parties' obligations remain in place to be performed. But it is a very useful remedy which allows a party against whom a breach of contract has been committed to be released from the contract and, where appropriate, to negotiate a substitute contract elsewhere. The commercial usefulness of such a remedy lies at the heart of some of the rules which the courts have developed for it.

2. Availability of Termination

The innocent party may terminate the contract only if *either* the term which has been broken is a 'condition' of the contract *or* the breach is 'fundamental'.[29]

---

[25] Chancery Amendment Act 1858 s 2; now found in Senior Courts Act 1981 (formerly known as Supreme Court Act 1981) s 50.
[26] *Johnson v Agnew* [1980] AC 367 (HL) 400.
[27] Above, p 266.
[28] *Photo Production Ltd v Securicor Ltd* [1980] AC 827 (HL) 849; see also above, p 274.
[29] *Ibid*.

(a) Breach of Condition

The word 'condition' is used in various different senses in the law of contract.[30] In this context it means a term of the contract which the parties have agreed will give the innocent party the right to terminate on the occurrence of any breach, whether or not the consequences of the breach are serious for him. Just as a term of the contract may itself be express or implied,[31] so the characterisation of a term as a condition may be express or implied. If the parties expressly identify a term as a condition it will be given effect as such, although the name which the parties attach to a term is not conclusive and does not prevent the court from looking behind the label to see whether it was really intended to be a condition in the sense that it was to give rise to the right to terminate.[32] Sometimes the courts will infer on the facts that the parties must have intended a term to be a condition; and they have held that certain typical clauses will be characterised as conditions unless the parties indicate otherwise—for example, time stipulations in mercantile contracts are normally conditions.[33] And in many cases where a term is implied by statute, the statute also defines the nature of the term—and so the terms implied into a non-consumer contract of sale by the Sale of Goods Act 1979 as to the seller's title to the goods, their compliance with any description by which they are sold, and their quality and fitness for purpose are all there identified as conditions of the contract of sale.[34]

(b) Fundamental Breach

A 'fundamental breach' is one which 'has the effect of depriving the other party of substantially the whole benefit which it was the intention of the parties that he should obtain from the contract'.[35] That is, it is the fundamental *consequences* of the breach for the innocent party which make the breach itself 'fundamental'. The innocent party need only rely on the breach being fundamental where it is a breach of a term which is not a 'condition' in the sense discussed above. Until the early 1960s it was thought that contractual terms were all either 'conditions' (giving the right to terminate for breach)

---

[30] Eg a 'condition precedent' is a term which suspends the obligation(s) until the occurrence of a specified event.
[31] Above, ch 8.
[32] *Wickman Machine Tool Sales Ltd v L Schuler AG* [1974] AC 235 (HL).
[33] *Bunge Corporation, New York v Tradax Export SA Panama* [1981] 1 WLR 711 (HL).
[34] Sale of Goods Act 1979 ss 12(5A), 13(1A), 14(6). The Consumer Rights Act 2015, in the equivalent provisions for consumer contracts, does not define the terms which are treated as being included in the contract as 'conditions' because it provides a self-contained remedial regime for rejecting the goods and treating the contract as at an end, rather than using the common law remedy of (and test for) termination: below, p 298.
[35] *Photo Production Ltd v Securicor Ltd* above, n 28, 849 (Lord Diplock).

or 'warranties' (giving rise to only damages), but it is now well established that many (perhaps even most) terms of contracts are neither conditions nor warranties, but 'intermediate terms' where the remedy (termination or only damages) depends on the consequences of the breach.[36]

A fundamental breach will include an outright refusal of one party to perform all or substantially all of his obligations under the contract—often referred to as a 'repudiation' or 'renunciation' of the contract—as well as performance of the contract which is so defective as to deprive the other party of substantially the whole benefit of the bargain. It also includes a renunciation of the contract in advance of the time due for performance—an 'anticipatory breach'—which gives the innocent party the right to terminate the contract immediately and so enables him to make alternative arrangements without having to wait to see whether the other party changes his mind and in fact performs when the time due for performance arrives. It is efficient and commercially useful.[37]

3. Exercising the Right to Terminate

Even where there is a breach of condition or a fundamental breach, termination of the contract is not automatic.[38] As a general rule the innocent party may elect to keep the contract alive and sue only for damages for breach—and in such a case the whole contract remains enforceable, including the innocent party's own continuing obligations of performance. But he may elect to terminate the contract by giving notice to the party in breach—and if he does so the contract is terminated at that moment. No court order is necessary to effect termination, and the terminating party need not give the contract breaker an opportunity to remedy his breach before exercising his right to terminate.[39]

Once the innocent party has made his election, it is irrevocable; and his election not to terminate (his 'affirmation' of the contract) need not be express but may be inferred from his conduct as long as it can be shown that he knew of the right to terminate.[40]

Sometimes the innocent party has no practical choice but to accept the breach and terminate the contract—for example, where the breach of

---

[36] *Hongkong Fir Shipping Co Ltd v Kawasaki Kisen Kaisha Ltd* [1962] 2 QB 26 (CA).
[37] *Hochster v De La Tour* (1852) 2 El & Bl 678, 690; 118 ER 922, 926.
[38] *Geys v Société Générale, London Branch* [2012] UKSC 63, [2013] 1 AC 523 (employment contracts are not an exception to this rule).
[39] There is an exception to this in the cases of a lease, where the landlord's right to forfeit the lease for breach is sometimes subject to his giving the tenant an opportunity to remedy the breach: Law of Property Act 1925 s 146.
[40] *Peyman v Lanjani* [1985] Ch 457 (CA).

contract by a security firm resulted in their employee destroying the factory which he was guarding.[41] In a very limited category of cases the court may require the innocent party to terminate for a repudiatory breach—but only where it can be shown that he has no legitimate interest in insisting on continued performance, and so he would be penalising the contract-breaker by insisting on the contract being performed without having himself any good reason to do so,[42] or where the election to keep the contract alive would be wholly unreasonable and damages would be an adequate remedy.[43] In such cases the innocent party is required to terminate and take damages and so will succeed in his claim against the contract-breaker only for the measure of damages which would have been awarded if he had terminated the contract. The innocent party can of course only refuse to terminate if he can perform his own side of the contract without the co-operation of the party in breach (or can obtain specific performance—although we have already seen that this will be rare).

However, there are some statutory limits on the right to terminate. For example, if the contract is one of sale, the normal right of the buyer to reject goods for certain defects is varied in non-consumer contracts where the seller can show that the breach is so slight that it would be unreasonable for the buyer to reject the goods.[44]

Sometimes a party will purport to terminate when in fact the right has not arisen, or has already been lost by (implied) affirmation. The law here is not entirely settled, but it seems likely that the courts will not regard such a purported termination as itself a repudiatory breach of contract which can in turn be relied on by the other party to terminate the contract, as long as it was done by the first party in good faith, honestly (but mistakenly) believing that he had the right to do so.[45]

For one contracting party to be able lawfully to terminate for the other party's breach, the question is whether the conditions set by the law for termination have arisen. The party seeking to terminate need not give a valid reason (nor, indeed, any reason) in order for his termination to be valid, as long as there is fact then a valid reason. If he gives a bad reason, but later discovers that he had another—and good—reason for terminating the contract, he can rely on it to justify his earlier termination, which remains (from the time when it was effected) a valid termination.[46]

---

[41] *Photo Production Ltd v Securicor Ltd* above, n 28.
[42] *White & Carter (Councils) Ltd v McGregor* [1962] AC 413 (HL Sc) 431.
[43] *Reichman v Beveridge* [2006] EWCA Civ 1659, [2007] 1 P & CR 20, [17].
[44] Sale of Goods Act 1979 s 15A, introduced by Sale and Supply of Goods Act 1994.
[45] *Woodar Investment Development Ltd v Wimpey Construction UK Ltd* [1980] 1 WLR 277 (HL) 283.
[46] *Maredelanto Compania Naviera SA v Bergbau-Handel GmbH (The Mihalis Angelos)* [1971] 1 QB 164 (CA).

4. Consequences of Termination

Although it is common to speak of 'the contract' being terminated, this can be misleading: the effect of termination is to discharge only the future obligations of both parties which have not yet accrued, that is, have not yet come due to be performed. It is not retroactive.[47] If at the moment of termination there are obligations of which performance has already become due but which have not yet been performed, those obligations survive the termination of the contract and so performance of them can still be required. And (depending on the interpretation of the clauses in question) contractual terms other than performance obligations may survive the termination—such as an exemption or limitation clause, a dispute resolution clause or a choice of law clause.

If the innocent party terminates the contract, he is also entitled to damages for breach of contract. His losses are not simply for the particular breach which has given him the right to terminate, but also for all the losses which flow from the contract itself being terminated.[48]

5. Contractual Termination Clauses

It is common in commercial contracts for the parties to include a clause providing for termination of the contract in certain defined circumstances— and also making detailed provision for the consequences of the termination. Such a clause can either supplement or exclude the general common law right of termination, depending on how the clause is drafted.

There are some differences in the operation of such clauses in common law contracts, as compared with the civil law. Because of the general duty to perform the contract in good faith, civil law courts will generally not permit a party to take advantage of an express right of termination in bad faith— sometimes providing that the purported termination cannot take effect; sometimes treating it as an abusive exercise of contractual rights and therefore giving rise to a claim for damages. English law does not have any general rule that a contracting party must exercise his contractual rights reasonably, or in good faith, although it might sometimes reach a similar result by interpreting the clause as entitling the party to terminate only in certain circumstances—such as where the Court of Appeal interpreted a clause in a contract for the provision of gardening services by a small business in favour

---

[47] Older cases commonly referred to the remedy of termination as 'rescission' of the contract for breach, but this terminology is now disapproved because it can be confused with the remedy of rescission for misrepresentation, which is retroactive: above, p 179; *Johnson v Agnew* above, n 26, 392–93; *Photo Production Ltd v Securicor Ltd* above, n 28, 844.

[48] *Photo Production Ltd v Securicor Ltd* above, n 28, 849.

of a local authority, which allowed the authority to terminate the contract for 'breach of any of [the contractor's] obligations under the contract', as covering only fundamental breaches.[49]

However, particularly in commercial cases between parties of equal bargaining strength, the courts will generally interpret and apply termination clauses strictly. A good illustration is *Union Eagle Ltd v Golden Achievement Ltd*[50] where a contract for the purchase of property contained an express provision that the seller had the right to terminate it if the buyer did not tender the balance of the purchase price by 5pm on a particular date. The buyer tendered the price 10 minutes late, but the Privy Council held that the seller was entitled to terminate the contract and to treat the buyer's deposit as forfeited. Lord Hoffmann said:

> The principle that equity will restrain the enforcement of legal rights when it would be unconscionable to insist upon them has an attractive breadth. But the reasons why the courts have rejected such generalisations are founded not merely upon authority (see *per* Lord Radcliffe in *Campbell Discount Co. Ltd. v. Bridge* [1962] A.C. 600, 626) but also upon practical considerations of business. These are, in summary, that in many forms of transaction it is of great importance that if something happens for which the contract has made express provision, the parties should know with certainty that the terms of the contract will be enforced. The existence of an undefined discretion to refuse to enforce the contract on the ground that this would be 'unconscionable' is sufficient to create uncertainty.[51]

Even though it has recently been held that a duty to perform a contract in good faith may be implied as a matter of fact into a contract,[52] this will not affect the courts' approach to express termination clauses since the implied term would be excluded by the express term.[53]

6. Deposits; Relief against Forfeiture

The *Union Eagle* case, discussed above, demonstrates the rule that a sum of money which is paid by one party to the other, in advance of performance, as a *deposit* is security for performance and will normally be forfeited if the party who has paid the deposit fails to fulfil the contract. It makes no difference that the deposit was to count towards the price to be paid.[54] By contrast, a sum which is paid as simply a partial pre-payment of the money

---

[49] *Rice v Great Yarmouth BC* [2000] All ER (D) 902 (CA).
[50] [1997] AC 514 (PC).
[51] *Ibid* 519.
[52] *Yam Seng Pte Ltd v International Trade Corp Ltd* [2013] EWHC 111 (QB), [2013] 1 Lloyd's Rep 526, above, p 67.
[53] *Ibid* [149]; above, p 216.
[54] *Howe v Smith* (1884) 27 ChD 89 (CA).

due under the contract, and not as security for performance, will not be automatically forfeited; all therefore depends on the construction of the terms of the payment.[55]

However, there are certain circumstances in which the court will grant relief against forfeiture of the deposit. In the case of a contract for the sale of land, the court has a statutory discretion to order the return of any deposit that has been paid if the contract does not proceed.[56] More generally, the courts devised an equitable discretion to grant relief against forfeiture of deposits where the deposit is in the nature of a penalty[57] or where it would be unconscionable for the vendor to retain the money,[58] although this will not normally apply in practice between commercial parties. A non-negotiated contractual term which requires the payment of a non-returnable deposit by a consumer may also constitute an unfair term within Part 2 of the Consumer Rights Act 2015.[59]

The equitable jurisdiction to relieve against forfeiture also extends to granting relief to a party who by the terms of the contract would forfeit a proprietary or possessory interest in land or other property, and the jurisdiction may sometimes be exercised by the courts to allow the party in default further time to perform the contract in order to avoid losing his interest.[60] This can therefore sometimes cover situations in which the courts in some civil law jurisdictions might prevent a party from exercising his strict rights under the contract by the operation of the doctrines of good faith or abuse of rights. But in England it is a jurisdiction which is quite narrowly limited to rights in property and is sparingly exercised, particularly between commercial parties.[61]

7. No General Right of Suspension

There is no general right at common law to suspend performance of the contract, even in the case of the other party's non-performance. For example, in a lease the landlord's failure to fulfil his obligation to repair does not (in the absence of express provision in the lease) permit the tenant to withhold rent. However, where obligations are concurrent, or interdependent—as will often be the case—the failure by one party to perform entitles the other party to

---

[55] *Dies v British and International Mining and Finance Corp Ltd* [1939] 1 KB 724 (KB).
[56] Law of Property Act 1925 s 49(2).
[57] Below, p 300; *Workers Trust & Merchant Bank Ltd v Dojap Investments Ltd* [1993] AC 573 (PC) (25% deposit in contract for sale of land was a penalty; vendor has burden of showing why the deposit should be greater than the customary 10%).
[58] *Stockloser v Johnson* [1954] 1 QB 476 (CA).
[59] Above, p 230.
[60] *BICC plc v Burndy Corporation* [1985] Ch 232.
[61] *Scandinavian Trading Tanker Co AB v Flota Petrolera Ecuatoriana (The Scaptrade)* [1983] 2 AC 694 (HL).

withhold the corresponding performance: for example, in a contract of sale, the seller's obligation to deliver and the buyer's obligation to pay the price are normally concurrent, and so the seller cannot require payment of the price where he is not himself able to offer his own performance. And where a party's obligations are entire and have not been fully performed, he cannot insist on performance of the other party's obligations: for example, one party cannot require the other to pay the price in return for his own incomplete performance where the contract requires entire performance before payment is due, although it can sometimes be a matter of interpretation of the contract to discover whether the obligation was 'entire', requiring complete and perfect performance before there is any entitlement to be paid.[62] If it was not an 'entire' obligation the party may be able to claim the price (subject to a reduction for defects) once he has substantially performed, even if his performance is in some way defective as to quality.[63]

IV. Damages

1. Damages are to Compensate the Claimant's Failed Expectation

Damages for breach of contract are calculated to put the claimant into the position in which he would have been if the contract had been properly performed—often called the 'expectation' measure:

> The rule of the common law is, that where a party sustains a loss by reason of a breach of contract, he is, so far as money can do it, to be placed in the same situation, with respect to damages, as if the contract had been performed.[64]

This contrasts with damages in tort, which are calculated so as to put the claimant into the position in which he would have been if the tort had not been committed.[65]

Sometimes the courts will award a different measure of damages for breach of contract calculated to reimburse the claimant's expenditure incurred in preparing for and performing the contract, but wasted as a result of the breach.[66]

---

[62] *Sumpter v Hedges* [1898] 1 QB 673 (CA).
[63] *Hoenig v Isaacs* [1953] 2 All ER 176 (CA).
[64] *Robinson v Harman* (1848) 1 Exch 850, 855; 154 ER 363, 365 (Parke B).
[65] Above, pp 180, 183 (liability in tort for misrepresentation, contrasted with liability in contract).
[66] *Anglia Television Ltd v Reed* [1972] 1 QB 60 (CA).

This is sometimes (rather unhelpfully) called the 'reliance' measure. However, such an award will only be made where the court does not have evidence of the proper valuation of the 'expectation': that is, where the claimant cannot prove his expectation or, at least, where if he claims the wasted expenditure, the defendant cannot show that he is claiming more than his expectation. If the court knows that the expenditure was greater than the sum which the claimant has failed to make by way of return from the contract, he will not be allowed to use this claim in order to escape a bad bargain.[67] The award of damages for wasted expenditure is therefore still based on the principle that the purpose of damages is to compensate the claimant's failed expectations.[68]

Even if the claimant can prove no substantial loss, he is entitled to at least nominal damages—a token sum, such as £5—for the fact that the defendant has broken the contract. The legal wrong is complete when the contract has been broken: it does not depend on there being any particular loss (or even any loss) flowing from the breach.

2. Valuing the Expectation

Sometimes it will be relatively straightforward to calculate what the claimant has failed to receive under the contract. In a contract for the sale of goods, the defendant's failure to deliver the goods is normally to be compensated by the additional cost to the claimant of going into the market to obtain goods of equivalent quality—that is, the difference between the contract price and the market price when the goods should have been delivered.[69] The assessment of the loss is generally made at the date of breach, but the court may depart from this where, at the time of trial, it has evidence that such an assessment would under- or over-compensate the claimant.[70]

However, there can sometimes be more than one way of making the calculation. For example, if the defendant promised a particular performance, damages for the *cost of curing* the defective performance will entitle him to obtain the factual equivalent of the defendant's promise by allowing him to pay for substitute performance by a third party. But, on the other hand, damages for the *difference in value* between the promised performance and the defective performance will enable him to have the financial equivalent, whilst not necessarily enabling him to pay for the factual equivalent. The difference between

---

[67] *CCC Films (London) Ltd v Impact Quadrant Films Ltd* [1985] QB 16 (QB).
[68] *Omak Maritime Ltd v Mamola Challenger Shipping Co Ltd* [2010] EWHC 2026 (Comm), [2010] 2 CLC 194.
[69] This is set out in Sale of Goods Act 1979 s 51, but that section restates the normal common law rule.
[70] *Golden Strait Corp v Nippon Yusen Kubishika Kaisha (The Golden Victory)* [2007] UKHL 12, [2007] 2 AC 353 (damages reduced to reflect event which occurred post-breach, which would have permitted party in breach to terminate the contract); *Bunge SA v Nidera BV* [2015] UKSC 43, [2015] 3 All ER 1082.

these two ways of calculating the failed expectation can be illustrated by *Ruxley Electronics & Construction Ltd v Forsyth*,[71] where Ruxley built a swimming pool for Mr Forsyth, but did not comply with the contractual specifications with the result that the pool had a maximum diving depth of six feet (roughly 1.8 metres) whereas the contract specified seven feet six inches (2.3 metres). The contract price was £18,000. The cost of demolishing the pool and rebuilding it to the contractual specification (the 'cost of cure') was £21,560. But the value of the pool, or of the house with the pool, as it was built by Ruxley was no less than it would have been had the contract been complied with (that is, the 'difference in value' was zero).

In the case of building contracts, such as *Ruxley*, the courts will generally lean in favour of awarding cost of cure damages. That was what the Court of Appeal awarded in that case. But it is not an absolute rule, and the decision of the Court of Appeal was reversed by the House of Lords which made clear that it is not appropriate to make such an award where it is not reasonable. The question is always how to characterise the claimant's loss; and the courts will take into account the reasonableness of the expenditure necessary to cure the defective performance as part of the assessment of the true nature of the loss. Where it is unreasonable to spend money (or so much money) curing the defect, or where the claimant does not intend to cure the defect even if 'cost of cure' damages are awarded, it might be more appropriate to characterise the claimant's loss as the difference in value between the works properly performed and the defective works. The trial judge had held that Mr Forsyth would not have spent the money on curing the defect, and the House of Lords took into account the fact that expenditure of such a sum would have been unreasonable in the circumstances.

The fact that English law seeks to protect the claimant's 'expectation' by an award of damages calculated to put him into the position in which he would have been if the contract had been performed points toward the use of damages as a substitute for performance. Indeed, some writers have even said that the damages for breach of contract are designed to protect the 'performance interest'.[72] So although, as we have seen, English courts rarely award specific performance of the contract, they use the award of damages for breach as a monetary substitute. But the decision in *Ruxley* shows that the approach is more nuanced than this. Just as the courts will not order specific performance when it would have the effect of penalising the defendant for his breach or would confer an excessive benefit on the claimant and would constitute a waste of resources to require performance to be made literally in accordance with the terms of the contract,[73] so the courts will not order the financial equivalent of performance (cost of cure) where it would punish

---

[71] [1996] AC 344 (HL).

[72] D Friedmann, 'The Performance Interest in Contract Damages' (1995) 111 LQR 628.

[73] *Co-operative Insurance Society Ltd v Argyll Stores (Holdings) Ltd* [1998] AC 1 (HL) 15–16 (Lord Hoffmann, quoted above, p 279).

the defendant, confer in substance a gratuitous benefit on the claimant and constitute an unreasonable award.

3. Damages for Distress and Other Intangible Losses

The approaches described above seek to find an economic substitute for performance. English law is normally concerned only with the economic consequences of breach of contract: damages are not often awarded for intangible losses in contract. But it might be appropriate sometimes to focus on a different (non-economic) characterisation of the loss: the intangible benefits which the claimant has lost as a result of the defective performance. This will tend to be in non-commercial contracts, where the claimant's interest in performance cannot properly be assessed simply in economic terms. This was actually the result in the *Ruxley* case. The trial judge had awarded Mr Forsyth £2,500 as damages for 'loss of amenity', which he identified as the proper loss rather than the cost of demolishing and reconstructing the swimming pool. The 'loss of amenity' award was reinstated by the House of Lords.

However, an award of damages for intangible loss is the exception rather than the rule. Damage to the claimant's person, property or economic interests can be compensated by damages for breach of contract. So can physical discomfort suffered by the claimant. But not normally distress or other intangible harm. The current state of the law was set out by the House of Lords in *Farley v Skinner*,[74] where a surveyor was engaged by a potential purchaser to investigate whether a house was seriously affected by aircraft noise, and failed in his contractual duty of care. The purchaser had no financial loss, since the price which he paid for the house corresponded to the market value after taking into account aircraft noise. But he was entitled to compensation for the lack of peace and tranquillity. The House of Lords held that, in general, compensation is awarded in contract only for financial loss resulting from the breach; but damages can be awarded for non-financial loss where a major or important object of the contract is to give pleasure, relaxation or peace of mind—such as in this case where the surveyor was retained not only on the usual basis (to investigate the physical state of the property) but also specifically to investigate the noise. But such an award must be moderate. The judge's award of £10,000 was allowed to stand, on the basis that although it was 'at the very top end of what could possibly be regarded as appropriate damages'[75] it was not so excessive that it should be overturned on appeal. The Court of Appeal has also emphasised that the level of awards for damages for physical inconvenience, discomfort and mental distress should not be out

---

[74] [2001] UKHL 49, [2002] 2 AC 732.
[75] *Ibid* [28] (Lord Steyn).

of line with the awards in other fields, such as for psychiatric damage in personal injury cases, for injury to feelings in cases of sex and race discrimination and damages for bereavement.[76]

Damages for distress are therefore not normally awarded for breach of contract in English law unless the contract was one of which an important object was to give pleasure (such as a holiday contract, where the holiday is a disaster)[77] or to avoid distress (such as a contract under which a lawyer is engaged to obtain a court order to protect his client against harassment, but no effective order is obtained and the harassment continues).[78] The *manner* of breaking the contract does not of itself normally give rise to damages.[79]

4. Whose Expectation? Losses Suffered by Third Parties

The normal rule is that a contracting party can sue only for his own loss. The courts have defined some particular situations in which a contracting party can sue for loss suffered by a third party to the contract, although these are regarded as exceptional cases, and are now perhaps less significant since under the Contracts

(Rights of Third Parties) Act 1999 it is possible for the parties in their contract to give a directly enforceable right to a third party who can then sue in his own name for his own loss.[80]

5. Punitive Damages

Punitive damages are not awarded in a claim for breach of contract. Sometimes (but only rarely) they can be awarded in tort in English law,[81] but the courts have made clear that there is no argument that they might be awarded in contract:

> [D]amages for breach of contract must reflect, as accurately as the circumstances allow, the loss which the claimant has sustained because he did not get what he bargained for. There is no question of punishing the contract breaker.[82]

---

[76] *Milner v Carnival plc* [2010] EWCA Civ 389, [2010] 3 All ER 701 [57].
[77] *Jarvis v Swans Tours Ltd* [1973] QB 233 (CA).
[78] *Heywood v Wellers* [1976] QB 446 (CA).
[79] *Addis v Gramophone Co Ltd* [1909] AC 488 (HL); *Johnson v Unisys Ltd* [2001] UKHL 13, [2003] 1 AC 518 (both cases concerned with abrupt dismissals from employment, alleged to have given rise to distress and other losses).
[80] Above, ch 10; for damages calculated to cover a third party's loss, see p 249.
[81] *Kuddus v Chief Constable of Leicestershire Constabulary* [2001] UKHL 29, [2002] 2 AC 122, including where the defendant calculated that he might make a profit from the tort exceeding the compensation payable to the claimant.
[82] *Ruxley Electronics & Construction Ltd v Forsyth* above, n 71, 353 (Lord Bridge of Harwich).

This is consistent with the general approach that remedies for breach of contract should not punish the party in breach.[83]

6. Damages to Deprive the Defendant of a Profit

Damages in contract are normally awarded only to compensate the claimant, and not to deprive the defendant of a benefit which he has obtained by reason of the breach of contract. However, in *Attorney-General v Blake*[84] the House of Lords accepted that a court may award an account of the defendant's profits as a remedy for breach of contract—but only in exceptional cases, and only where the remedies of compensatory damages, specific performance and injunction are inadequate. But it is not sufficient that the defendant broke the contract deliberately, or in such a way as to try to make a profit from it. The scope of this decision is still not clear, and it has not been explored very much in the cases.[85]

There is a different line of cases which might appear at first sight to involve the award of damages to deprive the defendant of part of his profits from his breach of contract, but where the courts have made clear that the award is designed to compensate the claimant's loss. In *Wrotham Park Estate Co Ltd v Parkside Homes Ltd*[86] the defendant began to build houses on a plot of land in circumstances where it was in breach of a covenant not to do so. Brightman J refused to award an injunction[87] in favour of the claimant, which had the benefit of the covenant, but awarded as damages in substitution for an injunction[88] such sum of money as might reasonably have been demanded by the claimant from the defendant as a quid pro quo for relaxing the covenant, which the Judge decided was five per cent of the profit which the defendant expected to make from the development (ie, from the breach of covenant). In spite of the calculation being made by reference to a share of the defendant's profit, it has been established that in such a case the damages—based on a hypothetical bargain between the parties as if they had both been willing to negotiate a reasonable price—are designed to compensate the claimant's loss

---

[83] See also above, p 279 (specific performance); below, p 300 (penalty clauses).

[84] [2001] 1 AC 268 (HL) (former member of the security services made a profit by publishing material in breach of his contractually binding undertaking to comply with the Official Secrets Act 1989).

[85] See, however, *Esso Petroleum Co Ltd v Niad Ltd* [2001] EWHC 6 (Ch), [2001] All ER (D) 324 (petrol company could recover profits made by company running one of its garages which had failed to reduce price to reflect local competition); *Experience Hendrix LLC v PPX Enterprises Inc* [2003] EWCA Civ 323, [2003] 1 All ER (Comm) 830 (award of profits under *Blake* is exceptional).

[86] Above, n 24.

[87] Above, p 280.

[88] Above, p 281.

of the right to bargain for a release or variation of the contractual term that has been broken.[89]

7. Limits on Recovery and Defences: Remoteness, Mitigation, Contributory Negligence and Limitation Periods

Once the core measure of damages has been ascertained, the claimant may not be allowed to recover the whole of the loss he has in fact suffered within the scope of that measure, because some or all of his loss is too remote, or has been suffered in circumstances where he has failed to mitigate it, or where he was contributorily negligent. His claim may also be barred by the passage of time.

(a) Remoteness of Damage

According to a rule developed in the mid-nineteenth century in *Hadley v Baxendale*, in a claim for breach of contract the defendant is liable only for the loss:

> [S]uch as may fairly and reasonably be considered either arising naturally, *i.e.*, according to the usual course of things, from [the] breach of contract itself, or such as may be supposed to have been in the contemplation of both parties, at the time they made the contract, as the probable result of it.[90]

That is, the defendant is liable only for loss which he could have had in contemplation at the time of the contract, either (1) because it is the normal kind of loss that any person in the claimant's position might be expected to suffer, or (2) because it arises from special circumstances which the claimant drew to the defendant's attention before the contract was concluded.

The inspiration for this test appears to have been the French Civil Code,[91] which contains a rule limiting the losses recoverable for non-performance of a contract to those which were foreseen or foreseeable at the time of the contract. However, under the French rule, in the case of deliberate non-performance the defendant must pay all the damage which he causes directly, even if it was not foreseeable. English law has not adopted the distinction

---

[89] *Pell Frischmann Engineering Ltd v Bow Valley Iran Ltd* [2009] UKPC 45, [2011] 1 WLR 2370 [47]–[49]. There are many cases, generally involving breaches of restrictive covenant or invasion of property rights (including intellectual property); eg *Experience Hendrix LLC v PPX Enterprises Inc*, above, n 85; *WWF—World Wide Fund for Nature v World Wrestling Federation Entertainment Inc* [2007] EWCA Civ 286, [2008] 1 WLR 445; but cf *Van der Garde v Force India Formula One Team Ltd* [2010] EWHC 2373 (QB) (breach of positive obligation).

[90] *Hadley v Baxendale* (1854) 9 Exch 341, 354; 156 ER 145, 151 (Alderson B).

[91] Articles 1150–51, referred to in argument in *Hadley v Baxendale* by Parke B at 346, 147–48.

between deliberate and non-deliberate breach in this context: even in the case of a deliberate breach of contract, the defendant is liable only for the losses which he could have had in contemplation at the time of the contract. English law distinguishes between intentional and non-intentional *torts* in its rules for remoteness of damage;[92] but not in contract. The remedy of damages for breach of contract is designed to reflect the economic risk allocation as it was settled by the parties when they entered into the contract.[93] It does not reflect the 'wrongfulness' of the breach.

The idea that the rule of remoteness of damage is based on the contractual risk allocation, and in particular the scope of the risk assumed by the defendant on entering into the contract, has been emphasised by Lord Hoffmann, who has even suggested that the traditional test set out in *Hadley v Baxendale* should be replaced by a broader test: for what kind of loss would the defendant reasonably be taken to have accepted liability?[94] However, the lower courts have generally preferred to retain the well-understood traditional test, and have said that the scope of Lord Hoffmann's new approach should be limited to unusual cases where the *Hadley v Baxendale* test would lead to an unacceptable result given of the context of the contract, the surrounding circumstances, or the general understanding in the market within which the contract is concluded.[95]

(b) Mitigation of Loss; Contributory Negligence

In addition to the rule of remoteness of damage, there are other reasons why a claimant may not receive full compensation for his losses in a claim for breach of contract. There is a balance to be struck, and the defendant will not be required to pay any part of the claimant's loss which the claimant would not have suffered if he had taken such steps as he ought reasonably to have taken to avoid or reduce his loss—the principle of *mitigation of loss*.[96] Once the defendant has committed the breach of contract, the claimant is required to take some responsibility to minimise its impact, but only to the standard that can be expected of a reasonable person in his position.

---

[92] Above, p 181.
[93] *Koufos v C Czarnikow Ltd (The Heron II)* [1969] 1 AC 350 (HL) 385–86.
[94] *Transfield Shipping Inc v Mercator Shipping Inc (The Achilleas)* [2008] UKHL 48, [2009] 1 AC 61 [12]; (2010) 14 Edin LR 47, 58.
[95] *Supershield Ltd v Siemens Building Technologies FE Ltd* [2010] EWCA Civ 7, [2010] 1 Lloyd's Rep 349 [43]; *Sylvia Shipping Co Ltd v Progress Bulk Carriers Ltd* [2010] EWHC 542 (Comm), [2010] 2 Lloyd's Rep 81 [40]; *John Grimes Partnership Ltd v Gubbins* [2013] EWCA Civ 37, [2013] BLR 126 [20].
[96] *British Westinghouse Electric and Manufacturing Co v Underground Electric Railways Co of London* [1912] AC 673 (HL).

Contributory negligence (the claimant's fault) is not generally available as a defence to a claim for breach of contract. It can only be raised in cases of concurrent liability in contract and tort, where the defence of contributory negligence is available to the defendant if sued in contract where he could equally have raised it had he been sued in tort.[97] In effect, it is allowed as a defence in the contract claim so as to avoid the claimant obtaining a better remedy by choosing to sue in tort when the essential nature of the concurrent contract and tort claims is identical.

(c) Limitation Periods

An action for breach of contract must be started before the end of the limitation period which applies to it—which means six years from the breach of contract, except in the case of a contract executed as a deed where the period is extended to 12 years, and an action for damages for personal injuries where the period is three years from the date when the claimant could have discovered his right to bring the action.[98] In 2001 the Law Commission proposed a general reform of this area, which would have introduced a new general limitation period for civil actions (including contracts, whether or not executed as a deed) of three years from the date when the defendant could have discovered his right to bring an action, with a long-stop period of 10 years from the act or omission giving rise to the claim.[99] In 2002 the Government accepted in principle this recommendation for reform, but after further consultation it announced in 2009 that it would not be taking the reforms forward.

8. Damages for Delay

In English law there is no requirement for the claimant to issue a notice of delay, or to give the defendant a second chance to perform, before claiming damages for delayed performance. In principle, a delay in performance is simply a breach of contract, and damages are available as of right at the moment the defendant fails to perform.[100]

---

[97] *Forsikringsaktieselskapet Vesta v Butcher* [1989] AC 852, 858–68, 875, 879 (CA).
[98] Limitation Act 1980 ss 5, 8, 11.
[99] Law Commission, 'Limitation of Actions' (Law Com No 270, 2001).
[100] In the case of late payment of money, the court can award interest as damages: *Sempra Metals Ltd v IRC* [2007] UKHL 34, [2008] 1 AC 561, although in commercial contracts there can also be an implied term that interest will be payable, under the Late Payment of Commercial Debts (Interest) Act 1998.

V. Debt

The action of debt is significantly different from a damages claim. In effect, it is an action for specific enforcement of the obligation: the court orders payment of the sum which was promised. However, this is an action which was devised by the common law: unlike the equitable remedy of specific performance it is available as of right if the debt is proved and does not depend on the court's discretion.

In a debt claim there are no issues about quantification of loss, remoteness of damage or mitigation of loss: if the debt is proved, then it is enforceable as a fixed sum, often called a 'liquidated' claim, by contrast with an 'unliquidated' claim for damages which have to be assessed and fixed ('liquidated') by the court. Enforcement of the debt can therefore be simpler and quicker than a claim for damages.

The action may be available for a simple money debt such as the repayment of a loan; or for a sum due under a contract as the price of goods or services, once the goods have been delivered or the services have been performed under the terms of the contract and therefore the price has been earned. A contractual provision for liquidated damages is an agreed sum and will be enforceable as a debt—as long as it *is* a liquidated damages clause and not a penalty.[101]

VI. Consumer Contracts for the Supply of Goods, Digital Content or Services: Rejection, Repair, Replacement, Reduction in Price and Repeat Performance

There is no general remedy at common law under which the court can order the defendant to repair or replace defective goods which have been delivered under a contract of sale or of supply of goods; nor to reduce the price to reflect the defect. Such a situation is not one in which specific performance

---

[101] Below, p 300.

will be ordered; and so the only remedies which are generally available for the buyer are termination of the contract and damages. In the context of contracts relating to goods, the remedy of termination involves the claimant rejecting the goods; and then he is entitled to claim back the price—not as a claim under the contract, but in restitution since his rejection of the goods means that he has paid but received nothing in return: there is a total failure of consideration.[102] Similarly, if defective services are provided under a contract for the supply of services, the court cannot at common law order a reduction in the price payable, nor can it generally order specific performance, since damages (to pay for the cost of obtaining substitute performance from a third party) will normally be an adequate remedy.[103]

These remedies are simply the operation of the normal rules relating to remedies for breach of contract, within the particular context of contracts of sale and supply of goods, and supply of services. In addition, however, there are now also certain provisions peculiar to contracts for the supply (including sale) of goods or digital content, and the supply of services, in favour of consumers. The Sale and Supply of Goods to Consumers Regulations 2002[104] amended the Sale of Goods Act 1979 and the Supply of Goods and Services Act 1982 by introducing new remedies for consumers in the case of non-conforming goods: to require the seller to repair or replace the goods, or to reduce the price. The Consumer Rights Act 2015 has replaced these provisions with new and broader rights for consumers. In the case of contracts for the supply of goods by a trader, the consumer generally no longer has the common law right to terminate the contract for breach of a term which is treated by the 2015 Act as being included in the contract;[105] instead he has rights to reject the goods and treat the contract as at an end—a 'short-term right to reject' which can generally be exercised for 30 days from delivery of the goods, and a 'final right to reject' where he has pursued other remedies also given by the Act (repair or replacement of the goods) without the goods yet conforming with the contract.[106] This develops the provisions originally introduced in 2002, but the 2015 Act has also gone beyond this and has introduced rights to repair or replacement, or price reduction, or a refund, in place of the common law remedy of termination, in the case of consumer contracts for the supply of *digital content*,[107] and in providing for the right to a price reduction, or to require repeat performance of a defective

---

[102] Cf above, p 267.
[103] If the contract is for personal services which cannot be replaced by third-party performance, specific performance will not be available because of the courts' reluctance to order the performance of personal services: above, p 277.
[104] SI 2002/3045 implementing Directive 1999/44/EC on Certain Aspects of the Sale of Consumer Goods and Associated Guarantees.
[105] Above, p 281.
[106] Consumer Rights Act 2015 ss 19(12), 20–24.
[107] *Ibid*, ss 42(8), 43–45.

service, in the case of consumer contracts for the supply of *services*.[108] The right to the repeat performance of a service is particularly significant: backed up by the remedy of specific performance,[109] it gives a much stronger claim for the consumer to have the contract performed in accordance with its terms, since the consumer's right is excluded only if performance in conformity with the contract is *impossible*.[110]

VII. Agreed Remedies

The parties are generally free to include in their contract provisions governing the remedial consequences of defective performance of the contract, as well as provisions defining the primary obligations of performance. Such clauses will of course be subject to the general controls on unfair terms, such as the Unfair Contract Terms Act 1977 and Part 2 of the Consumer Rights Act 2015.[111] But in addition there are some particular points to notice about clauses which provide for the remedies available for breach of the contract.

First, no contractual provision can guarantee that specific performance will be the remedy, since that is a matter for the court's discretion.

Secondly, commercial contracts will very often contain a provision defining the circumstances in which the contract can be terminated. We have already seen that such clauses are generally given full effect according to their terms, even in circumstances where many civil law systems would expect the defaulting party to be given a second opportunity to perform, or at least would require the 'innocent' party not to take advantage of the clause in bad faith. But there is no general principle of English law that a party must exercise his contractual rights in good faith.

Thirdly, the parties can include in their contract a provision quantifying the damages recoverable in the event of a specified breach. However, the courts are careful to analyse whether such a clause is a genuine attempt to quantify in advance the likely loss flowing from a breach (a 'liquidated damages'

---

[108] *Ibid*, ss 55–56. The common law remedy of termination is retained for consumer services contracts: s 54(7).

[109] *Ibid*, s 58. It remains to be seen in what circumstances the courts will be willing to order specific performance to give effect to the right to repeat performance, given that (outside the context of the Consumer Rights Act 2015) they will not normally order specific performance of a contract of services: above, p 277.

[110] *Ibid*, s 55.

[111] Above, ch 9.

clause—which is enforceable as a debt[112] in place of the normal rules for assessment of damages) or whether it is a penalty clause (designed to discourage breach, rather than estimate the likely loss; or, as the Supreme Court has recently put it, imposing a detriment on the contract-breaker out of all proportion to any legitimate interest of the innocent party in the enforcement of the primary obligation).[113] As we have already seen,[114] if a clause specifying a sum payable on breach is characterised as a penalty clause, it is struck out and the normal rules for assessment of damages are applied. However, the courts are rather reluctant to characterise a clause negotiated between commercial parties as a penalty: they regard as a good thing the parties' genuine attempt to avoid litigation by agreeing the remedy in advance.[115] But the fact that English law does not in principle allow penalty clauses is again consistent with the view that a contracting party should not be tied into the contract; and that he should not be punished for failure to perform. There is a much greater freedom to break contracts in the common law than in the civil law.

VIII. Learning About a Contract from the Remedies for Breach

At the beginning of this chapter we noted that the remedies for breach of contract reveal much about a legal system's notion of contract. This is true of the English law of contract; and some of the points which are revealed through the remedies re-emphasise aspects of the English law of contract already noted in earlier chapters of this book.

We have seen that there is significant special protection for the consumer in relation to remedies, as elsewhere,[116] although this is through the intervention of statute. The core rules of the English law of contract remain those

---

[112] Above, p 297.
[113] *Dunlop Pneumatic Tyre Co v New Garage and Motor Co Ltd* [1915] AC 79 (HL); *Cavendish Square Holdings BV v El Makdessi* and *ParkingEye Ltd v Beavis* [2015] UKSC 67, [2015] 3 WLR 1373.
[114] Above, p 225.
[115] *Robophone Facilities Ltd v Blank* [1966] 1 WLR 1428 (CA) 1447–49; *Philips Hong Kong Ltd v Attorney-General of Hong Kong* (1993) 61 BLR 41 (PC) 54–55, 58.
[116] Above, p 297 (remedies of rejection, repair, replacement, reduction of price and repeat performance in contracts for the supply of goods, digital content and services); for more general protection of consumers through statutory provisions see above, pp 126 (formation); 230 ff (terms).

of the common law—and the common law generally views a contract as a commercial instrument, to be entered into by parties bargaining at arm's length and protecting their own economic interests accordingly.[117] The remedies for breach of contract bear this out: the rules emphasise not literal performance but the economic equivalence of performance. The enforceable right under a contract is not to the defendant's performance itself—in the sense that an order of specific performance is rarely granted in favour of the innocent party, and is not even the primary remedy as a matter of principle. The normal remedy is damages: payment of money by the party in breach; it is only where damages cannot adequately compensate the claimant's loss that a court will even consider making an order of specific performance. However, the claimant's interest in receiving performance is protected by the award of damages, since the starting-point for the calculation of damages is the claimant's disappointed expectation, and so the purpose of the award is often to enable the claimant (if he so wishes) to obtain equivalent performance elsewhere.

The claimant's interest is analysed in economic terms. Damages are normally limited to losses which can be calculated in money, and the courts do not generally recognise non-economic losses—except in certain limited cases which will involve primarily non-commercial contracts.[118] But the claimant's full economic interest might not be protected: if he has acted unreasonably in incurring losses, or in failing to reduce them, his claim will be limited accordingly.[119] And the courts are sensitive to arguments based on the waste of resources which would follow from the award of a remedy—whether specific performance[120] or damages.[121]

The emphasis is firmly on compensation of the claimant, and the party in breach must not be punished, either directly or indirectly, by the remedies awarded for breach. Non-performance and defective performance are not seen as 'wrongs' in the same sense that a tort is a wrong. Penalty clauses are struck out and punitive damages are not awarded.[122] The defendant's culpability (such as whether his breach was intentional or unintentional) is generally irrelevant in the award of remedies: the scope of damages is fixed by the (economic) risk allocation of the contract as it stood at the moment of its formation, and the circumstances of the breach do not generally change that.[123]

The remedy of termination of the contract illustrates not only certain aspects of the contract in English law but also a view about the relationship between

---

[117] Above, pp 69–70.
[118] Above, p 291.
[119] Above, pp 284 (refusal to terminate); 290 (*Ruxley v Forsyth*); 295 (mitigation of loss).
[120] Above, p 279.
[121] Above, pp 290–91.
[122] Above, p 300.
[123] Above, pp 294–95 (remoteness of damage).

the contracting parties and the courts. Like rescission for misrepresentation[124] it is a remedy the innocent party can trigger by his own action—a 'self-help' remedy. Such remedies are designed to facilitate the claimant being released from the contract, in order to obtain another contract elsewhere. He is in control, and need not seek the assistance of the court to obtain release from the contract which has been broken—and even a contract which has not yet been broken but where the other party has indicated that he will not perform when the time comes ('anticipatory breach').[125] The claimant needs to be able to secure a speedy release in order to be able to maximise his commercial opportunities. Although there are some limited controls available to the courts over the unreasonable exercise of contractual rights by claimants,[126] there is a marked reluctance to inhibit the free termination by commercial parties of contracts where they have made express provision for it. Again, although the rule may not be so strictly applied in the case of non-commercial contracts, the starting-point is a rule which has been created and continues to be used with commercial parties in mind: the paradigm contract for the purpose of the English common law in the formulation of its remedies is the negotiated commercial contract.

---

[124] Above, p 179. Termination for frustration similarly does not require the intervention of the court: the parties are left to negotiate the consequences of supervening circumstances which are sufficiently serious to terminate the contract, and it is unthinkable in English law that the courts should intervene to modify the contract (except to provide consequential remedies, if frustration is established, such as under the Law Reform (Frustrated Contracts) Act 1943); the courts are not even called upon to take steps to discharge the parties from the contract, which is terminated automatically by the frustrating event: above, p 268.
[125] Above, p 283.
[126] Above, pp 285–86.

Appendix[1]
Contracts (Rights of Third Parties) Act 1999

1999 Chapter 31

An Act to make provision for the enforcement of contractual terms by third parties.

[11th November 1999]

BE IT ENACTED by the Queen's most Excellent Majesty, by and with the advice and consent of the Lords Spiritual and Temporal, and Commons, in this present Parliament assembled, and by the authority of the same, as follows:—

Right of third party to enforce contractual term.

1.—(1) Subject to the provisions of this Act, a person who is not a party to a contract (a "third party") may in his own right enforce a term of the contract if—
   (a) the contract expressly provides that he may, or
   (b) subject to subsection (2), the term purports to confer a benefit on him.
(2) Subsection (1)(b) does not apply if on a proper construction of the contract it appears that the parties did not intend the term to be enforceable by the third party.
(3) The third party must be expressly identified in the contract by name, as a member of a class or as answering a particular description but need not be in existence when the contract is entered into.
(4) This section does not confer a right on a third party to enforce a term of a contract otherwise than subject to and in accordance with any other relevant terms of the contract.

---

[1] This Act is reproduced under the terms of Crown Copyright Policy Guidance issued by HMSO.

(5) For the purpose of exercising his right to enforce a term of the contract, there shall be available to the third party any remedy that would have been available to him in an action for breach of contract if he had been a party to the contract (and the rules relating to damages, injunctions, specific performance and other relief shall apply accordingly).

(6) Where a term of a contract excludes or limits liability in relation to any matter references in this Act to the third party enforcing the term shall be construed as references to his availing himself of the exclusion or limitation.

(7) In this Act, in relation to a term of a contract which is enforceable by a third party—"the promisor" means the party to the contract against whom the term is enforceable by the third party, and

"the promisee" means the party to the contract by whom the term is enforceable against the promisor.

Variation and rescission of contract.

2.—(1) Subject to the provisions of this section, where a third party has a right under section 1 to enforce a term of the contract, the parties to the contract may not, by agreement, rescind the contract, or vary it in such a way as to extinguish or alter his entitlement under that right, without his consent if—

(a) the third party has communicated his assent to the term to the promisor,

(b) the promisor is aware that the third party has relied on the term, or

(c) the promisor can reasonably be expected to have foreseen that the third party would rely on the term and the third party has in fact relied on it.

(2) The assent referred to in subsection (1)(a)—

(a) may be by words or conduct, and

(b) if sent to the promisor by post or other means, shall not be regarded as communicated to the promisor until received by him.

(3) Subsection (1) is subject to any express term of the contract under which—

(a) the parties to the contract may by agreement rescind or vary the contract without the consent of the third party, or

(b) the consent of the third party is required in circumstances specified in the contract instead of those set out in subsection (1)(a) to (c).
(4) Where the consent of a third party is required under subsection (1) or (3), the court or arbitral tribunal may, on the application of the parties to the contract, dispense with his consent if satisfied—
  (a) that his consent cannot be obtained because his whereabouts cannot reasonably be ascertained, or
  (b) that he is mentally incapable of giving his consent.
(5) The court or arbitral tribunal may, on the application of the parties to a contract, dispense with any consent that may be required under subsection (1)(c) if satisfied that it cannot reasonably be ascertained whether or not the third party has in fact relied on the term.
(6) If the court or arbitral tribunal dispenses with a third party's consent, it may impose such conditions as it thinks fit, including a condition requiring the payment of compensation to the third party.
(7) The jurisdiction conferred on the court by subsections (4) to (6) is exercisable in England and Wales by both the High Court and the county court and in Northern Ireland by both the High Court and a county court.[2]

Defences etc. available to promisor.

3.—(1) Subsections (2) to (5) apply where, in reliance on section 1, proceedings for the enforcement of a term of a contract are brought by a third party.
(2) The promisor shall have available to him by way of defence or set-off any matter that—
  (a) arises from or in connection with the contract and is relevant to the term, and
  (b) would have been available to him by way of defence or set-off if the proceedings had been brought by the promisee.

---

[2] Amended by Crime and Courts Act 2013 sch 9(3), para 71.

(3) The promisor shall also have available to him by way of defence or set-off any matter if—
   (a) an express term of the contract provides for it to be available to him in proceedings brought by the third party, and
   (b) it would have been available to him by way of defence or set-off if the proceedings had been brought by the promisee.
(4) The promisor shall also have available to him—
   (a) by way of defence or set-off any matter, and
   (b) by way of counterclaim any matter not arising from the contract,
that would have been available to him by way of defence or set-off or, as the case may be, by way of counterclaim against the third party if the third party had been a party to the contract.
(5) Subsections (2) and (4) are subject to any express term of the contract as to the matters that are not to be available to the promisor by way of defence, set-off or counterclaim.
(6) Where in any proceedings brought against him a third party seeks in reliance on section 1 to enforce a term of a contract (including, in particular, a term purporting to exclude or limit liability), he may not do so if he could not have done so (whether by reason of any particular circumstances relating to him or otherwise) had he been a party to the contract.

Enforcement of contract by promisee.	**4.** Section 1 does not affect any right of the promisee to enforce any term of the contract.
Protection of promisor from double liability.	**5.** Where under section 1 a term of a contract is enforceable by a third party, and the promisee has recovered from the promisor a sum in respect of— (a) the third party's loss in respect of the term, or (b) the expense to the promisee of making good to the third party the default of the promisor, then, in any proceedings brought in reliance on that section by the third party, the court or arbitral tribunal shall reduce any award to the third party to such extent as it thinks appropriate to take account of the sum recovered by the promisee.

Exceptions.   **6.**—(1) Section 1 confers no rights on a third party in the case of a contract on a bill of exchange, promissory note or other negotiable instrument.

(2) Section 1 confers no rights on a third party in the case of any contract binding on a company and its members under section 33 of the Companies Act 2006 (effect of company's constitution).[3]

(2A)[4] Section 1 confers no rights on a third party in the case of any incorporation document of a limited liability partnership or any agreement (express or implied) between the members of a limited liability partnership, or between a limited liability partnership and its members, that determines the mutual rights and duties of the members and their rights and duties in relation to the limited liability partnership.

(3) Section 1 confers no right on a third party to enforce—
   (a) any term of a contract of employment against an employee,
   (b) any term of a worker's contract against a worker (including a home worker), or
   (c) any term of a relevant contract against an agency worker.

(4) In subsection (3)—
   (a) "contract of employment","employee", "worker's contract", and"worker" have the meaning given by section 54 of the National Minimum Wage Act 1998,
   (b) "home worker" has the meaning given by section 35(2) of that Act,
   (c) "agency worker" has the same meaning as in section 34(1) of that Act, and
   (d) "relevant contract" means a contract entered into, in a case where section 34 of that Act applies, by the agency worker as respects work falling within subsection (1)(a) of that section.

---

[3] Amended by Companies Act 2006 (Consequential Amendments, Transitional Provisions and Savings) Order 2009 SI 2009/1941, reg 2, sch 1, para 179.

[4] Inserted by Limited Liability Partnerships Regulations 2001 SI 2001/1090, reg 9(1), sch 5, para 20, and amended by Companies Act 2006 (Consequential Amendments, Transitional Provisions and Savings) Order 2009 SI 2009/1941, reg 2, sch 1, para 179.

(5) Section 1 confers no rights on a third party in the case of—
  (a) a contract for the carriage of goods by sea, or
  (b) a contract for the carriage of goods by rail or road, or for the carriage of cargo by air, which is subject to the rules of the appropriate international transport convention,
  except that a third party may in reliance on that section avail himself of an exclusion or limitation of liability in such a contract.

(6) In subsection (5) "contract for the carriage of goods by sea" means a contract of carriage—
  (a) contained in or evidenced by a bill of lading, sea waybill or a corresponding electronic transaction, or
  (b) under or for the purposes of which there is given an undertaking which is contained in a ship's delivery order or a corresponding electronic transaction.

(7) For the purposes of subsection (6)—
  (a) "bill of lading","sea waybill" and "ship's delivery order" have the same meaning as in the Carriage of Goods by Sea Act 1992, and
  (b) a corresponding electronic transaction is a transaction within section 1(5) of that Act which corresponds to the issue, indorsement, delivery or transfer of a bill of lading, sea waybill or ship's delivery order.

(8) In subsection (5) "the appropriate international transport convention" means—
  (a) in relation to a contract for the carriage of goods by rail, the Convention which has the force of law in the United Kingdom under regulation 3 of the Railways (Convention on International Carriage by Rail) Regulations 2005,[5]
  (b) in relation to a contract for the carriage of goods by road, the Convention which has the force of law in the United Kingdom under section 1 of the Carriage of Goods by Road Act 1965, and

---

[5] Amended by Railways (Convention on International Carriage by Rail) Regulations 2005 SI 2005/2092, reg 9(2), sch 3, para 3.

(c) in relation to a contract for the carriage of cargo by air—
  (i) the Convention which has the force of law in the United Kingdom under section 1 of the Carriage by Air Act 1961, or
  (ii) the Convention which has the force of law under section 1 of the Carriage by Air (Supplementary Provisions) Act 1962, or
  (iii) either of the amended Conventions set out in Part B of Schedule 2 or 3 to the Carriage by Air Acts (Application of Provisions) Order 1967.

Supplementary provisions relating to third party.

7.—(1) Section 1 does not affect any right or remedy of a third party that exists or is available apart from this Act.
(2) Section 2(2) of the Unfair Contract Terms Act 1977 (restriction on exclusion etc. of liability for negligence) shall not apply where the negligence consists of the breach of an obligation arising from a term of a contract and the person seeking to enforce it is a third party acting in reliance on section 1.
(3) In sections 5 and 8 of the Limitation Act 1980 the references to an action founded on a simple contract and an action upon a specialty shall respectively include references to an action brought in reliance on section 1 relating to a simple contract and an action brought in reliance on that section relating to a specialty.
(4) A third party shall not, by virtue of section 1(5) or 3(4) or (6), be treated as a party to the contract for the purposes of any other Act (or any instrument made under any other Act).

Arbitration provisions.

8.—(1) Where—
  (a) a right under section 1 to enforce a term ("the substantive term") is subject to a term providing for the submission of disputes to arbitration ("the arbitration agreement"), and
  (b) the arbitration agreement is an agreement in writing for the purposes of Part I of the Arbitration Act 1996,

the third party shall be treated for the purposes of that Act as a party to the arbitration agreement as regards disputes between himself and the promisor relating to the enforcement of the substantive term by the third party.

(2) Where—
  (a) a third party has a right under section 1 to enforce a term providing for one or more descriptions of dispute between the third party and the promisor to be submitted to arbitration ("the arbitration agreement"),
  (b) the arbitration agreement is an agreement in writing for the purposes of Part I of the Arbitration Act 1996, and
  (c) the third party does not fall to be treated under subsection (1) as a party to the arbitration agreement,

the third party shall, if he exercises the right, be treated for the purposes of that Act as a party to the arbitration agreement in relation to the matter with respect to which the right is exercised, and be treated as having been so immediately before the exercise of the right.

Northern Ireland.

9.—[provisions relating only to Northern Ireland].

Short title, commencement and extent.

10.—(1) This Act may be cited as the Contracts (Rights of Third Parties) Act 1999.

(2) This Act comes into force on the day on which it is passed but, subject to subsection (3), does not apply in relation to a contract entered into before the end of the period of six months beginning with that day.

(3) The restriction in subsection (2) does not apply in relation to a contract which—
  (a) is entered into on or after the day on which this Act is passed, and
  (b) expressly provides for the application of this Act.

(4) This Act extends as follows—
  (a) section 9 extends to Northern Ireland only;
  (b) the remaining provisions extend to England and Wales and Northern Ireland only.

Index

abuse of position *see under* **duress**
acceptance *see* **offer and acceptance**
agency *see under* **third party rights**
agreed remedies *see under* **breach of contract, remedies**
agreement
  communication between parties 95–96
  objective test
    English law 100–103
  objectivity/subjectivity
    arguments for 97–99
    distinction 96
  see also **offer and acceptance**
American law, estoppel *see under* **promissory estoppel**
assignment
  benefits only 256–57
  effect 258–59
  legal or equitable 257
  rights capable of 257–58
  third party rights 243
  see also **novation**
Australian law, estoppel *see under* **promissory estoppel**

bailment 54
battles of forms *see under* **offer and acceptance**
benefit of contract 235–36
  assignment/novation *see* **assignment; novation**
  see also **privity of contract; third party rights**
breach of confidence 94
breach of contract, remedies
  agreed remedies 299–300
  compensation of claimant 301
  consumer contracts, supply of goods/digital content/services, rejection/repair/replacement/reduction in price/repeat performance 297–99
  consumer, special protection for 297–99, 300–301
  damages
    claimant's failed expectation 288–89
    contributory negligence 296
    for delay 296
    for distress 291
    injunction, in place of 281
    intangible losses 291–92
    limitation periods 296
    profit (defendant's) deprivation 293–94
    punitive damages 292–93, 301
    remoteness of damage 294–95, 301
    specific performance 278, 281
    third party losses 292
    value of expectation 289–91
  debt action 297
  defendant's culpability 301
  injunction
    damages in place of 281
    discretionary remedy 280
    equitable remedy 275–76
  meaning of breach 272–74
  monetary losses 301
  non-performance 57, 258, 272–74, 287, 294, 301
  obligation to perform 273–74
  range of remedies 274–75
  rejection/repair/replacement/reduction in price/repeat performance, consumer contracts 297–99
  specific performance
    circumstances 279–80
    content of order 276
    and damages 278, 281
    as equitable remedy 275–76
    limitations 277–78
    modern law 277–80
    non-compliance with order 276–77
    reluctance to grant 278–79
    third party rights 247–49
  suspension 287–88
  termination for breach
    availability 281–83
    condition, breach of 282
    consequences 285
    contractual termination clauses 285–86
    deposits, relief against forfeiture 286–87
    and English law of contract 301–2
    exercising right 283–84
    fundamental breach 282–83
    nature of 281

capacity
  mental capacity 198
  minors 198
  statutory corporations 199
  vitiating factor 160

case-law *see under* **judge as interpreter/law-maker**
cassation   20*n*
certainty
   and commercial model   70
   good faith   65–66
   negotiations   76–78
   offer and acceptance   122–24
change of circumstances
   anticipation in contract terms   269–71
   background   260–61
   doctrine of frustration *see* **frustration**
   force majeure   264, 270
civil law system   8–9, 16, 45–46
Common Frame of Reference   72–73
common law
   and civil law   8–9
   and equity *see* **equity**
   as judge-made law   4–5
   meanings   3–5
common law systems
   academic writing   14
   case-law   13
   differences between   10–12
   English common law basis   12–13
   general features   12–14
   influence on each other   11–12
   judges' status   13–14
   legal reasoning   13
   Privy Council   12
   range of   9–10
confidence, breach of   94
consideration doctrine   69, 70
   basic principle   131–32
   detriment/benefit, promises involving   133–34
   disadvantageous contracts   135–36
   economic value, promises having   134–38
   existing obligation   138–42
   nominal consideration   136–37
   part-payment of debt   142–43
   particular rules   132–43
   past consideration   138
   request   132–33
   variation   137–38
   see also **formalities**; **intention**
consumer contracts *see under* **breach of contract, remedies**

damages
   liquidated damages clause   224–25, 299–300
   misrepresentation, in tort   180–82
   third party rights, calculation   249
   see also under **breach of contract, remedies**
debt action *see under* **breach of contract, remedies**

deed
   formality   127
   historical sources   128
   private formalities   129
   requirements   128–29
drafting features   71
duress
   economic duress   191–92
   pressure and abuse of position   189–91
   remedies   163
   rescission   193
   threats to the person   191, 193
   vitiating factor   160
   see also **undue influence**

economic duress *see under* **duress**
English law defined   3*n*
equity
   and common law   7–8
   historical background   5–6
   rights/remedies   6
estoppel
   liability, negotiations   82–83
   see also **promissory estoppel**
European context   5, 11, 17–18, 30, 66, 71–73, 233
express terms *see under* **terms**

finding the law   15
force majeure   264, 270
form, consideration and intention   125
formalities
   avoidance   129–31
   general *see* **deed**
   specific   126–27
   see also **consideration doctrine**; **intentions**
French law   16*n*, 34*n*, 46, 55*n*, 135*n*, 174, 246, 262*n*, 270, 294
frustration
   development of doctrine   70, 261–64
   disadvantaged party   267–68
   economic frustration   266
   foreseeable event   264–65
   frustrating event   265–66
   as implied term   261–63
   partial/temporary   268–69
   parties' control   265
   termination remedy   266–69
   test for   264–66

general law of contract
   drafting features   71
   economic instrument, contract as   69–70
   European context   71–73
   good faith *see* **good faith, role**
   intentions of the parties   68–69
   objectivity   67–68
   reasonableness/reliance   68

INDEX 313

special contracts
   distinction 57–58, 63
   significance of distinction 58, 62
German law 16*n*, 46, 55*n*, 56*n*
good faith, role 64–67
   certainty 65–66
   general duty 64–65
   negotiations 66–67, 77–78

Holmes, OW 273

identity *see under* **mistake**
illegality and public policy 199–200
implied terms *see under* **terms**
injunction *see under* **breach of contract, remedies**
intention
   parties' role 155–56
   significance 68–69
   terms of contract, special rules 59–60
   to create legal relations 156–57
   see also **consideration doctrine**; **formalities**
invitations to treat *see under* **offer and acceptance**

judge as interpreter/law-maker
   approaches to different sources 19–20
   legislative texts, interpretation 28–34
      background 28
      context at time of enactment 31–33
      European Law/European Convention on Human Rights 30–31
      normal/objective meaning 28–29
      Parliamentary material, use of 31–32
      reasoning beyond statute 33–34
      rules and presumptions 29–30
   precedent doctrine 20–27
      case-law as authority/binding 20–22
      Court of Appeal/Supreme Court decisions 25–27
      court hierarchy 22–25
      reason for the decision/ratio 22
      rules of precedent 22–27
      understanding case-law 27
   reasoning from cases
      background 34
      developing the common law 34–36
      Donoghue v Stevenson as illustration 38–44
      and interpretation of a code 37
      reasoning in the common law 36–38
Justinian, *Corpus Iuris Civilis* 9

land
   lease 56–57
   transfer of interest 56
law of obligations, contract within 52
lease of land 56–57

legislative texts, interpretation *see under* **judge as interpreter/law-maker**
letters of intent 89–90
liquidated damages clause 224–25, 299–300
lock-out contract 88–89

misrepresentation
   breach of contract, remedies 183–84
   damages in tort 180–82
   fraud 180–81
   inducement 176, 178
   law/fact distinction 177–78
   mistake, contrast 176–77
   negligence 181
   non-disclosure *see* **non-disclosure**
   precontractual 182
   remedies 84–86, 162–63, 177–78
      choice 184–85
      exclusion 185–86
   rescission *see* **rescission**
   unfair commercial practices 183
   vitiating factor 159
   voidable contract 179–80
mistake 70
   categories 163–64
   common (shared), on subject matter 172–76
   formation 164
   identity
      face-to-face contract 168
      formation prevention 168–70
      other contracts 169–70
      significance 167–68
   misrepresentation, contrast 176–77
   remedies 162, 163
   risk allocation 172–73
   subject-matter 171–76
   terms 164–67
   unilateral
      rectification 166
      on subject matter 171–72
   vitiating factor 159
   written contracts
      non est factum 167
      rectification 165–66

negotiations
   adversarial relationship, risk allocation 78–79
   background 74–75
   breach of confidence 94
   breaking off, as tort 81–82
   case by case approach 75–76
   disclosure, general duty, absence 80–81
   estoppel liability 82–83
   good faith, role 66–67
   letters of intent 89–90
   lock-out contract 88–89

misrepresentation, remedies in tort   84–86, 162–63
option contract   86–87
particular liabilities/general duties, distinction   83–84
pre-emption right   87–88
precontractual liabilities   86–92
preliminary contracts   86–90
subject to contract   79–80
tenders, duties to consider   90–91
unilateral contract, implied duty to maintain offer   91–92
unjust enrichment   52, 92–94
non-disclosure
duties of disclosure   186–89
mistake/misrepresentation, contrast   186
relationship between parties   188–89
tort liability   188
non-performance   57, 258, 272–74, 287, 294, 301
notaries   129
novation   259
see also **assignment**

objectivity   67–68
offer and acceptance
acceptance
e-mail/internet contracts   119–20
offeror's requirements   116
overt act/actual communication   114–15
postal rule   117–18
silence   115–16
telephone/telex   118–19
time and place   117–20
analysis
broad approach   107
insistence on   107–8
overriding rule   106
problems/benefits   104–6
battles of forms, unresolved negotiations   120–22
certainty requirement   122–24
completeness requirement   122
invitations to treat   110–13
offer
invitations to treat   110–13
meaning   110
termination by offeror/offeree   113–14
particular rules   109–10
as rule   103–4, 109
unresolved negotiations, battles of forms   120–22
see also **agreement**
option contract   86–87

pre-emption right   87–88
precedent doctrine *see under* **judge as interpreter/law-maker**

pressure and abuse of position *see under* **duress**
private law
basic structure   51–52
law of obligations, contract within   52
property *see* **property, and contract**
tort *see* **tort, and contract**
privity of contract
avoidance *see* **third party rights**
consideration, link with   237–39
judicial attitudes to   239–41
party, meaning   236–37
see also **third party rights**
promissory estoppel
American law   153
Australian law   153–55
common law differences   153–55
development of doctrine   145–47
elements in English law   147–53
estoppel by representation   144
estoppel, core principle   143–44
irrevocable representation   150–52
proprietary estoppel   144–45
reliance on representation   149–50
representation   149
shield, use as   152–53
temporary nature   150
variation of existing contract   148
property, and contract   55–57
land lease   56–57
land, transfer of interest   56
passing of property   55–56
public policy *see* **illegality and public policy**

reasonableness   68
reasoning from cases *see under* **judge as interpreter/law-maker**
Regulation on a Common European Sales Law (CESL), proposal   72–73
remedies
breach *see* **breach of contract, remedies**
consumer contracts *see under* **breach of contract, remedies**
damages *see under* **breach of contract, remedies; misrepresentation**
duress   163
equity   6
frustration, termination   266–69
misrepresentation *see under* **misrepresentation**
mistake   162, 163
negotiations, misrepresentation, in tort   84–86, 162–63
rescission *see* **rescission**
special contracts   61–62
specific performance *see under* **breach of contract, remedies**
termination *see under* **breach of contract, remedies; frustration, termination remedy**

INDEX 315

tort, misrepresentation 84–86, 162–63
vitiating factors 162–63
rescission
  bars to 180
  duress 193
  equitable rule 179
  self-help remedy 179
  third party issues 179–80
restitution 52
Roman law
  general law/special law, distinction 57–58
  principles 9

sources of law
  legislation and case law 17–19
  starting-point 15–17
  tabular illustration 4 *Fig.*
special contracts
  formation 58–59
  general rule, distinction *see under* **general law of contract**
  remedies 61–62
  terms *see* **terms of contract, special rules**
specific performance *see under* **breach of contract, remedies**
statutory drafting
  Contracts (Rights of Third Parties) Act 1999, as illustration 45–47, 303 *Appendix*
  general style 44–45
Supreme Court
  decisions 25–27
  and House of Lords 7*n*, 275*n*

tenders, duties to consider 90–91
termination for breach *see under* **breach of contract, remedies**
termination for frustration *see* **frustration, termination remedy**
terms
  background 201
  express terms
    collateral contracts 206
    commercial expectations 209–10
    context of document 208–9
    entire agreement clause 206
    intention test 203–4
    key issues 202
    not reduced to writing 203–5
    other written terms 204–5
    signature binding 206–7
    unfair contracts 220–24
    written contracts
      finding terms 205–7
      interpretation 207–10
  implied terms
    background 210
    business efficacy 212–13

    at common law 213–14
    drafting exclusions 215–17
    main tests 210–11
    officious bystander test 211
    particular types of contract 213–15
    regular/customary terms 211–12
    sale of goods 214
    standard terms 211–12
    statutory 214–15
    supply of service 215
    tenancy 215
  key issues 201–2
  special rules 59–61
    contexts 64
    intention of parties 59–60
    types of contract 60–61
third party rights
  agency 243–44
  assignment 243
  avoidance of privity 241–49
  by statute 247
  Contracts (Rights of Third Parties) Act 1999 250–56, 303 *Appendix*
    contracts covered 251
    enforcement circumstances 251–52
    enforcement right removal 253
    exemption clauses, application 253
    express contracting out 252
    other remedies, interaction 254
    privity of contract/consideration interaction 255–56
    promisee's position 254
    promisor's position 253–54
    reform proposals 250
    rights acquired 252
  creation of 242
  damages calculation 249
  enforcement by promisee 247–49
  loss by third party 247
  privity of contract/consideration interaction, post 1999 Act 255–56
  property law 245–47
  reform proposals 250
  specific performance 247–49
  tort 244–45
  trusts 242–43
  see also **benefit of contract**; **privity of contract**
threats to the person *see under* **duress**
tort 38–39
  and contract
    delivery of chattel 54
    differences 53–54
    overlap 53
    temporal context 54–55
  misrepresentation, remedies 84–86, 162–63

negotiations, breaking off 81–82
third party rights 244–45
trusts, third party rights 242–43

unconscionable bargains
meaning 197–98
pressure and abuse of position 189–91
vitiating factor 160
undue influence
actual/presumed 194–95
pressure and abuse of position 189–91
rescission 196
scope 194
terms 195–96
vitiating factor 160
voidable contract 196
see also **duress**
unfair contracts
background 218–19
common law control 224–26
construction *contra proferentem* 222–24
consumer contracts
exclusion/limitation clauses 230
unfair terms in 230–33
direct controls 224–34
employee protection 233–34
exclusion clauses 224
incorporation of term 221
indirect controls 219–24
interpretation of term 221–24
judicial control 220–24

liquidated damages clause 224–25, 299–300
loan agreements, statutory controls 234
non-consumer contracts, exclusion/limitation clauses 227–29
misrepresentation clauses 229
penalty clauses 224–25
procedural unfairness 220
special controls 225–26
statutory controls 226–34
substantive unfairness 219–20
unilateral contract, implied duty to maintain offer 91–92
unjust enrichment 52, 92–94

vitiating factors
background 158–59
illegality and public policy 160
overview 159–60
remedies 162–63
void contracts/voidable contracts, distinction 160–62
see also **capacity**; **duress**; **illegality and public policy**; **misrepresentation**; **mistake**
void contracts/voidable contracts, distinction 160–62

writing
as formality 58–59
see also under **mistake**; **terms**